DIMINI RESPONSIBILITY

My life as a U.K. Sub, and other strange stories

Volume III

ALVIN GIBBS

DIMINISHED RESPONSIBILITY
My life as a U.K. Sub, and other strange stories
Volume III

T&M 063

ISBN: 978-1-8380116-5-9

First Edition Published 2024 by Tome & Metre Books
© Tome & Metre Publishing

Photographs (unless stated) Copyright © Alvin Gibbs.

Printed by Stephens & George Print Group
Goat Mill Road, Dowlais, Merthyr Tydfil, CF48 3TD.

T&M Books Artwork: Rob Cook
T&M Books Editor: Mark Chadderton
Consulting Editor: Chris Coleman
T&M Proofing Team: Steve Creech

Tome & Metre Books and Tome & Metre Publishing
are wholly owned subsidiaries of Time & Matter Recordings.

Tome & Metre Publishing, Bedfordshire/Dorset

timematterrecordings.bigcartel.com
timematterrecordings.bandcamp.com
uksubstimeandmatter.net

"This book is dedicated to the gods Bacchus and Dionysus, and their elixir of love... wine!"

I must once more express my gratitude to Mark Chadderton and Rob Cook of Tome and Metre Publishing for their editorial talents, design skills and invaluable assistance in bringing to fruition this book and the previous duo of associated volumes, which all share the Diminished Responsibility title. Thanks fellas, now about that historical novel I sent you some time ago …

My profuse appreciation goes to Gaye Black for taking the time to write the Foreword she's supplied for this concluding volume, as well as for her lengthy friendship, her generosity, support and provision of my downtime accommodation whilst in the U.K.; not forgetting, the superb artwork she's bestowed for three Alvin Gibbs and the Disobedient Servants' record sleeves in recent years. No doubt, there will be yet more delightful evenings of wine, conversation, Death Metal music, and horror flicks, at Chez Black to come.

Salutations to my fellow U.K. Subs: Charlie Harper, Stephen Straughan, Stefan Häublein, and the irreplaceable fifth member of the Subs, Yuko Morinaga, for the music, fellowship and fun we've enjoyed together in both recent and past years. Kudos also to the hardest working and most genial roadie/driver I've ever had the pleasure of touring with – Gwinny Punk. May your wine glass always be full, your tattoos remain pristine and your love of all things Punk, never wane.

Take a bow the Bristol crew: Jon Murray, Ziggy, Chris Long, Stubbsy, Jess Spice and Bob, Mad Danny and our most excellent U.K. agent, Darren Griffiths of Crucial Talent fame, who also happens to be based in the Gloucestershire area. To each my sincere gratitude for the help and friendship you've all provided to me personally, as well as to the Subs and Servants, over the past decades. Merits of commendation are in order too for my talented Disobedient Servants: 'Soho' Steve Crittall, Christophe Sauniere, Leigh Heggarty, Steve Schmidt, and Barry 'Barrington' Francis; and to Time & Matter Records for having released all our recorded output since 2018.

Big shout out to Skull Strings France for their generous endorsement, Black Star amplification for the incredible freebie rig, and Fender Guitars, London, for gifting me a bass when they heard I'd had one stolen whilst on tour – how cool is that?

To my long-time friends Mel and Nicola Wesson, Patrick and Sarah Kerrane and our American neighbours Roger and Linda Bullock who, by general consensus, serve the best Manhattan cocktails to be had on this side of the Atlantic.

And lastly, to the woman who has completed my life and (goddammit!) actually put a smile on my face: Rosamunde Parsons – it's only just begun.

CONTENTS

FOREWORD

I have known Alvin for many years as a friend and contemporary.

We both played bass in punk bands, and of course, Alvin still very much does, namely the U.K. Subs and Alvin Gibbs and the Disobedient Servants.

We both toured with Iggy Pop, he as a member of Iggy's band and I in the Adverts, who were support on the Lust For Life tour. These days my involvement is mainly art related.

I have designed the sleeve art for Alvin's three solo singles and been in, and put on, various art shows featuring the Subs' Charlie Harper, and am regularly in attendance at both the Subs and Disobedient Servants' live shows.

I am always impressed with Alvin's boundless enthusiasm for history, literature and music, and his copious writings keep fans and associates up to date with the U.K. Subs and his solo career, and much more.

This, the third volume of his memoirs promises to be as beautifully written and absorbing as his previous volumes and will be eagerly awaited by his legions of followers.

GAYE BLACK, LONDON 2024.

PRELUDE

And so – a roll of burst drums, the collision of fractured cymbals and a loud fanfare of discordant trumpets – we finally reach the third and concluding volume of my memoir trilogy: My Life as a U.K. Sub, and other strange stories.

When Volume I emerged in 2020, I had envisaged being able to cover the tale of my lifelong involvement in the Punk genre and Rock music in general via a concise two book series. However, as I began researching and writing about my encounters and experiences both on and off the venue stages of the world, I realised another tome was necessary in order to complete the telling of this personally significant and sustained aspect of my anomalous presence on planet earth – hence the necessity for an additional volume, this chapter-rich piece of work you presently hold in your hands.

Volume I recounted my childhood fascination with Rock music, my escapades on the road as a semi-professional prior to upgrading to wholly-professional musician; and of my joining the U.K. Subs in 1980, leading up to the unforeseen circumstances of quitting the band in 1983.

Volume II detailed the aftermath of my departure from the Subs and the farcical tale of my almost joining Hanoi Rocks, followed by relocation to the U.S.A. and the ensuing Los Angeles years; which included my stint as touring bassist for Iggy Pop up until my subsequent move back to London to record and tour with Hanoi Rocks' spinoff outfit, Cheap And Nasty.

Volume III completes the cycle by divulging the circumstances of my return to playing with the U.K. Subversives and the personal and professional peaks and nadirs which occurred as a result of that restoration, right up to the present day – thus bringing everything up to date in this three-act literary drama; or, perhaps, founded on their curious contents, what some of you might sooner adjudge to be a three-act psychodrama?

Written memoir is all about the art of omission – what to include and what to exclude. There were many additional stories I could have shared with you in my book trio but, for the purposes of conciseness and a balanced narrative flow, a decision had to be made as to what anecdotes took precedent over others. The accounts to be found in all three volumes are the culmination of that editorial process, and hopefully my choices have provided the reader with the juiciest and most interesting events drawn from the catacombs of my remembrance and the various entries I've utilised from my diaries.

Don't worry, this isn't a preamble to revealing a fourth volume is now on the horizon featuring these rejected tales – there will be no Reverse Engineering-style volte-face regarding the Diminished Responsibility series. I just want you to know that so much more could have been shared, all of which has now been set aside and will remain so.

As for the disclosures which did make it onto the page, as in my previous two volumes, I've endeavoured to keep inaccuracies to an absolute minimum and striven to be fair in my assessments and depictions of others.

Despite this attempt at exactitude and objectivity, I expect there will still be those who'll maintain their portrayals in past and forthcoming chapters are inexact and erroneous. To them and to you I can truly affirm I have no motive or desire to depict anyone in a way which is fictitious or unflattering. All characterisations and incidents are exactly how I recall them and my thorough examination of diary records and subsequent verification of details with those who were present at these events has proven invaluable in substantiating my recollections. The reader should therefore be assured my testimony is as genuine and supportable as can be found in all other reliable memoirs which have been published in modern times.

It must also be noted that I have been as critical – if not more so – of myself and my behaviours throughout the three volume series as anyone I might be accused of being judgemental towards. There's light and shade in all human beings and I'm no more exempt from this duality as the next man or woman. Revealing my faults as well as any scarce virtues I might possess became an essential part of my role as author and archivist from the very beginning of this literary project.

Regarding the dialogue: I can't claim that every conversation or verbal exchange recorded in this book is word perfect as apart from those uncommon occasions I'd managed to document any discussions in my journal immediately afterwards, being able to recall every spoken interchange exactly as articulated after multiple years have elapsed is obviously an impossible task. However, I promise that if not verbatim, the substance and spirit of all the discourse recorded in this and my two prior books is as authentic and accurate as can be proffered when taking into account the passage of time.

Disclaimers dealt with, it now only remains for me to sincerely thank you for bearing witness to my servitude to the addictions, practises, perils, failures, triumphs, and cartwheels of fate I've experienced as a Rock musician. I also fervently hope that this final instalment, along with its predecessors, have delivered the correct balance of information, entertainment, and escapism to provide some transient relief from the increasingly perplexing and volatile world we inhabit in this third decade of the 21st century.

It would seem the fairgrounds are shutting down, but some rides can still exhilarate.

Enjoy your ride.

ALVIN GIBBS, Bordeaux, France, 2024

WHAT ARE YOU DOING TOMORROW?

What is it with the unanticipated telephone calls that jumpstart my music career at crucial times and go on to modify the landscape of my life?

Although not as immediately significant as the Brian James and Nicky Garratt phone enquiries that led to my joining Brian James and the Brains in 1979 and the U.K. Subs in 1980 respectively; or from Andy McCoy in the mid-'80s whilst I was living in California, which instigated my playing bass guitar for over eight months and seven continents with the Iggy Pop Band – nor even as timely and decisive as the long-distance question posed by Nasty Suicide via a transatlantic phone line to my Los Angeles home in 1990, prompting my relocation to London to record and tour with Cheap And Nasty – nonetheless, Charlie Harper's telephone proposition in the Summer of '94 would kick start the incremental process that would see me in the fullness of time returning to the U.K. Subs as a permanent player and song writer.

"Alvin, it's Charlie… what are you doing tomorrow?"

Those words were how it began. It seemed Harper was in a bit of a predicament. His then regular Subs' guitarist, Alan Campbell, wasn't able, for reasons unexpressed, to play two shows which had been booked for the Netherlands, plus a third in Germany; and so it was decided that his current bassist Brian Barnes would, as a short-term measure, switch to guitar and that a bass player be drafted in to fill the vacant spot. The thing was, Chas, being Chas, characteristically left finding a replacement four-string adept to the night before the band was due to set out for Calais, thereafter to travel to Nijmegen in the Netherlands for a rehearsal prior to the first gig, which was due to take place the following evening.

I'm pretty sure I was the first replacement candidate he contacted and, luckily for him, despite the eleventh-hour nature of his request, the timing was actually very good for me.

Those of you who previously bought and read Volume II of my trio of memoir books will already be aware that my marriage at this particular junction of my life was gradually, but assuredly, falling apart. My wife Mary Jordan and I were now living in separate locations – she had moved into a flat in Bayswater, which then allowed me to return to our former shared apartment in the West Hampstead district of London – and although we were still tentatively a functioning couple, I knew it was only a matter of time before a definitive break occurred.

The weird thing was, despite Mary being the one who was initially discontented with our marriage and critical of a lifestyle that she once found exciting, after we'd detached our living arrangements, she became the prime mover in trying to salvage our union and starting afresh.

To this end, my spouse signed us up for weekly matrimonial guidance counselling with an organisation called Relate and seemed very keen on sharing her 'issues' with our counsellor at each session, whilst I mostly sat and listened to her inventory of dissatisfaction. But after one such hour-long rendezvous at the Relate offices in the West End of London, an incident occurred that finally convinced me that any attempt at reconciliation would ultimately be doomed.

Following this particular session, at Mary's suggestion, we went to a bar in nearby Soho for a glass of wine. Sitting at a table opposite our own was a young woman vividly dressed in New Romantic-style fashion with multi-coloured braided hair and heavy makeup. As we sipped our drinks, Mary kept surreptitiously glancing over at this colourful female after which, she would snigger and then roll her eyes in a disparaging way, as if to say, 'What the fuck is that sitting over there?'

Now, as a youthful Punk rocker, I'd been the subject of that kind of mocking, dismissive, even sometimes aggressive behaviour from intolerant arseholes, due to my unconventional clothes and my irregular appearance – as faithfully recorded in Volume I – and so, wife or no, I wasn't having any of it…

"Listen, just because that girl likes to dress in a different way to how you like to clothe yourself, there's no need to put her down and take the piss."

I then, in vigorous terms, continued to counter what I considered her bigoted behaviour and bad manners:

"A few years back you would have championed her individuality. Well, I still do, so why do you think that I would be interested in joining in with your disrespectful scoffing of this woman simply because she expresses herself in a way you don't approve of. You call yourself a feminist Mary, but I don't see any signs of sisterhood in your attitude towards her."

This, as you may have anticipated, didn't go down at all well and we got into a quarrel that she artfully expanded to include those 'issues' she had been banging on about at our earlier Relate session – my having, Buddha forbid, been the architect of taking her to Los Angeles, a city she claimed to hate but where she'd studied acting at the prestigious Lee Strasberg Theatre and Film Institute and consequentially became passionate about wanting to become a professional actress. And then, having returned to London, which I'd only agreed to as a means of appeasing her, accusing me of not taking these acting ambitions seriously, despite my having sold my remaining Ampeg SVT amp head and 8 x 10 cabinet to fund her continued classes, and to pay for her publicity headshots and other acting related expenses.

Plus, as a general beef, casually enhancing her menu of discontent by mentioning what she considered my inability to provide the kind of secure, middle-class existence my wife had now decided she was entitled to, even though it was Mary who had the golden Harvard University degree that could have snagged her a good paying professional-grade job, which would have put us in a much more realistic position for a lifestyle upgrade.

Charlie's invitation then would deliver a short term but blissful vacation from these personal woes and allow me to play music again in a live setting in continental Europe. So, without hesitation, I said: "I'll do it."

Harper had assured me that he and the rest of the band would pick me up at West Hampstead tube station at 10am sharp. At 11am there was still no sign of either Charlie or his hastily assembled duo of musicians. I used a pay phone at the station to call him and wasn't that surprised when he answered and explained "Yeah, sorry, we're running a bit behind schedule, just waiting for the drummer to turn up and then we'll set off to collect you."

After another hour of hanging around the station, a battered, rust-tarnished van arrived and I was bundled into its interior, where I discovered two hard wooden benches on either side of the vehicle for Ison (drummer for the occasion), Brian Barnes and me to perch ourselves on. Charlie, naturally, was in the comfortable passenger seat upfront with the driver, who was a very sweet natured, archetypal 1990s crusty type, with dreadlock hair and clothes that evidently hadn't been anywhere near a laundrette for several months.

Together, we set off for Dover and after a mercifully vomit-free Channel crossing (I was very prone to sea sickness back then) reached Calais and drove on in beautiful summer weather through France and Belgium, to eventually reach our Nijmegen rehearsal room destination in the Netherlands at around 10pm.

Having only been asked to do these shows the previous evening, I thought Chas would have chosen for my benefit a set of Subs' standards that would've been pretty much locked into my memory vault from my earlier playing days with the band; but no, instead I was expected to learn a bunch of songs from their most recent album release, Normal

Service Resumed, including Squat the World, Lydia and Here Comes Alex – which I later discovered was a cover of a Die Toten Hosen track – with each tune being completely unknown to me as I hadn't even heard the NSR album, nor some of the other unfamiliar songs Harper had wilfully selected for the set.

By 2am though, I'd managed to nail the bass lines down for these newbies, and we slept overnight in the rehearsal facility – a club that had been closed for the evening – in bunk beds in the upper floor of the building, which were provided by the owners for visiting touring bands whose budgets didn't run to hotel rooms.

The following day we headed to Groningen. I knew we were in trouble when Barnes told me this was the one show that Charlie had booked himself – the other two shows having been arranged by Subs agent, Steve Harnett (aka Toxin) – and my premonition proved to be correct when it turned out Harper didn't even have an address for the venue.

"What the hell Chas," I protested "how are we going to find this place without an address?"

"We're bound to come across some Punks who can tell us where it is," was his mysterious reply.

And so, having reached Groningen, we drove around for a couple of hours, clueless to where the venue resided, until, incredibly, a Punk rocker on a pushbike, complete with Mohawk haircut, anarchy-sign emblazed leather jacket and bondage strides, appeared in the distance on a narrow rural road, in a farms and fields dominated district, situated some distance from the centre of town.

Now completely vindicated by his numinous assertion that a Punk rocker would appear from nowhere and save the day, Charlie rolled down his window and via this Groningen Punk, received the information that he should have obtained and written down before we'd even left the U.K.

As directed by the Punk on a bike, we drove a couple of kilometres or so further up that same lonesome country road and uncovered a former post office that had been turned into a squat by a bunch of Dutch Hippies. One of these longhaired free-spirits, an apparent acid casualty of the late 1960s, came out to greet us, having been alerted to our presence by the noise generated by the engine of our tour van. He bid us enter the graffiti adorned building and introduced us to a couple of other Hippie types from the commune.

They were all pleasant, welcoming, well-meaning folk, but the interior of their squat was as much a disaster area as the outside. The rooms were filthy, the smell of sewage and mouldy walls mixed with that of marijuana smoke, and a mangy old dog with various open sores where its fur had fallen away was wandering about the place, occasionally cocking its leg up to take a quick piss against various pieces of dilapidated furniture.

"Where's the gig taking place?" I asked.

I expected him to lead us to a purpose-built venue attached to the squat, but instead he reached for a very large, ancient iron key on a table shrouded in dog hair and said, "Follow me."

We trailed out after him, away from the main building across a muddy field that at one time would have probably been used to grow cereal grains or potatoes, or, since they'd been squatting there, cannabis plants. About 300 metres away was an old wooden barn, the sight of which caused me to start thinking: 'That can't be it, really, that CAN'T be it, can it? Surely they don't expect us to play in a fucking derelict barn?'

Things got bleaker when we reached this outbuilding. Our guide took the giant key from his pocket and unlocked the barn doors. This provoked a bunch of noisy chickens to dart out from the gloom, where they proceeded to run in-between and around our legs and out onto the field, delighted at having now been liberated from their coop. We went inside.

There was a single light bulb hanging from a wire, above a crudely fabricated stage made from wooden pallets, situated at the far end of the structure. Our guide thoughtfully switched on this solitary light source so that we could fully appreciate the truly shambolic nature of the space. To our right was a very badly constructed bar which, if you dared lean against it, would almost certainly have collapsed and destroyed any drinks it might have held. To our left, totally unconcerned about the intrusion was a large, tethered horse munching on root vegetables, its recent faecal evacuations liberally positioned around the straw-strewn barn floor in large putrid clumps – yes, the place stank of horseshit.

"Charlie, we can't play a show in a shithole like this," I protested.

Chas surveyed the interior of the barn before calmly proclaiming "Oh, I don't know, I think it will be alright, once they get the horse out."

It was a crazy gig. The electrical power kept cutting out, the bar inevitably collapsed in a heap of splintered wood and shattered beer glasses after one of the revellers fell into it; the sole swinging bulb hardly shed enough light to allow us to see each other, let alone keep track of what our hands were doing on the fretboards of our instruments. However, it has to be stated, the audience of local Hippies and Punks and their canines – there were dogs on string everywhere, who added to the general disorder by barking and growling at the band – seemed to really enjoy it, so I guess it wasn't all bad.

The following day we took a long drive to a location south of Hamburg, Germany, in order to headline the Wacken Rock Festival that Saturday evening. This festival in recent times has become a huge event with 100,000 attendees or more from all over the world, but in the early 1990s, it was a much more modest affair, held in a large tent with an audience of 2,000 noise seekers at most.

We played OK, went down extremely well and I was gratified to discover the festival organisers had booked us into a nearby hotel where we, according to my diary, had a party with some of the other musicians, staying up until 7am. This contrasted with the previous night, when the rest of the Subs slept at the squat, lured there by free marijuana. I however, directly after our soundcheck in the Hippie's barn, had walked 30 minutes into the nearest town to get myself a hotel room as I wasn't interested in smoking weed, or sleeping in a squat; nor did I want to wake up to find that poor mangy old hound pissing on me as I lay on a sullied mattress on the floor trying to get some sleep, as had happened to Ison.

Yeah, I'm weird like that.

This minor Euro gigging sojourn was completed the next evening following another tiring drive from Hamburg back into the Netherlands, this time to the town of Arnhem. It was a competent, reasonably attended show and we again made a late night of it by visiting a bar and drinking beer and chatting to the local Punks until 5am.

A bit sore headed, but having savoured this jaunt with the Subs, I and the rest of the band headed back to the U.K. via Calais and a ferry ride across the Channel to Dover. Whilst travelling, Charlie asked if I could again play with the band that coming Saturday at a Punk festival being staged at Brixton Academy. Naturally, I said "yes" – I was enjoying the camaraderie and being able to play some Punk rock music again after my four-year stint with the more traditional Rock outfit, Cheap And Nasty.

There were a lot of old friends and erstwhile faces from the Punk scene either attending or playing the Fuck Reading Punk festival in Brixton. I visited the dressing rooms of the Exploited and Anti-Nowhere League to say hi and catch up on what these bands had been doing in recent years, and around 8pm, we Subs served up a decent set to a receptive crowd.

Immediately upon leaving the stage, Charlie suddenly announced we

Back on bass with the U.K. Subs, mid-1990s.

were doing a second show at the Canterbury Arms pub, directly across the road from the Academy. Unfazed by this last-minute alteration, we trooped over there with our instruments and repeated our performance for an appreciative full house, most of which hadn't been able to afford the ticket price for the Academy.

It would be quite a stretch of time before I again got to play bass guitar for the U.K. Subs – Alan Campbell re-joined the band on guitar, Brian Barnes resumed bass duties and Charlie basically toured on with that line-up for another couple of years with some intermittent alterations – but it was a beginning; and what's more, an unanticipated opportunity to branch out into a new creative direction was just about to come my way along with a precipitous input of cash and the achievement of a long held ambition.

PUBLISHED

Let's deal with the trio of life enhancements which occurred at this time, before moving onto murkier personal territory and some less than advantageous developments.

Firstly, the source of the injection of money I referenced was the royalty and PRS payments I started to receive for having been the principal composer of the song Down on the Farm – which had auspiciously been recorded and released by what at that time was considered one of the foremost Rock bands in the world, Guns N' Roses.

Those of you who have already read Volume II, may recall our publishers of the period, Sparta Florida, had for over a decade, reneged on paying any U.K. Subs' songwriters their dues, necessitating Charlie Harper, Nicky Garratt and I to hire a legal firm called Clintons to take the fraudulent bastardos to court to correct this injustice. We were of course doubly spurred on to get these swindlers convicted and the royalty stream rolling again after I'd learned of G N' R's intension to include Down on the Farm on their salute to Punk album, The Spaghetti Incident? – a platinum status record released in 1993 which sold in excess of five million copies worldwide.

But before the original owners of the publishing company could be convicted of deceitfully pocketing monies intended for their composers, they promptly sold off the company to a set of honest and honourable proprietors who began paying out royalties once they'd taken possession of the business.

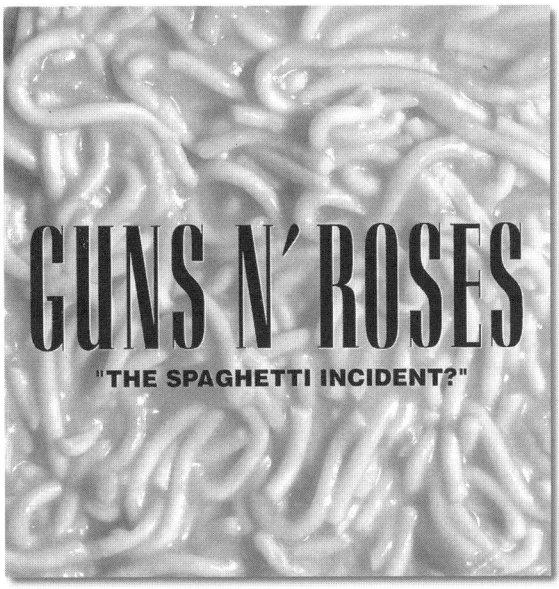

I was disappointed that the scumbags who had overseen the previous incarnation of Sparta Florida hadn't been criminally charged and convicted; and although by shifting the company on to new executors before they inevitably lost the looming court hearing meant that we would never recover the decade's worth of royalties owed us, it did at least guarantee that all future earnings would be forthcoming on a twice-yearly basis, along with accurately accounted statements.

Six months after Sparta Florida changed ownership, I was grateful to receive a cheque for over £8,000 as my first payment from the Guns N' Roses dividend, with other substantial disbursements coming my way over the next few years from this same royalty source. Furthermore, the new creative direction which I touched upon in the previous chapter occurred at the same time.

I've always been a voracious reader. In my teens, I read a lot of classic novels by the likes of Hemingway, F. Scott Fitzgerald, William Golding and Anthony Burgess – the latter two names being the authors of Lord of the Flies and Clockwork Orange. In my twenties, I got into more unconventional writers, such as Albert Camus, Jack Kerouac, Charles Bukowski, Hunter S. Thompson, William Burroughs, and Yukio Mishima.

By my late twenties and thirties, on any given week, you'd discover me reading concurrently, say, Voltaire's Candide along with The Twelve Caesars by Suetonius as well as Jorge Castañeda's Compañero: The Life and Death of Che Guevara; or an eclectic mix along the lines of The Dark Stuff, by Rock music journalist Nick Kent, a copy of Christopher Hibbert's brilliant King Mob – a retelling of the anarchy and wanton destruction caused by the Lord Gordon riots in 18th century London – offset for a different reading experience by George Orwell's prophetic masterpiece, 1984.

Books had educated me – I'd attended a typically uninspiring comprehensive secondary school and had been a notorious truant – and had instilled a real curiosity for a larger and far more fascinating world than the one I had grown up in. In later life they'd become a constant source of inspiration for lyrical ideas. As The Clash's Joe Strummer had once righteously observed: "In order to have output, you must first have input."

This regard for books and their influence had me figuring that one day I might even attempt to write one myself. But on what subject, and more crucially, would I really have the skills and discipline to accomplish something page-turning and compelling, which would be significantly more word heavy and in-depth than a school essay?

I'd read somewhere that first time authors should always write something from personal experience. And so, at the age of 36, I reviewed my life and came to the conclusion that the time I'd spent touring the world with Iggy Pop would be a fitting subject for a maiden outing into the realm of published literature. It seemingly had all the ingredients for a good read: world travel, noteworthy experiences and, hopefully, entertaining stories; plus, it would be a unique insight into working in close proximity with one of the undisputed heavyweight champions of raw, napalm-hearted Rock music, as a member of his band.

Having convinced myself of its worthiness as the subject for an intriguing book, I unearthed and read my diaries from that period and set about writing a synopsis for a prospective publisher, along with that vital first chapter – the one which any future reader would decide whether to plough on with the book or abandon it for something more stimulating.

The initial problem I encountered though was not what to write, but rather, what not to write. So much had happened during the numerous Iggy tours I'd been a part of that it became apparent I would have to edit out a lot of what had occurred, and not just for the sake of keeping the narrative treasonably compact either.

My essential dilemma was this: in 1994, when I began writing about my adventures on the road with Pop, I was still married to the woman from that Iggy touring period – Mary Jordan; and, to put it bluntly, I didn't want to humiliate her with disclosures of my adulteries in a book that might end up in the public domain.

I was also fully in agreement at that stage in life with Lenny Bruce's contention that "confessions of infidelity are a sophisticated form of sadism."

Iggy was also still wedded to the spouse who'd travelled with him for most of the time when we were on the road together and I certainly wasn't going to write about his rare infidelities during her uncommon absence and be held responsible for the negative marital repercussions my revelations might trigger. I considered Jim Osterberg a friend and would rather have devoured my own bones than to have any adulterous exposés potentially be the catalyst for a separation, or worse, a divorce from his then wife, Suchi Asano.

Andy McCoy on the other hand had, by 1994, divorced the woman he'd been married to during his tenure with the Iggy Pop Band and had since remarried. There would be no negative matrimonial consequences for him to deal with, being as the events recorded in the manuscript would have taken place before he had even met Angela Nicoletti, his new wife. This is why when the publisher who originally issued the first edition of my book kept exhorting me to add some touring sex stories along with the duly submitted drugs and rock 'n' roll to the initial proof

Neighbourhood Threat
by Alvin Gibbs

On Tour With
IGGY POP

WITH OVER 40 PHOTOGRAPHS NEVER PUBLISHED BEFORE

galleys, I ended up anaemically providing meagre mention of a couple
of McCoy trysts and then resolutely refused to give them any more
flesh-on-the-road revelations.

   But this was an issue for a future time – at this point I still didn't have
a publisher, just a synopsis and a first draft chapter: so I set up a meeting
with Carl Miller who, along with Nigel Ross-Scott, had attempted to
negotiate a third album deal for Cheap And Nasty (the Rock band
I'd been a member of from 1990-1994) before that possibility was
scuppered by lead singer Nasty Suicide who quit and bagged himself a
solo record deal instead.

   Having liked what I'd given him to read, Carl suggested we go visit
a friend of his who'd had two titles published with a company called
Britannia Press. He wanted to get a second opinion and to find out
if this experienced author thought the project was worthy of further
pursuance.

   David Evans and his life partner, Nigel, lived in a large, beautiful
Georgian house in Islington. Over lunch there, Carl and I outlined for

David the idea behind the proposed book. After reading the chapter I'd provided for him, he enthusiastically agreed that recalling my escapades on a lengthy world tour with the Igmeister would be a compelling read. He gratifyingly added that the chapter I'd given him to peruse was well written and had engendered the desirable effect on him of wanting to read more. Despite this favourable response, I was still amazed at Evans' generosity when he proposed handing on what I'd written to the head honcho at Britannia Press, Andre Delauchy, to see if he'd be interested in publishing the finished manuscript.

I'm really incapable of fully couriering to you the immense excitement I felt a couple of days later – having checked all incoming communications on my old-school landline message machine – after hearing Delauchy's voice stating he wanted me to phone him back ASAP, so we could discuss publishing the book (my book!) once I'd completed it.

After returning his call, he invited me to Belgo restaurant in Camden, a business which he had a financial investment in, for dinner, during which time he handed over to me the contract for my book's publication. This document quantified the per-sale percentage I would receive and stipulated a six-month deadline for finalisation. Upon receipt of the finished book, I'd be awarded an advance of £1,000. I went directly home after the shared bottle of champagne Andre had ordered to celebrate my signing of the agreement, and back in my London flat got on with writing freehand on a series of lined notepads the subsequent pages for the book which would eventually be published as Neighbourhood Threat: On Tour With Iggy Pop.

Just before 1994 reached its conclusion, I took my last ever trip abroad in the company of my wife in the unlikely hope that Christmas in Paris might somehow arouse some semblance of togetherness and romance in us. It didn't. Although our five days in that beautiful city was an enjoyable escape from London life, it certainly didn't ignite any desire in me to salvage our marriage. All I fundamentally kept thinking about during our time together there was how I needed to get back to work on the book to fulfil my six-month contractual obligation.

On our return, David Evans once again demonstrated his innate generosity when he phoned to ask how the book was shaping up. I told him it was coming along, but I didn't have a typewriter or home PC (still rare in those days), and so was getting words down using a biro on paper that at some stage would need to be typed out.

"Bring over each chapter as you finish them and I'll type and print them out from my PC," he said.

Not only would David accordingly do the keyboard and printing duties but he also proved to be a really helpful editor, challenging certain aspects of my naïve writing style and aiding me in trimming the more unnecessarily expansive sections into more concise pieces of prose. His assistance in achieving a final draft of the manuscript was immense.

Having handed over the finished book to Britannia Press with its working designation of Neighbourhood Threat, I then remembered that the very first song I'd learned from the list given to me to work on for the initial Iggy Pop Band's North American tour of 1988 was Some Weird Sin, which I consequently thought would make a much better title. I phoned Delauchy and told him to change it; but he didn't, and it emerged in the spring of 1995 with its original moniker on the front cover.

I can't be too critical of this oversight. Andre had given me my first break as a published and paid author – as contractually agreed, he cut me a cheque for £1,000 when I turned up at the Britannia Press' office above Belgo restaurant to pass on the finished manuscript – and his publicity people did a good job of getting the book reviewed in the Rock music journals, where it achieved a unified degree of praise.

They also got me onto MTV, where I was interviewed for 30 minutes about the contents of Neighbourhood Threat by one of that popular cable station's glamorous female presenters; plus numerous radio programmes, including Entertainment Superhighway, a live broadcast on BBC 5 with a large attending audience, on which the magician Paul Daniels and I were the main guests. Presented by Katie Puckrik – who I later learned had taken a bit of a romantic shine to me – I answered questions and told stories from my book whilst Daniels did magic tricks, on radio. Having spent time in his company in the Green Room and during the show, I can confirm that Paul Daniels really was as pompous, egotistic and smug as he appeared on television.

The final beneficial development of the troika that sustained me as my marriage continued to unravel and my personal life reached a crisis point, was the attainment of Shodan (1st Dan Black Belt) in the Japanese martial art of Shrorinji Kempo. After five years of regular training and study Mizuno Sensei, the 7th Dan head of the British Kempo Association, decided I was ready to move up from brown to black belt and had me apply for the Shodan grading test which took place at a large sports centre in Brixton. There, along with over 150 other students from various parts of the country who were testing for green to black belt status, I embarked on a four-hour grading that began with having to complete 100 knuckle push-ups.

Alvin's Shodan Black Belt, displaying his name in Japanese, mid-1990s.

This opening part of the Shodan trial was absolute. Anyone who couldn't achieve that 100 target would immediately fail the grading. Now, to some people, 100 knuckle push-ups sounds like a very difficult feat, but Mizuno Sensei had given me prior good advice on how to achieve it when I first started training in 1990: "You begin" he told me, "by starting with just three knuckle push-ups twice a day for three days. Then, you add one more, and so keep with four knuckle push-ups for three days, then add another and so on until you reach a hundred. What you will find" he asserted, "is that you can always force one more push-up after three days and in time a hundred will come comfortably to you."

That accomplished, I then had to demonstrate my proficiency at the various kicks, punches and strikes as they were called out to me by one of the British Sensei. This was then followed by a test of my knowledge of throws, sweeps, leverages, locks, and restraints on a fellow Shodan grading student, before switching to playing the attacker so they could display the same on me, which, in turn, allowed me to exhibit my ability to roll safely out of a throw or to land without injury when pitched high over a shoulder onto the hard parquet floor.

Set techniques were next, with the last 30 minutes being dedicated to randori – free fighting. Thinly padded gloves and an equally slender chest protector were worn as brown and black belts (some as highly graded as 3rd Dan) were sent, one after the other, to attack me in a taped off fighting space in order to test my self-defence skills. I have no recollection of battling with either my eleventh or twelfth opponent during the final minutes of that randori trial. I guess I was fighting

Kempo Karate certificates, Green Belt to Black.

solely on muscle memory and adrenaline during those last bouts. Despite my latter amnesia, I was told by my club Sensei, who'd watched all my matches, that I'd given a good account of myself and won the majority. A week later, after a practise session at Abbey Dojo, Jee Sensei informed me I'd attained Shodan status and a month following that, I received my certificate and Black Belt – embroidered with my name in Japanese katakana and kanji – from the Shorinji Kempo World Organisation headquarters based in the island of Shikoku, located on the south-western edge of Japan.

Along with becoming a published author, this was yet another ambition fulfilled; and, what with the cash injection from the Down on the Farm royalties, I was feeling pretty good about how things were shaping up that year. But then a complication arose that directly led to my having to come to terms with the now unchallengeable fact that my marriage to Mary Jordan was over – I met a woman.

DESTROY!

To be completely honest, when my wife and I stopped cohabitating together, and despite still being nominally married, I met and had relations with a number of women which lasted for varying durations.

I'd slept with the 30-year-old sister of the Britannia Press' publicist who worked in a secretarial capacity at her brother's office; then there was a German girl called Dina, who spent the night with me after we met at a one-off Subs London show where I'd filled in on bass; yet another German woman, this time an air hostess named Sabrina, subsequently became my short-term amour. There was the artist, whose sketches and paintings were regularly featured in publications; and then, most promisingly, one of the fashion editors of The Independent newspaper, an affair that lasted a reasonably long time – at least six months I think – and could have (ought to have) morphed into something far more substantial.

Having already reached the conclusion that my marriage was unsalvageable, the fashion editor was exactly the kind of woman I should have formed an enduring relationship with. She was attractive, had a great job, a nice apartment, was intelligent, educated and liked me a lot. She wanted to start an exclusive, settled life together, not just our regular nights of wine, cocaine and sex which, at that time, were actually my idea of the perfect romantic get together.

She was in many ways the ideal woman for me, but my emotionally fucked-up self wasn't looking for idyllic; it was looking for difficult, problematic and doomed.

So, after terminating my affair with the fashion editor; and subsequently visiting Mary to tell her that I no longer wanted to be involved in rescuing our marriage, I invited Lisa V to move into my West Hampstead flat.

I'd met Lisa at a gig I'd played at the Epsom Playhouse Theatre. Carl Miller had decided to promote some shows there and asked me to put a band together to perform on a Sunday evening. I got my former Cheap And Nasty band mate Timo Kaltio to join on guitar, recruited occasional U.K. Sub, Ison, to play the drums, and asked a singer/guitarist named Rob Reynolds, who I'd been introduced to by Carl, to enrol. The bass duties and intermittent lead vocals were my jurisdiction.

Also on the bill was blues singer Simon Whitaker and opening up proceedings was Lisa V and her musical partner Joanna McCaul – this acoustic guitar and vocal duo having previously played some gigs together locally.

After the headline performance of my hastily assembled band of musicians, Carl invited all the participants over to his house for post-

Leisure

Music

Make a trip to The Crossing

A former member of Iggy
Pop's band tops the bill at
The Crossing – a series of
live concerts at the Epsom
Playhouse.
Alvin Gibbs performs a one-
off acoustic set with vocalist
Rob Reynolds this Sunday.
Alvin was a founder member
and bassist with UK Subs
and went on to join Iggy
Pop's band for the Instinct
album and tour.

He has also written a book
called Neighbourhood Threat –
A World Tour With Iggy
Pop, due to be released
through Britannia Press next
Thursday.
Joining Gibbs and Reynolds
for the evening is European
festival regular Simon
Whitaker.
Simon is described as an
innovative and talented multi-
instrumentalist who plays
bass drum and hi hat, guitar
and steel drums. His debut
album I Fall U Fall has
recently been released on
Whitaker Records.
Opening the entertainment
will be Lisa Von Hasenburg
and Joanna McCaul who have
performed their vocal
harmonies on cable TV.
Tickets are priced £5 and
include a complimentary
lager.
Doors open 7.30pm. First
act on stage at 7.30pm.
Box office: 01372 742555.

Gene Pitney delights fans

Legendary singer Gene Pitney
makes a welcome return to
the Fairfield Halls with
special guest Bobby Crush.
Gene Pitney comes to the
Fairfield Halls on Wednesday,
May 24, at 8pm.
Tickets are £11, £13.50 and
£15. Call the box office on
0181 688 9291.

Alvin Gibbs and Rob Reynolds lead the musical line-up at Epsom Playhouse.

Guardian article re the Epsom Playhouse gig, 1995.

show drinks. There I got talking to V, who was a pretty woman in her mid-twenties with an amazing figure. Based on what I'd overheard earlier, she was moreover a talented songwriter, singer and guitarist. Lisa gave me her phone number and a few days later I called and asked her over to my place to share a bottle of wine. She ended up staying the night, and, within two months, Lisa V had moved in.

1996 was fast approaching and seeing as Neighbourhood Threat had garnered good reviews and been purchased in decent amounts, I thought I would pitch the idea of a follow-up book to Andre Delauchy, this time chronicling the history of Punk rock for its forthcoming twentieth anniversary year. He fancied the idea and offered me the same contractual terms with matching six-month deadline and an equivalent advance for this new writing project.

This time around though I didn't want to impose on David Evans and so got myself down to Tottenham Court Road where I purchased a Sharp word processor for £245, thereby being able to type the pages of my new book directly onto floppy disks (remember floppy disks?) whilst also cutting out the need to write everything out in longhand for David Evans to copy onto his PC. I also bought a desk and an office chair which I positioned together in a corner of my bedroom, so I could type away at any time of night or day without distraction.

In retrospect, this was a mistake. Evans, as I've already written, was a good editor and an insightful critic – having him look over what I'd transcribed would have helped ensure the book was a decent and thoughtful read, rather than the shambolic, drunken, inaccurate scrawl that it became.

The initial problem though was trying to write on a regular daily schedule now that Lisa was living with me. She had no job and no income which meant not only did I pay for everything, but we were together 24-7.

V wanted to spend a lot of time with me now that we were cohabiting and at first, I acquiesced, watched soap operas on TV with her that I had no interest in and patiently listened to her going on about how we should move to a new household as the present apartment was the same one I'd once (horror of horrors) shared with my wife – all to be financed by me of course. She quickly became a vampiric presence, sucking away at my time and energy whilst the clock kept-a-ticking and my new word processor continued to be underused.

When Lisa had first relocated to my place from her parents' house in Woking, I'd envisioned she would be keenly occupied in writing new songs and playing her guitar in the lounge whilst I got on with my twentieth anniversary Punk book and composed new tunes of my own in the bedroom; after which, following our respective separate activities during the day, we would reconvene in the evenings to eat dinner, drink some wine, chat, play records or watch a video movie together.

This turned out to be a delusional fantasy. There was always some vital necessity or trivial problem coming my way from her that required my full consideration at all hours. I eventually became ensnared in her relentless need for attention and wasn't taking care of essential business.

Now, I'll be totally upfront with you: the only reason I tolerated this situation for as long as I did was because the sex was really good. Yes, I'm quite aware this disclosure doesn't reflect well on my character and could well suggest that I was a deceitful and shallow man – I don't care, it's the truth.

So I appeased Lisa, by going with her to view some alternative apartments that weren't cursed by having once been inhabited by my soon to be ex-wife, although with absolutely no intension of renting them. I continued to be attentive to her needs and whims before coming up with a plan which I naively believed could recalibrate our relations – I took V to Rome for a week thinking that the city's architecture, food, wine, and history might instil in her a different sensibility and get us seeing things in a more compatible way.

It didn't. She wasn't keen on the food, nor the wine, and it turned out the most impressive aspect of Rome for her was not the magnificence of the Coliseum, but the fact that a lot of feral cats lived there.

Still, I persevered. On our return I tried to get her to work more on her music and get some shows together with her duo partner, Joanna. I even phoned Carl and asked him to book some gigs for them so she would have something to aim for. Instead of concentrating on playing guitar and singing in public again, her singular focus became pushing for us to get engaged. The fact that I wasn't even divorced yet didn't seem to matter to her. I tried to explain that it may be some time before I would be free to marry, but Lisa was determined we should make a commitment to do so, even though we had been living together for only a few months.

When the divorce papers arrived from Mary Jordan – who'd finally acknowledged that our marriage was over and taken the initiative by hiring a lawyer to obtain a Decree Nisi – Lisa's campaign for us to be formally engaged intensified. I got myself a lawyer and the divorce negotiations began in earnest, although I knew it would be a while before my marriage to Mary Jordan was irrevocably terminated.

By the early months of 1996, I'd still not made a decent stab at writing the book I'd pitched to Andre. I was getting stressed out, not only through my failure to make headway with my writing, but because of the divorce situation and Lisa's persistent crusade for our engagement, along with her needy and changeable ways – having asked Carl Miller to book a series of shows for her and Joanna to play, V suddenly decided she didn't want to fulfil these commitments, even though she'd been keen when I'd first proposed the idea.

I had to call Carl and tell him his time and efforts had been wasted. He, understandably, wasn't best pleased to hear this news and we got into an argument as I was trying to play the role of protective boyfriend and endeavoured to defend Lisa's indefensible changeability. So the way I began to deal with these pressures and discords was to drink – a lot. Not just wine or beer but large amounts of hard liquor too.

The other factor for this acceleration of drinking was guilt. I felt guilty for the breakup of my marriage; for not having been honest with Lisa about the true nature of my interest in her; for allowing myself to become so unproductive, distracted and, well, lost.

Those of you who have read my two previous memoir volumes will already know that my relationship with alcohol had, since my teens, been an adoring and devoted one. But it had mainly been what I like to term 'joyful drinking' – as part of the culture that is customary when a Rock band socialises, bonds together and tries to deal with post-show adrenaline during the touring cycle; whilst off the road, as an adjunct to the camaraderie when out and about with friends and acquaintances in a pub, bar or attending a gig; for celebrations; for the accompaniment of good food or a relaxing indulgence after a productive day.

Those are all examples of what I mean by 'joyful drinking': the imbibing of alcoholic beverages as a pleasurable enhancer as opposed to an addictive necessity or a means of defiling and abdicating from oneself because of loss, self-loathing, unhappiness or acute feelings of culpability.

As a young boy, I loved it when my parents threw intermittent parties. I enjoyed the music, the grown-up conversation, jokes, laughter, the adult flirting, the cigarette smoking and carefree drinking of the guests – that agreeable hum which pervaded a room when people abandon the shackles and cares of their everyday lives to let loose and have some fun for a while.

For these occasions my father would hand me a Martini Rossi bottle top, which he would occasionally plunge into his glass of beer and then hand it to me so I could sample a small portion of the brew. What he didn't know was I was also covertly going round cheekily asking his party guests if I could do the same with their drinks, some of which contained liquids a lot stronger than beer. They hadn't realised my dad was sporadically topping up my bottle top and so would laughingly dunk it into their tumblers when I offered it and allow me to sample their chosen beverages.

Although this only amounted each time to a mere thimble-full of tipple, by the time I'd sampled the drinks of several guests in conjunction with the mouthfuls of my father's beer, I would be quite merry by the end of the evening. I loved that buzz, the way it would make me giddy and cheerful and untroubled.

The next day I would always ask my father the same question: "Dad, why can't we have another party tonight?" To which he would answer "Son, if we had a party every night you wouldn't enjoy it," to which I always replied "Yes, I would."

That response is very revealing – even at that early age, it formed part of my desire to live a life that was counter to the commonplace, conventional experience. Why shouldn't people have a party every night if they wanted to? How come people's lives were primarily dedicated to drudgery and mundane repetition interspersed by rare occasions of release and gratification? Why couldn't you flip it round so that pleasure becomes the norm and the grind of life a rarity?

Although I had no knowledge of this learned sage as a young boy, the 4th century BC Greek philosopher Epicurus famously pronounced that 'Pleasure is the beginning and end of living happily.' Even as a seven-year-old child I would have agreed with that proclamation. I still agree with it now, although pleasure should in no way be interpreted as overindulgence: I get pleasure from being creative and industrious, working hard on my music and writing projects, not only from sharing wine and having fun with my friends and family.

But the caustic truth was, in the early months of 1996, due to the pressures and anxieties I'd listed previously, my drinking had shifted from pleasurable consumption to ingesting alcohol in much larger quantities for darker motives.

When at last I agreed to marry Lisa once my divorce was finalised – primarily as a means of getting her to stop her incessant offensive on the subject so I could make headway with the book – I felt even more ashamed for acceding to the engagement as a stalling tactic rather than from an authentic aspiration. Consequently, I drank even more, disgusted with myself for not having been truthful with her, or myself.

I would often consume till the point of unconsciousness at home; and, when out on the town with friends, until I was a stumbling mess, sometimes waking up in bed fully clothed alongside Lisa with no knowledge of how I'd got back to the flat or what had occurred earlier in the evening. My drinking became a way of self-harming, and it was whilst in the grip of this alcoholic debasement that I completed the book that would shortly be published under its apropos title – Destroy.

I've expressed before in interviews and in print my dislike for this failed attempt at merging the history of the Punk movement with my own involvement in the genre. Because of my depressed mental state, exacerbated by my prodigious alcohol intake, I made comments about certain bands and personalities in the book which were either distortions of the truth, or simply unfair and uncalled for. There were also a number of factual and spelling errors, although in my defence, when I handed over the completed manuscript to Britannia Press, I asked Delauchy to make sure everything was fact-checked and told him that it had to be proof-read, at least twice, by independent readers before going to print.

But that didn't happen. When I received the published book, I was horrified to discover it had been reproduced exactly as given and so vented my anger at Andre over the telephone in a loud and uncompromising way before, once again, reaching for the vodka bottle which, naturally, only made matters worse.

Despite my disappointment and anger at being let down by my publisher, I still felt compelled to promote the book on radio shows, in magazine interviews and cable TV stations. Luckily, most interviewers and hosts, such as Phill Jupitus on his BBC GLR show, were more interested in stories from my Subs and Iggy Pop days than in the actual contents of the book.

I was amazed then when Britannia's publicist, Tony Riley, received a letter from Punk rock fan and England football team defender Stuart 'Psycho' Pearce after having judiciously sent him a copy of the book knowing of his predilection for all things Punk. Pearce wrote that Destroy had been his sole reading during the Euro '96 tournament and just how much he'd enjoyed and been fired up by it.

L to R – Lisa V, me and my mother, Portugal, 1995.

For me though, Destroy: The Definitive History of Punk, remains an embarrassing failure, and a constant reminder of a very bleak period of my life.

The one good thing about Destroy was the £1,000 advance I received upon its completion. This funded, among other things, a much needed holiday in Portugal along with certain members of my family. Lisa, I, and the other vacationers were all based at the house my mother had inherited from her parents in the northern Portuguese town of Chaves.

Towards the end of our two weeks there, my sister Rosa and brother-in-law Andrew, having first-hand witnessed how needy and difficult Lisa was, waited for a private moment when she was in another part of the house, to ask me if this was truly the sort of woman I wanted to get hitched to once my divorce was finalised. I knew they wouldn't have said anything unless they were concerned about me making a bad decision – my family have always been supportive of each other's choices, so it took a lot for them to ask me such a forthright question. But I also appreciated their honesty and the fact that they were right. If I'd married Lisa, it would have been an unmitigated disaster.

Once you took sex out of the equation, we were entirely unsuited, despite both being musicians – although with very different work ethics and levels of ambition. She was a fine singer and guitar player; her songs were very good; but Lisa had no talent for tenacity or doing what was necessary to reach the professional level. At that time in her life, she simply wanted to be catered to, looked after and securely married.

And so, back in London after this conclusive vacation together, I had to tell her that our engagement was off and marrying her was now out of the question. It was an awful admission, but it had to be done, for both our sakes. She eventually accepted my rationale for discontinuing our betrothal and decided to go back to Woking to again live with her parents.

This eased the pressure on one front, but there was still my divorce to deal with. Just before flying out to Portugal, I attended my first annulment court hearing with my lawyer. Mary was there with her brief and a list of 'wants', which included my paying off a hefty outstanding joint tax bill from our time in the U.S.A. and ownership of 50% of my royalties for all of my published songs in perpetuity – virtually all of which I'd composed before I'd even met her. There was also a fee for all the years she had apparently sacrificed her life for the sake of my career.

It was weird seeing Mary sitting across the table from me, an unceasing scowl on her face, devoid of any traces of the genial, reasonable woman I'd fallen in love with.

I had discovered that Mary's father had paid out for a flat for her in the Bayswater area of London, a location near Hyde Park and consequently a pretty pricey area for property. When I revealed this to my lawyer, he said I had every right to make a claim for 50% of the value of the apartment as part of any divorce settlement, especially since I lived in mere rented accommodation – but I wouldn't hear of it.

"I'm not going to make any claim on a property that I've not put a single penny into," I told him.

"Well, let's at least use it as a bargaining point to get some of her financial requests dropped," he countered.

"No" I insisted, "let's leave the Bayswater flat out of it and concentrate on making the case for why she's not entitled to half my royalties for the rest of her life."

What I couldn't have predicted following this initial encounter with the woman who had been my wife for 14 years, was that when our next and final divorce hearing took place, I would be in a very different physical and mental condition to the man who sat across from her and wondered: "How did it come to this?"

GOING BACK TO CALI

October 1996. I'm suspended around 35,000 feet somewhere over the Atlantic Ocean, destination Los Angeles where, according to LL Cool J, 'the AC's cold, but the girls still strip.'

Reclined in my window seat on a Virgin Airlines flight whilst sipping my third glass of wine, I'm trying my upmost not to stare at the über-hot hostess who'd just served up the Italian red and handed out the peanuts. She had engagingly sashayed past me along the aisle in her wetsuit-tight scarlet uniform on numerous occasions and, although I knew nothing would come of it, the urge to engage her in conversation with a view to obtaining a future date in the so called City of Angels, kept up its relentless campaign and required some serious resisting.

This was the siren's song – the biological and psychological impulse to be physically connected with another human being as a means of getting back to the primitive essence of the human/animal condition, and as an agency for gratification and the loss of self.

Gautama Buddha confessed that if there had been another drive as powerful as sex, he wouldn't have attained enlightenment. Athenian philosopher Plato likened the power of the sexual urge as being chained to a madman and was thankful when he reached his seventies and impotence, brought on by old age, finally killed off the maniac.

I say, long live the maniac. He's the madcap that biology and evolution bequeathed us; and, as far as I'm concerned, science and evolutionary principles are sacrosanct.

These were the offbeat, wine-induced thoughts that scurried around my skull as the Boeing 747 I'd boarded that afternoon at Heathrow Airport winged ever closer to my Californian destination.

So what led me to taking this flight to the city that I'd lived and revelled in during a prior decade? To answer that enigma we've got to time slip a few months, to when Lisa departed from my life and I started to play more and drink less.

V's parting and my completion of Destroy freed up the time for me to get into other things. I was invited by my friend Greg Radcliffe to perform as a member of his band Razor Babies in the video film they were making as a visual commercial for their latest single release. I also filled in on bass for an enjoyable duo of live shows with the U.K. Subs in London. Shortly thereafter, Charlie Harper called and offered me three additional consecutive gigs with the Subs. The first was definitely in Swindon but, for some reason, I've neglected to record in my '96 diary the other two venues and cities, or how these shows fared. A week later, he again phoned and asked me to play a late show at the Canterbury

Arms in Brixton, which provided me with another opportunity to utilise the four-string machine to serve up some Old School Punk rock.

The most significant phone call of them all though, came from the U.S.A. some weeks before that Brixton gig, as I was restringing one of the basses at my flat whilst simultaneously watching Match of the Day on the TV.

"Alvin, it's Nicky Garratt."

Credentials established and customary small talk dispensed with, Nicky then relayed the principal purpose for his call:

"I've been talking to Charlie about doing a reunion album with you and Steve Roberts which, we're both agreed, was our favourite line-up of the Subs. He tells me though that Steve is too risky a proposition these days…"

I could certainly vouch for what Charlie had disclosed to Garratt. When Lisa had initially moved in with me, before my own drinking became problematic, Roberts had contacted me to say he was heading down south shortly and could he visit to chat about a band he was putting together that he wanted me to get involved with. Seems Stevie boy had transformed himself from drummer to lead singer and sole songwriter of a modern-day Glam rock styled outfit which he wanted to relocate from his present York base to London.

"Let's talk a bit of business," he kept saying.

"Sure, it would be good to see you again after all these years," I told him. "Get over to my flat for seven p.m. on the day of your arrival, and my girlfriend and I will have dinner waiting for you."

"Great matey," he replied, "can't wait."

Unfortunately, we did.

On the evening of his expected visit 7pm came and went, likewise 8pm. Then, around 9.45pm the flat's intercom buzzed to alert us that someone wanted entry into the building. I hit the button that allowed me to talk to whoever was seeking access and heard a voice with a distinct Yorkshire accent that I didn't recognise:

"Hello, this is Steve here. I'm the drummer in Steve Roberts' band. I drove him down to London. We're both outside but I think I'll need a hand getting him in."

I opened the front door from the intercom panel and bounded down the stairs to the communal entrance hall to witness a semi-conscious Roberts being helped in by the man who will now be referred to as 'the other Steve'.

"What the fuck happened to him?" I asked.

"I think he got nervous about seeing you and he ended up drinking a bottle of whisky on the drive down from York," the other Steve explained.

Together we hauled the wannabe Glam rock star up the stairs and having got him into my apartment, lowered him onto the couch where he started mumbling drunken nonsense in between lapsing in and out of consciousness. The other Steve was mightily apologetic: "I'm so sorry Alvin. He's been looking forward to seeing you for months. I guess he was worried he would make a bad impression, and now look."

"It's alright," I told him, "none of this is your fault. The original dinner we cooked is ruined but Lisa and I can whip up something so we can eat together."

He was grateful for the offer and by the time the meal was ready Steve Roberts had revived a little from his alcoholic stupor and staggered across the room to join us at the dining table. I kept the wine out of his reach but put a bowl of pasta in front of him.

Ignoring the provided cutlery, Roberts used his hands to scoop up large portions of the food, which he attempted to cram into his mouth only for sizeable amounts to either end up on his lap, the table, or the floor. Lisa and the other Steve were horrified at his boorish behaviour, but I laughed it off and chatted to Roberts' drummer until it was time for the two Steves to leave. I then assisted the other Steve in physically supporting the intoxicated former U.K. Sub and together we got him safely down the stairs, out of the building and into the car that had been parked in a neighbouring street.

Roberts did phone me the next day to offer apologies for his lateness and conduct; and I did meet up with him on a couple of occasions whilst he was still in London. For those encounters, he was reasonably sober and present, but that first reunion had convinced me he couldn't be relied on and that all his former protestations of being "a changed man" were mere words designed to reassure rather than a sign of genuine reformation. This was the reason I was in complete agreement with Charlie's estimation of Steve Roberts being a chancy prospect.

Nicky Garratt had obviously taken on board Harper's forewarning:

"So, having discounted Steve for the album, I've lined up a really good drummer who lives here in San Francisco."

The musician in question was Dave Ayer, who'd played with northern Californian Punk outfit Samiam (pronounced Sam-I-am) and contributed drums to three of their long playing records, each of which had been released on Garratt's New Red Archives record label.

"The question is: are you interested enough to fly to San Francisco to play bass on this album; and, if so, do you also have some songs to contribute?"

My answer to his double-barrelled inquiry was "Yes" and "Yes."

Recording wasn't due to start until October, so I had plenty of time to write a couple of tunes for the LP – Lost Not Found and Cyberjunk – and as there was now a tangible project to work towards, I put aside my depression and heavy drinking and initiated a healthier weekly routine.

I upped my Shorinji Kempo training schedule at Abbey dojo, joined a gym, where I worked out four afternoons a week; and enrolled with a Kendo dojo which held weekend classes at a school hall in Camden Town.

Kendo is a traditional form of Japanese fencing that utilises a split bamboo sword (the shinai) and protective armour (bōgu), both of which I acquired from a martial arts shop in the West End of London having been severely bitten by the Kendo bug.

Most importantly, I also cut down my drinking from reckless to a glass or two of wine late in the evening, after my various training sessions or following a productive day of book reading and working on the historical novel I'd started; or subsequent to playing my acoustic guitar, this having become a regular activity for me which often led to new ideas for songs.

I was also back up to professional form, bass playing wise, having completed recent shows with the Razor Babies and the Subs. And so, with this restored condition of mind and body, I considered my trip to the U.S.A. and decided before heading to San Francisco to record the proposed re-union album, I would firstly visit the city I'd foolishly left six years before to appease the woman I subsequently divorced.

Despite the wearisome 11-hour flight, as soon as the 747 touched down at LAX Airport, I was instantaneously energised and excited to be back in Los Angeles.

Once I'd got out of the internal part of the airport, the Californian October sunshine and dry heat warmed my bones and spirits as I looked about for the man who was due to collect me for the drive to Hollywood. The hombre in question was patiently waiting for me beside his car adjacent the exit. After an embrace and a sincere welcome, he put my suitcase in the trunk and we set off, firstly losing the labyrinth of roads that surround LAX, before heading east, then north, on the 110 Freeway.

I'd previously phoned a number of my old friends from the time I'd

On the balcony of the Harte-Wilhoite Hollywood residence, 1996.

lived in the Wiltshire District of North Hollywood in the 1980s to let them know I would be returning for a visit; but it was the drummer of one of the bands I'd played with during that period, Dave Harte, who was the first to offer me a ride and who'd also generously proposed I stay with him and his wife in their smart house up in the Hollywood Hills whilst I remained in LA.

During the drive Dave told me of all the immense changes that had occurred in his life since we'd played together in the Rock band Broken Glass. He'd married the actress Kathleen Wilhoite, who'd starred alongside Charles Bronson in the film Murphy's Law, had been awarded roles with Robert De Niro in Angel Heart, Patrick Swayze in Roadhouse, and Susan Sarandon and Nick Nolte in Lorenzo's Oil; plus numerous other movie appearances that would take up far too much page space for me to document. She'd also had parts in successful TV series such as Twin Peaks, LA Law, Ally McBeal, and ER. Kathleen was also a musician who would later release two albums, on both of which Dave took care of the production duties as well as providing the drum parts.

They'd had their first child the year before – Jimmy-Ray – and I learned from my friend that he was now moving away from music and getting into television production, this being a more secure and lucrative form of making a living than the notoriously unstable profession I was still a part of.

I then disclosed the essentials about my life after I'd traded LA for

London in 1990 – tales of my time with Cheap And Nasty and the circumstances of our eventual demise; the Guns N' Roses windfall; my impending divorce and unsuccessful attempt at domesticity with Lisa V.

My room at the Harte-Wilhoite residence was comfortable and spacious with a picturesque window view across the hills to Griffith Park. Kathleen was very welcoming and had plenty of juicy stories about the actors she'd worked with over the years. We had dinners in restaurants, saw a couple of local bands and visited some of the bars I'd habitually frequented when I'd lived in the Big Orange. I got to meet up with other old friends, notably another alumni of Broken Glass, Tim Mosher, and the always entertaining Ike Baruch, who I'd played bass with in the clubs of Cali for his band Revolver, and who'd recently split up from his wife Darcy – I'd been best man at their traditional Jewish wedding just prior to my returning to the U.K.

When I quizzed Ike about the circumstances of their break-up his explanation was very enlightening:

"Hey, take a look, before we got married Darcy and I would have sex all the time, but once I'd married her, I didn't want to fuck her anymore. Wha-do-ya make of that?"

"It sounds to me like a classic case of Madonna-whore complex."

"What's that?"

"It's a Freudian concept – basically the inability of certain men to maintain sexual arousal once they're in a committed and caring relationship. They regard their pre-marriage partners as desirable, free and easy women but once married, they start to see them as mother-like saintly figures and their sexual appeal dissipates to the point where sex eventually becomes less pleasing, and then downright impossible... or something like that."

"Sounds about right," mused Ike, who then told me about how he punched out the lead guitarist for the band he'd formed after Revolver whilst they were playing together onstage.

"When I split from Darcy because I couldn't fuck her anymore, I found out that my guitar player was seeing her. I tried to forget it but one night, when we were halfway through our set at the Roxy, I looked at him and thought 'hey, you're fucking my wife,' so I went across stage and hit the cabrón in the face as hard as I could. The pussy went down pretty easy."

"What the fuck! You were the one who left Darcy because you couldn't have sex with her anymore. If she started up with your guitarist and they were having sexual relations neither he nor she were in the wrong. You were the one out of order mate."

His final justification was classic Ike.

"You're probably right, but what-ya expect from a Brooklyn-bred Puerto Rican Jew?"

My trip to LA was exactly what I'd needed to get away from the stress of my on-going divorce and to conclusively put aside the failure of my attempted relationship with Lisa. It was with some sorrow then, after a most excellent week there, that I was obliged to return to LAX, again courtesy of a ride from Dave Harte, to catch a flight to a more northerly part of the state where Nicky Garratt was waiting for my arrival at San Francisco International Airport.

This was another city I'd lived in for a while and I relished seeing again the familiar colourfully painted Victorian houses with their bay windows and neo-gothic architecture, as we drove in Nicky's jeep up and down those notoriously steep SF roads – made famous in the Steve McQueen movie Bullitt – until we eventually reached his house in the Sunset district of the metropolis.

Charlie was flying in from London two days hence, so Nicky and I got the proverbial ball-a-rolling with him firstly acquainting himself with my two pre-written songs and then having me learn a Burt Bacharach tune he wanted us to cover entitled Little Red Book. Now I love, love, love the amazing recorded output of Bacharach and his principal lyricist Hal David; but of all the fine songs the Silver Fox had composed, Little Red Book definitely wasn't among the best. Not only was it a second-rate pick, but it also struck me as being a particularly unsuitable choice for a Punk rock makeover. When Harper turned up, he was of the same mind, but Garratt was determined to keep it for the recording schedule.

After Chas' arrival we all got down to some serious song writing. Being similarly jetlagged from our transatlantic flights, Harper and I would wake anytime between 5 and 6am and then head off together to a wonderful café, just an easy walk down from Nicky's place on 41st Avenue. Simple Pleasures was owned and frequented by a lot of 1960s era hippie, beardy, Grateful Dead-types, but, by common consent, it served the best coffee, raisin muffins and eggs over easy with hash browns in the area.

Following our daily breakfast there, Harper and I always took a stroll to the beach to watch the morning mist evaporate as the sun gained strength, which allowed the ocean to gradually reveal itself along with its cargo of ghostly transient ships on the distant horizon. After a more extensive walk along the sea wall, we would return to the house to write something together before Garratt had even risen from his bed. Charlie and I wrote Mouth on a Stick, AK47, Psychosis, Bitter & Twisted (my divorce song) and Squat 96 in our first week in Frisco as a consequence of this routine.

Once this initial writing phase was over, Nicky booked us a rehearsal room in a pretty rough and hazardous part of the city – all the store fronts were wire meshed and iron barred to prevent break-ins and drug dealers were on just about every street corner conspicuously selling their wares to the local crackheads and junkies. It was in one of the practise rooms located in a vast concrete building set in this insalubrious area that I first got to meet Dave Ayer.

I instantly liked Dave. He was easy-going, had a partiality for smiling, was evidently bright and possessed a correspondingly sardonic sense of humour to my own, plus we kind of looked similar – in fact when we got to tour together the following year, a lot of people would ask us if we were brothers. He was also a very good drummer.

During our three days of preparations for recording in the rehearsal facility we worked on the post-breakfast songs that Chas and I had co-written, plus my self-penned tunes and a quartet of Nicky's musical offerings – to which Harper appended some appropriate lyrics – as well as, lest we forget, the uninspiring Bacharach cover.

All four of us threw in arrangement ideas and worked in unison to compress the most listenable juice out of each track; and this genial sense of unity and industry meant that as well as being creative and productive, these practice sessions were really enjoyable. Now armed with enough rehearsed material for the album, we were ready to begin the recording process.

On the 21st of October '96 we convened at The Wally Sound Studio, which was situated in the basement of one of those large archetypal Frisco Victorian houses, this one being set in the birthplace of the 1960s counterculture movement – Haight-Ashbury. Its owner and the engineer for these recordings was Wally Heider, who'd been overseeing various recording studios since 1969 and was a pleasant and professional man to work with.

Wally Sound's control room and live space were both on the smallish side, but still adequate for our needs; and once Dave had set up his drums, he, Nicky and I began putting onto tape the material we'd rehearsed earlier that week.

Mass backing vocals (including goose!), SF, U.S.A., 1996.

The backing track playbacks corroborated that we were on the correct sonic path, so we pressed on over the next couple of days until all the foundation work was done and Charlie could start adding some lead vocals and Garratt commence affixing his rhythm guitar overdubs and lead solos to these solid sounding musical constructs. Nicky then kept pressing for more songs, even though we had a more than satisfactory number for an album's worth already.

When Charlie and I challenged him about this back at his house one evening, Nicky revealed that he wanted to record enough material for not one, but two LPs, to which Harper reasonably asked "Why?"

"Well," explained Garratt "I need a major release for my New Red Archives label for next year and I thought if we had enough tracks for that and then recorded the same amount again, we could sell those to Cleopatra Records as a companion album, which would then cover the recording costs."

Before I get back to moving the narrative forward again, let me first offer you some contextual information regarding Nicky Garratt's record label, New Red Archives:

After Garratt moved to New York City from London in the 1980s, he decided to start a label specialising in Punk rock music. Launched as

New Red Archives in 1987, one of Nicky's first releases was the U.K. Subs' Harper/Garratt/Gibbs reunion album Killing Time, to which I'd contributed my bass playing and a trio of songs whilst in New York on a short hiatus between tours when still a member of the Iggy Pop Band.

Shortly thereafter, Garratt relocated the label to Los Angeles and then moved it again to San Francisco whilst signing to NRA, among others, Ultraman, Crucial Youth, Kraut, Samiam, and Reagan Youth – this band in particular turning out to be a real cash cow for the label. Nicky told me that in spite of Reagan Youth officially disbanding in 1989, a member of the outfit asked Garratt to just go ahead and release a compilation record he'd compiled utilising songs from previous albums without any deal having been agreed between them. It was issued as Reagan Youth Volume I in 1990 and sold in such numbers that Nicky cleared more than $100,000 from the record. Seeing as there had been no contract, NRA were not obliged to and did not pay any royalties to the band, plus there had been no recording costs, so the label's financial outlay was solely for its manufacturing and packaging.

By the time we were recording in San Francisco, NRA had also received a huge money injection after Garratt signed an exclusive deal with the distribution company East India Trading. He never disclosed exactly how much they dished out as an advance, but he did say it basically paid for his house in SF, plus the record company offices he'd had constructed on its ground floor and the other expensive refurbishments he'd overseen. And yet there he was trying to eke out more songs from us in order to record two albums so that one of them covered the recording costs of the LP that was due to be released on New Red Archives.

Now, that would all be for the good if it meant Charlie and I would receive larger royalty payments as a result of the money saved, but, as you will learn, this wasn't going to be the case.

Anyhow, these were all considerations for the future and although still taken aback by this sudden change of strategy, Charlie and I nevertheless dived deep into our reservoir of creativity and managed to solo write and co-write together, and with Nicky, some additional songs for the suggested second LP.

My favourite of the Harper/Garratt/Gibbs writing collaborations – and the best song to emerge from all of those SF recordings in my estimation – was a tense, sinister sounding track called Day of the Dead.

This began as a fast four-note bass riff I'd played to Garratt, an obvious verse progression, to which he added some suitably theatrical chords for a punchy chorus. Chas then worked on the words, which were inspired by the stack of horror comic books Wally kept in the control room, which he'd been delving into during the sessions. His vocals for

Day of the Dead were pitched with the perfect degree of repulsion and surprise – 'I heard a scream – can this be! This woman she had no head! How was I to know this was the day of the dead?' – whilst Nicky's taut, dissonant guitar pattern at the start of each verse section heightened the song's inherent tensions.

It was evident that the Harper/Garratt/Gibbs alliance, along with new recruit Dave Ayer, was capable of writing and recording some fine music. How it would fare in the tough and gruelling crucible of being on the road though, was another matter.

HEAVEN'S GATE

As the San Francisco recording sessions neared their conclusion and, having now pretty much reached our tally of necessary material for Garratt's two LP initiative rather than the originally planned solitary release, it occurred to me that it might be a nice gesture to get Dave Ayer on the writing credits, seeing as he had done such an excellent job in the drumming department. To this end I asked Dave to come up with a drum pattern. I then added two distinct bass lines as verse and chorus parts to give structure to this embryotic song. When Nicky was called upon to add rhythm guitar he aimlessly hacked about on the strings of his Gordon Smith for a while and then, having unplugged it, claimed he couldn't come up with anything fitting.

This was weird. Garratt was normally a very creative guitarist, capable of embellishing any piece of music with interesting chops and textures. His attitude was seemingly 'let's move on and get into something else'; but I felt sorry for Ayer, his one chance of getting a song credit seemingly vanishing because Nicky couldn't, or wouldn't, add some guitar to this nascent co-write.

I took the guitar off Garratt, re-plugged it into the amp, and started putting together some chords that I thought might mesh with the drums and bass. Within 30 minutes or so we had a completed backing track. Charlie then sang the lyrics he'd been working on whilst I'd been adding the rhythm guitar to tape and, thus, Beggars & Bums emerged, destined as a track on the Riot album, released by Cleopatra the following year.

Dave thanked me for my salvage operation and Nicky even complimented me on what I'd managed to put down utilising his axe. He did eventually add some superb lead guitar to it, but I still don't understand why he had given up on the song so easily, nor why it was subsequently credited as Harper/Garratt/Gibbs/Ayer. As I've already noted – weird.

It's quite something to consider that in just two weeks we were able to write and record 31 songs for the two albums Quintessentials and Riot, both of which would emerge in 1997 – this being the 20th anniversary year of the formation of the U.K. Subs.

Nicky mixed the songs at Wally Sound after Chas and I returned to the U.K., and did a fine job of obtaining instrumental clarity without the usual consequential loss of power and sinew. The effects he used on Harper's voice were also in keeping with the edgy, menacing atmospheres that largely prevail on both albums and I, of course, especially liked the fact that the bass was suitably punchy and to the fore in the mix.

Recording the Quintessentials/Riot albums, SF, U.S.A., 1996.

As far as I'm concerned, those two records are as favourably comparable to anything the Subs had done previously or have achieved since. American magazine and radio reviews for the album duo were as enthusiastic and complimentary as any band could wish for – the only winged insect in the proverbial ointment being the money aspect, which we will get to the nub of in a future chapter.

Having flown into London from SF on the 8th of November, I again got myself down to Heathrow Airport for the 29th, this time for a British Airways flight to Düsseldorf, Germany. Two years before, when playing with the Subs at the Wacken Rock Festival near Hamburg, I'd met an attractive German woman named Sari, who I stayed in touch with via occasional phone calls and who'd invited me to visit her. So I did.

It wasn't an entirely successful trip – her boyfriend (I really didn't have a clue) turned up one night, drunk, understandably angry, and demanding entry to her flat as we lay in bed together, post coitus. It really put a spoiler on the trip. The next day I got myself a hotel and ended up spending the rest of my Düsseldorf week with another pretty blonde girl, who just happened to be one of Sari's apartment block neighbours. As I've opined in Volume I, after the Pascale and Simone Parisian debacle: the female of the species can be every bit as duplicitous as the male.

The early months of 1997 were taken up with my on-going divorce settlement vacillations, martial arts training and working for the Labour Party, of which, at that point, I'd been a member for going on seven years. This work consisted of leafleting the Hampstead and Highgate constituency with Labour literature, helping to write press statements and accompanying our Labour MP, Glenda Jackson, as she went door-to-door to make the case for re-election later that year.

I'd also been occupied with negotiating terms, in a series of phone calls with Nicky Garratt, for the proposed U.K. Subs' tour of the U.S.A. to promote the Quintessentials and Riot albums, which were both shortly to be released there. He'd started his own booking agency to reserve the shows – 34 gigs, starting 3rd April and finishing 14th May, with Garratt's NRA agency taking 10% gross of the tour's total income. He'd also disclosed that Charlie Harper and Dave Ayer had already signed up for the venture and he just needed me on board to proceed.

"I'm up for it in principle," I told him "but here are my terms: I want a month's rent covered for when I'm away. Secondly, I need to have the round-trip airfare to San Francisco in advance."

I hadn't been reimbursed for the return airfare from London to the U.S. I'd paid out to record Quintessentials and Riot, and, to this very day, still haven't been compensated.

"I also want your guarantee that this will be a properly put together, professionally run tour with hotels in each city pre-booked and at least one roadie," (without an actual day off for the tour's six weeks duration things would be gruelling enough, so another pair of hands to help carry the equipment was vital) "plus a decent per diem payment as both a wage and to cover touring expenses."

"No problem," answered Garratt, "I promise you it will be a professionally run tour and I'll wire the rent and airfare money to you next week."

"In that case, I'm in."

As promised, the money for both my initial stipulations appeared in my bank account a week later and I swiftly booked my air ticket in conjunction with Charlie so we could fly together to California from London.

Prior to setting off for the States, Chas had me play a U.K. Subs' show at the Forum in Kentish Town, London, with Darrell Bath on guitar and Ison on drums. It was a very good gig. From the C.I.D opener to our final song Warhead, the crowd were fervently with us, demanding encores and chanting the band's name in customary fashion.

It turned out to be a superb night all round as Düsseldorf-based band B. Bang Cider were on the bill and my occasional German air hostess girlfriend Sabrina – a pal of B. Bang's lead singer Monique Maasen – happened to be backstage in the shared dressing room following our set.

Intermittent German girlfriends seem to have been the in-thing with me in the 1990s.

Shortly after we ran into each other, a taxi was shared to a French restaurant just down the road from my flat in West Hampstead. After some food and wine, Sabrina spent the night, leaving the next morning wearing the Lufthansa uniform she carried in her holdall as she was due back on airline duty at Gatwick Airport a couple of hours later. Occasionally, just occasionally, the universe bestows you a perfect day – that was one of them.

On Wednesday 26th of March 1997 I met up with Charlie Harper at Heathrow Airport. 14 hours or so later we were standing together in line with the other passengers at the arrivals section of San Francisco International Airport waiting for the immigration people to stamp our passports and for the customs Rottweilers (human, not canine) to pull apart our suitcases in search of possible contraband. Having mercifully made it through without difficulties, Nicky Garratt whisked us off to his house and gave us the lowdown on the what-was-what, concerning the impending tour.

We learned a number of things: that he'd booked a room in that same facility where we'd worked the album material into shape for another trio of rehearsals to construct a set of new and more familiar Subs' songs for the tour; that our support band for the entire caper was to be Anti-Flag, who'd just released their debut album Die For the Government on Nicky's New Red Archives label; that he'd purchased a former airport shuttle bus for us to travel in which had previously been converted into an extremely basic touring vehicle, with elementary bunk beds for sleeping, plus a few seats and a TV and video player, neither of which worked. And that he'd hired a roadie/driver called Gavin for the duration, who ordinarily was the bass player for ex-Sub Karl Morris'

Texas based band, Billyclub.

Harper and I had arrived over a week before the tour was due to kick off, so we had plenty of time to acclimatise, making our morning visits to the Simple Pleasures café and visiting a favourite local sushi restaurant in the evenings. Nicky was a vegetarian who didn't allow guests to bring anything to eat with meat or fish involved into his house, which was fair enough; so Chas and I always went out to eat whilst staying there.

One memorable night, after a rehearsal, we walked to the beach to view the dazzling comet Hale-Bopp, complete with fiery tail, illuminating the dark ether above the ocean. March 1997 was the closest it would get to planet Earth, and to date, it's the most visible and brightest comet to be seen in the northern hemisphere skies, since modern astronomers began observing such heavenly entities.

The next day, on television, we watched with incredulity the various American news network reports of a futile and tragic incident related to the comet we'd witnessed the night before.

Marshall Applewhite had founded a quasi-religious cult faction called Heaven's Gate, which had recruited a generally affluent but highly credulous group of followers who'd chosen to hand over all their wealth to him in order to share a communal life at a large mansion house in Rancho Santa Fe, with Applewhite performing the role of paternal guru.

Heaven's Gate beliefs were a hell's-broth of New Age mysticism, Christian revisionism and ufology – belief in extra-terrestrial visitations and the certainty that sightings of unexplained lights and any unusually shaped craft in the sky were space ships from other worlds. And the absolute conviction that by following the teachings of their leader, devotees would soon graduate from the human evolutionary stage to a higher level in order to be invited aboard a UFO and thereafter, transported through Heaven's Gate to live an eternal, blissful life on some divine planet in the wider universe, whereabouts unspecified.

At first Applewhite taught they would achieve this whilst still inhabiting their living bodies; but following the death of his partner, suddenly altered it from a physical transformation to a spiritual one. With the appearance of Hale-Bopp and having now designated himself as 'Jesus' successor' this would-be messiah then claimed that the comet was really camouflage for a UFO, which was artfully hidden behind it awaiting the arrival of all the members of the Heaven's Gate community to convey them to their assured cosmic destination of blessedness – but if that wasn't ludicrous enough, here's the truly screwy and sinister part: in order to rendezvous successfully with the spaceship they must first all die.

On the day we'd been on the beach to witness the Hale-Bopp comet, the 38 adherents of the group, along with their leader, took their own lives using phenobarbital to induce stupor and breathing difficulties, after which, they secured plastic bags over their heads to inflict fatal asphyxiation. An autopsy later revealed that Applewhite had terminal cancer. Seeing as he had so little time left to live, he'd simply decided to terminate the cult via a mass suicide event. 21 women and 18 men between the ages of 26 and 72 had sufficiently believed in his insane assertions to kill themselves.

What the fuck had happened to their critical thinking? How is it that when it comes to established religions or quasi-religious belief systems, people so easily abandon their incredulity and accept as factual the most absurd, jaw-dropping childish nonsense?

The great Spanish film director Luis Buñuel once quipped "Thank God I'm an atheist" – a paradoxical statement that is both a typical surrealist Buñuel-ism and a witty testament to his disapproval of religion.

In my case, "I'm an atheist" will suffice.

On the morning prior to our first rehearsal, I started to feel unwell. By the evening I had all the symptoms of a virulent flu infection: high temperature, sweats, a persistent cough, perpetually runny nose, fatigue. I figured I'd caught the bastard on the flight over – aircraft ventilation systems are notorious for spreading viruses – but where or how were irrelevant issues having spent a sleepless, feverish night, because ill or not I was obliged to drag myself out of bed in the morning to rehearse with the band in that sweatbox of a room in the concrete compound situated in a very unsavoury part of the city.

I should have been resting up and giving my immune system time to conquer the pathogen that had invaded my body, but we had a tour to do. So I struggled in for the three booked days and, despite being in a kind of sweaty, influenza induced trance most of the time, managed to help assemble and rehearse up a set of songs for the shows ahead – a mixture of Subs classics such as C.I.D, Endangered Species, Party in Paris and Warhead, along with plenty of fresh material from the two new albums: Cyberjunk, Mouth on a Stick, Bitter & Twisted and Squat 96, being among them.

Before we headed off for the opening gig of the tour in Bakersfield to test the set in front of a live audience, there were a couple of outstanding matters which needed resolving. We'd still not been told what we were going to receive as a per diem, so Charlie, Nicky and I huddled together in Garratt's kitchen to talk it out. Two of us were very unimpressed with the answer.

"I thought ten dollars a day would be adequate," Garratt told us.

U.K. Subs at the San Francisco beach, 1997.

Harper was outraged: "Ten dollars is ridiculous Nicky! I thought we'd get fifty dollars a show at least."

Garratt, in turn, was outraged at this suggestion: "Oh yeah, then take all my money... Go on, take all my money!"

With that, he took his wallet out of a trouser pocket and launched it at Chas. It bounced off his chest, where it remained untouched on the kitchen floor awhile.

Following this histrionic gesture, we continued with some heated haggling until he upped it to $15 a day but refused to go any higher. $15 meant the combined wage allowance for the entire band per day was a mere $60. Now we didn't know what Nicky's agency had negotiated per show because he never shared this information with us – an educated guess being around $1,000 a performance as an overall average; but even after having paid both our airfares (£1,000 in total) and my rent for one month (£600), $15 a day as an allowance was a pitiful recompense when considering the potential income from the tour.

There were just five non-playing driving days – a necessary 10 to 12 hours of travel due to the long distances between certain destinations – during which the band would not be earning any money, but 36 gigs where we would. Using my very reasonable average figure, this amounted to at least $36,000 that was due to be accrued from the entire tour. Even allowing for the airfares and my rent outlay, Nicky's agency's 10% ($3,600), gas money and a wage for Gavin the roadie/driver (perhaps $30, certainly no more than $50 a day), that still left a substantial amount of money unaccounted for.

Then things got worse. When I asked about the pre-booked hotels, it turned out there weren't any.

"I bought a bus for us to travel in with bunk beds, why would we need hotels?" was Garratt's response.

"Well, let's see… how about somewhere to shower and bath, an occasional real bed to sleep in, a toilet, a sink to wash our clothes (many American motels also had coin operated laundry facilities), you know, stuff like that," I acerbically replied.

Despite these perfectly reasonable expectations, Garratt was adamant that the bus was adequate, that we would discover Subs' fans along the way that would let us use their bathrooms. Feeling very flu-sick, I felt in no condition to continue arguing and gave up, then went to my room and tried to sleep off the fever and crushing headache that still hadn't shifted despite the painkillers I'd consumed a couple of hours earlier.

It wasn't like I wanted luxury accommodation. Just two cheap motel twin rooms for us all to get a decent night's sleep in, with a shower in order to keep clean and a sink to wash my smalls and T-shirts so that I didn't end up smelling like some vagrant. The other thing that twisted my melon was Nicky hadn't suggested the idea of sleeping in the shuttle-bus as an alternative to hotels until we got to SF, by which time it was a case of fait accompli.

It was too late now to back out. I had travelled over 5,000 miles to California to tour the U.S.A. and despite feeling let down about the money and the reneging on hotels, I really had no choice but to accept the situation and adapt to whatever lay ahead.

There was no way of foreseeing at the time that this decision would go on to have a huge impact on my life and health. The consequences of going on this tour were going to be very severe indeed.

EL PASO

Bakersfield is an unexceptional Californian town that resides to the north of Los Angeles. Because of its relative anonymity, it had been selected by Nicky Garratt for what would essentially be the warm-up gig for the tour. This inaugural show took place on the 3rd of April 1997, at a suitably nondescript bar with a (chortle, snigger) double entendre name – Bottoms Up.

I was still in a grim condition from the acquired virus but imbued with that time-worn 'the show must go on' attitude and, later, when the beneficial effects of a large dose of adrenaline kicked in after we'd started our set, I succeeded in disregarding the worst aspects of the influenza to focus on my playing.

There were around 70 mainly Punk-unaware but mildly curious locals in the bar to witness this 20th Anniversary Tour opening gambit. Firstly, Anti-Flag showcased a dozen or so of their Punk protest songs, the pick of the yield being the magnificent anti-war anthem, You've Got to Die for the Government. We then took to the playing area which, seeing as there was no stage for bands to perform on in the venue, was merely a rectangle of ground-level tiled floor near the entrance doors.

We started off with a short, sharp instrumental piece that Nicky had written for the Quintessentials album entitled Jump On It, then launched into Cyberjunk and tore on through the rest of our song list at a lively pace.

It was the first time I'd performed with Harper and Garratt since the Polish Tour of 1983, but we intuitively adopted our onstage roles from that period, Nicky and I leaping around and throwing shapes whilst Charlie held the middle spot, dancing and singing in his typically idiosyncratic fashion. Despite Dave Ayer being plainly taken aback by the unfamiliar physicality of the performance – when Garratt jumped backward into his drum kit whilst throwing his axe in the air, I thought Dave was going to have a seizure – he nevertheless maintained rhythmic solidity, his kick drum pounding like a cardiovascular muscle in unison with my bass parts to provide the necessary underpinning for Nicky's guitar antics.

Post-show, another piece of familiar behaviour resurfaced from times past. There was a return journey to San Francisco that night of 283 miles (455 kilometres) which meant, as soon as all the gear was squared away in the bus, it was imperative to get driving ASAP as we had an even longer trip the following morning to San Diego. However, Charlie had made friends with a group of Mexican farm workers who regularly imbibed at Bottoms Up and consequently, was getting very drunk with his new amigos, downing beers with tequila chasers, and sampling some

Charlie on the dreaded tour bus, U.S.A. tour, 1997.

of their highly potent hand-rolled sensimilla ciggies.

When Nicky approached to say we had to split, he waved him away and tossed another shot-glass worth of cactus juice into his mouth. Then it was my turn to try to reason with him:

"Chas, it's an eight-hour drive tomorrow, we've got to leave early doors. Say farewell to your new mates and let's get out of here."

Charlie responded by going into his customary inebriated belligerent mode, a genre of reaction which in later times would be termed by those of us who frequently worked with him and knew Harper well as his 'obnoxious granddad' persona.

"Oh fucking 'ell, I don't care about all that, call yourselves Punks, I'm not going anywhere…" – blah de blah, de blah, de blah.

There was no point in arguing with him when he'd reached this pig-headed, accusatory frame of mind owing to intoxication; so I went over to Nicky and said: "You know what we've got to do, right?" To which he replied "Yep, let's do it."

Having returned to where Charlie was ordering yet another round of tequilas for himself and los Mexicanos, Garratt snatched the beer bottle out of his hand, placed it on the bar and together – standing either side of Harper – we slid a forearm apiece under his armpits and literally lifted him off the ground, after which we carried him onto the bus, whilst all the while Chas yelled obscenities at us, writhed and demanded to be let loose.

This wouldn't be the last time such drastic action would be required to prise our illustrious singer out of a club or bar in the early hours of the morning on that tour. In fact, it was to become pretty much the norm rather than the exception.

The next day, just before setting off for San Diego, we met Gavin, our driver/roadie for the coming weeks. He seemed OK, but I could tell from our conversation over coffee at the Simple Pleasures café, that the main attraction of the job for him was not the work but the possibilities that touring with the U.K. Subs would generate for partying and meeting women.

Gavin wasn't the only new member of our touring party. Nicky had loaded up the back of the bus where the equipment resided with boxes of 20th Anniversary 1997 Tour T-Shirts and NRA merchandise – mostly vinyl records and CDs – and had invited an employee of his record company to join us in order to sell all this swag at gigs until after the Los Angeles show, when Chick (obviously a nickname, no idea what her real moniker was) would return to SF and Garratt would then take on the vending role himself.

When we got to San Diego, I was astounded to find among Garratt's huge amount of saleable product a trio of different singles with titles taken from the Quintessentials' album – A-side single one: Day of the Dead, which had a pic of Charlie on the back cover; A-side single two: War on the Pentagon, featuring a live snapshot of Nicky; and A-side single three, Cyberjunk, with an old action photo of me on the record sleeve.

Neither Harper nor I had any idea that NRA had pressed-up these records and certainly Garratt didn't mention any extra money for us as a corollary after I made my discovery and asked him about them. All the merchandise money he garnered from the tour – including the T-shirts' sales and any purchases of the Killing Time, A.W.O.L. and Quintessentials albums, all of which Chas and I had contributed to as bassist, singers and as writers, plus those three separate singles I'd uncovered on his merch stall – went directly into his pocket. This was yet another issue that sat badly with me. But it was a case of having to accept this irritating state of affairs or quit; and seeing as I was financially in too deep at that point, plus not being a quitter by nature, I rejected the latter course of action, and toured on.

I was amazed the following day to see how many young people attended our gig at the Showcase Theatre on Main Street, Corona,

California. The venue was packed solid with teenage Punks who gave Anti-Flag a great reception before they mosh pit stomped and leapt around to our set in that structured aggressive American way we'd noted during previous Subs' tours of the States.

Pete Dee, guitarist with splendid British Punk outfit The Adicts, came backstage with his American wife to chat. He, and lead singer Keith 'Monkey' Warren, had immigrated to California some years before. I hadn't shared a beer with Pete since 1983, so it was cool to reconnect with my old friend and to hear about how well The Adicts were doing in the U.S.A.

This was also the first time that we met the owner of the Showcase Theatre, the benevolent, generous and charming Ezzat Soliman, who would become a good friend and benefactor to the Subs in the future.

Both Dave Ayer and I had tried sleeping overnight in the wretched shuttle-bus, but it wasn't happening. I'd been in a floor level bunk, which was like trying to sleep in a coffin placed atop a sauna, and moreover, having parked up after the San Diego show in an area mainly occupied by trucks adjacent a freeway service station, we discovered that the noise of interstate traffic combined with the coming and goings of the HGVs guaranteed neither of us could get any reasonable rest. Later in the tour, after we started heading east, we also learnt that the bus leaked like a fucked tap when it rained.

So, following the Corona gig and thereafter, apart from one or two necessary exceptions or an offered satisfactory alternative, Dave and I would go halves on a twin bedded motel room in order to get some decent sleep and to have access to a shower, toilet and sink – Charlie was usually too loaded at the end of the night to care where he slept, whilst Nicky was far too parsimonious to contemplate actually paying for a hotel room when there was a cramped bunk in a leaking bus to be had.

Now, the cheapest rooms on the American road were generally to be found via a chain called Motel 6; but even so, the most modestly priced of their twin rooms were still $25 to $35 a night, and seeing that we were only receiving $15 a day, this would have left us with no money to pay for food and drink. It became necessary then to use our credit cards to pay the motel fees so we would still have enough cash available in order to eat.

What really started to annoy Dave and I though, was that having booked into a motel, Garratt would regularly knock on our room door and ask to use the toilet and shower facilities that we'd paid for. Despite becoming increasingly resentful of this penny-pinching tactic, we would nevertheless allow him entry in the interest of maintaining some kind of band esprit de corps.

Billboard, Whisky A Go Go, LA, 1997.

The Los Angeles gig at The Whisky a Go Go was outstanding. Ike Baruch and Tim Mosher – who thoughtfully invited me to stay over in the spare room of the small house he shared with his wife Gretchen in Laurel Canyon – were guest-listed and had obviously enjoyed our brand of noise: Tim's appraisal of our set when he came backstage was "all killer, no filler!"

A long drive to Scottsdale Arizona was then endured, and after we'd played there the following night, the Subs' touring party rolled into Albuquerque New Mexico for what I've recorded in my diary as a 'so-so gig.' Next up was El Paso.

El Paso Texas sits beside the Rio Grande, this being the river which separates it from the Mexican town of Ciudad Juárez. Just by looking across the border to the outskirts of Juárez, the economic disparity in infrastructure, housing and transportation between the U.S.A. and Mexican sides was starkly evident, and readily revealed why so many on the poor side of that boundary would want to cross the divide to start a better life in more affluent America.

Our venue was in the city centre and had a stage situated towards the entrance of the establishment with no back wall to it, meaning we could be viewed from both the front and the rear of this podium. Behind the stage there was a number of pool tables for those who wanted to play

Eight Ball rather than watch the show whilst, in front, there was the standard audience space with a bar that stretched its full length. This was where the vast majority of ticket buyers would assemble.

Adjacent stage left there was also a narrow passageway that connected both areas so that people could transfer from pool room to main room for access to the bar.

After our soundcheck we received a number of reports that many of the local Punk rockers heading for the gig were being harassed and arrested under ridiculous pretexts by meathead El Paso cops. Still, this didn't hinder the venue from becoming filled to capacity come show time.

At 11.45pm we took our places onstage and started our set. It was a lively crowd and the temperature had risen to sweltering. In amongst the animated audience we could see a couple of waitresses carrying trays of drinks from the bar to those who'd ordered them. Around the midway point of our set, Nicky broke a string and we took a break whilst he tuned up his spare axe using, as was his way, a traditional metal tuning fork.

Upon seeing we had come to a stop, one of these cute waitresses came down to my side of the stage, looked up at me, and in her broad Texan accent said, "Hi honey, being as you-all taking a respite, I thought I would ask if there's anything I can get you from the bar?"

"Sure," I replied, "it's really hot up here so a beer would be very much appreciated – and I'm sure our singer and drummer might like a cold one apiece too."

"No problem honey, I'll get those to you in a jiff."

Guitar now tuned; we got back to playing. After a few minutes, despite the fierce volume of the band, I became aware of some shouting and a commotion emanating from behind me. I looked about and saw a man breaking a pool cue over another player's skull. Friends of the assaulted then entered the fray wielding their pool cues which, in turn, led to the assailant's companions getting physically involved too. This ruckus then quickly made its way from the pool room into the main room via the connecting passageway.

Then it really kicked off.

Whilst we continued to provide a soundtrack for the affray, like rolling thunder the fighting rapidly multiplied to involve the majority of the audience. Beer glasses and bottles soared through the air; barstools were employed as weapons; fists pounded into faces, people wrestled each

U.S.A. tour, 1997.

other to the floor – it was like watching a movie-style Wild West saloon bar brawl, but for real.

We kept on playing.

In the midst of this violent, chaotic scene I saw a tray being upheld with a large pitcher of beer and three tankards on it. It weaved its way around the brawlers, expertly avoiding the hurled glass objects until the waitress who'd asked what I'd wanted to drink arrived directly in front of me and placed my beer order on the stage at my feet, not a drop of the brew having been spilled. We took an adjournment to pour out the beers and brimming with admiration and wonder at her skilful waltz around the combatants, I lent down and asked her "How the hell did you do that?"

"Honey, when you've worked this place as long as I have, your reflexes and peripheral vision get real sharp, real quick. This sort of thing happens all the time here darling, I'm a veteran. Just let me know when you want another pitcher."

I was in love.
Regretfully, nothing came of my amorous interest in the Texan waitress. After the show – once the audience had dissipated, the broken glass had been swept away and the blood mopped up – we shared a couple of drinks together. But alas, the Subs were driving 635 miles (1,021 kilometres) through the night to Dallas in order to reach that city in

Sharing vocals with Justin Sane of Anti-Flag, U.S.A. tour, 1997.

good time for our gig there the following evening; and so a lingering kiss had to suffice along with a promise, never kept, that I would seek her out the next time we played El Paso.

Real shame, because as Eddie Cochran had exalted in a song that could've been written about her – 'she (was) sure fine lookin' man, she's something else.'

Gavin, as I suspected he might, had become a problem. He was often missing at load in and load out times and his main focus seemed to be drinking as much beer as possible at venues – not appreciated behaviour, seeing as he was the driver – and doing his upmost to hit on women, which didn't seem to work out too well for him as he always returned to the bus alone to complain about "frigid bitches" and suchlike. Having tolerated this for far too long, his inevitable dismissal came as a consequence of his actions (or rather inactions) during our Dallas show.

There was a minor stage invasion in Dallas for Warhead – six or seven over-excited Punks joined us to dance around and sing the chorus along with Charlie, during which time they'd inadvertently knocked over a microphone stand and a cymbal stand, and somehow upended Nicky's amplifier. I looked desperately around for Gavin in order to signal to him that he needed to sort this carnage out whilst we continued playing; but he was nowhere to be seen – that is until I noticed him standing in the audience, casually watching the band with a beer in one hand and an arm around a girl he was trying to seduce.

When we'd finished the show, I found him in the same spot, minus the girl, who'd sensibly gone home. I told him to get his lazy arse into our dressing room sharpish, and, grasping I was in no mood for debate, he sheepishly followed me there. Nicky and I then proceeded to explain in robust language why his services were no longer required. He put up some pathetic defence like "Come on guys, this is supposed to be a Punk rock tour, loosen up," but we disabused him of the notion that being Punk meant acting like an unreliable and indolent arsehole, paid him off and sent him on his way.

Garratt though was in no hurry to replace him because having one less person to pay equalled more money saved. We ended up having to do all the equipment carrying and driving ourselves for the next seven shows. Eventually, after I'd kept on at him to find a replacement on a thrice-daily basis, he contacted someone who was to fly to Atlanta and meet up with us there, thereafter taking on the driver/roadie duties.

Prior to Atlanta, we'd gigged in Houston Texas, completed five shows in five different Florida cities and played in New Orleans. It was following this New Orleans performance that the band's shuttle-bus dropped me off at the super-cheap motel on the outskirts of the city which I'd already checked into earlier that day. Ayer had some friends to stay with, so I'd got myself a solo room.

Having showered and got into bed, I checked my watch and noted it was gone 3am – American club concerts routinely start late: midnight and even 1am are not unusual stage times.

Just as I started to drift off to sleep, I became aware that the door handle to my room was turning back and forth in conjunction with an inexplicable scratching noise. I pulled on my strides, crossed the room, swung open the door and came face-to-face with some sunken-eyed black fella who appeared more shocked than I did and who swiftly bolted up the corridor and out onto the exterior stairwell.

There was a bent wire coat hanger on the floor. This was obviously the crude tool by which he was trying to unlock my door, so I picked it up and went back into the room. Having returned to bed, I was astounded and severely pissed off to again see the handle flipping from side-to-side a few minutes later. For a second time I opened the door, and for a second time he scarpered. This maddening game continued two, maybe three times more before I thought 'Fuck this, I'm getting in security.'

I'd noticed an armed guard in the reception booth situated across from the car park when I'd arrived, so I went over there and told the security officer what'd been occurring.

"Oh, that motherfucker, yeahs, I knows him. He's a crack-head looking to swipe a wallet or whatever else he can steal; and so fucked up on that shit he don't care whether someone's in the room or not."

"Is he dangerous?" I inquired.

"Can be, all depends how desperate he is for money for crack, know what I'm saying?"

I knew what he was saying.

"Have you got a firearm with yah?" he asked.

"Certainly not, I'm British! We don't carry guns. I do have a Swiss army knife though."

After he'd laughed at this for an awkwardly long length of time, he said: "Well I guess that's something, though I suspect if that tweaker is packing some heat, it won't be enough. Still, seeing he's not shot you yet, chances are he hasn't got a piece on him tonight. Probably sold it for some snow, know what I'm saying?"

I knew what he was saying.

"Tell's yas what sir, I'll come up there with you and patrol your corridor for a while. That should scare that motherfucker off, but if that don't do it – at which point he started up with the laughing again – it will be down to you and your Swiss army knife. Know what I'm saying?"

The Hartsfield-Jackson Atlanta International Airport was where we were supposed to meet the newest member of our touring party. We were late for the pickup so Nicky and I started scouring the domestic arrivals area for any sign of him, being as his plane had touched down an hour before. Problem was, we didn't actually know what he looked like as he'd been recommended to Garratt, sight unseen.

Having combed the place to no avail Nicky understandably wanted to give up, but as we were about to leave, I glanced over at a line of wheelchairs provided for passengers needing assistance and noticed a pair of leopard-print brothel creepers sticking out from one of the chairs, the creeper wearer having reclined into a sleeping position in the seat. We'd found our man.

Drew was the antithesis of Gavin – hardworking, reliable, sharp, immensely likeable and funny. As we were leaving the airport, he pointed out to me a very uptight business type with a metaphorical stick up his arse and said "If you are what you eat, that guy's definitely eating a lot of pussy."

That night we played an Atlanta venue called The Point, which by show time, was heaving and hot. It was only after completing Jump On It and launching into Cyberjunk that we became aware that Charlie wasn't actually onstage with us. He'd been in the dressing room 20 minutes or so before we'd walked on but had now mysteriously vanished.

The explanation for his disappearance revealed itself when, way back at the rear of the club, I was able to identify Chas sitting on a stool nonchalantly drinking something stronger than beer whilst chatting to an attendee sat beside him at the bar. We eventually had to abandon playing Cyberjunk to plead with him to reunite with the band utilising the house PA, but he didn't seem in any rush to comply. Dave, Nicky and I were therefore forced to abandon performing and return to the dressing room.

Sometime later, Lord Harper deigned to leave his bar stool to join the hired help – that was the general vibe of his attitude – and when quizzed about his behaviour went into an inebriated tirade: "Fucking place was packed, what did you lot expect? I couldn't get through all those people; fucking Rock stars, you should have just carried on…" – Blah de blah, de blah, de blah.

'Obnoxious granddad' was alive and well and ranting in Atlanta Georgia.

Garner, North Carolina and Richmond, Virginia were the next gigging destinations, then Allentown, Pennsylvania, where Nicky relayed a message to me that had just been conveyed to him via the promoter's phone from his NRA office in San Francisco. I'd given my lawyer Garratt's business number in case of any divorce issues that might arise whilst I was in America. Apparently, our next court hearing date had been brought forward and it was crucial I be there, not only to avoid being lumbered with a non-attendance fine, but more importantly, to defend my interests alongside my brief.

The rescheduled date was for the 3rd of May but the tour was due to continue until the 13th, which meant having to quit and return to London from an appropriate city in the near future. We had Newark, New Jersey and Washington DC to play after Allentown, followed by two consecutive shows at Coney Island High in New York City.

NYC was definitely the best place to take a flight back to the U.K. from, so I used my overworked credit card to purchase a ticket from JFK to Heathrow Airport. This transatlantic journey was booked for

Dave Ayer 1968-2012.

the day after the last gig of the Big Apple duo. It cost me £500 which, when added to the money I'd already had to spend on motel rooms and other necessary expenses – restaurant meals and drinks, bass strings, guitar straps, picks, guitar stand, etc – meant I would end up making no money whatsoever from a tour that had been a lot of work and a fair amount of grief.

I was leaving the tour two weeks before it was due to end which, despite the difficult nature of the sojourn, was something that still rankled with me as it's not in my nature to abandon anything until it reaches its completion, unless that is, it becomes absolutely impossible not to do so. My replacement was to be Carly Guarino who, I believe, travelled with Anti-Flag as their merchandise seller. She was apparently a good bassist, and from what I understand, did a fine job playing out the tour with the remaining Subs.

After my final performance at Coney Island High, I got to share a twin room with Dave Ayer for the last time. We'd become really good mates over the past weeks and he had often confided that he thought we were the only two sane members of the band. With me leaving the expedition, he wasn't at all looking forward to playing on with an untried bassist. It was to be the last time I saw him. After the tour, and, I hope not as a direct consequence of it, his life took a severe downward spiral.

Later, back in the U.K., I learned from Charlie that Dave had started taking drugs during that remaining fortnight of shows. As an outcome, in due course, he ended up being estranged from his wife which in turn led to his addiction to the most corrosive narcotic of all – heroin.

Dave battled his dependency for many years. According to his sister Lisa, he did eventually succeed in breaking free of heroin's insidious hook, although I believe the accumulated damage the brown had inflicted on his body was the main contributing cause of his premature death in 2012. He was only 44 years old and I was very saddened to hear of his demise.

The depth of his talent will live on though via those great drumming performances on the Quintessentials and Riot albums; and in the memories of anyone who saw him playing live with the U.K. Subs in the American spring of '97.

C.I.D... P

There were definitely positives connected to the 1997 Subs' American tour. It gave me the opportunity to once more perform across the length and breadth of the U.S.A. and to again experience that nation's diverse topography in all its grandeur; to get reacquainted with old friends and to make some new ones; plus it got me back into the methodology of being a professional touring musician for a lengthy stretch of time. But, as you've no doubt figured out already, there were negatives too.

Charlie had been a difficult band mate on occasions, getting loaded, being belligerent if challenged when intoxicated and sometimes adopting a frivolous attitude to shows, as was demonstrated at the Atlanta gig when he seemed more interested in drinking at the bar than joining us onstage. This was very frustrating because when Chas had fully committed to a performance, he was commanding, charismatic and in fine voice.

Nicky Garratt seemed to be in a constant state of anxiety about money although he was the one who by far, was accruing the most income from the tour. As well as his daily $15 per diem, his agency had procured 10% of the charged fees for all 36 gigs as well as him having taken in large amounts of cash from tour T-shirts and NRA merchandise sales, every dollar of which he'd kept for himself. At the Corona show alone, I observed that his pockets were so swollen with merch-acquired dollar bills that he had to eventually transfer all the notes into a plastic carrier bag which, by the end of the night, was filled with cash.

He had also, without consulting me or Charlie, appointed Anti-Flag as our tour support band. They'd just released their inaugural album on NRA, so promoting that record at our gigs would bring in further revenue for Garratt as their label's owner. There was also the vexed question of the shuttle bus purchase.

Nicky had told us he'd paid $10,000 for the vehicle and this had been his justification for not booking hotel rooms and offering such a meagre daily wage. However, just a couple of months after the tour had concluded, he'd told me during a phone conversation that he'd sold the bus on for exactly what he'd paid for it. Years later, when Garratt started playing guitar more frequently with the Subs on European tours, he would bring us an annual sum in cash royalties for the Killing Time, A.W.O.L. and Quintessentials albums and all other accumulated NRA income from the various licensing deals he'd made for these records – plus their offshoot singles – of around €50 apiece.

A decade or so later, I insisted on getting a written accounting statement from him to see why these payments had been so low for so long. After he handed it to me along with a derisory €35 NRA royalty payment for the previous 12 months, it made for some very interesting reading.

It was clear Nicky had cross-collateralised these records with the tour – in other words, he'd offset any claimed 1997 U.S.A. tour expenses by retaining a substantial amount of income from record sales and licensing deals to cover them. This is certainly not ethical music business practice. Tour income and expenses are just that, and record income and costs are a separate entity, but he'd mixed these in together in order to justify garnering money from our royalties.

Worse still, having studied the statement further, I saw the biggest amount he was applying to warrant paying myself and Harper these insubstantial royalty sums, was the $10,000 fee for the shuttle bus – the very bus he'd sold all those years before for what he'd paid for it.

Having shown this accounting sheet to Charlie and his wife Yuko (this would have been around 2009) Chas and I then confronted Garratt about these huge inaccuracies. He got pretty flustered about it, said things like "OK, I see what you're saying… err, let me look into it… maybe we can just discard this from now on and I'll pay whatever royalties are owing in the future with these expenses removed?"

He didn't, of course, offer to pay back the money he'd been incorrectly withholding since 1997, and after the decision was made to use Jet for all future European and American tours in 2011, he stopped paying any royalties.

In order to be absolutely certain that my diary entries and memories were correct about this before I committed them to print, I contacted Charlie to ask for his recollections regarding the subject. It has to be stated that my memories of certain events (in conjunction with my diary evidence) and Charlie's recall of those same events do not always tally. However, concerning the financials for that 1997 U.S.A. tour and the subsequent contentious royalty/tour expenses entanglement, his remembrances correspond exactly with my own.

Although these issues are now the discarded debris of the past, I have decided to reveal them because I believe it's important to have the facts on record. My high regard for Nicky Garratt as a musician, producer, songwriter, and performer was, and still is, unstinting, and we did continue to regularly play gigs and record together under the U.K. Subs' banner up until 2011. Nonetheless, it did bequeath a measure of disappointment and irritation that lingered with me for quite a while.

However, by far the worst legacy of the 20th Anniversary American Tour had nothing to do with financial issues or Charlie's sometimes wayward behaviour; and this most unpleasant aspect of its inheritance was soon to reveal itself in all its wretchedness upon my return to the U.K.

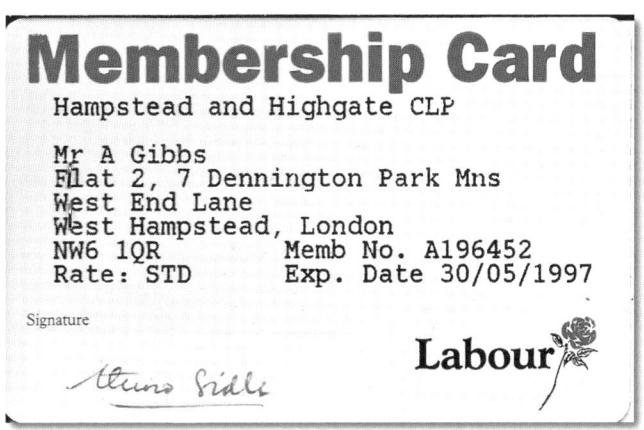

I landed at Heathrow Airport from New York City on the 30th of April 1997. The next day, 1st May, was the date for the much anticipated U.K. General Election. The Tony Blair led Labour Party were still ahead in the opinion polls and although I could hardly bring myself to believe it, a change of government was now looking the most likely outcome.

Despite having only three hours sleep due to jetlag, I got myself down to the Labour Party Hampstead and Highgate constituency HQ at 8am, pinned on my red rosette, and went door-to-door, street-by-street, to make sure those who'd told our canvassers they would be voting Labour, did so. I also organised transport for anyone who through infirmity or disability needed a vehicle to get them to their nearest polling station.

I worked all day, right up until two hours prior to the polls closing at 10pm, after which I took a tube and a train to East Croydon Station, where my awaiting father – who was also rooting for a Labour win – drove me to his place to watch the election coverage whilst sharing a number of glasses of wine. The earlier BBC exit poll predicted a Labour victory with a swing of 12% but as the night progressed, it became clear they'd underestimated the magnitude of Labour's eventual success. It was a landslide, with a swing of 16% from the Conservatives to Labour and a parliamentary majority for Blair of 179 seats.

I was both relieved and euphoric at the extent of this triumph; and when the much-detested Conservative minister for defence, Michael Portillo, lost his seat to his Labour challenger in the early hours of the morning, I just couldn't contain myself, leaping around my father's front room, wineglass in hand, yelling "Yes! Fucking amazing, even Portillo's got the sack," whilst my dad added "That's the best thing I've seen on television for a very long time son."

After 18 long years of Tory governance, the Labour election victory of 1997 was considered to be one of the great political triumphs of modern times; and I was grateful to have been able to play my modest part in it.

The only reason I'd been in the U.K. for this election rather than still on tour with the Subs in the States, was because my second divorce hearing had been brought forward to the 3rd of May, this being a meeting that my lawyer had messaged as being crucial for me to attend. But the day before our court appearance it was abruptly postponed and rescheduled for a later date. This was frustrating, but it also meant I could now put the depressing divorce dispute on the back burner for a while and get on with more enjoyable fixations.

These included going to see Crystal Palace FC clinch getting into the 1st Division playoff final by beating Wolves at Selhurst Park and subsequently, watching them at Wembley Stadium achieve promotion to the Premier League, after a spectacular David Hopkin goal in the final minute of regular time earned the Eagles a 1-0 victory over Sheffield United. The year before, I'd had to suffer the mortification of witnessing them tragically lose 2-1 to Leicester City at Wembley in the 1996 playoff final due to an extra time goal by Steve Claridge.

I also went to see a number of bands perform in various clubs and venues, which included an Ian Hunter show at the Shepherd's Bush Empire with occasional U.K. Subs' axe man, Darrell Bath, playing guitar for the ex-Mott The Hoople legend – an occasion that has reminded me of an interesting encounter with Ian Hunter that'd occurred in the fading days of Cheap And Nasty:

Back in 1994, a co-headline show with our former label mates Dogs D'Amour had been hastily put together for the Moonlight Club in West Hampstead, London. We used their backline for our set but approximately midway through our performance the bass amp I was utilising decided to fart and splutter and smoulder before it finally succumbed to whatever was ailing it and refused to function. There was no spare bass amp to be had, so we were obliged to abandon the stage.

I'd seen that Darrell was in the audience so, after we'd forsaken performing, I made my way through the crowd to say "hi" to him. As I approached the guitarist, I abruptly became aware that he was standing with someone who I instantly recognised from my Glam rock, pre-Punk years.

Ian Hunter hadn't seemingly physically changed at all since I'd seen Mott The Hoople for the first time in a promo film for their breakthrough single, All The Young Dudes, on Top of the Pops in 1972 – same blond corkscrew hair, same slim build, same omnipresent dark shades.

Darrell introduced me to him and after shaking hands, Hunter asked me what had occurred with the bass amp. I explained it was mechanical failure and he told me "That's a shame; I was enjoying your set," which

was something wonderful to hear coming from one of my teenage Rock music heroes. I then told him I was an acquaintance of Buffin and Pete Overend Watts (ex-drummer and bassist of MTH) and that I'd been good friends with Guy Stevens, Mott's Svengali and the producer of their early albums for Island Records. We chatted for a fair while about Guy and his eccentricities before Nasty Suicide joined us to pay his respects to Hunter – they had already met, when Nasty had still been a member of Hanoi Rocks.

Ian told us he was recording at Abbey Road Studios with Bath, ex-Sex Pistol Glen Matlock, Vom Ritchie and 'Honest' John Plain (providing bass, drums and guitar respectively) along with guests such as Casino Steel and Blue Weaver on keyboard duties.

"Why don't you both come down to the studio tomorrow around lunchtime and I'll show you around," he proposed.

Nasty and I didn't need to be invited twice. Next day, after a quick coffee at my flat which was only a 20 minute walk from Abbey Road, we both set off for this world famous studio. Having arrived and gained entry at the time Hunter had suggested, we discovered the recording musicians were having a lunch break, so we chatted to the various participants. I'd met Matlock a number of times before and Bath and Ritchie were friends. Ian shortly thereafter emerged from the control room and took us on a tour of the facility.

Having led us to the live room of Studio 2 – a large space with its famed staircase and grand piano resting on a gleaming parquet floor, the same piano on which Paul McCartney had composed Let it Be – Ian said "There you go, this is where The Beatles

Passport pics, just prior to my illness, 1997.

recorded all those amazing songs in the Nineteen-Sixties and Seventies," whilst I kept thinking 'how fucking cool is this, being guided about such a hallowed location, by Ian Hunter of all people.'

After the tour, Hunter invited us into the control room to listen to a couple of near-completed songs. They both sounded great, which is what you'd expect considering the quality of those involved. Nasty and I then escorted Ian out of the main studio building and said farewell to him as he climbed the steps to the front door of an adjacent house. This is where he would be staying whilst working on the record.

The album that emerged from those sessions was released the following year by Cherry Red Records. Dirty Laundry is a fine LP, one that should have got a lot more attention and praise.

I didn't see Ian Hunter again in the flesh until I attended a Mott The Hoople reunion concert in 2013 at the O2 Arena in London. It was to be the last time that the original bassist and guitarist, Pete Overend Watts and Mick Ralphs, would appear with the band. Ralphs suffered a severe stroke that ended his gigging days in 2016, whilst Watts – an early-1970s bass playing protagonist of mine – died of throat cancer in 2017.

In late May '97, Charlie enquired if I would be up for playing three shows in Europe with the Subs. Alan Campbell was on guitar, Ison the drummer. During this brief Euro excursion, I noticed that my lips and the tips of my fingers and toes were feeling numb. This deadening of my body's extremities persisted upon my return to London where, a week or so later, I also started to get stomach and neck pains.

My GP made an appointment for me to see a neurologist at the Royal Free Hospital in Hampstead. There, blood samples were extracted, reflexes were checked and a further full physical examination undertaken. I was told additional investigations were necessary and to report any changes in my condition. Things got worse.

The pains in my stomach and neck increased and I started to feel really weak, with diminished strength in my arms and legs. I knew I was in serious trouble when one morning I made myself a cup of tea and after attempting to lift the mug to my lips discovered my hand wasn't strong enough to support it. The hot liquid poured out of the receptacle onto the kitchen counter. It was a fast downward slide from then on.

Every successive week another corrosive aspect of my illness would emerge, so by the time my father drove me to the Royal Free for admittance as an in-patient in late June, I could hardly walk. My fingers had curled up into the palms of my hands and refused to unfurl, my speech had become slurred due to my tongue's incapacity to work correctly and my head was being forced ever downwards towards my chest due to the severe pain in my neck.

Having secured a bed in the neurological ward at the hospital and following on from my first full night there, a battery of tests commenced the next morning which would continue for a fortnight in anticipation of uncovering what had caused these disturbing disorders. During my first week at the Royal Free, as well as having blood taken from a vein for analysis twice a day, I was also regularly transported in a wheelchair to have an EMG (Electromyography) test. This consisted of a long, sharp needle electrode being inserted into my tongue, my arms, and my legs, in order to estimate the electrical activity in my muscles. From this investigation the doctors were able to ascertain any nerve damage or electrical reduction.

The EMG results revealed that my nerves were not servicing my muscles correctly, thereby creating muscular degeneration with the effect of serious weakness to my limbs and other parts of my body. Further tests then followed – a HIV check, which proved negative, and more physical examinations to assess the true extent to which my body had become enfeebled.

This was the most psychologically difficult aspect of what had occurred: the not knowing what was responsible for my debilitated state. It could have been something as adversely life-changing as the onset of Parkinson's Disease, Guillain-Barre syndrome or Multiple Sclerosis; but one of the doctors had a theory as to what had happened to my health based on information that I'd given him regarding the influenza I'd contracted just before the U.S.A. tour.

In order to prove his speculative diagnosis, he told me I needed to have a Lumbar Puncture (also known as a Spinal Tap), which I readily agreed to even though I knew it was not a pleasant process and could, if things went awry, result in paralysis.

The next morning I was wheeled from the ward to a room kept for such procedures, helped up onto an examination table and told to lie on my side with my legs pulled up in a foetal position. This would allow the long thin needle that would shortly be inserted into my spine to get between the bones more easily.

A local anaesthetic was administered whilst a nurse, who sat on a stool beside me and grasped my hand throughout, told me to squeeze her palm tightly if the pain got really bad. The neurologist then pushed the needle into my spinal column, all the while reminding me to keep as still as possible as one abrupt move could result in my being paralysed. Cerebrospinal fluid was then withdrawn from my spinal canal for diagnostic testing.

Two days later the doctor with the disorder theory, turned up at my bedside and affirmed, based on the test results from the extracted cerebrospinal fluid, that his hypothesis had been proved accurate. He then enlightened me as to why I'd ended up in such an appalling state.

It seems having not rested and taken care of myself in San Francisco when I'd acquired the flu virus; instead ignoring my illness to go on a gruelling tour of the U.S.A., meant that this pathogen hadn't been fought and destroyed by my immune system, as would have normally been the case. The dilapidated state of virus resistance was a result of the constant daily travel, touring fatigue and my ever increasing disenchantment with various aspects of the tour, plus the stresses triggered by my problematic divorce. Physiological factors and adverse mental states can be just as responsible for lowering immune system responses as physical influences.

As a consequence, this unchecked virus stayed in my body and camouflaged itself in my nerves' myelin. If you think of nerves as being a collection of wires which convey electrical impulses to different parts of the body from the brain, then myelin is the all-important insulation that shields these transmitters. Having returned to London and rested-up, my revived immune system, which had remarkably retained memory of the virus it formerly was unable to annihilate, deduced this deception and directed antibodies to attack my nerve protecting myelin.

These antibody raids had led to acute polyneuropathy – the simultaneous malfunction of numerous peripheral nerves throughout the body, hence the first symptoms I'd detected being the numbness in my fingers, lips, toes, and other extremities. The hostile antibodies then started to assault other parts of my physique as they intensified and widened their search and destroy mission, hence the withering of muscular tissue in my arms and legs, my leaden tongue and my stomach and neck pains.

If left unchecked, this autoimmune aggression would progress to the point where my entire body would close down.

The designation for this type of neural onslaught was Chronic Inflammatory Demyelinating Polyneuropathy, or, in shorthand, CIDP. I was told it was a rare disease (a piece of information that became the inspiration for a song title a couple of years later) and a variant of Guillain-Barre syndrome. The good news though was that the neurological team had also come up with a treatment they believed could help turn my health around.

This consisted of pumping into my body an intravenous infusion of immunoglobulin day and night for two weeks, dispensed from a bedside machine. Immunoglobulin is a liquid substance containing live antibodies. The design behind this treatment was to introduce these new antibodies to kill off the destructive autoimmune ones and, once they'd succeeded in performing their coup d'etat, I'd begin a long-term course of steroid immune suppressants to prevent these fresh antigens from also going into attack mode.

The side effect of this treatment was that within a few days of commencing the infusion, I started to feel really nauseous and would have to regularly vomit into the cardboard bowls the nurses had to constantly empty and replace. This meant I was incapable of retaining any of the food I tried to eat and led to them putting me on a drip to replace the nutrition and hydration I wasn't getting from meals and drink; but, here's the positive side of the medication – around the sixth day I awoke to find I could unfurl my fingers and my speech was not as slurred as it had been.

From then on, in the same way my body had slowly begun to shut down before my immunoglobulin therapy, it began to gradually revive again, although in an incomplete way. Nonetheless, I was eventually able, with limited assistance, to get to the ward toilet rather than having to use the urinal bottle or a pan for defecating. Then, to achieve a short if unsteady walk out of the ward and back – whilst still attached to my wheel-fitted infusion machine which trundled alongside me – and even eventually, joy of joys, to finally be able to have an unsupervised hot shower.

The key neurologist looking after my case, Doctor Cox, was very pleased with my progress and said she would prescribe immune suppressants as soon as the immunoglobulin had achieved all it could in my Lazarus-like return from immobility and disease. She told me this treatment could only get me back to 70% of where I'd been prior to the onset of CIDP; the other 30% would be down to the result of regular physiotherapy and my mental determination to fully recover. The good doctor had seen other patients never fully recuperate from this disorder, but I had a couple of important factors working in my favour. At 38 years old I was still relatively young and, furthermore, I had been an exceptionally fit person for my age, a consequence I guess of my regular martial art training.

On the day I was discharged and a friend of mine came to drive me to my mother and stepfather's home in South Norwood London, I'd been an in-patient in the Royal Free hospital for close on five weeks; but I was still in need of some home care and assistance, so unhappily had to relinquish my West Hampstead flat.

It was now down to mental toughness and physiotherapy in order to realise my complete physical rehabilitation – a feat that would take nearly two years of my life to wholly accomplish.

WIPEOUT BEACH

So how did this illness mentally and emotionally affect me as I lay incapacitated in my hospital bed at the Royal Free? I guess I should have been in a psychologically dark place, fearful for my future, anxious for my life. But truthfully, I was actually very composed as I descended further and further into neurological perdition.

The initial stage of not knowing what had triggered my body to damage itself in such an appalling way had been the most testing part of the experience, but even then, with a conceivably permanent disabled future ahead of me, I remained positive that I would overcome whatever disease had afflicted my body and emerge to play gigs, write, record, tour and travel as before. These feelings were nothing more than bravado and optimistic conjecture, but it's amazing how positive attitudes can assist in the healing process and be a beneficial reassurance during difficult times.

At that early stage, I'd also come to terms with the prospect I might even die. Having already experienced such a full and enjoyable life, I was quite prepared, if it came to it, to relinquish my mortal self at 39 years old without any regrets or resentment about my passing. In fact, some of my closest friends and family, having witnessed my terrible condition during their hospital visits, had thought the worst and were more disturbed and troubled about this possibility than I.

The thing with acute illness is that it's often more difficult for loved ones and others to deal with than for the patient themselves. Anyway, that was my experience. I was far more concerned about the emotional impact of my condition on my parents, my stepfather, sisters and long-term friends than I was about my own personal situation, having reached a point of acceptance, and moreover, as I've already confided, still believing I would fully recover to again ride the possibilities and realities of our sentient world.

It was thanks to the incredibly knowledgeable, devoted and caring neurological doctors and nursing staff at the Royal Free that I'd avoided either death or facing the remainder of my life in a wheelchair whilst wasting away from a gravely degenerative disease; and so, upon my release from hospital, I figured the very least I owed these remarkable people was the courtesy of applying positive determination to get myself back to full health and complete the work they'd initiated.

Still too weak to function normally – the lack of service to my muscles from the nerves meant they'd severely atrophied – my mother and stepfather Leroy, cared for me and a kind friend drove me four times a week to physiotherapy sessions at the Mayday Hospital in Croydon, the very same hospital I was born in. There, I worked on regaining muscle

Campeonato Nacional
1a Divisão

G.D. CHAVES
S.C. CAMPOMAIORENSE

ESTADIO MUNICIPAL DE CHAVES
3 DE MAIO 1998   1.000$00

SECTOR	FILA	LUGAR
SUPERIOR LATERAL		

incluida taxa do Iva

10000521

fibre in my upper body, arms, and legs via various exercises and time spent on the weight machines.

After a couple of months, I was at least able to walk passably well for a reasonable distance with the aid of a stick and so asked my physiotherapist if it might be beneficial for me to take time out to travel to northern Portugal with my mum and Leroy, where I could take long walks in the mountainous region known as Trás-os-Montes, which is where my mother's hometown of Chaves is situated. She said it might be a good way of accelerating my rehabilitation but stipulated I must also do my muscle building exercises every day whilst there.

I spent three months convalescing in Portugal, living in the house my mother had inherited from her parents. Each day I walked to the centre of Chaves for lunch, then back up the long, steep hill that needed to be negotiated to journey from one location to the other – a round-trip distance of some 20 kilometres. As instructed, I also did my daily exercises, ate well – I had been 11½ stone (73 kilos) before the onslaught of CIDP, less than 8½ stone (52 kilos) upon leaving hospital – inhaled as much mountain-fresh air as possible, and even started drinking some local wine. After a month of this regime, I was able to lose the stick and walk comparatively long distances unaided.

Despite the important muscle recovery aspect of the trip, it also turned out to be a very enjoyable visit. Leroy and I would go to home games of the local professional football team GD Chaves (whose strip was gratifyingly identical to that of Crystal Palace FC – red and blue stripes) at their Estádio Municipal de Chaves stadium. I would shop at the town market, where everything from food, wine, linens, North African carpets and Portuguese majolica ceramics could be purchased at very good prices after a bit of customary haggling. And I relished some amazing meals, favourites being polvo dressed with chilli-suffused olive oil, baked or boiled bacalhau with raw garlic or bolinhos (a traditional type of fish cake), all ordered from the menus of the restaurants that lined the edge of the Tâmaga River, adjacent to the ancient Roman bridge constructed in the reign of the Emperor Trajan.

However, towards the end of my Portuguese stay, I made an error of judgement that almost proved fatal. One sun drenched afternoon; we took a taxi to a popular picnic spot by a stretch of the Tâmaga that separates Portugal from Spain. The river there was as placid as a garden pool and despite not being the strongest swimmer at the best of times, and still being in a muscle weakened state, I nonetheless got it into my head that swimming from one country to another would be a cool thing to do.

When I told my mother of my intention, she warned that a lot of people had drowned in this spot believing, as I did, that this part of the tributary was tranquil and not realising there was a deceptive undertow which had undone many a swimmer. Of course, being the dogged idiot I am, I ignored the caution, waded into the water and began swimming in the direction of Spain.

The river was approximately 100 metres wide at that location point and at first, I was doing fine, utilising a breaststroke to propel myself through the water and feeling confident about comfortably getting to the other side. About halfway across I suddenly became aware of a force that was dragging me along with the directional flow of the river, whilst simultaneously drawing me downwards to its depths. The undertow my mum had warned me about had made its dangerous presence known and I tried not to panic as I fought against its powerful pull, swimming on in the hope I could break free of its influence and that I still had enough strength to make it to the shallow parts of the outlying embankment.

It took every fragment of my CIDP depleted vigour to fight off the fierce undercurrent and reach the other bank. Even so, I was so exhausted by the effort and so devoid of the muscle power to clamber out of the river, that I almost drowned in the couple of feet of water I'd ended up immobile in, just in front of the slope of terrain which constituted the Spanish boundary.

Luckily, someone walking by saw my predicament and scrambled down to haul me out. They kindly waited beside me as I lay inert and breathless on the bankside until I'd recovered enough to thank them in Spanish, after which, I made my way back to Portugal utilising the nearby bridge which spanned the Tâmaga, rather than crazily chancing

Convalescing in Portugal, by the River Tâmaga, 1997.

its perilous waters for a second time.

My flagrant lack of judgement disturbed me. What was I thinking in attempting to swim across a notoriously unsafe river, having so recently emerged from hospital with wasted muscles and weakened limbs from an acute neurological disease? After a while though, I began to perversely see it as yet more proof that I was destined to regain full health and live and work as exactly before. I rationalised these experiences as verification that if I applied myself and set my mind to a course of action, anything could be achieved, no matter how adverse the odds. Again, this was more a case of swagger than rational thinking but, as before, it was these fanciful attitudes that aided me in accomplishing total recovery from CIDP in the months ahead.

Whilst I'd still been getting treatment in hospital, my lawyer passed on the revised date for my divorce hearing. I wasn't sure if I would be discharged by then so asked my friend Mel Wesson to call Mary Jordan to explain my situation and request for a deferral until I'd made at least a partial recovery from my illness. Mel did as I asked but when he next visited me, was angry and upset at her response.

After firstly accusing him of harassing her by phoning, she then said my disclosed neurological disease was the direct consequence of karma – apparently the universe had inflicted CIDP on me because I'd been a bad husband – and no way would she countenance changing the hearing date on my account. Mary also threw in for good measure, the threat that if Mel contacted her again, she would call the police and have him arrested. This was the friend who'd been Best Man at our wedding and, along with his wife Nicola, had socialised with us and been a part of our lives since we'd first dated.

But the thing was, as a result of her unpleasant intransience, I'd only just emerged from the Royal Free when I attended the hearing, thereby having to use a stick to walk into court, looking hospital thin and affliction gaunt. My brief also submitted documents signed by the neurological team that detailed the explicit affects that CIDP would have on my present and future health. These factors all worked in my favour. The judge was appalled I'd had to attend so soon after being discharged and ruled sympathetically in my favour, only one of her demands was granted. So what kind of karma was that?

14 years of marriage had been dissolved in an afternoon and I'd become a single man again. Despite the bruising nature of our break-up and divorce, it's strange to think that not that far in the future I would again get hitched and, some years subsequent, divorced again, although this time to a different kind of woman, in very dissimilar circumstances.

Upon its commencement, 1998 saw me persevere with my physiotherapy exercises, my regular visits to the Royal Free for check-ups and the steroid medication regime. I had put on some weight, was getting stronger and had started socialising again, going to The Albion pub on South Norwood High Street twice a week to drink beer and play dominoes with Leroy and his fellow Jamaicans and other West Indian mates. Where I lived with my mother and stepfather, Whitworth Road, was just a couple streets down from Selhurst Park (Crystal Palace FC's stadium) so I began attending all the home games, just as I'd done as a young boy and teenager, afterwards having a couple of beers at The Albion or Cherry Tree pubs with my fellow Eagles supporters.

February came around and I celebrated my 40th birthday with my old friend Mel Wesson, whose own 40th birthday had been just a few days before mine. Seeing it was such a milestone occasion, we splurged out and had lunch at the expensive Michel Roux junior's double Michelin-starred restaurant, Le Gavroche, in the Mayfair district of London. After an incredible meal and lots of wine we gadded about the West End, visiting pubs and old haunts from our younger days and saw a bawdy Restoration-period play at the Royal National Theatre: The London Cuckolds. It was a good birthday.

I was slowly reclaiming myself, getting back into my normality groove, but something had been missing from my life for a while – sex. Living with my mother and stepfather had certainly made things awkward in that regard, although I'd nevertheless managed to eventually 'date' a nurse who was a friend of one of my sisters and had several 'dates' with a young woman who worked as a bar waitress at the Hilton Hotel in Croydon. These liaisons had had to take place at their abodes and seeing that I was pretty much self-reliant again, I figured the time had come to move out and find a place of my own.

I was still in contact with one of my former paramours – a fashion editor of The Independent newspaper – who'd thoughtfully visited me in hospital a couple of times. She told me one of the news editors at the paper had recently split from her partner and was looking to rent out the basement of her house as a living space in Stoke Newington, North-East London. I met up with her, and within a week had moved in.

I could easily write a whole separate book about my time living in the same house as this woman in Stokey – which was what she routinely called the district – and maybe sometime I will; but let's just say things got so complicated and bizarre there that I decided after six months, or thereabouts, to get out and relocate to my father's place on the Monk's Hill council estate in Croydon.

Prior to hospitalisation, the worst day by far had been when I discovered my fingers were too weak to hold down the strings in order to accomplish any notes and runs on the fretboard of my bass guitar. Having now regained some of that muscular strength, I was excited when Charlie Harper phoned and proposed recording a new Urban Dogs album with the original line-up of himself, Ian 'Knox' Carnochan, Matthew Best and I. He revealed producer/engineer Dave Goodman would be at the helm for this one – I'd worked with Goodman once before, when he'd recorded my 1978 Punk band, The Users – and that we would be making the record at Goodman's Mandala Studio in the Forest Hill district of South-East London.

The album was being funded by a Swedish-based indie company called Raw Power Records, which was run by Stockholm resident Alf Olofsson. No contracts were forthcoming and the whole thing, business-wise, seemed somewhat shady, but for me just being able to play my bass guitar and contribute songs to a record again was the essential thing. It would be an important step in my rehabilitation, with money being of secondary consideration.

I already had a trio of songs written before my illness – State of Grace, Don't Jump My Train and Destroy. I recorded the electric rhythm guitars for these tracks with Matthew accompanying me on his kit before affixing the bass lines. Charlie opted to only sing Destroy as he felt my voice would be more suitable for the other two. Consequently, I provided the lead and backing vocals for those and one more, yet unwritten.

I savoured recording at Dave's studio, which was situated in the basement of his house. There was a very bohemian, relaxed vibe to the place, a bit like Dave himself. His lovely wife Cathy would make us all wonderful meals for lunch and dinner, and we always ate together in their kitchen, the food being accompanied by lots of red wine, also generously provided by the Goodmans.

After one of these excellent meals, whilst the rest of the Urban Dogs were sharing a couple of Dave's marijuana ciggies in the garden, I went into the studio's live room, picked up Knox's guitar and instantly wrote the music for the song Rare Disease. Later I added the words but, yet again, Harper decided the track would benefit more from my singing than his; and so I did as requested and managed to get the entire vocal performance onto tape in one take.

We recorded 17 songs in total: four solo compositions of mine; two Harper/Best collaborations – Junkie Hell and Step the Mind Gap; five of Knox's solo compositions – Punk Rock City, Whip Me Whip Me, Police State (not to be confused with the U.K. Subs' song with the same title), Schizophrenia and Millennium Dome; a pair of Charlie Harper songs

– Quarantine and This Machine; a Harper/Carnochan collaboration – Baby Marley (Charlie's ode to his new born grandson); and three cover songs – Wipeout Beach, Hey Joe and Punk Rock Ist Nicht Tot – written by Alan Vega, Billy Roberts and Billy Childish, respectively.

This new Urban Dogs' album sounded good, with some great songs and performances, and had been the ideal way for me to resume playing and recording. My fellow Dogs were supportive, upbeat and fun to be with throughout: I was constantly laughing at Knox's screwy jokes and hilarious observations. Dave Goodman was also a joy to spend time with. His Mandala Studio might not have been the most hi-tech or roomy place I'd recorded in, but it was certainly the friendliest, most generous and relaxed environment for creating and recording music that I'd experienced thus far.

Having been given the title Wipeout Beach by Olofsson, the album was mixed, manufactured and subsequently released on the 23rd of November 1998. On this release date, as a promotional stratagem, he organised a launch gig at the Dublin Castle in Camden, London. Playing on a record was one thing, with its stops and starts and rest periods, but having to constantly pound away at the fat strings of a bass guitar for an hour or so with little respite, was something else.

Come the night of the show, I was nervous about being able to consistently play throughout the performance whilst still being partially CIDP weak.

The venue was packed, which ramped up my anxiety, but, despite my qualms, it all went well. We worked our way through a set of Urban Dogs' debut album songs and new material from Wipeout Beach. I even played guitar and took the lead vocal for Rare Disease, whilst Knox took over on bass. Some favourite cover tunes were also included, among them, The Velvet Underground's I'm Waiting For The Man, and Pills, originally written and performed by Bo Diddley, before becoming substantially more famous via the raucous version the New York Dolls recorded for their debut album.

Alf had set up a stall selling Wipeout Beach CDs, and I'd noted he'd managed to offload the majority by the time our performance was over. Even though I hadn't got involved with this project to make money, I thought it a bit mean for him to do so without passing something on to the band. With this in mind, I asked Olofsson to meet us all the next day to talk about some recompense for the work we'd put in.

The following evening, at the Intrepid Fox pub in Wardour Street, we four Dogs gathered to see what kind of deal Alf was offering. He kept on saying he would pay out royalties founded on record sales but I knew, based on the location and size of his record company, that we would never see a penny of that income, and so I pushed for some kind

Urban Dogs' Wipeout Beach album launch show, London, 1998.

of advance. I suggested £250 each, this being a gesture amount rather than a serious up-front payment. Despite the low level of my proposal, Olofsson kept trying to argue the royalty route, but I was having none of it.

I'm always amazed how some of those involved at the business end of Rock music view professional musicians. In any other occupation, payment is always a given. If you hired a brick layer to construct a garden wall, when the wall is built you wouldn't dream of saying "Well, let's just see how it does. If it proves sturdy enough and I have no forthcoming problems with it, I'll pay you something later on."

If you got a plumber in to fix a leak, would you tell them "Thanks for that, I'll let you know about some possible money in the future once I'm reassured the repair holds and it doesn't leak again."

Of course not.

Each of us had travelled back and forth spending dosh on bus and train fares, had written songs for and played and sung on the album and devoted two entire working weeks to create Wipeout Beach. So why then would Alf think it unreasonable to ask for £250 apiece as a sign of his appreciation, especially since the chances of receiving any more dough, or even a single accounting statement from him, was zilch.

Now, you might argue that seeing as he had paid out for the studio time that this financial input was sufficient. However, applying the 'other professions' analogy again, that would be like taking your car to a garage to have some work done to it, paying out for the necessary parts but then refusing to pay the labour costs and giving a sketchy "Let's see how things pan out Mr Grease Monkey; maybe, just maybe, something will come your way at a later date."

The difference between a professional and an amateur is that the professional gets paid. Hence, unless you've already had dealings with, know and trust those involved in a music business transaction – especially when it comes to making records – it's always better to get some money upfront rather than hope something will turn up later, and I'd only recently met Olofsson, so had no idea whether he was trustworthy or not.

However, Knox was a friend of his, thus, Alf's involvement, although this in itself wasn't necessarily a positive recommendation. Knox was notorious for making bad deals with manipulators and giving away his services and songs for no recompense, many examples of which I could reveal for you here, but for brevity's sake, I'll skip. Just trust me on that.

And so I kept to my pay us something upfront mantra. Charlie then said he would forgo his share of the advance, which sounded very accommodating and charitable, but I later found out he'd already made a deal with Alf for gratis boxes of CDs to sell with his T-shirts and other swag on the Subs' merchandise stall, the profits of which, he would retain without sharing any accrued cash with his fellow Dogs. I don't blame Chas for this, he was taking care of himself, which is fair enough, but I'd wished he'd revealed it at the time rather than make it sound as if he was above such sordid considerations as money.

Knox, being the man he is, told Olofsson he didn't want anything, and I'm pretty sure, unlike Harper, he hadn't made his own clandestine deal with Raw Power. Although this seems very noble of him, it could have undermined my negotiation with Alf by making me look as if I was the only money-centric Medici in the band for merely asking £250 for the fortnight of time, effort, playing, and travel I'd put into helping to realise the album. And anyway, I wasn't just bargaining for myself, I was negotiating on behalf of us all.

Despite my arbitration being destabilised by these interventions, I stuck to my demand and Alf eventually agreed to pay Matthew and I what I'd asked for. He duly handed over the cash to us the following day.

I've gone into quite a lot of detail about this because I want to convey to you the machinations and looseness of the business side of things during that period of time. Just scrabbling about for small amounts of money for work already achieved required a lot of resolve and bloody mindedness.

Those of you who've already read Volume I and II of my memoir series will know how many times the bands I've played for were financially fleeced, and I was determined not to let it happen again. From then on it was a case of 'if I play, I'm paid'; unless that is, I'd agreed to do a charity event or record, or I was playing purely for the fun of it.

And by the way, Raw Power Records haven't to this day added a single penny more to the £250 I'd had to argue so tenaciously for back in 1998, and I've yet to receive one accounting statement from them to clarify why.

SOCIAL CHAOS

1999 was a transformative year. I returned to London with yet more augmented strength after another three month recuperative spell in northern Portugal and a doctor-instigated decrease in my immune suppressant medication – it's dangerous to just quit steroid treatment, a slow withdrawal is necessary, otherwise seizures and other serious physical malfunctions can occur – both of which accorded me another level of optimism for an absolute recovery from CIDP. These advances made me mad keen to get back to regularly making music for a live audience and the resumption of some kind of consistent mind and body exercise training.

I wasn't yet ready to return to Abbey Dojo and Kempo classes. Having now reached black belt status, I knew when it came to randori (free fighting practise) there would always be some cocky brown belt students who were looking to prove themselves against a Shodan and utilise everything in their attack technique's locker (as they should), in the hope of being awarded a black belt grading in the near future by Sensei Jee.

Although having made great strides in regaining my vigour, I figured I needed another form of training before I was ready to get back in the dojo to give a good account of myself in a fighting contest. To this end I joined the Swash and Buckle Fencing Club in the Westminster district of London, which taught traditional European fencing. There was a warm-up exercise period before instruction and then, for beginners like me, direction in how to attack and defend with a foil – a sword with hand guard and a thin blade that measured 110 cm (roughly three-and-a-half feet) from guard to tip.

Six months of regular attendance at the club wearing the obligatory metal-meshed Kevlar mask, gauntlets and a lamé – a high necked jacket made of tough cotton that helps protect the groin, chest, and throat – ensured I learned the all-important defensive parry and lunge counter-attack foil techniques and also absorb some of the time-honoured skills of swordsmanship to become a reasonably good novice fencer. Nonetheless, there was one aspect of this martial discipline which I found very difficult to acquire as a reflex.

As with my Kendo Japanese fencing training, the customary practise in the European version is to move backwards and forwards in a linear way whilst engaged in a match. In Shoriniji Kempo though, I'd been taught not to retreat backwards, but to use correct footwork to side step an advancing attacker. This causes them to necessarily adjust their position and provides the correct angle and time to counter attack with strikes to the left or right sides of their temple, jaw or floating rib, based on a rapid estimation of their weaker flank.

Having practised this method of countering an attack for more than six years, I ended up being continually told off by the Swash and Buckle instructors for side-stepping my fencing opponent in order to thrust the tip of my foil into their ribs, which seemed to me a very sensible thing to do. However, those were the fencing rules, and I ended up finding it so frustrating that I eventually left the club as I had no wish to unlearn the automatic defensive behaviour which had taken all those years of Kempo training to be ingrained in me.

In July, after three warm-up shows were offered to me by Charlie Harper – The Lincoln Inn in Scunthorpe, Lincoln's Grafton Labour Club and an unrecorded venue in Llandudno, Wales, with Darrell Bath taking the guitar role and the Subs' latest recruit, Gary Baldy, occupying the drum stool – I hooked up with Chas at Gatwick Airport to take a flight to the U.S.A.

This was to be my first American excursion since the U.K. Subs' 20th anniversary tour of 1997, where the seeds for my neurological illness were decisively sown and despite a lot of hard work and difficulties, no money had been made after taking into account my expenses, which didn't exactly motivate me to be again involved in a States-side tour with the band.

I was assured though, by Charlie and the originator of this proposed tour, that things would be very different this time around.

A young, enthusiastic booking agent from Florida named Randy Wolpin had decided to utilise the Lollapapalooza and the Warped travelling festival concepts to construct a similar roving carnival of bands which he'd engaged to open up at the Palace Theatre in New Orleans on the 16th of July, thereafter to traverse North America playing a series of shows until the tour's finale on the 9th of August at the Place des nations Amphitheatre in Montreal, Canada. Wolpin titled this extravaganza the Social Chaos tour, a suitably anarchic designation in consideration of the pedigrees of the bands he had hired for his moveable Punk rock feast.

Headlining would be the American Punk outfit T.S.O.L.; British Oi band The Business were selected to be second on the bill; the Subs were awarded third from top, with Chelsea (U.K.), D.O.A. (Canada), Vice Squad (U.K.), Murphy's Law (U.S.), The Vibrators (U.K.), D.R.I. (U.S.), One Way System (U.K.), Lower East Side Stitches (U.S.), Anti-Heros (U.S.), Sloppy Seconds (U.S.), Gang Green (U.S.) and ex-Dead Kennedys drummer D. H. Peligro's solo band, all being subject to a fluctuating bill order as we progressed across the North American landmass.

It was an intriguing package alright, but when I spoke to Randy on the phone, I still needed some convincing that the tour was viable and that I wouldn't again return home penniless as, among other initial outlays, I had to pay my air tickets upfront and it would be a long way from home if things went badly. Although he couldn't categorically assure me that one, maybe even two, of the shows he'd booked might not happen, Wolpin pledged that Social Chaos was essentially solid and there was some money to be made, plus it would re-engage American and Canadian audiences with the U.K. Subs in a major way. I took him at his word and booked my flights in conjunction with Harper so we could sit together on the plane.

As well as being reassured by talking to Randy, there were other key modifications from the Subs' previous tour of the States that I appreciated. I was to be acting tour manager, which meant, based on the band's day-to-day income and expenses, I could decide what to pay out as wages as we gigged along. Also, this time around, all the backline (amps, speakers, drum kit etc) would be provided at each venue, so no heavy lifting up and down stairways would be necessary and we could, if we so wished, leave the venues to get onto the freeway to head towards our next destination directly after I'd collected our fee.

Nicky Garratt was to provide his dynamic guitar work again but for this fresh caper, a Californian drummer, Gizz Navarro – a member of Dead Lazlo's Place, a Hardcore Punk outfit, which had released its debut album on Garratt's NRA record label – would replace Dave Ayer, who'd become a heroin user and was tragically no longer capable of playing. Having two members already based in the U.S.A. also made sound economic sense, as there would be no need for air tickets to-and-from the States for Garratt and Navarro, saving the band more than £1,200 in initial outlay, which would have had to have been deducted from our eventual overall profit.

And so on the morning of the 13th of July 1999, I got to Gatwick and met up with Charlie at the Virgin Atlantic check-in counter where we discovered standing in the same line waiting to collect their tickets, old friends Knox and Eddie Edwards of The Vibrators. Once we'd boarded the plane, I also noticed across the aisle Beki Bondage and the rest of her band, Vice Squad, who I visited for a brief chat before take-off. I also clocked Micky Fitz and other members of The Business sitting a couple of rows behind us, who nodded and gave the thumbs up knowing we were to be travelling companions all the way to New Orleans and beyond.

I'll now duplicate for you what I recorded in my 1999 diary regarding this notable tour. You may find some of the writing descriptively brief due to the fact that we were mostly in motion and there weren't enough inactive occasions to have been more expressive with my pen. Still, I think these entries provide a sincere, if truncated account of the daily events during the nomadic Social Chaos tour of '99:

13th July – Atlanta, Georgia via Boston, Massachusetts

Seven hours after take-off we land in Boston, Massachusetts. No hassles with customs and a couple of hours to annihilate whilst awaiting a connecting flight to Atlanta, all spent discussing the tour-to-be with Charlie, Knox and Eddie – "have enough tickets been sold to sustain this multi-bill tour?" "Will we get paid what's been agreed, or forced to take a reduction if things don't go to plan?" "Is this Randy guy really up to organising such a large event and might it not be the case that we'll have to cut and run and suffer a financial hiding if the tour goes tits up in a week or two?" Etc, etc, etc.

We board our linking flight to Atlanta. It's a really dilapidated, dirty aircraft with threadbare seats in need of either being completely refurbished or retired from service. After two-and-a-half hours of flying time it gets us to Atlanta, Georgia without falling apart. We troop off to hang around the airport for our third flight of the day.

Get a beer at the bar and risk a hot dog with Chas, Knox, Eddie and a couple of the Vice Squad contingent. A four hour interval follows before we are called to the gate for our final journey to New Orleans. Just about to board the plane when the airline announces over the intercom that this flight is cancelled, but then adds there's a Delta Airlines' flight leaving for our destination in a matter of minutes, for which our tickets are now valid.

A crazy dash ensues for this alternative gate which, of course, just had to be situated on the far side of the airport from where we'd been patiently awaiting our original flight. Vice Squad, The Business, Knox, Eddie, Harper and I breathlessly make it onto the aircraft with seconds to spare before its doors are sealed for take-off. It has now gone midnight in Atlanta.

14th July – New Orleans, Louisiana

Our third and final flight lasted approximately an hour, during which time I lapsed into a kind of semi-sleep state. Wake to the shudder of the plane hitting tarmac and for one fearful moment, believe we'd crashed rather than safely landed in Louisiana. File out of the aircraft and into the disembarkation building of the Louis Armstrong Airport in New Orleans. Nicky Garratt and our drummer for the tour, Gizz Navarro, are waiting for Charlie and me in the arrivals zone, along with the man who's been hired by Wolpin to tour manage his pageant of Punk – the aptly name Tool.

Tool wears a wife-beater vest, shorts, cowboy boots and a plastic Viking's helmet, complete with fake horns, which he believes bestows a dash of eccentricity and wackiness to his personality. Our immediate collective estimation is that he's a dickhead. Micky Fitz, Steve Whale, Harper and I start making bets on how long this evidently unsuitable coordinator will last.

The odds for his survival get considerably slimmer when he tells us that he's going to buy everybody a drink of their choice at an airport bar, only for him to discover, after we've followed him around the place for more than 20 minutes, that all the airport bars have shut for the night. He then informs us he's organised transport which will arrive in 15 minutes time to convey everybody to the pre-booked hotel. Three hours later, with no suitable vehicle in sight, we are all obliged to get taxis from the outside rank to take us to the accommodation.

It's close to 5am local time when we get there. The chosen motel is in a very rough part of the city, the very same area where I got myself a motel room on the '97 tour, only to have some crackhead trying to repeatedly pick the lock of my door to break in despite the fucker knowing I was in residence; so no hanging around outside, we go straight into the lobby and check-in.

Our smiling child-faced impresario, Randy Wolpin, is there to greet us, and after polite introductions, Chas and I take one of the twin rooms booked for the Subs, whilst Nicky and Gizz take the other. After a necessary shower, I set my head down on my pillow and succumb to instant sleep.

15th July – New Orleans, Louisiana

Wake at 8am having only managed to accomplish two hours sleep due to extreme jetlag. Harper sleeps on in the bed across the room from me, so I wander out into the lobby to see if anyone I recognise is up for getting some breakfast. Eddie Edwards had just hired a car as The Vibrators' means of getting around North America, and he's happy to drive me, Knox and Vice Squad's drummer Pumpy, to a diner a couple of miles away from our decidedly hazardous location.

Our friendly, toothless, black waiter asks, "Where you all from?" Eddie replies "London, England." The waiter says "Oh, that's nice, have you all driven from there for some fishing?" We leave him a good tip and head back to our HQ.

Watch TV with Chas, shower and shave and then step outside, where the sun is high and the humidity sticks to the skin like a damp towel.

The young American lad who'd been hired to drive The Business about in their Winnebago camper van tells me that earlier he'd been approached in the car park by some local crack addicts with menaces and just managed to avoid a mugging thanks to two arriving motel residents who put them off their criminal stride.

We rehearse in the evening in a small room with a drum kit, amps etc, courtesy of some friends of Gizz who play together in a band called Disco Bombs. They sit around on stools and watch us go through the set, which sounds pretty rough to these ears, although this is not a surprise, seeing as Navarro has only had the chance to run through the songs a couple of times with Nicky in San Francisco prior to flying here.

After three hours of practice, I declare I've had enough and we pack away the guitars. I'm playing the black Gibson Thunderbird bass that Charlie purchased in 1997 for the 20th anniversary tour, which had been left at Garratt's house for future stateside gigging use. Back at the motel, Chas and Gizz take a taxi to join up with the Disco Bombs' fellas on Bourbon Street for bars and booze. I stay to get some sleep, but I'm awoken at 4am when Harper stumbles into the room, turns on the air conditioning, the TV and clatters about until he finally gets into his bed around 5am.

16th July – New Orleans, Louisiana

Gig day. Wake at 9am (wow, a whole four hours' sleep!) and go fetch some coffee for me and Chas from the machine in the motel lobby. Take a walk around the block to a Wallgreens' pharmacy, where I buy a box of Garcia and Vega cigars with my credit card. [Yep, back then, American pharmacies sold smoking products.]

When I return, Nicky has picked up the Subs' mini-van as there's no need for anything bigger due to the backline being provided at each show, and sets off to collect his and Harper's merchandise, telling us he'll be back to help carry out the instruments and luggage from the rooms prior to checkout time. With an hour-and-a-half to go until we have to vacate the motel or pay for another night, Charlie decides he wants to get some breakfast. He promises to return in 30 minutes.

Checkout time comes around, but there's no sign of Garratt or Harper, so Gizz and I have to transport all the guitars, bags and suitcases out into the brutal sun. An hour later Nicky arrives, and a few minutes thereafter, Charlie strolls into view. Both get a tongue lashing from me and after loading up the van, which is a difficult proposition as Garratt and Harper's swag boxes take up much of the space at the rear of the vehicle, we head off for the State Palace Theatre – the location for the opening night of the Social Chaos tour.

The venue is impressive: big, big stage, many tiers of seats that reach up into the gods, with rows of balconies and private boxes along the sides above our heads.

Say "Hello" to Gene October and the Chelsea guys, all of whom had just flown in from London. Eat some veggie chilli backstage, drink a beer and take to the stage after D.R.I. finish, with eight other bands having already unveiled their musical wares for the mainly young, teenage-plus audience.

Sloppy show, Gizz makes some glaring mistakes and after breaking some strings, Nicky knocks over his amp and fucks up his guitar in an anarchic salvage operation. The Business and T.S.O.L. follow us to finish. We wait around until, as designated Subs' TM, I finally get paid by Randy. Into the van and head off into the night for Texas. Try to find a motel to stay at around 3am, but there's a baseball tournament going on so there are no rooms to be had. We have no choice but to drive on into the southern night.

17th July – Austin, Texas

Cross the Stateline into Texas at 6am and pull over at a rest stop. Charlie lays on a stone picnic table and sleeps; Nicky takes a nap in the van, Sandra, who Charlie employed yesterday to sell merchandise, is laid out on the grass, whilst Gizz and I wander round in a dazed state. Get back in the van after an hour of trying to snatch some sleep, continue our journey to Austin.

Pass ramshackle houses, a large hand-painted sign that reads 'Gang raped while dying, still no arrests.' Texas swings by and we eventually stop at a Denny's diner to eat.

When we reach tonight's venue, the Backroom Club in Austin, real chaos reigns. No one knows what's going on. Tool is running around growling and acting the fool to no good effect. We retreat to find a reasonable motel and book in. I share a room with Chas again, shower, and try to catch some sleep whilst Harper TV channel hops. When we return to the venue Tool wants us to play last. The reason for this is because last night T.S.O.L. went on to an almost empty theatre, most of the audience having left after The Business finished to head home, being as some previous bands had overrun and the headliners were obliged to go on at a very late hour.

I say, "OK Tool, pay us headline money, whatever you're paying T.S.O.L, and we'll do it."

Tool doesn't like this idea, instead he offers us a fully paid up day off

L to R: Nicky, Alvin, Gizz and Charlie, Social Chaos tour, 1999.

instead of having to perform tomorrow. We laugh and tell him, think again, we've not come all this way NOT to play. We finally reach a compromise – Subs will be second to the headliners with, for tonight only, Vice Squad agreeing to take the graveyard shift.

It turns out to be an excellent gig for us. The crowd love it and the playing is so much better than yesterday.

18th July – Lawrence, Kansas

Set off early. Brutal 800 mile (1,287 kilometres) drive during which, we have a front tyre blow out whilst travelling at 75 mph. We unload the van. I help Nicky fit on the spare, and onwards. Pass time having quizzes and verbal competitions, which are a lot of fun and help take our minds off the gruelling nature of today's epic journey. 14 hours after leaving Austin we reach Lawrence, Kansas.

We go straight from the van onto the stage to perform, where the playing improvements of yesterday have evaporated due to our road weariness. We go down OK though. Collect money from Randy, and Chas decides to stay in Kansas for a barbecue at the house of Terrence 'Tezz' Roberts, acting bassist for The Business. There's a day off tomorrow and The Business are happy to drive Harper to Denver, this being where the next show is scheduled for that following evening.

To my relief Sandra also decides on this barbeque option. Having renamed her Fifi – for no other good reason than she's French – it's obvious to me she's terminally useless. Her selling technique at the merch stall consists of leaning languidly against a wall whilst chain-smoking cigarettes and looking perennially bored. She's travelling in the van with us, sleeping in one or other of our rooms (on a couch or a put-up bed) as she doesn't want to pay out for her own room; and additionally, eating our rider food, drinking our drink and it's not as if Gizz or I have anything for her to sell for us.

As on the last U.S.A. tour, Garratt and Harper are retailing Subs' T-shirts, plus other wares, and putting the proceeds directly into their own pockets. I'm not complaining about them making the extra dinero per se, but it's a bit much to expect me and Gizz to yield room for, and to accommodate someone who is travelling with us to facilitate making money solely for them.

20th July – Denver, Colorado

Yesterday's gig-free 24 hours was pleasant enough. Nicky, Gizz and I drove in beautiful sunshine to a motel which was just a couple of miles short of Denver. We book one room costing $50, with me and Gizz paying $20 apiece to get a bed each, whilst Garratt coughs up $10 to take the couch.

This morning we are awoken at 9am to the hellish sound of loud hammering and power drills directly beneath our room. Never one to miss an opportunity, I storm into the lobby and demand recompense from the desk clerk for our rude awakening. He's sympathetic to my reasoning and awards us a total refund. That's a night in a good motel for free, which pleases Garratt and Navarro no end.

Arrive in Denver and roll up at the venue, a large Art Deco period theatre called The Artisan. D.O.A. are already there and we challenge them to play us in a game of a just invented sport christened 'Socky', a hybrid of British soccer and Canadian ice hockey, which we kick off in an alley adjacent to the theatre. The game is fast and furious, Joey Shithead and his men trying to prise the football away from our feet with their hockey sticks, whilst Nicky and I attempt to dribble past them to get a scoring opportunity. Gizz, being of a decent girth, is our goal keeper. It ends in an honourable 3-3 draw. Every member of D.O.A. is easy going and cool to hang with, I like them immensely.

James Stevenson turns up, having just flown in from Portugal to join Chelsea as second guitarist. It has been at least 10 years since we last shared a beer together, and it's good to see the fella and catch up on things.

Subs and D.O.A., post-game of 'Socky', Social Chaos tour, 1999.

I end up getting a little too much sun hanging out with all the band affiliates on the outside patio that adjoins the venue. Beki Bondage comes to my rescue with some moisturiser and hydrating block, which she liberally applies to my sun-reddened face with relish. There's definitely a cooperative and mutually supportive spirit being exhibited by most of the band members towards each other on this tour. We chat, drink and eat together, lend each other guitar leads, straps, stands, and tuners, the only major exception being the D.R.I. guys, who keep to themselves and seem uninterested in socialising, although their guitar tech is always talkative and friendly to us.

Much relieved when Charlie safely arrives with The Business. We take to the stage at the perfect time of 10pm and immediately win the approval of tonight's spectators. A huge mosh pit develops with the onset of our opening number and the audience stomp and slam dance right up until the conclusion of our final song. The collective playing tonight was faultless, so there's a genuine feeling of mutual gratification when we get back to the dressing room to debrief.

After a swift beer, I wander out into the auditorium to watch The Business and T.S.O.L. Both bands play blinding sets but, for me, the London outfit edge the honours tonight. I'm always astonished at just how good a front man Micky Fitz is, masterful and engaging throughout, one of the best in the business, excuse the pun.

Whilst standing amongst the punters, a stream of 18, 19 and 20-something year-olds come up to me to say what a great band the Subs are and how much they love our music. I'm amazed that people of that age even know who the U.K. Subs are. There's definitely a much younger audience here for British Punk rock than in the U.K., where it's mainly people from my age-group who attend our gigs. This gives me huge optimism that Punk rock will continually attract a new generation of enthusiasts in the coming decades and that, with continuing youthful support, the U.K. Subs and some of the other groups on this tour will be able to play and prosper for many years to come.

GET OUT OF DENVER BABY

We began picking up serious road rhythm as the Social Chaos tour pressed on from the Rocky Mountains of Colorado, onwards towards the deserts of Nevada – at which point, let's get back to my diary entries for more day-by-day action:

21st July – Colorado to Las Vegas, Nevada

'Get out of Denver baby, get out of Denver, you look like a commie and you just might be a member, get out of Denver baby, get out of Denver.' Charlie Harper repeatedly sang this Bob Seger tune as we sped away from the city last night before stopping a couple of hours west of Denver to book ourselves two twin motel rooms, which we vacated at 9am this morning. After breakfast in a local diner, it was all aboard the Chrysler mini-van for the lengthy drive to Las Vegas.

Amazing scenery: firstly turbulent rivers and vast mountains, then deep canyons, a multiplicity of cacti, some majestic eagles circling overhead. We get out at an especially scenic point to have some group photos taken on the perilous edge of a breathtaking canyon. Drive on, and as evening darkness begins to intrude, pull over into a service station car park to eat the foods that we'd purchased earlier at a supermarket close to our former motel. Then continue headlong into the inscrutable parts of the Mojave desert.

The van's headlights pick out endless amounts of cacti, a few sizeable scampering lizards and the desert's immeasurable solitudes. I drift off to sleep and awake to see what I assumed was the morning sun rising up on the desert horizon. Having glanced at my watch and seen it was only just after 1am, I lean forward in my seat towards Gizz, who's upfront taking his turn at the steering wheel, and in a perplexed voice ask:

"Gizz, why the fuck is the sun coming up at 1am?"

He laughed, nodded towards the brilliant glow beyond the rock ridge and tells me "That's not the sun, that's Las Vegas."

Soon enough, Vegas is spread out before us in all its neon eccentricity. We drive along its main artery – the Strip – flanked by hotel-casinos of various sizes and renown. Around 2.30am, we leave the sensory assault of flashing illuminations behind us to reach one of the suburbs of the city where Gizz's friend's house is situated. We'll all be staying here for two nights, sleeping on sofas and wherever a comfortable spot can be claimed in its numerous rooms, until it's time again to move on.

Vegas bound, U.S.A., Social Chaos tour, 1999.

22nd July – Las Vegas, Nevada

Wake at 10am and join Charlie and Fifi for a swim and some sunbathing around the pool located in the backyard of the house. Even at this time of the morning, the strength of the sun is such that we have to retreat back into the house after 45 minutes or risk being badly burned by ferocious solar rays. Make for our venue de jour in the afternoon, the Huntridge Theatre. It's another vast space where, after the doors open for the punters, only about a quarter of the auditorium gets filled. All the other venues have been well attended, so I guess Punk rock is not the attraction here that it has been in the other cities we've already played.

Take a beer and make the acquaintance of a blonde beauty in the bar, who then pleasingly attaches herself to me for the duration of my time at the Huntridge. Trouble in the foyer when a member of One Way System gets his camera film confiscated by the owner of the theatre: a puritanical Mormon who became enraged because an affiliate of the band took a picture of a female fan who'd lifted up her T-shirt to reveal her breasts and then encouraged the guitarist to photograph away. A fight almost breaks out between the band and the owner and his security goons, but Randy arrives to smooth things over and avert any fisticuffs.

D.H. Peligro also gets threatened by a bouncer for smoking a cigarette in the foyer. It seems that just about everyone who works at the Huntridge is either surly or positively hostile towards the bands and punters alike.

We Subs get on stage at 9pm to perform a workmanlike set. Back to the blonde, who unfortunately has to travel out of town that night with a girlfriend who'd given her a ride to the venue. We find an empty dressing room to make out for a bit, and then reluctantly say our goodbyes. Quit the Huntridge for our Vegas base, where I manage to cop a bedroom for myself and within minutes of our arrival, have showered and fallen into a luxurious deep sleep in a comfortable double-sized bed.

23rd July – Mesa, Arizona

Seems there was a party at the house after I'd got to sleep, with Nicky being forced to escape to the van to get some shut-eye due to the noise and activities in the lounge, which was where he'd previously been sleeping on a couch. I lucked out getting that unclaimed bedroom.

Swop the Mojave for the Arizona Desert and drive, according to our vehicle's dashboard visual display, in 109° Fahrenheit heat to the city of Mesa, for tonight's Punk rock frivolities. Get to the Nile Theatre, this evening's house of fun, and glad for the air conditioning, which was keeping the venue cool and contrasted greatly with the extreme outside temperature.

Watch the earlier bands play their sets, and notice that Nicky Garratt is in a very cheerful mood because a female friend has turned up: a girl who, apparently, helps him with his "sex projects".

I remember her from one of the gigs on the 1997 tour. I'd happened to unsuspectingly barge into our dressing room – Garratt had tried to bar the door with a chair – whilst they were engaged in one of these so-called projects, about which I'm not going to share the details as that would be perfidious of me, seeing as it's private stuff and Nicky was, and remains, a friend of mine. Let's just say it was the sort of thing Iggy Pop had in mind when he wrote Some Weird Sin.

It was a notable show for us, lots of movement from Chas, Nicky and I, good playing all round and a satisfactory audience reaction. After leaving the stage, I drank some beer and chatted to assorted member of The Business, Vice Squad, One Way System and T.S.O.L., although D.R.I., apart from their affable guitar tec, are still being unfriendly and acting like they're somehow above it all.

Onstage, San Bernardino, California, 1999.

24th July – San Bernardino, California

The entire band stayed over at Nicky's 'sex projects' girl's house last night. This morning, we're joined by all-round good guy Tim Jamison, lead singer for St. Louis, Missouri based Punk outfit, Ultraman, who'd recorded an album for Garratt's NRA record label in the late 1980s. Tim was along to take on the driving duties and generally help out for a couple of days.

With Jamison now in the driver's seat, we accomplish a typically long journey in hot sunshine to the Orange Pavilion – a massive aircraft hangar of a venue –which is filled with thousands of young, Hardcore Punk rockers, Skinheads and San Berdoo Latino gang members. From our dressing room and just before we get to play, the sound of gunfire can be heard and we later learn that two rival gangs had a shoot-out in one of the outdoor bars of the venue, although we don't get to discover if there were any injuries or fatalities.

Subs go on to a great reception and we play a sharp, unrestrained show for the assembled thousands, who respond in typical Hardcore Californian fashion – moshing, stomping around and generally responding to our music in a very physical manner. Afterwards, backstage, we discover that liggers and freeloaders outnumber the bands by three-to-one, and a fair few are doing their best to drink rider beer, steal whatever merchandise is around and pilfer anything else that wasn't being kept a watchful eye on. I'm much relieved when my friend Dave Harte turns up to whisk me away from this disarray and thievery to Los Angeles, and thereafter on to a Mexican restaurant in the Valley.

Following a delicious meal and a pitcher of margaritas, another alumni of Broken Glass (the group I played with in LA in the late 1980s) turns up. Tim Mosher, Dave and I go on to Studio City to have a couple of beers and reminisce about those heady LA days at a bar called Residuals. Say our goodbyes to Tim, and Dave drives me to his and his wife Kathleen's house in the Hollywood Hills, where I spend a comfortable night in their spare bedroom.

25th July – San Francisco, California

Following breakfast with Dave and Kathleen, I get driven to Gizz's house, where the rest of the Subs had spent the night after the San Bernardino show. All in the van for the 382 mile (614 kilometres) ride north to San Francisco, our initial destination being Nicky's house.

After unloading some of Garratt's merchandise boxes into his garage for restocking, Chas and I take a short walk to our favourite sushi restaurant for lunch and then onwards to the 3,000 punter capacity Maritime Hall, where this evening's Punk rock action will be taking place. Upon our arrival I run into Randy, who tells me he'd finally had enough of Tool and has dismissed him as the Social Chaos' tour manager. I tell Wolpin that I'm amazed Tool lasted this long, seeing as he's without doubt the most inept TM I've ever had the displeasure of working with.

Nicky's girlfriend Dolores and his jogging partner Arabella – blonde, slim, pretty, German – turn up just before we perform our set, which was what the Americans would have referred to, in former times, as 'a doozy', with prodigious energy and faultless playing. Take a beer with Arabella at the bar whilst watching The Business work the crowd to an even higher level of frenzy.

I collect our fee from Randy then continue to get even friendlier with Arabella, so much so, I end up spending the night with the attractive Teutonic blonde at her house in the Richmond district of SF.

Now, at this point, my diary entries get very imprecise and a number of touring days are not recorded at all; probably due to the new punishing levels of travel required and the subsequent lack of opportunities to find a suitable occasion to write about the events of these hectic 24 hour periods on the American road. Despite that, there was certainly enough diary information to reconstruct the remainder of the tour:

Seattle, on the 27th of July, was our next rendezvous city, and although I have no recollection of our gig at the venue there, I do remember sitting with Micky, Steve and Tezz from The Business drinking in a bar beforehand and having Paul Rooney from Vice Squad present himself at our booth in a very distressed state, blood oozing from his nose onto his T-shirt. It seems he'd got into an argument with his bassist, who'd abruptly ended the dispute with a punch to Paul's snout.

Having reported this to us, the understandably unhappy guitarist then tried to get us to form a posse to seek out and take revenge on the now absconded bass player on his behalf. Micky's view, which was shared by the rest of us, was that this was an internal band matter and, despite us all having sympathy for Rooney's plight, it wouldn't be right to hunt down the assailant for a beating based on one punch and a now fast drying bloodied nose. I seem to recall the pugnacious bassist didn't return to complete the tour and Vice Squad got in a substitute player whose name escapes me due to the corrosive effects of time.

Portland, Oregon, and the Roseland Theatre was the next city and venue to host the Social Chaos Punk pageant, followed by a mammoth 2,064 mile (3,321 kilometres) drive across America, from its west coast to Lake Michigan in the east, destination Milwaukee, Wisconsin. We had two days in which to accomplish this journey, all the bands being required to meet up there at the Eagle Ballroom for a show on the 31st of July.

The 40 hour drive was brutal. There simply wasn't enough time to book into motels, so we would only stop to eat, fuel up, piss, crap and get clean at the numerous trucker-friendly service stations which, thankfully, provided showering facilities for long-haul drivers on the I-90 freeway. Whilst in motion, we took it in turns to either sleep, drive or ride shotgun, so that if whoever was driving lapsed into sleep whilst at the wheel, the shotgun occupant could shake them awake before we veered off the road. Heavily fatigued but in one collective piece, we made it to our final destination with just a couple of hours to spare before the Subs were obliged to get onstage to earn our fee.

A 452 mile (727 kilometres) ride was required the next day to attain Columbus, Ohio, play a gig there, and 24 hours later, undertake yet another show at the Phoenix Theatre in Detroit. This was followed by a Pittsburgh performance, before transferring the travelling circus to New York City, with Coney Island High being the place to be in the Big Apple for some gritty alternative music on the 6th of August.

New York to Providence, Rhode Island, was a thankfully meagre 108 mile (174 kilometres) trip, where the Social Chaos cast played their penultimate gig before the finale of the entire enterprise, set for Toronto on the 8th. The concluding show was originally meant to be in Montreal on the 9th, but this had been cancelled for reasons that were never revealed – poor ticket sales being the most likely motive.

Wet and windy night time visit to Niagara Falls, U.S.A., 1999.

We'd driven straight after the Providence show to Niagara Falls, which is on the border of New York State and Ontario, Canada. Even though we arrived in darkness at around 11pm, being as none of us had ever seen the Falls before, we abandoned the van for a while to get a close-up look of this magnificent cascade from Terrapin Point viewing platform, adjacent to the torrent.

The Falls were lit up and were everything you would want them to be, but there was also a strong wind going on, which meant we got drenched whilst oohing and aahing at this natural wonder. Curiosity now satisfied and still fully intending to cross the border for the drive to Toronto the following day, we headed back in sodden clothes to the van and set about trying to find a hotel on the American side for the night. Problem was, there was some sort of convention going on, and not a single room was available for occupation at the dozen or more hotels we tried to check into.

We eventually had to give up and spend the night sleeping in the van in our water-drenched garments. When I awoke, I felt the water which had evaporated from our clothes during the night and collected on the inside roof of the van, dripping back down onto my face, which only added another layer of discomfort to an already unpleasant situation. Mercifully, it soon became a typically gorgeous August day, so we gathered outside in order to let our still damp clothes dry via the heat of the sun.

The Toronto show was a bit of an anti-climax. It definitely lacked the fire and vigour of our earlier performances. I guess the thousands of miles we'd travelled, the lack of sleep and physical wear and tear finally got to us, but that was fine, the playing was good enough and the audience was approving of what we offered them. I collected our fee off Randy Wolpin for the last time. He had been a solid friend to the Subs throughout the Social Chaos experiment, always cheerful and positive, always available to sort out any practical problems; and after many hugs and handshakes with, and goodbyes to, our fellow touring comrades – minus, obviously, the dour members of D.R.I. – we found a motel for the night and slept.

The next day Nicky and Gizz drove me and Charlie to my Portuguese aunt and uncle's house in Shelton, Connecticut. Like most of my mother's brothers and sisters, they'd immigrated to the U.S.A. whilst still relatively young to start a new life for themselves and become part of the thriving Connecticut Portuguese community.

After dropping Chas and I off there, Garratt and Gizz drove on to JFK Airport in NY City to return the van to the hire company and thereafter take a flight back to California. Harper and I stayed with my aunt, uncle and my two cousins, Carlos and Dennis, in Shelton for three days eating good Portuguese home-cooked meals and drinking decent Portuguese wine before, on the 12th of August, getting a ride from Carlos to JFK for our flights back to Blighty, where good ol' time-twisting, jet lag-induced disorientation was waiting to ambush me upon my return to my father's house in Croydon.

Despite its crazy travel schedules, the sleep deprivation and occasional physical discomforts – trying to get a night's sleep in wet clothes whilst propped up in a van seat was certainly a new uncomfortable touring low – I nevertheless really enjoyed the Social Chaos Tour of 1999. Unlike on the previous American sojourn, Nicky Garratt hadn't been in a constant state of anxiety about money, was far more relaxed and proved to be good company throughout.

This time around, Charlie was more reliable, cooperative and focused on performing and singing rather than partying and doing what he wanted to do, when he wanted to do it, despite whatever detrimental circumstances meant he shouldn't; and Gizz Navarro had been a delight to work with throughout – consistently pleasant, trustworthy and sunnily enthusiastic from day one of the tour right up to its conclusion.

As TM, I'd also made sure we all made some money. Starting off by paying a daily wage of around $50 until we'd got the van hire fee sorted, I then, having already repaid the air fares and taken the motel payments, fuel and other expenses into account, gradually increased this amount so that by the mid-point of the tour, we were making more or less $150 apiece per show. This meant that each member took home roughly the net amount $2,500 after personal expenses such as food and drink – although Nicky and Charlie would have each made twice that for themselves from merchandise sales. It wasn't a huge windfall, but it was certainly a lot better than what Harper, Dave Ayer and I made on the 1997 tour, and I was therefore called upon to TM the U.K. Subs, along with providing the bass lines, on a number of subsequent North American ventures.

The other very satisfying aspect to this tour, the first major excursion I'd undertaken since my illness, was that, despite the intense physical exertions of playing and travelling and the scarcity of any consistent rest time, I hadn't lapsed back into an unwell state and had managed to stay reasonably robust throughout; although, once back in Croydon I started to feel some numbness in my extremities again and so, on the advice of my neurologist, as a precaution, returned to the Royal Free Hospital for an in-patient top-up treatment of immunoglobulin for five days and nights. This supplementary set of infusions definitely worked, as I never needed to return to hospital for any additional treatments from then on. Henceforth, I would be free of any punitive aspects of CIDP.

After my stay at the Royal Free, I flew to Portugal for two weeks of fresh mountain air and sunshine with my father for company. One night we were drinking brandy outside on the porch of my mother's house when a large pack of village dogs of various breeds and sizes raced past the front gate, leaving a cloud of road dust behind them. I looked to my dad and said, "What the hell were they running from?" Just as I finished my question, a huge grey wolf came bounding down the path directly in front of us and loped on after them.

I knew it was not unusual for wolves to come down from the mountains to the village to try to get themselves a chicken from a pen or, in this case, to make a meal of one of the stray dogs that roamed the area, but it was the first time I'd seen a wild wolf up close. It was a large, magnificent looking animal and for the rest of our stay I relished hearing it, or another of its kind, howling away in that deep expression of lamentation on the outskirts of the village in the dead of night.

By 1999 I'd also got back into regular dating again, but with the usual results – new women, old story. Then, in October, I went to see Michael Monroe play a typically energetic, rocking show at the Borderline in

London in the company of Charlie Harper and Darrell Bath. There were a lot of people I knew attending, including a girl who had been part of the female Scottish contingent which had followed my old Hanoi Rocks' spin-off band Cheap And Nasty from gig-to-gig, whenever we'd played north of the border. She was with another young woman who I'd met at a birthday party five years previously and had thought very beautiful.

I bought them both a drink at the bar and then spent most of my time speaking to the birthday party beauty who hailed from Oslo, Norway. Trine Karlsen and I experienced an immediate amatory rapport and after the show had concluded, we swapped phone numbers with the intention of getting together for a drink sometime in the near future. I was elated a couple of days later when, after picking up the reverberating telephone assuming it to be Charlie asking me to play some last minute show, I instead discovered it was Trine asking about the possibly of us meeting up that week.

That following evening, after many glasses of Bordeaux red were shared at a wine bar on the Charing Cross Road, I went back to her flat, where we spent our first night together – the initiation of a relationship that was to endure for a further six years.

END OF THE CENTURY

Following on from the challenging but ultimately enjoyable Social Chaos North American tour, my new steady relationship with Trine Karlsen had also raised my spirits like a séance. I was similarly pleased to be asked to play yet more shows as a U.K. Sub at a variety of cities and venues with Gary Baldy and Darrell Bath handling the drums and guitar tasks. A couple of months later, in November 1999, Charlie proposed getting Nicky Garratt over from San Francisco to take on the guitar role for a series of U.K.-wide gigs, starting at the Fleece and Firkin in Bristol on the 18th and finishing up with a show in Swindon, precisely one month later.

After two rehearsals in London, the band set off westward to play this opening date with Gary driving, plus then Subs' agent, Steve 'Toxin' Harnett, and newly hired merchandise seller Zowie Huxley for company. It was on this journey to Bristol that I discovered that Zowie's uncle was Aldous Huxley, author of such seminal books as Brave New World and The Doors of Perception (from which Jim Morrison procured the name for his band) whilst her grandfather, Thomas Henry Huxley, had been a close friend of Charles Darwin and an early proponent of evolutionary theory. And now there was his granddaughter, travelling to a gig in a van full of Punk rockers to sell T-shirts for Charlie Harper. How weird and wonderful is that?

Toxin wasn't one for details such as post show lodgings and Charlie also didn't consider pre-booked hotels as a necessary adjunct to the tour, so we mostly had to rely on the generosity of fans, friends or promoters for places to stay after each gig, which was a real hit or miss accommodation lottery. It was a very cold U.K. winter and I remember someone kindly offering us a share of their flat in York to spend the night.

The front room was heated by a coal fire, but the rest of the dwelling was freezing, including the small bedroom where they said I could sleep. The room was so Arctic-like that despite getting into the bed with all my clothes on and wrapping myself in the provided blankets, I just couldn't get warm enough to achieve any reasonable sleep and spent most of the night shivering and longing for the dawn. Next morning they revealed that particular bedroom sat directly above the icy meat locker of the ground floor butcher's shop, which made it the coldest space in the flat. Not surprisingly, within days, I succumbed to a bad bout of flu and as a protective measure due to my former neurological illness, returned to my father's place in Croydon to convalesce after which I re-joined the tour having fully recovered a week later.

As well as this shambolic, clueless approach to having somewhere to

Zowie Huxley, merch and wigs.

stay after each gig, there was also a problem with Gary Baldy. I knew that it must have been an even more difficult tour for him, seeing as he was not only drumming but taking care of all the driving, although this was mainly because he wasn't too keen on anyone else taking control of the steering wheel; but even so, he acted as if he wasn't a part of the group.

He hardly spoke to any of us and was distant and detached. I think he was resentful of the evident bond between Chas, Nicky and I that had been forged over many years of working together and somehow saw himself as an outsider or intruder even. He was also having personal relationship problems – in the process of separating from his wife, I seem to recall – which must have only added another level of unhappiness to his already melancholic state of mind.

This unfortunate situation came to a head when he left us with the van in Portsmouth to return to London by train on some urgent business having said he would drive his car to Nottingham for that evening's performance at the Running Horse pub, which is still a functioning venue that continues to host live music. However, Gary didn't show up and couldn't be reached by telephone, despite numerous attempts by Harper, who'd commandeered the landlord's phone in the pub in an attempt to discover the reason for his absence.

Stage time came around and Charlie was forced to get on the microphone to ask the audience if there was anyone present who played drums and knew some Subs' tunes. A young man of about 18 years came over to where Chas and I were trying to alleviate our sorrows with beer, to offer his services. He did his best but, in all honesty, the performance was deeply embarrassing and I felt we'd cheated those who'd paid to see us, although Harper seemed quite relaxed about the horror show we'd just served up and said, considering the circumstances, it was good enough.

I disagreed and told Nicky Garratt that it was the worst experience of my music career to date and that I wouldn't be interested in appearing with the Subs again unless the disorganised and chaotic nature of this tour was changed to something more structured and better prepared for the future. After that shabby recital had concluded, Charlie put up a handwritten sign on the merch table which read: **The U.K. Subs are looking for somewhere to stay tonight, can you help?** Thankfully, at that stage, we had just three more gigs to fulfil.

Gary Baldy did return for the final trio of shows with an obviously fictional story about his car having malfunctioned on the motorway on his way to Nottingham but continued to be just as unresponsive and withdrawn as before. The final gig in Swindon would be the last show he'd play as a U.K. Sub.

Trine had gone to Oslo to spend Christmas and celebrate the start of a new year with her family and friends. I spent the holiday with my own family and, on New Year's Eve, went to a party given by one of my father's neighbours and joined in the customary drinking, intoxicated behaviour and conversations that are a traditional part of these occasions. It was the beginning of a new century and a new millennium so I was eager to get back on the road to play music, although not in the

Trine Karlsen, London, 2000.

manner of that last shambolic U.K. winter tour, but with a reliable set of band members, pre-arranged hotels and some properly organised travel preparations. Either that, or my days of playing with the Subs were over.

Toxin had been solely interested in booking us shows to earn his commission and always passed on to Charlie the responsibility of arranging transportation, accommodation and assembling a viable line-up of the band for every event. The undiminished truth was that Harper didn't have (still hasn't) any aptitude for those kinds of tasks. The man is devoid of a single organisational bone in his entire body. That's not a criticism, it's just a fact.

Now, if you're looking for someone to write great songs, to be an excellent vocalist and live performer, then Chas is your man; but if you're seeking someone to make good financial deals, book decent shows and ensure that a van and hotels are reserved and all the musicians are all lined up for a gig or a tour in good time, then he's categorically not your guy. In fact, he's hopeless.

Here's what I mean:

Just 10 days after the concluding Swindon show, Charlie asked me to play at the Half Moon club in Putney, London. Nicky Garratt had returned to San Francisco by then so Harper had asked Darrell Bath to re-join for that show at late notice. Luckily, Darrell hadn't already arranged to be busy doing something else. Likewise with me, seeing as Chas had only asked for my participation the night before this Half Moon event.

When I stopped by Harper's flat in Crouch End to get a ride to the venue on the afternoon of the show, he let me in and asked me to sit on the couch whilst he took care of something he was attempting to sort out on the telephone. Seems Gary Baldy hadn't been answering his calls, which he'd only started making just before my arrival, and so he was now trying to find a substitute drummer a mere hour before we were due to soundcheck at the venue.

Ison couldn't do it, yet another drummer he tried was unavailable but, fortunately, Eddie Edwards was not gigging with The Vibrators that evening and was up for the challenge. Now Eddie is a brilliant drummer, for a band like The Vibrators that is, but his idiosyncratic playing style is not compatible with the meatier and faster music of the U.K. Subs. During the Half Moon show, I had to keep stamping my feet to try to get him to speed up his playing, to no avail. When we got around to performing the usually blistering track Endangered Species, he played it at the speed of a waltz and I recall that two members of the audience satirically danced arm-in-arm to it, as if in a ballroom.

Of course, none of this was Eddie's fault. It was Charlie's for not confirming an apt drummer ahead of time for the gig; and there had been a recent similar failure of organisation, although on that occasion the problem was regarding transportation rather than band personnel:

Same drill, Chas makes a last ditch phone call to me to play bass for a one-off gig in Newcastle of all places, with Alan Campbell on guitar and Ison drumming.

"Come to my flat at midday tomorrow," he instructed.

I get there at the requested time and, sure enough, Harper's on the phone, late doors, trying to sort out yet another issue. This time around he hadn't booked a van to drive us and the equipment to our venue in the north-east and was desperately calling anybody he knew who might have a vehicle for hire. The rest of the guys were there too, so we hung around and listened as either the person he'd called does not pick-up or, if they do, tell Chas they're already engaged in another activity and are unable to take on the driving job. Eventually I spoke up:

"Charlie, you've left this too late, what are we going to do?"

His solution was for Alan and me to take our instruments on the Tube with him and Ison and then for us all to catch a train to Newcastle from Euston Station, hoping that whoever was supporting the Subs that night would allow us to use their amps and drum kit in order to play the gig. There was no guarantee that whoever was opening for us would consent to this and, even if they did, that their equipment would be good enough to achieve a decent band sound; but just as with the disastrous Running Horse last-ditch drummer incident and the Eddie Edwards eleventh-hour fiasco, Charlie simply didn't care what kind of quality of sound and performance we would be able to offer a paying audience. He seemed to think that just turning up and winging it was good enough.

After a long and expensive train journey to Newcastle, the support group did agree to the Subs using their gear that night, although none of it was of a proper professional calibre. They were all helpful and friendly local amateur musicians, whilst we were supposed to be the career band, which meant suffering a frustrating lack of volume due to the inadequate wattage of the amplifiers and having to try to work with a consequently weak onstage sound.

The post show experience wasn't a happy one either. We had no choice but to cram into the promoter's front room in order to find a spot to catch some sleep that night, the next day arriving in London tired and sore from sleeping in chairs or directly on the floor with just a £20 note each for our troubles due to the exorbitant price of the train tickets.

Having therefore experienced these Harper-inflicted tribulations, when he asked me to do a 40 date European tour beginning in the Netherlands on the 7th January 2000, which would include visiting 10 other nations before wrapping things up with a show in Germany on the 20th of February, I needed to make sure that if I said yes, there would be a good, compatible drummer working with us and that the transport and hotels were all pre-booked and guaranteed.

Charlie assured me that the Euro tour was the responsibility of a Munich-based agency called IBD (International Booking Department) and that they'd made sure the promoters from each venue had reserved hotel rooms ahead of time for us, plus, on a rare day off, the agency themselves had already taken care of booking suitable accommodation. He also pledged that the transport would be first-rate. IBD had hired a professional German driver/Tour Manager named Kurt to take care of us on the road. Kurt drove a new Mercedes Sprinter van with comfortable airline-style seats in the passenger part of the vehicle and a large separate space at the rear for equipment, instruments and merchandise – so far, so good. The only unresolved issue was who the drummer was going to be.

I spoke to Nicky Garratt about this via a call to his San Francisco

L to R: Chas, me, Nicky, and Tommy Couch, Warsaw, Poland, 2000.

home. He brought up the possibility of Steve Roberts returning to the Subs' fold but, knowing full well that this could turn out to be a disastrous idea I quickly nixed it and suggested some more reliable candidates. The drummer of the Punk band One Way System, Tommy Couch, was one of Nicky's proposals and I immediately liked the notion. I'd seen Couch playing with his band on a couple of occasions and had admired his hard-hitting style. We then recommended him to Chas, who also liked the suggestion and, after he'd completed a call to Tommy, phoned me back to say we had our drummer for the forthcoming Euro excursion.

Early in the morning of the 7th of January 2000, Kurt's Mercedes Sprinter arrived outside Trine's flat in Belsize Park to pick me up for what had been billed as the U.K. Subs' Millennium European tour by IBD Booking. Having spent a very satisfactory, very passionate farewell night with my girlfriend, I was ready to get back on the road again to play music and revisit many of the Euro cities I'd performed in with Brian James and the Hellions, the Subs, Iggy Pop and Cheap And Nasty.

Waiting for me in the bus was Tommy Couch, Nicky Garratt, Zowie Huxley – again along to sell T-shirts for Harper, as well as the New Red Archive vinyl records and CDs Garratt had transported over from the U.S.A. – a Psychobilly enthusiast named Paul (can't remember his surname) who'd been hired to hump the equipment from van to stage and vice versa; plus Charlie and his new squeeze Lula, a young Italian woman who liked nothing better than chain-smoking marijuana spliffs and, consequently, proved to be a laid back and easy going member of the travelling contingent rather than the usual problematic on-tour girlfriend.

That same day we travelled to Dover, crossed the Channel to Calais, and drove onwards to Rotterdam in the Netherlands to play our inaugural Euro gig at a club called Baroeg, which is still open for business and now describes itself as a 'subcultural pop venue'.

After the show, back at the hotel, I shared a twin room with Kurt and there, much to my mortification, learned from him that Charlie was only going to be paying Nicky, Tommy and me €30 a day, less than £20 according to the exchange rate of the time. This was my fault for not asking Harper before the tour started what my wage was going to be and yet another reminder of the importance of finding out what the band was going to be paid before committing to any show or tour.

Still, as pitiful as this stipend was, playing on this tour did provide me with the opportunity to firmly establish myself as the go-to U.K. Subs' bassist and acquainted and reintroduce me to venues that I would go on to play many times over in the following decades: notably, Hamburg's Fabrik; Berlin's SO36; Warsaw's Proxima; Luzern's Sedel and Aachen's Musikbunker – a WW II German underground military emplacement which had been converted at some point, post war, as a location for Rock concerts.

During the trip I got to be great friends with Tommy Couch with whom, if there wasn't a hotel single room up for grabs, I would often share a twin room. Tommy had been a boxer in his younger days and his sister, Jane Couch, had the distinction of being the first licensed female pugilist in the U.K. She had gone on to win numerous world titles, latterly receiving an MBE from the Queen of England for her achievements. I also got to know a lot more about my other travelling partners as the tour progressed.

Kurt was a man devoid of any sense of irony. For example, he hated going to Croatia and moaned and bitched when we were there because he claimed the country had supported the Nazis during the Second World War. Paradoxically, his favourite nation to visit was Italy – part of Hitler's Axis alliance and an active affiliate of Nazi Germany – whilst the country he most wanted to visit was Japan – the other member of the Axis and a formidable ally of the Nazis – and, wait for it, Kurt was German and lived in Munich!

Although he had a thriving business with a fleet of Mercedes vans and a large house in Bavaria, he considered himself a communist and was always spouting far-left conspiracy theories and irrational anarchist

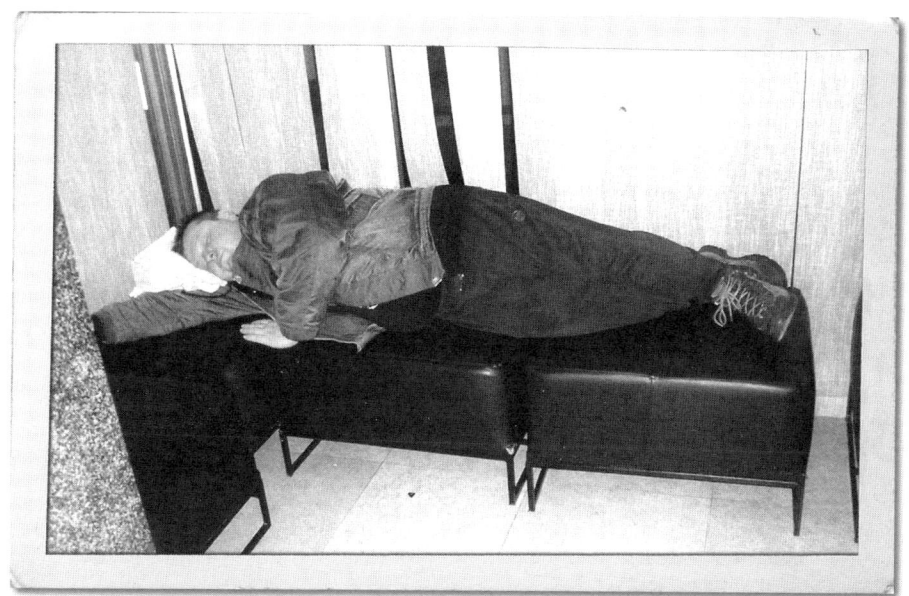

TM Kurt, dreaming up more conspiracy theories, Euro tour, 2000.

propaganda. For instance, what were merely aircraft water vapour trails were, according to Kurt, chemicals that were being sprayed by western governments to mentally neuter and pacify their peoples so that they could be more easily manipulated.

He proselytized the ridiculous and discredited hypothesis that the Apollo moon landings never took place and were merely hoaxes perpetrated by America to humiliate Soviet Russia. And, on a future Euro tour, post 9/11, proclaimed the attacks on the World Trade Center towers and the Pentagon were in fact the work of the American government who'd destroyed their own buildings and killed their own people as an excuse to invade Iraq, even though it was Afghanistan – where the actual perpetrators were trained in Al-Qaeda camps protected by the Taliban – that had been invaded as a consequence of those terrible terrorist assaults. But hey, why let facts get in the way of an idiotic conspiracy theory?

The tour itself was pretty good with the shows in the main being well attended and the hotel accommodation generally decent apart from a few notable exceptions – what is it with some promoters who think because you're in a Punk rock band that you'd be content to stay at any shithole they've booked you into?

Trine flew over from London to attend our gigs in Lillehammer, Oslo (her home city) and Drammen in Norway and would stay overnight with me at the hotel afterwards; a pleasurable three-day visit that broke the usual touring routine and which we both made the most of.

It was on this Euro campaign that Nicky Garratt met a German woman after our show at the Glocksee Club in Hannover with whom he would go on to form a long-term relationship. Manu had initially made a play for Tommy Couch but when he rejected her advances, she quickly used her odd, opaque charms to snare Nicky.

Charlie had witnessed Manu start a fight with the coat-check girl upon her arrival at the club and we both couldn't see anything about the woman that was at all attractive, either physically or in the personality department; but Garratt seemed smitten and off they went to her flat after our performance to spend the night together. The following day Nicky noticed some money was missing from the case he'd carried to Manu's.

This would be a feature of their relationship over the next six years. During Euro tours he would stay with her in Hannover or she would spend the night in his hotel room and then the next day Garratt would discover €100 or €200 had mysteriously evaporated from his wallet. After Manu went to San Francisco to spend some time with him at his home he told me he later noticed that €1,500 in cash he'd stored away in his wardrobe had gone walkabout, and yet he refused to countenance the possibility that she was responsible for these thefts.

When the Subs were gigging in Europe during this period, it led to a very unpleasant atmosphere whenever Nicky found cash had gone missing and a general sense of paranoia that there might be a thief among us. In denial about his girlfriend's involvement, the suspicion would then fall on the band or crew members, although he claimed he didn't believe that Charlie, I or any other affiliate of the Subs was responsible for these disappearing amounts which to me, was irrational thinking. If he was so sure it wasn't Manu, someone in the touring party must have been accountable.

It was years later, after he'd spent two days off with her in a hotel in Berlin and following her departure, he'd again noticed cash which had been in his wallet was no longer there, that I felt compelled to have it out with him:

"For fuck sake Nicky, when are you going to accept that your girlfriend is stealing from you? Every time Manu turns up some of your money goes missing and you always act astonished and make us all feel under suspicion. It's too much of a coincidence mate; it has got to be her."

I felt bad for him, but it needed to be said. Imagine trusting someone you've been intimate with for years and then having to admit to yourself they've habitually stolen money from you whenever you'd got together. What a terrible self-admission that must have been. It was the final stake in the muscle of love.

U.K. Subs' Euro tour, 2000.

    He eventually agreed it could only have been Manu all along and subsequently sent her an email saying he was now aware she'd been pilfering his cash and couldn't believe how it was possible for her to have done that to him after all the intimate times they'd had together, to which he received no reply.

We never saw her again.

TOMMY, YOU CUNT!

The Subs' Millennium European Tour was, for me, the first of what had been a recently established mammoth recurring January/February continental-wide excursion for the U.K. Subs – a yearly tradition which has continued right up to present times. Chas told me his reasoning for choosing these winter months to go on the Euro road was because most bands wouldn't consider travelling during this period due to the inevitable extreme cold and icy conditions to be encountered in such countries as Norway, Finland and Denmark, as well as the correspondingly harsh winter weather territories of the East, such as Poland, Slovakia, Slovenia, Lithuania, and the Czech Republic. Playing during this unpopular touring season awarded us the choice venues and attracted to our shows those normally starved of live music during this gig-barren time of year.

After Tommy Couch declined to sign on for another tour, Jason Willer was given the percussion role until Jamie Oliver took over drumming responsibilities in 2005. Nicky Garratt originally played guitar for these annual campaigns but was eventually replaced by Jet – the circumstances behind that transition to be revealed later – with The Vibrators being our regular Euro support act for most of this Garratt-active time period.

TV Smith then superseded the Vibrators as opening act in 2014 and continued in that role until we returned to our former policy of using local support groups to activate proceedings. After Jet stopped working with the band in 2015, the new axe man for the U.K. Subs, Stephen Straughan – once he'd fulfilled his gigging obligations to former employers the Angelic Upstarts – became the permanent guitarist for all Subs' gigs and tours, domestic and abroad.

IBD continued to be the agency that booked and organised these working excursions, with Kurt always being appointed by them as our driver and TM. Typically, we would play 14 or 15 different countries during the course of these European jaunts, but some of IBD's routing was wilfully bonkers. You'd be doing a gig in, say, Munich in southern Germany, and then the next day's show would be in Barcelona, north-eastern Spain. Because of the frequency of these long harrowing journeys between countries and venues, we soon started referring to IBD as 'I Be Driving', although this wasn't the primary reason for our change of agency in 2014. TV Smith had recommended changing to Berlin-based Muttis Booking Büro and some other positive noises were thereafter relayed to us about this agency from various bands on Muttis' roster. We therefore terminated the Subs' relationship with IBD and began exclusively working with Muttis for all our future European tours and Euro festival appearances.

U.K. Subs filling to capacity the SO36, Berlin, Germany, 2011.

Having been the first Punk band to play Poland in 1983 guaranteed upon returning to that nation for the first time in 2000, that there would be a lot of Polish media interest based on Charlie, Nicky and my own perceptions as to how the country had changed since our first Soviet-era visit. As well as returning to some of the cities we'd played 17 years before to again share with the Polish people our brand of Punk rock in venues which didn't exist that first time around, we spent much of our schedule being interviewed by the press and receiving invitations to radio and TV stations to compare modern Poland with the nation we'd toured in previously.

My personal view was although the country had changed considerably during the intervening years – no long queues for food or other basic commodities, regular legitimate democratic election and a vastly improved infrastructure – it was still a state in transition; although it has to be acknowledged that since 2000, thanks in large part to its EU membership, Poland has become a fully modernised European nation and Warsaw, in particular, has transformed from its former grim and dishevelled condition into a thriving capital city.

It is almost certainly due to this historical link that the country has maintained to this day a special connection with the U.K. Subs – an enduring and affectionate bond which is shared by the band.

The relentless touring involved in these annual revisits of Europe resulted in the band progressively building a considerable following

Double bass – me and Pete Vibrator, Venice, Italy, Euro tour, 2008.

on the continent, especially in Germany and the eastern European countries. Within a couple of years, we were selling out large venues like the Fabrik in Hamburg and the SO36 in Berlin, as well as doing good business in other eminent cities such as Vienna, Paris, Madrid, Rome, and Prague.

There are numerous noteworthy incidents and anecdotes I could relate to you from the various Subs' Euro tours I've undertaken over the last two decades, but that would require so much book space I wouldn't be able get on to all the other events and stories I want to share with you regarding additional aspects of the U.K. Subversives' career since the year 2000 until now. With this in mind, I'll simply offer up a couple of particularly memorable tales, starting with the occasion Charlie Harper decided to singlehandedly sabotage a show in front of a sell-out crowd at the prestigious Boogaloo Club, in Zagreb, Croatia, 2007:

We'd been instructed to get ourselves down to the venue much earlier than was routine for our Euro gigs, the reason being that Chas was due to be interviewed by a journalist for a local paper in a bar adjacent to our performance location. The Subs' soundcheck was set for 5pm but he'd been asked to meet up with this native scribbler some three hours beforehand and, seeing the meeting was at a bar and the newspaper was picking up the tab, he started ordering cocktails whilst answering all proffered questions and enunciating his views on Punk, politics and other related subjects to the man who was paying the bill. After he'd returned to join the band for soundcheck, it became apparent a lot of cocktails had been consumed during this rendezvous as our singer was now in a very intoxicated state.

The way it usually works with Charlie after he's consumed too much alcohol is that he adopts a manner which those of us who have worked consistently with the man over many years have come to refer to as his 'Obnoxious Granddad' persona. He's also quite capable of taking on that guise from time-to-time without the stimulus of booze but drinking definitely guarantees and exacerbates this personality transformation. Sure enough, his belligerent comments upon his return regarding the sound system, the stage lighting and pretty much everything else about this excellent venue indicated we were in for the full OG experience.

After the check, Harper started guzzling the rider beer. This, of course, only assisted in magnifying his displeasure at everything and everybody. The Boogaloo has a house limit of 1,500 punters and, shortly after the doors opened, the room had filled to capacity.

Our main support band, The Vibrators, went on to a rousing reception and played a fine collection of classic songs including Baby Baby, this being their most recognisable tune and one that the audience joyfully sang the chorus to whilst being conducted by lead singer Knox. After their well-received performance it was time for the Subs to build on the escalating excitement and appreciation shown by the Croatian crowd engendered by The Vibrators' set.

It was not to be.

The instant we stepped onstage; Charlie started yelling through his microphone that the overhead lighting was "Fucking shit." This was a man who had thought an old ramshackle barn in a muddy field in Holland which contained a carthorse and chickens, a miniscule stage made of discarded pallets with a single 100-watt light bulb swaying on a slender wire to illuminate the entire playing area, was a good enough venue for the Subs to perform in whereas the Boogaloo, with its up-to-date multi-coloured lighting rig, vast stage and modern, powerful sound system, was not.

Being drunk, he muffed his cues, mangled his vocals, forgot most of the lyrics and seemed more concerned with haranguing the lighting engineer, soundman, the promoter, and the large assemblage of people who had paid for a ticket to see us, than actually singing. He then escalated this inebriated routine by throwing cans of beer in the direction of what he thought were those operating the light and the sound desks but instead sent these projectiles flying perilously close to the skulls of his wife Yuko and Vibrator Eddie Edwards, who had watched the unfolding fiasco from the merchandise area in the auditorium with mounting horror.

Nicky Garratt, who was still on board for the European tours at that time, exchanged glances with me which reflected our growing certainty that this was not going to end well. We were correct.

Charlie raged on, telling the puzzled crowd that they'd all been "fucking ripped off" by the promoter before reducing some young girl to tears who'd taken up a position of adoration directly below him at the front of the stage, after he'd berated her for being a "fucking plastic Punk." It was at this point that he decided to call the man who he'd accused of fleecing everybody present to join him onstage:

"Tommy, you cunt! Where are you, Tommy? You're a cunt Tommy. Come down here and let me tell you what a cunt you are."

The promoter was a Croatian who everyone applied the more western designation Tommy to – real name, Tomi Edvard Sega. He'd also earlier opened the show with his own band Eksodus and seeing that his English language skills were not so good at that time, overheard his name being hollered by Chas and assumed he was being called to the stage so that our eminent singer could thank him for the wonderful gig he'd arranged for us.

"Tommy, come up here. Stop hiding you fucking cunt!" continued Harper, at which point Tommy, with his arms raised in a combined gesture of triumph and appreciation, unexpectedly walked out on to the stage from the wings. Charlie, who was completely unaware that Tommy was approaching him from the rear, sustained his character assassination of the Croatian until the victim of his ire slipped unnoticed beside him and put an arm around Harper, whilst all the while waving to the audience with his free hand and smiling the innocent smile of the oblivious.

Now in a state of shock that 'Tommy the cunt' had actually taken up the challenge and was stood there beside him, Chas' critical tone abruptly changed from that of fury to a much more conciliatory tenor:

"Er… yeah… I was just saying Tommy… that, er, these lights (pointing to the amazing array of multihued stage lamps, lasers and strobes above our heads) aren't very good."

Our promoter responded by continuing to wave and smile, before vacating the podium after giving Charlie an affectionate hug. Once he'd disappeared back into the wings, Harper returned to his previous disposition of outrage: "He's fucking ripped you off, the sound is shit too…" at which instant he picked up his stage monitor and threw it into the crowd.

"Tommy, you cunt, that's what I think about your sound system."

He then came over to my side and did the same to my monitor. I'd had enough at that point, as had Nicky and Jamie. Together we trooped off stage, each livid that the show had been ruined by our vocalist's alcohol-fuelled rants, his abusive behaviour and now, his wilful destruction of equipment. We were forced to terminate the performance having barely made it to the middle of our set.

Charlie, unconcerned by our refusal to play on, continued to throw microphone stands, monitors and other pieces of important stage paraphernalia off the podium. The audience was entirely bewildered by what it was they were witnessing and having eventually realised the show was done, filed out of the venue. Back in the dressing room, after he'd finished slinging everything of technical necessity belonging to the venue from the stage, the inquest began.

Harper was completely unrepentant, insisting the lights and sound were "total shit." When I countered by listing some of the hundreds of venues that he'd happily played in over the years with far inferior stage illuminations and PA systems than those of the Boogaloo, he venomously sneered "What do you know about it? You never go to big shows, so how the fuck would you know what is good and what is shit?"

I responded by sarcastically calling him Elton John, told him he had acted like some privileged spoiled Rock star who'd had a tantrum for no reason and managed to ruin through his selfishness what should have been a triumphant gig for the band and an enjoyable evening for the audience. He responded by flouncing out of the dressing room, where he immediately encountered a tearful Yuko who had been stunned and saddened at her husband's unhinged behaviour. She laid into him too, but he waved her away and went to the now empty bar of the venue to get himself yet another drink, still convinced that his crazy accusations and actions were entirely justified. There were more tears later when the sound crew menacingly insisted on receiving financial compensation for the equipment he'd damaged and he was forced to pay out €1,000 in cash to placate them.

The next day, a hung-over Chas tried to blame the whole debacle on Tommy. Apparently, it was our promoter's fault for asking him to turn up at the venue so early and arranging the newspaper interview in a bar "where he fucking should of known I would get drunk." Yes, there are times when Harper's logic becomes so Kafkaesque that even the most gibbering, irrational, lithium-deprived hypo-maniac would seem reasonable in comparison, although his natural charm and charisma always seemingly counteract these occasional episodes of bizarre thinking.

Simply put, it's a Charlie thing.

As for the poor, publicly maligned Tomi Edvard Sega, he continued to organise future shows for us in Zagreb, the last being again at the Boogaloo Club back in 2018 – all without the onstage behaviour that had marred our previous aborted show there. However, it's a strange detail that to this day whenever any member of the Subs has reason to mention our Croatian friend and facilitator, he is still referred to as 'Tommy the cunt'; and now that his English has improved substantially, he remarkably calls himself 'Tommy the cunt' too. So, maybe, Charlie was right after all.

Another interesting Euro recollection concerns the first and only time the U.K. Subs were booked to play in Bulgaria. This was back in 2006 when The Vibrators were still our support act, although for that tour they only opened the initial 11 shows, after which we went on to play 12 of our own using local bands to kick-start the evening's revels.

Following a series of Italian dates that culminated with a performance in Bari – a handsome port city, situated beside the Adriatic Sea – our IBD itineraries informed us that the next destination on the list was Sofia, the capital conurbation of Bulgaria.

True to the 'I Be Driving' practice of ridiculous routing, reaching Sofia would entail a long and arduous journey out of Italy, into Slovenia, onwards across Croatia and then entry into Serbia where, having traversed that country, we would many hours later reach our Bulgarian border crossing point located near the Serbian district of Pirot. It turned out to be a very educational drive.

Whilst travelling through Croatia on the E70 highway heading towards Serbia, we witnessed some of the residual scars of the 1990s Balkan Wars – discarded factories and other former large structures such as grain storage facilities, which had been reduced to rubble owing to extensive shelling and missile fire. House after abandoned house was pitted with bullet holes or completely burned out due to receiving artillery rounds; and every 500 metres there was a sign, warning travellers not to venture out of their vehicles on to the land either side of the road, as these areas were still riddled with the anti-personnel mines that had been buried there by Serbian forces wanting to maim and kill Croatian combatants and civilians alike. There were also other dangerous relics of this conflict.

Our promoter for the Sofia show and our forthcoming gigs in Belgrade, Zagreb and Ljubljana, was travelling with us in the Mercedes

Playing Belgrade, Serbia, Euro tour, 2009.

Sprinter. As we crossed Serbia on its main E75 artery, he cautioned our driver Kurt against veering from the highway for any reason.

"After the war many Serbian soldiers kept their assault rifles and other weapons. Some have formed militias and wait for drivers and their passengers to come off the main road so they can rob them of their money, passports and anything else they can use to raise money. Women have been raped too, and in a few cases, they have killed their victims simply for fun."

Even if you kept to the E75, you could still be subjected to brigandage of another sort. On no less than three occasions on our Serbian journey, we were pulled over by the police for a trio of concocted infractions. Firstly, it was for running a red light, even though there were no traffic lights on the motorway.

Then it was the old 'we caught you speeding' con, despite the fact most other cars, vans and buses were racing past us just before we got pulled over, with Kurt having already told us that at no time would he exceed the speed limit as he didn't want to give the local constabulary a reason to stop and fine us. On the third occasion we became victims of the classic overweight vehicle accusation, a charge that we could not disprove as there was nowhere to weigh the Sprinter along with its passengers and equipment load, thus leaving us without any recourse to refute their fabricated allegation.

This final mugging was a classic heist. Not only did we have to pay off these uniformed thieves or risk being taken off to the local police station, but just to add a large scoop of effrontery to grievance, after Kurt offered them Euro notes, one of the crooks told him they would only accept Serbian Dinars.

"But I don't have any Dinars," Kurt protested.

"That's not a problem," said one of the police officers in reasonable English. "You can follow us to my brother-in-law's service station, just a kilometre up the highway from here. There he can change the money for you, for a commission of course."

Not only were we being fleeced by these predatory policemen on a trumped-up charge, but one of them even had his brother-in-law in on the scam, making money from any unfortunate foreign traveller pulled over by these shady arseholes by obliging them to pay exorbitant exchange rates to trade their Euros, Dollars or Pounds sterling into Serbian Dinars, or go to jail. What a caper.

To be fair, this sort of thing didn't just happen in Serbia during the first decade of the 2000s but also in the various countries that made up what we then called The Wild East; and, upon reaching the Bulgarian border, we encountered yet more corruption.

Our promoter had already informed us that he'd pre-paid the Bulgarian border guards and customs officers an amount of money "not to fuck with us," as he put it. A smooth entry into the country should therefore have been a given.

After flashing our passports to the official on the Serbian side, we crossed the minor stretch of terrain that constituted No Man's Land and arrived in front of the Bulgarian border post where we noticed a couple of old, heavily stained mattresses had been laid out just in front of the entry gate. A guard saw our approach, walked out of the guardhouse and started sparingly scattering some disinfectant from a large plastic container onto the mattresses.

"What's he doing?" asked Kurt, thereby verbalising the same unsaid thought shared by the rest of us. The guard then came over to the van and started talking to the promoter in what must have been some shared eastern European language. After their conversation ended, our impresario said we must drive over the disinfected mattresses in case we had somehow acquired on our tyres the rare Bird Flu virus which had just emerged in the U.S.A. For this precaution, every vehicle was to be charged two Euros.

It was obviously a piece of nonsense concocted by these venal sentinels in order to raise money for their own pockets. Can you imagine the revenue which would have been generated from the constant stream of trucks, cars, buses, and vans entering the country via that entry point having to pay out two Euros to these bandits day and night to disinfect their tyres? Having handed over the coins and driven over the mattresses as instructed we motored on through the gate and stopped beside the customs office, fully expecting to be immediately waved on so we could proceed towards Sofia. Instead, a dour-faced, portly customs official came out and told us to park up in one of a series of spaces reserved for vehicle inspections.

He then asked for our passports and Carnet – Bulgaria was not yet a member of the EU, they joined the following year (2007) and their customs laws required a typed list of equipment, instruments and all other goods we'd transported into the country, which they were then supposed to check off from the same Carnet when we left.

I turned to the promoter: "I thought you said you'd paid off these people to give us an easy ride?" He didn't look too happy.

"Fucking Bulgarians, they're hoping to get even more money from me by holding us up. Don't worry, I'll sort this out."

With that he followed the customs minion into his office to privately remind him of all the palms that had already been greased and being detained was definitely not what he'd paid for. A long negotiation must have ensued as 20 minutes later we were still hanging around outside the van waiting for a resolution, at which point I felt a dire need to urinate.

When I asked a guard if there was a toilet I could use, he pointed to a café adjacent to the guard house. There, I discovered a couple of truckers drinking coffee at a table, whilst across the room sat six or seven women, who all turned to look at me as I entered and collectively smiled these weird, woeful smiles. I ignored their attentions and headed straight to the men's urinal to relieve my bladder. Having vacated the lavatory the guard who had directed me there came in and beckoned me over to the café's counter, where he ordered himself something a lot stronger than coffee to drink and lit up a cigarette.

"Hey, you see those women over there," he nodded in the direction of the group of smiley females across the way: "if you want you can choose one of them for some sexy time (Yes, really, he used that exact expression.) We have a place here you can go with a woman for, say, thirty minutes: Just forty euros for a fuck or twenty for sucking."

This was unbelievable. Not only were the border guards and customs officials charging motorists to drive over their ridiculous mattresses and taking bribes not to make problems for outsiders entering the country, but these state-paid criminals were also running a prostitution ring, pimping out women to truckers and travellers and, no doubt, taking a hefty percentage of what was paid to these sex workers for themselves.

I firmly declined his offer and made for the van, thankfully to witness our promoter emerging from the office clutching the Carnet and passports shouting, "Let's get out of here." But just after we boarded the Sprinter and prepared to leave, the plump, sour-faced customs officer walked over to the open driver-side window and ordered Kurt to pay him €20.

"What for?" demanded Kurt.

"Parking fee," came the reply.

TWIN PEAKS

As for any additional Euro Winter Tour stories I might have shared with you from 20 years of repeated visitations, there was the time the windshield of our van shattered in Finland due to plummeting temperatures, before the heating refused to work and the vehicle succumbed to the icy air and ceased to function altogether on a narrow road which snaked through a forest, just as night's darkness was descending. It was minus 30 degrees centigrade outside and we had to vacate the van for safety reasons, stand in the deep snow and wave down passing cars to beg a ride to warmth and safety before hyperthermia set in – luckily the Finns driving on that desolate stretch proved to be friendly and obliging people.

Alternatively, I could have expanded on the occasion I got sucker punched by the psychotically jealous ex-boyfriend of a young woman I'd got very friendly with as we departed from a Hamburg club at 4am. Intending to take a cab to my hotel, I'd only fleetingly noticed a figure in the shadows moving my way before the blow was struck, so I'm quite proud of myself for not ending up on my arse, instead staying on my feet and getting in a counter punch to my assailant's face as he moved in for his second assault.

Unfortunately, just as my fist connected with his nose, two German police officers came out of nowhere and grabbed me, believing I had just instigated an attack rather than the reality, which was I'd merely been defending myself from an aggressor. It won't surprise you to learn that the man who'd bloodied my lip then tried to subvert the truth by telling the law I'd wantonly attacked him.

Fortunately, the woman I was with and a couple of other witnesses who'd seen what had really occurred put them right and my female companion and I were allowed to hail a cab whilst the policemen detained her obsessive ex. A short time later we consummate our mutual attraction back in my hotel room. I'd won, he'd lost. Good. What is it with these screwy possessive men and women who just can't accept the will of a former partner to move on?

Alright, enough: let's now return to the year 2000 and get on to the other momentous events of that 12-month period, firstly focusing on the never-ending saga of trying to find and hold on to a drummer who had the right attitude and abilities to be a permanent member of the U.K. Subs.

I'd been disappointed that Tommy Couch didn't want to continue his association with the Subs. He was a fine drummer who I got on really well with on a personal level, but he wanted to return to the familiarity of gigging with One Way System and despite my best efforts, I was unable to change his mind.

We had some recording time booked at Dave Goodman's Mandala studios in South London and a pending tour of the U.S.A. – put together by the Pouch agency run by Randy Wolpin, who'd organised the North American Social Chaos travelling festival the year before. It was therefore imperative we get a new sticks wielder, ASAP.

A few names were banded about, and then I remembered we'd got quite friendly on the Social Chaos tour with Vice Squad's drummer, Pumpy, who'd just left the Squad, for causes yet undiscovered. He seemed an adequate player and seeing as the issue was pressing, I put his name forward and received agreement from Harper and Garratt to give him a shot.

Shortly after this became common knowledge, Rebecca Bond – aka Beki Bondage, the lead singer of Vice Squad – phoned Nicky to warn him about our new band member. When Garratt asked her exactly why we should be concerned about employing him, she enigmatically disclosed: "I don't want to go into it, but if you do work with the guy, you'll find out soon enough."

We didn't heed Beki's warning and Pumpy debuted as a U.K. Sub providing the percussion for the recording of the Revolution's Here EP, which featured two solo Harper songs – Reclaim the Street and Metro – two Harper/Garratt compositions – Go Home and The Revolution's Here – plus a reworking of the lush Thunderclap Newman classic: Something in the Air. This EP was released later that millennial year, to no great fanfare or financial reward, by French indie label Combat Rock.

Whilst at Mandala Studios we also covered Nirvana's Stay Away for a tribute album dedicated to Kurt Cobain and co which featured other Punk outfits such as Agent Orange and The Vibrators. This record was also released in the year 2000 by Cleopatra Records with the curious title Smells Like Bleach.

It was during the recording of Stay Away that I started to consider the possibility that we'd made a mistake in hiring Pumpy. He was having trouble coming up with a compatible drum pattern for the track – Cleopatra didn't want an exact reproduction of the original, asking instead for a version that was inherently U.K. Subs in essence and different in execution – so Nicky offered him some alternatives, none of which he was successful at emulating with the result being that he became increasingly frustrated and defensive. When I suggested the configuration that was eventually used, he initially huffed and puffed in a manner that we would soon get to know all too well, as he told Garratt and I that we should make up our minds and not put him through "all this stress."

"This is how we work in a studio," I countered. "We allow each other the freedom to come up with something that works but if one of us is having difficulties, we pitch in to help. You should see it as a positive thing, not a personal attack."

After my interjection he calmed down and eventually mastered my proposed drum pattern, which is the one you can hear on the record. Still, his defensive attitude and lack of aptitude for the work didn't exactly inspire confidence; but the U.S.A. tour was looming so we begrudgingly accepted the fact he was going to be our drummer for the foreseeable future.

The States' tour of 2000 was a 30-date marathon, opening with a show in Seattle on the 3rd of October, concluding with a gig in Sacramento on the 12th of November. As with all our previous American expeditions, a lot of the drives were brutal and sleep was a rare commodity but, as ever, there were also compensations.

From the West Coast we gradually made our way into the Mid-West and onwards to the eastern seaboard. We put in some good performances and enjoyed a few interesting experiences along the way, which helped lift the morale when our physical bodies began flagging.

I had in my head that my new, if still burgeoning, amorous involvement with Trine Karlsen was nonetheless a tenuous thing that was likely to end in failure, just like every other romantic relationship I'd previously embarked on. Accordingly I adopted an attitude of not actively looking for any short-term liaisons on this tour whilst simultaneously remaining open to the possibility of some overnight female company if an attractive enough woman demonstrated any sincere interest in me. This occurred in the Midwestern capital city of Iowa: Des Moines.

After soundcheck at our club venue on University Avenue I was playing pool in the front bar with Dave our young American tour driver, when a very pretty young woman who, fatally for me, had a slim physique with curvaceous additions, approached the table and asked if she could play the winner of the game in progress. We agreed, but even though I ended up being the victor I insisted she play Dave instead, as I figured she was about half my age. I was 42 at the time and it transpired she was 22, so pretty much a spot-on assumption. My thinking was that seeing as their ages were more comparable, they might hit it off and become a till-dawn-do-they-part couple; but Trudy was having none of it.

"You won, so I want to play you," she insisted.

U.S.A. tour, 2000.

After our game of pool and while still endeavouring to play cupid to the two twenty-somethings, I asked them what they wanted to drink, thereafter procuring their requested beverages which I then handed on to the duo before moving to another part of the bar to take up residence on a comfortable couch to sip my beer and ready myself for the show. Five minutes later, Trudy came over and sat down next to me. After she'd initiated conversation, it became obvious she was interested in me rather than Dave; so, after we Subs had completed our performance, I accepted an invitation to go back to her apartment to share some wine. Sure enough, after a couple of glasses of Italian red an initiating move on her part led to more intimate interchanges which, in turn, led to us spending the night together.

Early the next morning Trudy had to get to the café that she waitressed at but said she would firstly drop me off at the hotel where the rest of the Subs had slept. After we got in her car, she switched on the dashboard radio whereupon a song in progress by Eagle-Eye Cherry emerged from the speakers containing these words:

"… Well I know I'm going away and how I wish it wasn't so. So take this wine and drink with me, let's delay our misery. Save tonight, fight the break of dawn, come tomorrow, tomorrow I'll be gone. Save tonight, fight the break of dawn, come tomorrow, tomorrow I'll be gone."

We both smiled at the synchronicity of this song, which was the perfect

U.K. Subs at the Little Big Horn, Montana, U.S.A. tour, 2000.

soundtrack for our brief liaison. After reaching the hotel we embraced, kissed and told each other we would stay in contact; but as is customary with these sorts of impetuous one-night flings, personal circumstances altered and I never got to drink wine nor fight the break of dawn with Trudy again.

Perhaps the most bizarre recollection from that tour occurred in South Carolina, whilst another memorable episode transpired during our travels in Virginia. I'll recount the more surreal remembrance first:

It had been an early start and we'd been driving for a couple of hours when Dave pulled into a ramshackle gas station as the vehicle was in need of a top-up of fuel for the rest of that day's journey – another 300 miles traversing the sultry State of South Carolina to Spartanburg. Having to get petrol into the van gave me an opportunity to purchase some coffee from the shop behind the gas pumps, so I made my way into the store, hoping that there would be an air conditioning unit in operation so I could cool my boots for a while.

Instead of a humming AC machine pumping out chilled air inside, there was a single overhead fan which made a piercing animalistic screech after every rotation of its shaky axis. This device had absolutely no influence on the hot and humid interior temperature and was merely a source of annoyance, its systematic squeal being the equivalent of running long fingernails over the surface of a chalkboard. Another irritating element was the faulty fluorescent ceiling light. It sporadically flickered on and off conferring an eerie, strobe-like effect and would have been anathema to anyone prone to epilepsy.

I looked around and spotted a coffee dispensing area. Two glass pitchers of black java sat on their warmers with a stack of Styrofoam cups and other related accoutrements off to the side. I poured myself a cup but noticed there was no milk available, just some of that creamer powder that bleaches the coffee white while simultaneously turning your drink into a lump-filled mess.

As I approached the counter I observed two middle-aged women at a cash register, one of whom was trying to instruct the other in how to operate it, although she was evidently having a very hard time conveying the information to that part of the instructee's mind responsible for comprehension.

"Now see, you've got it wrong again honey. After you put in the amount using these buttons, you open the register using this button..."

Figuring I shouldn't disturb them whilst they were engaged in this failing tutorial, I went to another part of the counter where a young woman with the strangest backcombed hair I'd ever seen, complete with a red velvet bow resting on its summit, wearing green eye shadow, face warts and luminous purple nail polish, stared blankly into the empty space beyond the counter. I entered the space the Carolinian had moments before been gaping mindlessly into and said, "Excuse me, I've got myself a coffee but there's only creamer available, could I get some milk instead?"

It took her some time to even register my presence, but when she did and I'd repeated my request, the young woman simply replied in a dense southern drawl: "We've got creemer."

"Yes, I know, but I would like to get some milk, as I don't like creamer."

She was utterly thrown by this unexpected response and in the same monophonic tone of voice she'd deployed before, started up again with her "We've got creemer" mantra.

"Yep, creamer you most certain have," I confirmed, "but I do want some milk for my coffee, can I buy some from you?"

This really must have fucked with her mind as she started bellowing "Creemer!" over and over, like a scratched vinyl record, whilst to our

U.K. Subs at the Whisky A Go Go, LA, U.S.A. tour, 2000.

right the long-suffering instructor was still endeavouring to get her student to understand the unfathomable complexities of an analog cash register – "Oh, see, you've pressed the wrong button again honey, let's start again…"

"Creemer!"

"I know you've got that, but you're not listening…"

"Creemer!"

"Stop with the creamer, please."

"You're still hitting the wrong buttons honey, let's start over…"

"Creemer!"

These mad exchanges were taking place as the ceiling fan rhythmically generated its discordant feral shriek and the faulty florescent light sputtered and flickered at an ever-increasing speed, and I thought to myself 'Fuck me, I've ended up in a David Lynch movie.'

And so I placed the required dollar bill for the coffee onto the counter and got out of there before the backward speaking dwarf or Killer Bob or psychotic Frank Booth turned up, carried my beverage to the van and announced to my fellow travellers "It seems we've arrived in Twin Peaks, let's get the fuck out of here."

I've drunk black coffee ever since.

As established on the Social Chaos North American Tour, when driving from city to city in the U.S.A., we would often check the map to see if there was a lake or river en route so that Charlie could do some fishing and we could all have a picnic lunch in picturesque surroundings, time allowing. On our way to Springfield, Virginia, we figured we could afford an hour or so for this indulgence at a suitable location called Lake Claytor, which we'd spotted in our American atlas.

When we reached the outskirts of this body of water it became necessary to drive down a narrow road that led to a gate operated by whoever was sat in the guard-box adjacent the barricade. As soon as we pulled up alongside the cabin, an elderly man emerged from its interior. He noted Charlie's green hair, Pumpy's twin red-dyed Mohicans and our general atypical dress sense, smiled, pointed in a westerly direction and declared in his pronounced southern accent: "California's that aways fellas." We appreciated the joke, laughed at it, and got chatting to the affable sentinel of the lake who, after warning us about staying away from those areas which were the habitats of certain venomous snakes, raised the gate and said "enjoy."

After the picnic, Harper got out his expensive rod and reels, his box of floats, hooks and other angling accessories from the van, and got down to some serious fishing. We watched as he kept casting out his bait into the lake to no effect. Eventually, out of boredom, Nicky and I asked Charlie for a length of line and a small hook apiece. After attaching to our hooks a pair of maggots taken from a box of grubs Chas had earlier acquired from a bait shop, we cast our lines out into the water in unison and both immediately felt a tug on our individual nylon cords. Having pulled them back out of the water we were both shocked to find we'd both instantaneously caught ourselves a fish each, after which we carefully unhooked the barbs from their mouths and returned them to the lake.

Virtually every time Garratt and I cast our lines into the water we secured a fish whilst Charlie, with his costly angling equipment and years of experience, was catching nada. I started joking about it – "Hey, Charlie, I've caught myself yet another fish, oh, look, Nicky's just caught another trout too. I've lost count of the number of fish we've returned to the lake Chas; it's getting to be hard work." Knowing full well he wasn't even getting a nibble I mischievously added "How's it going for you mate, hooked anything yet?" All of which inspired a lot of laughter from Dave and Pumpy whilst Harper continued to cast his fishing line into the lake only to reel it back sometime later, minus any water species attached.

Charlie fishing, a forgotten lake, U.S.A.

Eventually he got fed up with all the ribbing and shouted at us "Fucking amateurs! I'm trying to hook something special, not just any old trout. Anyone can get one of those." To which Nicky countered "Well, apart from you of course." Even Charlie was compelled to laugh, at which point he packed up his equipment and we headed off in the direction of that evening's venue as nothing trumps the work whilst on the road.

LAS VEGAS WEDDING

Charlie continued to use the drumming services of Pumpy for a short visit we made to the Czech Republic immediately after the U.S.A. tour, with Simon Rankin replacing Nicky Garratt on guitar. Some U.K. dates then followed with Alan Campbell taking up the axe-man role.

It was during this series of shows that a troubling incident involving misuse of my credit card occurred. Whilst in America, some of Nicky's merchandise had gone missing and the culprit for both of these alarming events obviously was – for reasons I'll not get into here – someone within the band's orbit. Neither Garratt nor I had absolute proof of this person's wrongdoing, only circumstantial evidence, so we let it go. However, from then on, I kept a wary eye on this individual and considered them nothing more than an untrustworthy functionary.

On a personal level, things were definitely on the up. I'd found a very nice one-bedroom flat to rent in Agamemnon Road, West Hampstead, via my former landlord, which Trine and I moved into together. We started cohabitating and living a contented life there. She had a good job as a graphic designer with a major design company called Black Sun and when not touring with the Subs, I would have dinner ready for us when she got in at 6pm and took care of the shopping and housework during the day. We both loved this area of North-West London and often strolled up to Hampstead Village to browse the book stores, take walks on the heath and have drinks on the way back at the Holly Bush pub, which was built in 1790 and was still being illuminated by its original 19th century gas lamps. With its wood panelling, fireplaces and nicotine-stained ceiling, the interior of the Holly Bush resembled a set from a Victorian-era movie drama. If you're ever in that part of London, take a drink there and see it for yourself.

Leaving behind our domestic harmony in London for a while, we spent Christmas with Trine's family and friends in Oslo and saw in the New Year there with the Norwegian traditional meal of a smoked salmon starter and a main of Pinnekjøtt lamb ribs (also known as Stick Meat,) washed down with beer, wine and the national firewater, Akvavit – a strong spirit made from potatoes, sometimes grain, traditionally flavoured with caraway seeds. It was a good start to 2001.

Things got even better on our return home. Trine and I had been discussing the possibility of getting married. I knew that if we did get hitched, I'd finally reached a stage of life where I could fully commit to her and be sexually faithful. And I guess Trine was at a lifecycle point where she was also looking for fidelity and some relationship security.

At first we considered getting spliced in London, but when we

Trine and I, 2001.

contemplated the expense of putting up her family and friends in hotels, the cost of a reception and all those other customary wedding additions, it made far more sense for us to just go to an overseas location for the ceremony and spend that money on ourselves, having some fun and adventures in an exciting location; which is why I suggested flying to my old stomping ground of Los Angeles, firstly to see friends of mine there, then to drive on to Las Vegas to stay a few days in one of the famous casino hotels, thereafter to get married in one of the chapels on the

Vegas strip. This would free us from all the obligations and stress that a conventional ceremony in London would have entailed.

After yet another series of Subs' dates in the U.K. had concluded, we set off by taxi to Heathrow Airport on the 5th of May 2001. An 11 hour flight to LAX Airport then ensued. After we'd cleared customs, we got into an awaiting pre-arranged Lincoln Continental limousine which transported us to Tim Mosher and his then wife Gretchen's house in Laurel Canyon.

Those of you who have read Volume II of my memoir trilogy may recall that Mosher was the lead singer and guitar player in Broken Glass, the Rock outfit I was with just prior to joining The Iggy Pop Band in 1988. Since then, he'd married and taken to writing music for U.S. TV shows whilst simultaneously playing guitar with greasy rockers Junkyard, who he continues to be a member of to this day.

Having spent the night in the Mosher household, Tim took me and Trine to his nearest Avis car rental lot the following morning. There I shelled out for a nice ride for the remainder of our U.S. stay – a black Chevrolet Camaro – and immediately drove my wife-to-be along Sunset Boulevard, pointing out to her the various venues I'd played when I'd lived in LA, showing her the house in North Hollywood where I'd resided with my first wife and onward to Santa Monica Beach, where we discovered a classic 1950s-style American diner to have breakfast.

After another night at Tim and Gretchen's, we set off in the Camaro early in the morning for the five hour I-40 highway excursion to Las Vegas. Having passed the Joshua Tree, we continued on through the scorching Mojave Desert until the cacti, rattlesnakes, lizards, and sandstone rock formations receded and the Vegas skyline came into view.

On reaching the strip, I swung our ride into the main driveway of the famed Caesars Palace Hotel and brought the noire beast to a halt. As soon as we emerged from the vehicle, a uniformed valet offered to park the Camaro for us in the hotel garage. I handed him the keys and a $5 note, but before he could carry out his designated task, another Palace employee arrived, hauled our suitcases from the trunk and carried them into the hotel's impressive, marbled foyer, which necessitated another $5 tip.

That's the thing about these Vegas casino hotels. Since they figure you're gonna drop thousands of dollars at their slot machines, roulette, dice, and black jack tables, their rooms are always well priced and the food and bar drinks inexpensive – but, unless you want to garner disapproving looks because the hotel staff and your fellow guests think you're a cheapskate, you're required to give a hefty tip for every drink, every meal and every service provided which means by the time your stay is finally done, it isn't a low-cost stopover at all.

Anyway, here was the Vegas plan: spend two days on our own at Caesars having fun and a flutter before Tim – who I'd asked to be our witness – flew in from LA to stay over for two nights in the room I'd paid out for him at the Palace. On the evening of his arrival we'd have dinner together and the following day, after Trine and I had obtained our marriage license from the courthouse, all three of us would take the hired stretch limo from the hotel to the matrimonial venue on Las Vegas Boulevard.

Following the ceremony, we would then limo it back to Caesars for a wedding meal at one of their exclusive restaurants and Tim would return to LA the next day whilst my new bride and I stayed on at the Palace for a further three days, thereafter, to reclaim the Camaro and take the drive out of Nevada to the neighbouring state of Arizona to visit the Grand Canyon.

However, having got to the Caesars Palace check-in desk to claim the keys to our room, it seemed the receptionist had other immediate plans for us.

"Yes, we have your reservation here but unfortunately there's a problem with the wing of the hotel where the room you've booked is situated. We're having some necessary building work done in that location, which will not be completed for some time; and I'm afraid we have no other rooms available at present. The hotel is fully booked out."

When I'd made this booking online on my laptop from London six weeks before, I'd read about this proposed construction and phoned Caesars especially to make sure it wouldn't be problematic for us. I was told by the hotel representative at the end of the line that all the work would be finished long before we arrived and our reservation was solid. Having relayed this conversation to the receptionist she firstly apologised, then said they could offer us a series of alternatives which she believed, we would be very happy with.

"Firstly, we'll put you in the Hilton Hotel directly across the road from here for four nights, free of charge. We will also give you meal vouchers for our buffet restaurant for breakfast, lunch and dinner; and when you return to Caesars you will be given an executive suite rather than the standard double room you'd originally booked at no extra charge. Each evening you are here we will deliver to your suite a bottle of champagne, chocolates and a variety of other delicacies as an extra thank you for your understanding."

This all sounded mighty fine to me, but Trine had a counter opinion:

"This is disgusting, we made this booking weeks ago and we're told everything would be OK, what kind of fucking place is this?"

I was shocked at her reaction. They were proffering gratis accommodation at the Hilton just a short walk from Caesars for four nights, free food and an upgrade to a suite upon our return that we'd have never been able to afford, unless that is, we purchased a winning ticket for the National Lottery draw. Her swearing had also given the receptionist all the ammunition she needed to have us evicted from the hotel.

"I don't have to put up with that kind of language ma'am, so if you're not satisfied with our generous offer, you can find somewhere else to spend your stay…"

"Whoa!" I interjected, "Absolutely not, you've been extremely generous."

At which point I told Trine to go sit on a couch on the other side of the reception hall so I could mitigate the damage. She did what I'd asked, but walked away still muttering under her breath all the expletives she could muster about the situation, which to my mind, was nothing less than a very fortunate modification to our visit. We would be saving ourselves hundreds of dollars and anyway, wasn't it all about us getting married rather than whether we resided in the more prestigious hotel every night? This was my first insight into an aspect of my future wife's psyche that I'd not experienced before, and it worried me.

Having apologised for my fiancée's inappropriate language, I managed to re-engage the desk operative in civil conversation, during which time I thanked her for these financially beneficial alterations to our Vegas stay. She then had a bellhop take our luggage to a corporate limo. Some minutes later it dropped us off at the Hilton Hotel, where we were escorted to a huge room on one of the upper floors containing a bed the size of a Premier League football pitch and a bathroom larger than most of the hotel rooms I've stayed in over the years. There was also a floor to ceiling window which provided an amazing panoramic viewpoint of the neon-lit strip and the high-rise casino buildings around us.

Result.

But still Trine whined and sulked that we were not in the hotel we'd originally wanted, and I had to take her back over to Caesars to drink cocktails in the main bar whilst watching a live show entitled Frankly

Speaking – featuring a very realistic Frank Sinatra sound-alike singing classic Old Blue Eyes' tunes such as Night and Day, Fly me to the Moon and, of course, My Way – in order to get her smiling again. We also had a go at the slot machines and I managed to lose $60 after being $180 up at one point playing black jack.

I'd put aside $500 purely for gambling with the agreement that once that was gone, not another cent would be used for wagering by either one of us. We easily managed to surrender that amount to the house in less than a couple of hours, but there were others who were evidently devoid of the sort of fiscal discipline we'd adhered to.

The next day, whilst on our way to use a couple of our meal vouchers to partake of the Caesars' lunch buffet, we passed through the vast space where the majority of the roulette games were located. There, we noticed a large crowd of people who would intermittently clap and cheer, all gathered around one particular table. Curious as to what was going on, we joined the spectators and saw that there was only one player active in this roulette game.

He had obviously been riding a lucky streak for quite a while, seeing as there was a high wall of $500 chips that must have amounted to $65,000 or more in front of him. Once again, the roulette wheel was spun, the croupier activated the marker ball and to more applause and whoops from the onlookers, the player with the Midas touch added another $10,000 worth of chips to his ever increasing stack. We would have watched some more but hunger took a hold of us and instead made our way to the restaurant, where we spent around two hours eating lunch and drinking wine.

When we returned to the roulette room, we discovered the man with the Midas touch – this having now been replaced by the Medusa effect – was still venturing his tokens on the wheel of chance at the same table. But the crowd had since dispersed and instead of the mountain of chips we'd witness two hours earlier, fanned out in front of him on the green baize was what I estimated to be a paltry 17 or 18, $500 gaming pieces. In the time it had taken for us to have lunch, he'd forfeited around $60,000 back to the house. That's how quickly fortunes can be made and lost in Las Vegas.

Trine and I got married at the Little White Chapel on the strip in the late morning of the 12th of May 2001. I'd booked that particular wedding venue because it had glamorous historical form. Frank Sinatra, Joan Collins, Slash from Guns N' Roses, Judy Garland, Paul Newman, and a long list of other famous names, had all been matrimonially yoked there. Following the short ceremony with Tim officiating as our witness, we emerged from the chapel into the Nevada sunlight. A car passed us

Vegas wedding, U.S.A., 2001.

on the adjacent road and some guy in the passenger seat shouted at me through his opened window "Don't do it buddy!" believing we were just about to be married, rather than the reality that we'd already been hitched.

As omens go, it was a pretty accurate one.

The people at Caesars Palace were good to their word. When we returned there the day after our marriage to finally obtain a room for the remainder of our Vegas stay, we were taken to an enormous suite that consisted of a spacious lounge, kitchen, TV room, a bedroom with more square footage than all the rooms in our London flat combined and a bathroom containing a Jacuzzi, as well as a large bathtub and a walk-in shower. When the champagne was delivered, we fired up the Jacuzzi and drank our wine whilst luxuriating in its warm aerated water, then dried off, dressed, and set about discovering what else this eminent hotel had to offer.

There were a lot of shops that sold luxury goods. In one particular expensive men's clothing store, we spotted the store owner who'd been drafted in by director Martin Scorsese to play a small part in the film Casino – he's the sharp suited middle-aged man with the distinctive quiff who gets into an argument with Ginger (played by actress Sharon Stone) at a craps table and ends up having all his winnings thrown up in the air by the courtesan. And, in the basement, to our initial amazement, the city of Rome had been recreated, complete with duplications of the Coliseum, the Spanish Steps, Trevi Fountain, and other popular Roman landmarks.

If you glanced up above your head there was also a convincing sky that had moving clouds to add some realism to what was, after all, nothing more than a Disneyland-style ersatz fabrication of the wondrous original, although it would seem some people preferred this fake version of Rome.

As we ambled through the faux Forum, a couple walking just in front of us with American mid-western accents had this to say about Caesars' plaster and plastic eternal city:

Man: "Why would anybody bother with the expense of travelling to Europe when we've got this Rome right here in the U.S.A.?"

Woman: "Yep, and the best thing about it is that everybody speaks English, and there are no crooked Italians to deal with."

And people still wonder by what conceivable means Donald Trump was able to become president of the United States of America.

AMERICAN HIGHWAY

After our stay at Caesars Palace had run its course, we took the Interstate Highway to a city in Arizona called Williams, some 60 miles south of the Grand Canyon. There we booked into a motel for the night, leaving the next morning to drive the additional distance to the spectacular 6-million-year-old geological formation.

Trine and I spent a couple of hours admiring the magnificent views from the Canyon's south rim whilst making sure we took lots of photographs to commemorate our visit, then returned to the Camaro and looked at the map I'd bought in Vegas. Having worked out a route, I ignited the engine, heavy footed the accelerator and launched the vehicle due west onto the CA-58 freeway to avoid any interstate tolls, destination California.

As we cruised along on this seemingly endless asphalt artery, amazing landscapes glided past like the painted backdrops of a 1960s cowboy movie. By late afternoon I noticed we were running low on fuel. I'd filled it up in Williams before setting off but the map hadn't reflected the actual time it would take to get to California nor the fact there hadn't been a gas station to be seen on this route for five hours. Just desert terrain, distant rust-coloured mountains, cacti and bush weed.

This road was no place to run out of petrol. We hadn't glimpsed another vehicle either up front, behind, or on the other side of the freeway, for more than 100 miles and if the car had come to a standstill because of a lack of gasoline, Trine and I walking away from our means of transportation in the hope of coming across somewhere ahead to fill up a couple of plastic jerry cans to return with, wasn't a viable option.

Heatstroke, rattlesnakes or venomous scorpions would most likely have got to us before we'd found a station to buy some portable fuel, or maybe some crazed gun toting serial killer in the mould of Jeffrey Dahmer would have bundled us into the boot of his car, later shot and dismembered us, then buried our body parts in a hole dug somewhere out in the desert.

OK, I admit my having these macabre thoughts was more likely to be the consequence of severe driving fatigue and low blood sugar levels rather than any realistic likelihood of these gruesome musings happening. Plus, I do possess an overactive imagination: but Trine couldn't drive back then, and I'd been behind the wheel for a solid eight hours at that point with the last food we'd consumed being the previous evening at a Denny's diner in Williams, things were looking dire.

The engine must have been running on mere vapours when an hour later, my new wife exclaimed in triumph and relief: "A petrol station, over there!" I gazed in the direction of her extended finger and, sure

Our visit to the Grand Canyon, Arizona, U.S.A., 2001.

enough, clocked the welcome sight of somewhere to fuel-up just up ahead to our right, at the end of a dusty track that led to its forecourt.

Having taken the necessary sharp turn and whipped up the sand on that narrow side-road into a mini Khamsin, I pulled up in front of a gas pump. In my frenzied enthusiasm, I stupidly overfilled the vehicle to a point where the fuel started to seep back out of the tank onto my Converse shoes. I then went inside to pay the woman sitting behind a cash register for the petrol I'd extracted, plus the bottle of water, a couple of Hershey chocolate bars and the large pack of Cheetos cheese puffs I'd picked up from the aisles. When I disclosed to the attendant the number of the pump I'd used, she gave me a sideways glance and said "Hey, are you English?"

"Guilty as charged," I replied.

"Me too," she said.

"Really? Where from?

"Croydon," she answered.

What were the odds that this septuagenarian woman, sitting unaccompanied in a garage in the middle of no-wheres-ville Arizona,

One of the endless highways of the American West.

having originated from my home town? She was equally astonished to learn that I was a Croydonian and got into the story of how she met her now deceased American husband in the U.K. and had immigrated with him to that south-western state over 40 years before our chance meeting.

This sort of unlikely far-flung coincidence had only happened once before. On that occasion I was staying at a Hong Kong hotel in the mid-1980s when it was raided by the Royal HK Police looking to bust any prostitutes and their Johns renting rooms there. The Caucasian policeman, who banged on our door and demanded to inspect my then wife's passport and mine as proof we were legitimate guests, saw that my place of birth on my passport was Croydon. "I'm from Croydon too," he said, before asking "Has it changed much in recent years?" "Let's hope so," I replied, which elicited a smile from the constable before he wished us a good stay in what was still at that time, a British colonial protectorate.

Back to Arizona:

The expatriate lady and I chatted awhile. After wishing her well, I headed back to the car. As I exited, I noticed what must have been at least a hundred large cockroaches milling around a side door of the building. Looking at the barren desert landscape as darkness encroached and the extant rays of the sun receded behind one of the distant red mountains, I felt sorry for her being all alone in such a desolate place. Croydon is hardly the jewel in the international conurbation crown, but having to live and work in that isolated environment as an older widowed woman must have been a very lonely and forlorn existence.

When I got back in the driver's seat, Trine asked me why it had taken me so long to pay the fuel bill. "I'll explain on the ride," I told her, then added "It's a poignant story about how life doesn't always go the way you want it to."

By the time we crossed the state line into California, I was so weary that I'd occasionally hallucinate a hitchhiker on the side of the road although, according to Trine, there was nobody thumbing for a ride on the hard shoulder; either that or I would glimpse in the beams of my headlights an illusory, abruptly vanishing desert-dwelling creature scuttling across the white lines of the freeway as we forged ahead in the hope of finding somewhere to spend the night in the midst of all this solitude.

Well aware I was badly in need of rest, my wife suggested we stop in a town which was 20 miles ahead called Needles. 'Thank fuck for that,' I thought, 'We can find a motel, get something to eat and maybe even discover a bar to have a couple of well-deserved beers'; but as soon as we pulled into Needles and drove around looking for somewhere to spend the night, I quickly realised there was no way we could consider staying there.

Hispanic gangs wearing their colours congregated in the streets and gave us predatory looks as we drove by. There were a lot of burned out and boarded-up buildings and the unmistakeable scent of privation and violence hung heavy in the air; so I got out of there fast, back onto the highway before something very bad happened to us in that forsaken town.

This of course meant driving on, which was something I wasn't happy about. Still, I managed to add another 180 miles to the odometer and got us safely to the orderly, well-tended city of Barstow, where we found a decent motel and there, after some store-bought food and a couple of Mexican beers, slept the best sleep of my entire life.

When we finally got to LA, Trine and I again lodged at Tim's place for a day and night before taking off to the pretty coastal town of Santa Barbara for a 48 hour stay in a hotel near the Pacific Ocean. On returning to the Big Orange, we transferred ourselves to my other ex-Broken Glass friend, Dave Harte, and his wife Kathleen's new house in

Me, Alan Campbell and Pumpy, Spain, 2001.

Culver City, this being a relatively affluent suburban community in Los Angeles County, not far from Marina Del Ray. It was there we resided for the remaining 10 days of our marital vacation, then flew back to London to begin married life together, blissfully unaware that in just a couple of years, what had been undertaken in the U.S.A. would be undone in France.

Shortly after returning to the U.K., Nicky Garratt phoned from San Francisco to propose we take an offer from LA label Cleopatra to re-record 16 Subs' songs of our choice for an album. Unless we were going to radically rework these tunes – maybe a Reggae version of Crash Course, or perhaps a pulsating Electro a-la-Killing Joke adaptation of Countdown – I didn't really see the point; but Nicky said Charlie was keen and there would be some money in it, so I agreed.

Garratt flew to Heathrow, where I picked him up in my dodgy second-hand Ford Sierra and drove him directly over to Harper's flat in Finsbury Park. This is where he'd be staying whilst we were making the record at Dave Goodman's Mandala Studios in South London.

Cognac, France, 2001.

Having the originals to listen to rather than having to come up with something innovative of his own resulted in Pumpy providing adequate drums on these recordings, and 16 revisited tracks were duly captured by Goodman – including classic tunes such as Tomorrows Girls, Down on the Farm, Warhead and Endangered Species – thereafter being sent on to Cleopatra for manufacturing. This record emerged in 2001 with the given title of Time Warp: Greatest Hits.

I can't say I have any great affection for this album but, on the positive side, it did get Nicky, Charlie and I back in the studio and offered the three of us the opportunity to discuss the idea of finding a replacement drummer for some upcoming shows in Brazil and Argentina.

Meanwhile, with Garratt having returned to America, Alan Campbell resumed guitar responsibilities for a four day visit to Spain. This entailed staying in a small town called Bergara in the Basque Country. There, on our arrival night, we played a show on a stage in the town square at 3am as part of the musical entertainment for their week-long summer municipal fiesta. The other three days were spent just eating traditional Basque food, drinking and seeing the other bands perform, as well as getting a good view of a terrorist attack by the Basque separatist group ETA. We watched in a semi-state of disbelief as a bunch of hooded figures blew up the Bergara branch of the Banco de España, being as these Euskadi rebels considered this financial institution a repressive tool of the Spanish State.

Seeing as the Spanish caper had been little more than a paid holiday for the group, I told Trine we would travel to South-West France to visit ex-Subs' drummer Kim Wylie and his wife Katrina for a vacation of our own. As I've divulged before, Wylie had abandoned drumming to become a co-pilot for KLM airlines and had now moved from Essex to a small French hamlet near Bordeaux.

It was an eye-opening stay. I couldn't believe that their substantial three-bedroom house with its swimming pool, outbuildings and acres of land, had cost them far less than what the small one-bedroom apartment we were living in back in London was being valued at – I'd made enquiries about possibly acquiring it from the landlord, but the price he wanted was far too prohibitive. This visit got me thinking about also finding an affordable property in that beautiful region of France.

These were still pre-Brexit times of course, when British nationals had the right to work and live wherever they wanted within the European Union, an esteemed entitlement which has now been lost to an entire generation of young adults as a consequence of the 2016 referendum result – I will provide full disclosure regarding my take on this regressive vote in a future chapter.

I'd not been to South America since my visit there with Iggy Pop back in the 1980s and was keen to return. I was even more eager to start playing with a new Subs' drummer; someone more compatible and trustworthy than Pumpy had been.

Nicky Garratt had recruited a 23 year-old percussionist living in Oakland, California. Jason Willer had been in East Bay Punk bands since his teens and had earned himself a reputation as one of the more talented kit manipulators in the northern Californian Punk rock scene. The Brazilian and Argentine shows would effectively be his audition for full-time membership of the Subs.

Pumpy however, had seen on the U.K. Subs' website that his name was not included in the line-up for this overseas excursion. He phoned me up, his voice full of indignation and resentment, predictably delivered in the usual snorting, hyper-ventilating way he adopted when offended or stressed. I told him not to get his balls in an uproar, that we'd decided on using another drummer who'd be travelling with Garratt from the States as it made sense to do so to avoid the cost of a third expensive flight to Brazil from the U.K. – North America to South America plane tickets were a third of the price. Figuring I didn't owe him a truthful explanation anyway, I also added he would be contacted and given an update on what we were planning next when Chas and I returned to the U.K., although I already knew 'what we were planning next' was the appointment of a drummer to supersede him.

September came around and, after meeting up with Harper at Heathrow Airport, we embarked on the protracted flight to the most populous city of Brazil, São Paulo, with our British Airways Boeing 777 touching down on the hot tarmac of Guarulhos International Airport in the early afternoon of the 6th. As some of my diary entries from the time will demonstrate, it was the beginning of a very eventful visit.

6th September 2001: São Paulo, Brazil

Having collected our suitcases and my bass guitar from the airport's carousel, Charlie and I hang around in the sunshine outside the arrivals terminus for our pickup. Eventually our hosts and agents, Matthias Prill and Renato Martins, turn up in a vehicle and, after apologising for their late arrival, drove us to the Real Castilha Hotel, in the heart of this huge, bustling city. Chas and I are then taken up to our shared room on the 8th floor and 10 minutes later Nicky Garratt and Jason Willer, who'd both arrived together from San Francisco earlier, vacated the room they're sharing two floors below our own to pay us a call.

Our agents then take the band out for lunch followed by a visit to a store called London Calling which, as the name would imply, sells Punk clothing, records, books, plus tickets for our two consecutive shows at the Hangar 110 venue in central SP on the 14th and 15th. Onwards to a rehearsal room where we run through the set a few times to get gig prepared.

Jason is what I would call 'a power player'. He's very good but seems overly concerned with putting muscle into every drumming performance rather than providing the more multi-faceted playing that the differing songs require. Even so, he's a vast improvement on Pumpy. Finished up the evening at Matthias' apartment where we drank cocktails whilst admiring his signed movie star photo collection and Rat Pack (Sinatra, Dean Martin, Sammy Davis Jr., et al) memorabilia.

7th September 2001: Buenos Aires, Argentina

Hardly any sleep at all – up at 5am to be collectively driven from the hotel to the airport for our flight to Buenos Aires. Lots of turbulence on the way, which has the plane dipping and diving and led to a few white knuckles and jangled nerves amongst the passengers. Despite the bumpy flight, we make it safely to the capital of Argentina and once the equipment and bags have been collected, we're met and driven to the Americano Hotel by our promoter, Andre.

Just enough time to put the luggage in our rooms before we're whisked off to a radio station to play five songs live on air followed by an interview. A meal back at the Americano came next after which, another interview takes place in the hotel bar, complete with camera crew and lights for the biggest cable Rock show in South America – the interviewer told us it's watched by far more people than MTV there. Hardly enough time to shit and shave before we're taken to the concrete cavern which is the Cemento for a soundcheck.

At midnight we arrive back at the venue and discover there's no rider provided for us in our dressing room. We have to haggle with Andre for one large bottle of beer for Chas, Jason and I to share and a small plastic one with water for Nicky, which really sucks seeing as the Cemento is packed with punters and he's definitely making good money from this gig.

The crowd chant the band's name and we finally get to take to the stage at 2am. Despite Willer messing up on a couple of the songs – this being entirely understandable considering only one rehearsal day was feasible prior to the first show – we nevertheless played pretty well together. No encore is requested though; due to the fact that this Argentinian audience doesn't seem to understand the concept. We spend some time autographing records, CDs, etc, for the large contingent of punters hanging around the venue's bar and, consequently, don't make it back to our hotel until 5am, with a 7am start in order to fly back to São Paulo - this leaves, yet again, very little time for sleep.

Having returned to the sunshine of SP after the cold and wet weather of Buenos Aires, our third day of the tour had originally been designated a recording day, as Charlie and Nicky had written some new songs they wanted to demo and we'd subsequently booked a studio at our own cost for that afternoon/evening.
However, when we arrived there, the essential backline equipment that Matthias had hired for recording was nowhere to be seen and we were forced to cancel the entire session.

Mr. Som Recording Studios – which is the name of the facility we'd planned to record at – was located close to the airport in the midst of a series of tall office blocks. In my diary entry for that day, I wrote: 'I'm amazed at the low altitude at which aircraft fly in to land. They just about stay above the towering structures near the recording studio and I said to Charlie, that I wouldn't be surprised if one day a passenger plane tragically crashed into one of these buildings.'
We were just three days away from 9/11.

The following afternoon we travelled by road to the municipality of Campinas to play a show in a small venue called Bar 54. According to my diary, I'd estimate around 150 people had come to see us perform there, this being a number that was an evident disappointment to Prill and Martins although, as I pointed out to them, it was hardly Punk rock territory, plus the bar they'd booked us into was situated in a remote part of the city.

On the night ride back to São Paulo, our hired driver slowed down for a red traffic light at an intersection until suddenly, inexplicably, he put his foot down on the accelerator and drove on through the stop light. Luckily, we weren't side-swiped by a lawfully moving vehicle to our right or left but, nonetheless, we reacted to this reckless action by yelling at him and calling him names that threw doubt on the legitimacy of his birth and the low eminence of his mother.

He countered by asking: "Didn't you see those men with scarves wrapped around their faces just across the road from the traffic lights?" Charlie then claimed he'd seen a couple of suspicious homens in the shadows but didn't think anything of it.

"If I'd stopped for that light, they would have run over with their handguns drawn to rob us; then, most likely would have shot some of us for kicks before making off into the night. It was far less dangerous to drive through that stop light to take our chances with oncoming traffic than to wait for those bandits to hold us up and start shooting."

Matthias confirmed this was something that had been standard practise for some time in certain deprived and hazardous neighbourhoods like the one we'd just passed through. Feeling sorry about the insults we'd just hurled at him; we deferentially thanked our driver for potentially saving our lives and made sure he got a good tip on reaching the hotel.

The 10th was a low-key kind of day. No gig, but another interview, this time for a show on nationwide Radio Brazil, where we chatted live on air with the host and got to pick some of our favourite Punk tunes for broadcast.

We knew the following day was set to be a special occasion. The U.K. Subs were going to be playing live on Brazilian national television for an invited audience of São Paulo Punks; but what neither we nor the world could have possibly anticipated on the 10th, was just how shocking and politically transforming the 11th of September 2001 would turn out to be.

SÃO PAULO 9/11

11th September 2001, São Paulo, Brazil

A truly shocking day. Used the bathroom after getting up and hear Charlie switch on the TV. He then starts shouting something indecipherable to attract my attention. Stopped brushing my teeth to see what'd got him so verbally excited. There on the screen, via the BBC World News channel, I see live pictures of one of the World Trade Center towers in New York City exhaling smoke and fire after an airliner had collided with it. As we continue watching, a second passenger plane hurtles into its associate tower causing a fiery breach in that structure. This second event had us realising both collisions had not been accidents but a coordinated and deliberate double attack on these landmark buildings. We continue to watch in horror and disbelief as those trapped on the upper floors jump to their deaths rather than be burnt alive. As the inferno takes hold of both edifices, one tower, then the other, collapses down to a mound of dust and debris, killing all those who'd survived the initial crashes and any fire-fighters and rescue workers who'd ventured inside, as well as those who'd been directly beneath the disintegrating monoliths on the outside. Nicky and Jason had been watching the terrible events unfold on television too and together, in a mutually dazed state, we're driven to the TV station to accomplish our soundcheck for this evening's live on-air performance. Whilst on the way there, we debate whether we should include Warhead as one of the five songs we've been allocated.

The later news reports all indicated that Osama bin Laden's militant Islamic terrorist organisation, al-Qaeda, was almost certainly responsible for the atrocities and anyone who knows the lyrics to Warhead, will be aware that its first verse contains these words: "The soldiers of Islam are loading their guns, they're getting ready" and, later, "While the Islam armies are beckoning on, getting ready." Its chorus could also have been interpreted as a reflection of the day's events: "There's a burning sun and it sets in the western world, but it rises in the East and pretty soon it's gonna burn your temples down."
   Back to the remainder of my 9/11 diary entry:

Jason thinks it would be tactless to perform it after so many people have lost their lives in such horrific circumstances, a point of view that both Nicky and I are sympathetic to. Harper, predictably, is unconcerned with matters of sensitivity and thinks we should go ahead and play it anyway. After a couple of drinks in a nearby bar, we return for the Musichaos TV show to discover a large, young and extremely enthusiastic Punk audience surrounding the stage we're about to be let loose on. The subsequent raucous proceedings reminded me of the Beat Club TV show in Bremen, Germany, which Chas, Nicky and I had been a part of back in 1982. We'd still not resolved the Warhead issue so after the first three songs were done, I took the unilateral decision to go into the opening Warhead bass riff with the rest of the band following my lead. Later, in the restaurant we were taken to for dinner, they all agreed it had been a good call. Today's terrorism awarded Harper's words a contemporary relevance, although it was not the terrorists but their victims in and around the twin towers and those who'd subsequently died in the aircraft that crashed into the Pentagon and in UA flight 93 – which fell from the sky in Pennsylvania after its passengers and crew tried to take back control of the plane – that I'd had in mind when I'd initiated the song. What the fuck is going to happen next?

The answer to that diary question was the invasion of Afghanistan in 2001 and, indirectly, Iraq in 2003; plus, two more decades of religious militancy which engendered a lot of additional blood-letting; and, following the death of bin-Laden, the rise and fall of the Islamic fundamentalist death cult known as ISIS.

If you're interested, an audio-video recording of our 9/11 2001 Brazilian TV appearance can be found on YouTube. There you'll discover all five of the songs we performed, including our intense and poignant version of Warhead. And in Volume I of this trio of memoir books, you'll find an account of the time the Subs visited one of the World Trade towers whilst staying in New York City, just prior to the opening show of our North American Tour of 1982, along with a photograph of Nicky Garratt and I on the viewing floor at the very top of this now extinct structure.

Despite the traumatic events of the 11th, we kept to the tour itinerary and went on to play two consecutive sold-out shows in São Paulo, followed by a seven hour drive to Rio de Janeiro for our performance at a large, mainly open-air, venue in central Rio, the Fundição Progresso. The fact that the majority of this arena had no roofing is significant as, having completed our soundcheck and returned to the hotel to have dinner, a monsoon-style downpour flooded the vast audience area in front of the stage. This torrent also drastically reduced the number of paying attendees the promoter had been banking on.

Most of the deluge had abated by the time we kicked into our opening number a few hours later, but the 200 irrepressible punters in attendance in a venue capable of holding a couple of thousand, were obliged to stand in six inches of water and mud during the entire performance.

Sampling coconut milk, Brazil, 2001.

Matthias made sure we got our money but Marcos – the promoter of the show – must have lost thousands of dollars, what with the cost of hiring the Fundição Progresso, paying the security people, our fee, lights and equipment hire, etc. We felt sorry for the man, but that's how it goes if you're in the promoting game. Sometimes you make, sometimes you break, sometimes you forsake. The Rio rainstorm had unfortunately assured it was 'forsake' for Marcos on that occasion.

Later that night we did something that very few outsiders get to do without putting their lives at risk. Favelas are the lawless slum towns of Brazil. They emerged many decades ago when the needy and impoverished illegally occupied vacant land on the outskirts of cities, constructing their own alternative conurbations, which generally comprise of shanties and poorly fabricated buildings made from stolen or salvaged materials.

Over the years they've become havens for criminals, drug dealers and drug users, prostitutes and pimps, and have consequently become extremely dangerous places to venture into unless you know one of the top-ranking men – usually a drug lord – who enforces whatever code of conduct they deem fit on their Favela's population. Even the police and regular army wouldn't risk going into a Favela unless unequivocally ordered to do so.

It just so happened that Matthias knew the boss of bosses of the Mangueira Favela and he'd guaranteed our German-born agent and the Subs, safe passage to visit his domain if we so wished. This was a unique

U.K. Subs with promoter Renato Martins, Brazil/Argentina tour, 2001.

opportunity to go into an environment that we would normally avoid at all costs, so we were definitely up for it.

As arranged, two tough looking men met us on the periphery of Mangueira. They escorted us into a labyrinth of narrow alleyways, which passed through an assortment of crudely constructed dwellings made of wood pallets and hardboard, roofed with uneven panels of corrugated metal. After a while we reached the entrance to a large subterranean passage burrowed deep into a hill. We followed our guides through this wide, florescent lit tunnel and encountered a series of further passages, which had a number of diminutive bars where you could buy beer and cigarettes. Matthias said it would be rude not to buy a brew in one of these sparse, crudely constructed drinking dens, so we huddled together at the counter of a random choice and bought ourselves a beverage each.

Our guides/body guards then led us on to a much larger area where the entrance to a room was shrouded from view by some tattered drapes. Lifting the curtains and signalling for us to go inside, we did as our chaperons instructed and there discovered a space where a number of emaciated women sat on stools waiting for potential customers. It was a brothel of course, with another veiled room at the back where clients could take their chosen sex worker to claim what they'd paid for. We quickly made it known that none of us were remotely interested in what was on offer, then left and continued on, advancing ever deeper into this bizarre, almost otherworldly, underground metropolis.

The only comparison I can make for the Mangueira Favela is the Martian district called Venusville in the 1990 sci-fi film, Total Recall, which starred Arnold Schwarzenegger. Those of you who've seen this movie will recollect that Venusville was also a subterranean conurbation frequented by the poorest and most lawless on planet Mars and which, correspondingly, had bars and bordellos and was a place of constant potential danger. Although it has to be stated that Mangueira had neither the gritty charm nor sleazy allure of its comparable fictional film city. Going there had been an interesting, but ultimately, dispiriting experience.

Having returned to the U.K. after our South American visit, I again spent the Christmas holidays and saw in the New Year in Norway with Trine. The advent of 2002 brought with it two major changes on the private and professional fronts. The first modification was purchasing a house for the first time.

As revealed earlier, my holiday at Kim Wylie's place in South-West France got me thinking about buying a property in that region as the price difference between a flat or house there, in comparison to London, was astonishing. I'd arranged with Wylie for another flying visit so I could scout out properties in the hope of finding an affordable and worthy place to call home for the wife and I. Trine had been in total agreement with this course of action and had encouraged me to travel over to find something suitable for us.

Kim drove me to some Immobilier (estate agent) offices and we set up a number of viewings for various properties around the area in which he lived. One of the houses we viewed, located in a pretty little town not too far from Bordeaux, really got the hook into me.

It was a large three-storied maison bourgeoise, an archaic term for a dwelling that would have been traditionally occupied by someone with some sort of significant professional status, such as a doctor, lawyer, or army general. It had been built in the 1860s during the reign of Napoleon III, had high ceilings, wood floors and marble fireplaces throughout, plus a huge stone barn at the rear and a petite maison – a smaller version of the main house mirroring its imperial style – sited on the opposite side of the high and wide iron gates which, when unbolted, led to a spacious courtyard. The main residence contained seven bedrooms and numerous living spaces, although it would need some restoration work before it became fully liveable.

Never one to turn away from a challenge and, after conferring with Trine by phone, I put in an offer for considerably less than the already reasonable asking price in order to help offset the investment needed to fully renovate it. I then returned to London. A week later I received an email from the Immobilier informing us the owners had accepted my offer. I'd bought a house in France.

The second amendment to my life in 2002 was the adjustment to my membership of the U.K. Subs. Although having been a fairly regular member since 1999, Charlie Harper was having one of his occasional 'take control' episodes, which entailed changing the line-up of the band so that he could again be entirely in charge of its musical direction and business affairs.

To this end, he enlisted Jason Willer, Simon Rankin (who was to switch from guitar to bass) and had asked Alan Campbell to return to the fold as sole six-stringer. It was this version of the Subs that went on to record the album Universal, which was released in the early summer of that year by the Captain Oi! record label. This line-up also took on all gigging responsibilities.

I wasn't too bothered by Charlie's decision to alter the membership of the group. Having just purchased the French property, I knew a lot of time and energy would have to be spent in getting the main house into a wholly liveable condition, and it would require travelling back and forth from London to Bordeaux to hire and oversee an electrician, a plumber, a plasterer, as well as a roofer – the slate roof had a lot of perforations which allowed water to drizzle into the top floor when it rained – plus, someone to do the structural internal building work.

The original plan of action for the French house was for the work to take place piecemeal over a five year period, whilst Trine and I continued to reside in London at the rented West Hampstead flat. This was due to our money situation. We had to keep on earning there in order to pay for various parts of the overall renovation, as having now acquired the property we didn't have the resources to upgrade it. But seeing as the main house would be more than big enough for a couple and another resident to co-exist in it without encroaching on each other's privacy, my father, who wanted to sell up and move out of the Croydon council estate I'd grown up on, suggested providing the money for the majority of the renovations in order to be able to live there too.

Another discussion with my wife ensued and she agreed to the proposal as it would mean having the house in a habitable state so we could live permanently in France in a much shorter time period than the five years we'd originally planned for. I'd been apprehensive about my dad remaining on his own anyway, so this was also a good solution to that concern.

So how was I to know that this advantageous fast-track transition from one country to the next would ultimately lead to the ending of my marriage and a return to working full-time with the U.K. Subs?

Life can be mysterious like that.

REUNION

Universal was a good album with some fine songs – Fragile is one of my favourites to play live, and it's still regularly included in our set – although it was inevitable that Harper's new version of the U.K. Subs wouldn't be sustainable for long. This was mainly due to the fact that Charlie was again solely in charge and, as I've written before, the man has no aptitude for organisation, negotiation or planning.

Jason Willer later told me Chas had coaxed him over to the U.K. from America to play drums on the album by telling him on the phone that he could stay at his flat in Finsbury Park and would be taken care of financially whilst in the capital. Despite these assurances, a couple of days subsequent to his arrival, Willer was turfed out of Harper's apartment without a given reason, and not so much as a pound coin had been, nor would be, offered towards his London expenses.

Jason had to take to couch surfing at the homes of those he'd befriended and became so destitute that he was forced to fish out whatever was still edible from the various supermarket skips he found being used as receptacles for out of date, decaying foods.

This absurd state of affairs was because Charlie hadn't arranged an advance from the record company to cover any of the expenses for Willer, who'd spent what little money he'd had on air tickets to the U.K. I think Charlie must have done a product only deal with Captain Oi! for CDs and vinyl to sell on the Subs' merchandising stall, the proceeds from which would then go directly into his pocket, and that's why there was no advanced money to reimburse his band members for their outgoings whilst working in the studio.

As to why Rankin quit shortly thereafter, I can only surmise he too became dissatisfied with the chaotic way Harper did business, although Alan Campbell continued to work with Charlie and, in fact, played a festival show with me and new drummer, Jay Roni Moe (aka Jason Loadsman), in yet another configuration of the Subs in August 2002 – this performance, at the Lichfield Rock Festival, was recorded and subsequently released as a live album titled Staffordshire Bull, by Invisible Hands Music in 2003.

I was still travelling back and forth to France from West Hampstead to oversee the various renovations taking place at the Bordeaux house. After my only 2002 appearance with the Subs at Lichfield, I thought no more about working again with the band in the near future until Nicky Garratt phoned me with a proposal. He'd been talking with Charlie and Steve Roberts about getting together what was now being termed the 'classic' line-up of the Subs (Harper, Garratt, Gibbs, Roberts), for a

reunion show in London with a view to thereafter embarking on U.K. and continental Euro tours with the same cast if things went well.

I told Nicky that I didn't think it was a realistic idea seeing as my most recent experiences with Roberts hadn't exactly indicated he'd suddenly morphed into a reliable person. I also said I believed he was incapable of doing even a one-off show without beforehand consuming amounts of alcohol guaranteed to adversely affect his playing, let alone being temperate enough to get through an entire tour. But Garratt said Steve had assured him repeatedly that he'd become a "changed man" and was absolutely ready and willing to make a comeback with the U.K. Subs as a sober and serious musician.

As sceptical as I was, I figured I owed Roberts the opportunity to prove me wrong. After Charlie told me he'd been given the same assurances by Steve, I agreed to give it a go, although I intuitively knew the gamble of delivering a good live performance with our former percussionist back on the drum stool were at casino level odds against.

This reunification event was to take place at the short-lived Islington based Marquee Club, which had yet again changed its location, this time from Charing Cross Road in Soho to a building near the Angel tube station in North London. Steve was to travel from York to the capital for two days of rehearsals before the show, whilst Nicky was to fly in from San Francisco. I'd booked a TGV train from Bordeaux to Paris and onwards, via Eurostar, to The Smoke.

With all the elements for this comeback gig now in place, Roberts contacted a video film company and made a deal with them to capture the occasion for posterity. Despite the passable short-term money the subsequent DVD generated, I wish he hadn't.

Just before completing this chapter, I received the shocking news that Steve Roberts had sadly taken his own life. I know it's traditional not to speak ill of the dead, especially when that death is the result of a tragic suicide; but the truth endures and must be documented, although that truth should be delivered with charity. So here's the charity: Steve Roberts was, regrettably, a depressive, self-damaging alcoholic and, as we now know, depression and alcoholism are acute clinical diseases. These disorders badly affected his judgement – he was convicted of public racial abuse and other unacceptable civic order offences – and these same illnesses also diminished his self-knowledge: why did he continue trying to refashion himself as a Glam rock star in the mould of Ziggy Stardust-era David Bowie whilst in his sixties (Steve was 68 when he died,) especially as his real talent lay in playing the drums, which he could do exceptionally well when in a positive frame of mind and free of intoxication.

I want you to keep this in mind as I relate my account of the 2002 reunion show. Remember that Steve Roberts was a fragile, troubled and insecure man, fighting his demons as best he could, although ultimately being unable to resist their seductive, destructive influences.

As well as the heart-breaking personal loss for his wife and family, his death is doubly tragic because Steve's gift for drumming never got to fulfil its enormous potential. But I will always cherish his amazing performances both live and on record, and the good times we had together on the road, having both joined the U.K. Subs at approximately the same time as young men. To this day, Charlie, Nicky and I all agree that this early-1980s formation with Steve Roberts behind the kit in

Rehearsing for the Marquee reunion show, London, 2002.

his prime, pounding out the beats and pummelling his cymbals into submission, was the strongest line-up of the band. This is our personal preference although, as is their prerogative, we're aware there are those who favour earlier or later configurations of the Subs.

Day one of rehearsals

Roberts arrived at the rehearsal facility smiling, in a cheerful mood and ready for the day's exertions, which was comforting. We'd agreed a set beforehand that reflected the period we'd all worked together featuring songs which hadn't been heard by a Subs' audience for many years – Sensitive Boys, Countdown, You Don't Belong, Ice Age, Fear of Girls and other live rarities taken from the albums Diminished Responsibility and Endangered Species, all to be mixed in with older classic tunes.

When we started playing together, I couldn't believe how quickly we musically jelled after such an absence of time, and just how good it all sounded. Steve was on it, playing tight, taut and muscular beats which I either played off or accentuated with my bass, whilst Nicky filled in the sonic space with his erudite guitar work. Soon, we were all smiling.

After the practise run, a friend of Roberts turned up to go out for drinks with the drummer. When they'd left Garratt turned to me and said:

"See, I told you he wouldn't let us down. His drumming was great, just like back in the Nineteen-eighties, before he went off the rails."

"Nicky mate, this is day one," I reminded him. "Let's see how he is tomorrow and on the day of the gig, and then we'll find out if he's really the reformed character he claims to be."

Day two of rehearsals

Steve again turns up on time but he's bleary eyed and seems distracted. I ask him how his evening went and he says he'd visited with his friend a couple of London hangouts from his past for drinks, but nothing too crazy. When we get to rehearsing, Nicky and I can tell that he'd had more than just a few bevvies the night before. His timing is off, the energy of the day before is missing and he's making silly errors. Still, it's not so awful that we start to panic – yet.

Nico, a long-time acquaintance of Harper's, had invited the band over to his house for a meal and wine after we'd concluded the day's run through. Trine attends and Roberts has his friend from the previous night join us. After an evening together at Nico's, our drummer and his companion once again head off to visit the pubs and clubs of Soho.

Charlie was oblivious to the implications of those two hitting the town on the eve of our collective return to the stage but, after the day's decline in drum power and the inconsistent timing, Nicky and I were all too aware that another night of heavy drinking could seriously affect Roberts' playing and badly jeopardise the quality of our performance in front of what was expected to be a full-house at the Marquee Club. It was with a sense of foreboding then that I went home with my wife to consider the likelihood of a disaster or an improbable triumph for the erstwhile Harper/Garratt/Gibbs/Roberts alliance.

The reunion show

The plan was for us all to meet up at the Marquee Club at 5pm for soundcheck. When I got there at the agreed time, I discovered Steve Roberts and that same drinking lackey of his already ensconced in our dressing room, downing beers, surrounded by the empty bottles of the wine and brew they'd already consumed. I wasn't impressed.

"What are you doing Steve, isn't this precisely the sort of thing you promised Nicky and Charlie wouldn't happen? Aren't you supposed to be a 'changed man' now?"

"I'm just having a few drinks with my mate, what's the problem?"

Charlie and Steve Roberts, reunion Marquee show, 2002.

"Couldn't you at least have waited until after soundcheck to start pouring wine and beer down your neck?" I inquired.

"Oh, for fook sake, who are you, my mother?" he countered.

Nicky Garratt then came into the room, surveyed the empties on top of the depleted fridge, those arrayed on the table, on the floor, looked at me and said: "Yep, looks like you were right after all Alvin."
After a shaky soundcheck, things got worse. Having pretty much swigged down our entire drinks rider with his pal, I caught Steve emerging from the support band's dressing room carrying an armful of beers he'd pilfered from their fridge whilst they were still playing onstage. I admonished him for his thievery and told him that he should return the bottles to where he'd found them. He ignored me and continued carrying his plunder into the Subs' green room, where he and his still thirsty friend proceeded to guzzle the contents of these purloined bottles.
The show was a debacle. Roberts' playing was all over the place. He kept slowing down then speeding up to compensate, missed cues, forgot arrangements and by the halfway mark of the set, was flagging and out of breath. If you're unfortunate enough to own a copy of the DVD which was released containing the entire gig, you can see me intermittently jump up onto the drum riser to yell at Steve to get his "fucking shit

together," plus the numerous other expletives I aimed his way.

After this embarrassing performance, which was entirely the result of Roberts' inability to drink moderately before a show, I gave him the verbal hairdryer treatment; told him he was an idiot for fucking up a real opportunity to play regularly with the Subs again; that he'd embarrassed himself and the rest of us, and that he needed to get professional help for his drinking problem and seriously sort himself out.

He just scowled at me, said nothing and got into the van that would take him and his drum kit back to York that night.

I did see him fleetingly again, some years later, when Jet was the Subs' regular guitarist and we were waiting to do a soundcheck at a venue in York. I was sitting in the band bus reading a book when Charlie slid open the side-door and said, "Steve Roberts is here, why don't you come in and say hello to him, let bygones be bygones."

"He won't be interested in seeing me Chas" I told him, adding "It's because of what I said to him after the reunion fiasco. People who've met him since tell me he hates my guts for criticising him."

Harper went back into the building but returned a short time later to plead with me to make up with Steve. I eventually yielded; told him I'd go into the venue to see Roberts once I'd finished the chapter I'd reached in the book. Having concluded my reading, I walked into the live room, smiling, prepared to shake Steve's hand and put aside the memories of that mortifying Marquee night.

Roberts and Charlie had their backs to me as I entered. Steve must have heard my footsteps on the parquet floor. He looked about; saw who it was, rolled his eyes and exclaimed "Oh, for fook sake!" then turned his back on me and resumed his conversation with Harper.

I immediately returned to the bus. Even though I was ready to start anew with him, he obviously didn't want any kind of reconciliation with me. And that's how it was, on the very last occasion I saw Steve Roberts.

What a pitiful valediction.

I was devoting more time to Bordeaux than London as the essential revamps to the house were nearing completion. We still kept on the rental flat in West Hampstead which Trine, seeing as she continued to work for Black Sun at their Fulham Palace HQ, would spend more time at than me. My focus was on having the French property re-wired, re-plumbed, re-roofed and ready for full-time habitation come the spring of a fast-approaching New Year.

Yet again we spent the Christmas holidays in Oslo, but by May 2003, my wife and I, with my father in tow, made the transition to living permanently in rural France in pursuit of a better, more laid-back, more effortless, sort of life. Well, that was the intended idea, although it's a proven truism that men and women make plans while the gods laugh.

Kim Wylie, who lived just a 30-minute drive from our new Bordeaux abode and, who'd taken a break from co-piloting aircraft to be a stay-at-home father, had joined a local band called Blue House. As the name implies, this group played a lot of Blues-based material. As well as Kim, Blue House also had another member who was English – singer/guitarist Steve Blackman – plus a French bassist.

Having heard I was now living in the area, Blackman, who'd formed the band, sacked the bassist and then asked me to take on the four string role. I was mortified he'd axed the Frenchman in order to have me in the outfit, but it was a way of keeping up my bass chops and to play some local live shows, so I agreed to join.

We performed in a number of clubs and bars in the Aquitaine region during the summer, but I eventually came to the conclusion that the songs Steve selected for the set were all a bit too repetitive and tedious to maintain my interest long-term. I was therefore well pleased to receive a phone call from Charlie, enquiring if I would be interested in playing bass with the Subs for yet another tour of the U.S.A.

As well as wanting me to re-join for this American excursion, he also asked if I could recruit a drummer as Jason Willer – who was still too upset at that point about how he'd been treated in London to consider working with Harper – had declined. Normally Nicky Garratt would have been the obvious candidate for guitarist, but his girlfriend of the time, Manu – the woman who habitually stole money from him – was due to visit him in San Francisco just as the tour kicked off, so he wouldn't be able to participate. Consequently, Charlie requested that I should also think about a suitable guitarist who might replace Garratt.

When I told Kim Wylie about this, he expressed an interest in doing the tour. It had been 20 years since he'd last been on the road with the U.K. Subs and I cautioned him that it would be an arduous excursion, that the financial rewards would not be particularly good and chances were, at least a couple of shows would end up being cancelled (as routinely happened on these States-side capers) leading to an even further lowering of anticipated income.

I then reiterated that if he did enlist, it should definitely not be for the money aspect but for the pleasure of playing Punk rock music again in America and for the adventure and camaraderie which in the past at least, had always been a feature of our U.S.A. escapades. He said he was fine with signing up on that basis. The next day I called Chas to notify him that I'd found our tour drummer.

With Wylie on board, I then phoned my old Croydonian friend Steve Crittall in London to propose he enrol too. Steve was thrilled to be given the opportunity to experience playing his axe, coast-to-coast, in the States with the Subs; and so, with the guitarist vacancy having been filled, we had our finalised line-up for the 2003 U.S. tour.

It had been agreed that Steve would come over from the U.K. to France to rehearse at Wylie's house for the upcoming American jaunt. Following these rehearsals Crittall returned to London and a few days later, flew with Charlie from Heathrow to San Francisco.

Kim was married to an American Airlines' air hostess and he'd told me that this connection meant he could get us (me and him) round-trip tickets with this same airline to SF from France for $250 apiece, which sounded like a very good deal. He also said we would get an upgrade to either first class or business but, being as we were guests of one of the airline's employees, it was necessary to be smartly dressed or risk being denied entry to these exclusive cabin areas.

"What do you mean by smart?" I asked him.

"Wear a suit or a nice jacket with proper trousers, not jeans, and neat shoes, no sneakers; and a decent looking regular shirt 'cause if you put on a T-shirt, it won't cut it," was the reply.

I wasn't at all keen on these wardrobe regulations; but I did have a suit and so, in the interests of obtaining a far more comfortable seat, free flowing good wine and some genuinely edible airline food, I wore my two-piece to Bordeaux Airport with leather shoes and a crisp white shirt only to discover that Kim had already got himself upgraded to first class, while I was seated next to two corpulent Americans at the rear of the aircraft in Extremely Uncomfortable class. Thus, I ended up with my knees up around my ears for the 11-hour flight whilst simultaneously being repeatedly elbowed by the obese passenger to my left every time he shifted his weight around.

I also felt a right twat, sat there in my suit surrounded by people wearing casual clothes, who were no doubt wondering what the pretentious idiot in their midst was thinking wearing such a stiff get up.

Nicky Garratt was waiting for us at SF International with Charlie and Steve. We would all be staying overnight at Garratt's house, then return to the airport the next day to hire a mini-van for the sojourn from one of the rental companies there. Nicky drove us the following morning and offered to pay for the vehicle using his card. We would then repay him the hire fee at the end of the tour, after we'd returned to San

Francisco to take our flights home.

This wasn't as altruistic as it sounds. Garratt had a credit card that awarded one air mile for every dollar spent and, seeing as the stipend for the van was in excess of $3,000, he would accrue a lot of air miles plus get all the money back in cash, which is not a bad thing if you're looking for some non-declarable dough when submitting tax forms to the IRS.

Still, we were happy to go along with this arrangement and having taken possession of the van, set off for the first municipality of the tour, Sacramento, and our inaugural show at the Boardwalk in the Orangevale district of the capital city of California.

The reason we'd only needed a mini-van rather than something more spacious, was because we would just be carrying a guitar, a bass, Charlie's merchandise and our personal luggage for the duration of our visit. Providing the drums and backline for the entire tour would be our support band throughout, Toxic Narcotic – a Hardcore outfit from Boston, Massachusetts.

This first gig, playing wise, was ragged, which is what invariably happens when you pull together a group of musicians with varying degrees of live experience and then expect them to jell collectively in short order; but we got through it and received our first earned money, which I was then told by the promoter we had to share with Toxic Narcotic.

I was again designated tour manager and this split hadn't been specified in my personal itinerary containing all the financial information, although I had to accept our sudden halving of income after having phoned Roz Lynne – our Pooch Booking agency tour coordinator – who apologised for not including this important information in my tour book.

Having found us a motel for the night based on a recommendation from the club owner, I tried to grab some sleep whilst being plagued by the recurring thought that this was going to be one hell of a challenging tour indeed.

THE ALAMO

An hour to sunrise, but we're already on the road, motoring towards Salt Lake City, Utah, as we had some serious distance to travel and an early show there. At the wheel was the driver/roadie we'd hired in 'Frisco, a young Afro-American with a taste for British skinhead-style clothing named Max, who was actually a resident of Los Angeles and had been recommended to us by a former American tour driver.

He was a nice enough fella but, as with Gavin on the 1997 U.S.A. tour, it quickly became apparent that Max was more interested in the possibilities for partying and meeting and bedding young women than applying himself to the work – his mysterious disappearances at load-in and load-out times were an especially irritating habit.

We were getting on with our support band Toxic Narcotic in a reasonable if lukewarm sort of way, but their music was not at all compatible with ours. It was a Hardcore noise more suited to being performed ahead of bands like Discharge or The Exploited than the more song-led material of the U.K. Subs. Still, they were transporting and providing the hardware, so we accepted their musical appeal lay elsewhere, ignored the evident mismatch, and tried to find common ground with them on a personal level.

The best thing about that Salt Lake City show was the promoter's T-shirt – it read **I Eat Mormon Pussy** – and having got back in the van, post-performance, we drove on into the Utah night towards our next gig destination: Fort Collins, Colorado, which was once a military outpost for the U.S. Army during the Indian Wars of the 1860s.

Reno, Portland, Tacoma, and Bend Oregon, had already been played, followed by Denver, Omaha, Des Moines, Milwaukee, Detroit, and Toledo, where the duplicitous promoter ran off with the entire show's takings and neither band received their contracted fees. Albany, Ithaca, Allentown, Providence, and Boston came and went, with Philadelphia getting us to the midway point of the tour.

By this juncture certain realities had been established. Charlie was being a lot more easy-going and far less difficult to man-manage than had been the case on previous North American visits. Perhaps because of his advancing years he didn't seem to have the same energy or need to habitually over-drink and be sporadically obnoxious and difficult, as had been his way in the past. Whatever the reasons, as Shakespeare wrote regarding Henry V's reformation after he'd obtained the crown of England – 'We are blessed in the change.'

Chas may not have been the tour's enfant terrible this time around, but Kim Wylie was steadily on course to appropriate that title for himself.

Being a co-pilot for a well-known airline in his recent past must have instilled an arrogant sense of infallibility in him. He simply refused to acknowledge that he was predisposed to make mistakes, whether it was regarding his playing – which could be pretty sketchy at times – or in any other way.

For instance, having discovered and booked a hotel for when we'd finished our show at a venue no more than two kilometres from the hostelry, Kim decided he would take the wheel of the van to drive us back for the gig. When we reached the main road that led directly to the club, he turned right and drove on.

My immediate thought was he'd turned in the wrong direction and that he should have gone left instead of right and, obviously, I wasn't the only one to think the same as Steve Crittall spoke up to notify Wylie he'd made an error:

"Err, Kim, you went right when you should have turned left, you need to turn around as we're now travelling in the wrong direction."

Wylie wasn't having it: "No, this is the right direction; I know where I'm going. The club is east and we're going east, I know that from being able to navigate planes using the stars."

I couldn't let this go unchallenged: "I think Steve's right Kim, we should have gone left on the main road. You're taking us away from the venue, not towards it."

"Bullshit!" was his reply, adding "I'm going the right way and you two should let me just get on with the driving as you're both not only wrong, you're also being a distraction."

I looked at Steve and shrugged my shoulder to indicate that we should let him drive on until he realised he'd miscalculated. It had taken us 20 minutes from club to hotel, but just under an hour later we were still driving. Crittall made a comment about this. Wylie didn't like it.

"Shut up! I know what I'm doing, this is the right direction," at which point we ran out of road, having reached a harbour which enclosed various sailing yachts undulating in the large body of water that stretched out to the horizon in the fading light. Steve couldn't resist:

"See, you were wrong, we told you but you wouldn't listen."

And yet Wylie still wouldn't admit to his gaffe: "Ah, but we passed the club on the way down here, so I wasn't wrong, you were wrong."

Florida, U.S.A. tour, 2003.

At which stage I'd had enough: "No, we didn't Kim, now fucking turn us around and let's drive in the right direction to where we're playing tonight."

Even then Wylie kept insisting he was right and we were the ones in error all the way to the club that we would have arrived at two hours beforehand if he'd listened to us and not his ego.

The other Wylie annoyance was his continual gripes about the money situation even though prior to his committing to the tour I'd warned him about not doing it for purely financial reasons. We'd had, as per usual, two gigs cancelled plus the Toledo, Ohio incident where the promoter had run off with all the revenue, which constituted a loss of net income. But even so, the wages I paid were OK and I'd noticed Kim had been buying a lot of gifts to take back for his wife and daughter, so I couldn't see why he was daily busting my balls about this issue nor how I was expected to amend this predicted deficit – the answer to the latter conundrum would be revealed at a future date.

Steve Crittall was doing a sterling job on guitar and seemed to be enjoying himself, taking lots of photographs of the trip and appreciating the changes in topography as we travelled around America. Max was enjoying himself too much. He was getting drunk most nights, routinely chasing women and was always unavailable when we most needed his help. His days were numbered.

For my part, I'd discovered I could be faithful on the road, despite the opportunities, which occasionally presented themselves, to indulge in brief, adulterous sex. This was a really satisfying discovery. It signified I'd finally attained a maturity which put fidelity before indulgence and also meant that I no longer had to deal with the feelings of guilt and remorse I'd experienced in the past whenever I'd been unfaithful to a partner. I regularly phoned Trine whilst travelling around the States to chat and make sure things were alright with her in France and was actually looking forward to returning home to my wife.

Thus far it had been a tiring, sometimes problematic tour, and things were just about to get tetchier as we pressed on to New York City to play our Big Apple home-from-home on the Bowery, CBGBs.

It was good to be back at the birthplace of American Punk rock, but Kim Wylie was dissatisfied with the billing for that evening's show. Instead of Toxic Narcotic playing directly before the Subs, CBGBs' legendary owner Hilly Kristal, had put a local band in that spot and had relegated TN to first on stage. The reason for Wylie's discontent was this would mean TN would have to break down their drum kit after playing to make way for the middle band and Kim would have to restore it for our performance. He therefore asked me to get Kristal to change the playing order so the kit would already be in situ when it was our turn to gather together on that famous stage.

I told him I would request this alteration but couldn't guarantee a positive reaction. When I broached the subject with Hilly, he said he'd promised the local band the pre-headline slot and he wasn't about to change this arrangement just because our drummer was too lazy to assemble a drum kit prior to playing – a fair enough point. Wylie though, had a very different perspective:

"You're supposed to be the tour manager; your job is to get things done for the band. Go back and tell him he has to change it so Toxic Narcotic are on second."

I was incensed by this and my reply was as vociferous as it reads:

"First off, I'm not getting paid any extra money for being tour manager, for liaising with the promoters, collecting the money every night, paying the band every day after I've calculated what we can afford for wages based on our income and outgoings; recording every nickel and dime of expenditure and earnings with supporting receipts for each entry in the tour book so that ungrateful wretches like you can be assured that I'm scrupulously honest with the money…"

My voice may have then risen up a notch or two:

"I asked Hilly, he said no, and that's it. I may be tour manager but it's not my job to tell promoters how to do theirs. The running order is down to Hilly and he won't shift, so stop being a fucking pain in the arse and just get on with it."

He was still evidently dissatisfied with the situation but knew better than to pursue it further whilst I was in such an agitated frame of mind. And yet, he still tried to broach this same subject later, to which I dashed all his hopes with a one word answer: "No."

Our performance was competent – extracts from our set can be seen on the Punk from the Bowery compilation DVD, which also features performances at CBGBs by, among others, Agnostic Front, Cro-Mags and Poison Idea – and Kim managed to survive the terrible stress and exhaustion of having to erect a drum kit for the very first time on this tour.

We then headed south to Baltimore, where I took Max aside, told him his services were no longer required, paid him off and gave him some money for the airfare back to LA. Will Sullivan, the guitarist with Toxic Narcotic, who we'd become very friendly with over the course of the tour, took over the driving job and the Subs/TN road show continued on to Florida – Myrtle Beach, Augusta, Tampa, and Fort Lauderdale – before crossing the state line into Georgia for a duo of gigs, in Savannah and Atlanta.

When we got to Texas a more serious falling-out occurred between me

U.K. Subs at the Alamo, Texas, U.S.A., 2003.

and Wylie, although, just prior to this significant dispute, having arrived in San Antonio, we all visited the famed Alamo Mission, where in 1836 after a 13 day siege, Mexican President General Santa Anna took the Texan garrison and massacred most of its defenders. Having seen the classic John Wayne Alamo film, I was expecting the former fortress to be in a wilderness location and was more than surprised to find it in the middle of a plaza surrounded by office buildings, fast food restaurants and shops of various kinds. It was an interesting visit and we got Will to take a bunch of photos of the band at the Alamo monument and in front of the renowned mission's façade to memorialise the occasion using Steve's camera.

Dallas, Texas, in the twin motel room we were sharing that night, was the location for where Wylie and I really got into it. As I've already divulged, he was always bugging me about money and he'd now come up with a solution as to how we could make ourselves some extra cash. I'd put aside over $3,000 to pay Nicky Garratt back for hiring the mini-van for the tour on his credit card and it was this sum that Kim had now set his sights on as an additional top-up to our gig earnings.

"Let's not pay Nicky back when we get to San Francisco. Let's divide that money and let Charlie pay him back from a future U.K. Subs' tour," he proposed in all seriousness.

I was shocked. How could he suggest such an underhand and immoral scheme?

"No way; we assured Nicky we would pay him back at the end of the tour and that's exactly what we're going to do, so forget about it."

He wasn't going to give up that easily:

"That's the difference between you and me – I think outside the box and you don't…" he yelled back, and continued with "so, for a change, do what I say and use that money to pay ourselves. Charlie can reimburse him another time."

"Fuck that!" I snapped back "Nicky and Charlie are my friends and you don't cheat your friends Kim, or at least I don't. You shouldn't even treat strangers like that. I can't believe you're asking me to go back on our agreement with Nicky and then have Chas take on the debt. Don't talk to me about this again, or I'll really get angry with you, understand?"

Wylie didn't get his way on that occasion, but he did come up with another ruse to make himself some additional money. Having arrived in Los Angeles after our Austin, Oklahoma City, Phoenix, Tucson, and Corona appearances, we all stayed at my friend Isaac Baruch's house in North Hollywood to save on hotel room expenses. Being the generous host he is, Ike said we could help ourselves to any food or beer in his fridge and to utilise the telephone to ring home, as he paid a set monthly fee for American long distance and international calls. It struck me as

'Soho Steve' Crittall, U.S.A. tour, 2003.

strange then when Wylie said he was going out to find a pay phone to call his wife.

Sometime later he came back and announced forcefully: "I've just spoken to Katrina, she tells me the airfares for Alvin and I were not two hundred and fifty dollars apiece but five hundred each. So the band owes me an extra five hundred dollars."

He'd told me before leaving for the States that the originally priced cheap rate tickets were the same cost as those they'd used for family and friends on many previous occasions and yet now, suddenly, after this

U.K. Subs' line-up for the 2003 U.S.A. tour, Miami Beach.

mysterious pay-phone call to his wife, they had doubled.

I knew it had to be a fabrication, that he was just trying to scam us out of another $500 because I wouldn't go along with his earlier plan to renege on the deal with Nicky and stitch-up Charlie with the debt – $500 each for air tickets wasn't far off what I could have got us if I'd looked and booked online – but Harper said "Oh well, if that's what it is, that's what it is. Alvin will pay you the money," which completely undermined my planned response – it's bullshit! – and left me thinking: 'Alright, if he's shameful enough to con the rest of us out of $500 and Chas wants to let him get away with it, so be it,' but it really disturbed me. Why would a supposed friend do that?

There were four more shows after LA. The final one being in San Francisco, where I made sure Nicky Garratt got all his money as promised. Wylie and I flew back to France. It was effectively the end of our friendship. I'd met him when his name was still John Towe back in the 1970s. We'd toured together with Brian James and the Brains/Hellions in Europe and the U.K., and worldwide with the U.K. Subs. But I couldn't be mates with someone who would take money under false pretences from his fellow band members and who'd wanted to cheat

Garratt out of the sum we'd agreed to return to him and have the burden of payment transferred solely onto Charlie's shoulders.

Although we still live only 10 kilometres away from each other, I no longer have any dealings with him, or him with me – as Charlie Harper once lyricised: 'When the trust is gone, something's going very wrong'. How true that is.

What is it with goddamn drummers?

It seems to me I've been pre-occupied in highlighting the faults of others but have as yet not owned up to any of my own transgressions from this period of my life. So here goes:

Although Trine had got herself a job in France through a family connection with a Norwegian-owed cognac distilling company called Tiffon, who were based in the beautiful town of Jarnac, it became apparent she was unhappy living in my chosen country. Trine wanted us to sell up and move to Oslo, for me to get a regular job there, and for her to again be with her family and friends on a permanent basis.

I'd told her before our move to the Bordeaux region that if she had any doubts about leaving London we wouldn't go, to which she replied, "I'm fine with it." But it's only when a person starts to actually live day-to-day in a new environment that they discover if it's truly a suitable place for them to be or not. I'd seen signs of this discontent previously but hoped it was just a transitional response and nothing much to worry about.

However, one evening, quite matter-of-factly, my wife explained that although she still loved me, it was no longer possible for her to subsist in a place that she was no longer happy with. She again brought up the moving to Oslo idea which for me was a non-starter for a number of reasons, chief among them being my severe dislike of cold weather.

I took her to a nearby bar, bought us some drinks and effectively talked her out of leaving. This was wrong of me. I wasn't thinking about her interests or needs, just my own selfish requirements and aspirations. She agreed to stay and give it another go, and yet I knew it was the wrong choice for her.

Still, out of self-interest I kept insisting all would be fine, whilst in truth knowing that happiness is not an emotion which can simply be reasoned back into a person's psyche. I also knew it would be just a matter of time before the razor of reality severed the already frayed binds of matrimony, and we'd have to go our separate ways.

FIEND FEST

The way the marriage eventually ended was more a case of incremental drift than a decisive split. Despite all my best efforts to talk her around to my point of view and reassure her, I could see that Trine was still dissatisfied with living in rural France and wanted to return to Norway. I proposed she go to Oslo whilst I remained in Bordeaux so that we could travel back and forth between those two cities to see each other when possible.

My wife thought it a good compromise and moved back to her home city where she would live with her father until she'd found an apartment of her own.

As was our tradition, I flew to Oslo to see Trine and her family to celebrate the Christmas period and on my return embarked on a massive European tour which covered 12 nations, starting in Germany on the 9th of January 2004, finishing up on the 24th of February in France. The line-up for the 38 Euro-wide shows was the omnipresent Charlie Harper, Nicky Garratt, Jason Willer, back in the band having finally recovered from his Universal album recording trauma, and me.

It was a poorly paid tour. Harper was only offering us each €60 a day and, as ever, there was no share in any of the merchandise being sold, with these auxiliary takings often reaping more money per-show than the band's gig fee. To add to these bellyaches, in order to save additional income, there was no hired roadie this time around to help with the equipment for load-ins and load-outs; so Nicky, Jason, Yuko and I – Charlie never helped with the band's gear, ever – were expected to do all the heavy hauling prior to and after a show without any assistance. Still, I made a little money, relished playing live and enjoyed some of the travel, especially in Italy, where we got to perform in Rome, Padova and Brescia, before returning home to Bordeaux feeling road weary but gratified. I was firmly back in the touring game and first choice Subs' bassist once more, or so I thought.

Trine Karlsen and I managed to maintain our long distance marriage for most of 2004, but the sheer distance and consequent lack of intimacy between us became issues that needed to be addressed. I was due to play some shows in the U.K. with the Subs so we decided to meet up in London just prior to the tour, to discuss what the best way forward for both of us might be. Having spent two days deliberating this, we had to eventually concede our marriage was over but that we would remain friends and continue with regular communication by telephone and even visit each other from time-to-time. It was a difficult, emotional decision for the two of us, but we knew there was now no other option.

I wasn't going to sell up to live in Norway and she wasn't about to return to residing in France. Those were the irresolvable facts.

Sure enough, in later years, I visited Trine a couple times at her flat in Oslo and she on occasion, travelled over to stay at the French house. We also talked weekly by phone and frequently emailed each other with news about our detached lives. In 2006, we got divorced. It was a very different termination to the one I'd endured with my first wife, Mary Jordan. Trine never made any claims on any of my money or the Bordeaux property which I had wholly paid for and I, of course, didn't make any demands regarding her Oslo apartment, which she had singularly purchased.

The friendly back and forth continued for another couple of years until, inevitably, the phone chats became briefer and less commonplace, the emails stopped and visits were no longer planned in either direction. She'd moved on, I'd moved on. I recently learned Trine has remarried and I truly wish her and whoever her new husband might be a long and happy life together.

Charlie had again started up with his mix and mismatch approach to the U.K. Subs' membership. For some U.K. shows he would invite Brian Barnes to play bass and Alan Campbell to brandish his guitar, as well as a plethora of differing drummers to share the stage with him. For the European, U.S.A. and Canadian tours, it would be Nicky Garratt, Jason Willer and I in the main. And it was this line-up which embarked on the Subs' American tour in the autumn of 2005.

By Subs' standards, this October visit to the States was a fairly brief one – just 18 gigs in 18 different cities to contend with – and one of these, in Boise Idaho, got cancelled leaving us with a free day after a very rare early show at a venue called Hell's Kitchen located in Tacoma. Rather than moping around in a motel on a non-earning day, we asked the Hell's Kitchen promoter if he knew of a studio we could hire the next day to record. He recommended the curiously titled Jesse's Autopsy Room, which we then booked via his office phone.

The following morning we turned up at this basic but satisfactory-enough studio and chatted about what material we had amongst us to record. Jason had a rudimentary chord sequence which Garratt added a series of changes to, after which Charlie asked Willer to write some lyrics for him to sing. The result was the anti-capitalism song Product Supply.

Nicky and I had been working on a piece of Punk rock music during soundchecks. With Harper's lyrics attached, this final version was recorded and awarded the title Embryo. Charlie then suggested we re-record one of my Urban Dogs' Wipeout Beach album contributions,

Somewhere on the American road, U.S.A. tour, 2005.

Rare Disease, although this time around with Harper providing the lead vocals rather than me. We duly added that to our recorded yield and after mixing these tracks spent the entire night in the studio to save on motel costs. I chose to sleep on the floor of the vocal booth seeing as it was soundproof and would cancel out Garratt's and Harper's epic snoring. These Tacoma recordings would eventually be released as a vinyl 7-inch EP entitled Product Supply by Time & Matter Records in 2011.

This mid-to-late portion of the first decade of the new millennium was a patchy phase for me regarding my playing relationship with the Subs. However, there were a couple of interesting excursions during this variable period. The 2006 Euro tour for example, with our regular support band of that time The Vibrators in tow, during which Vibes' drummer Eddie Edwards – a passionate Arsenal FC supporter who consequently always derides local rival team Tottenham Hotspur – told me what has subsequently become my all-time favourite football-related joke.

Eddie: "Alvin, did you know there are three teams in the Football League that have swear words in their names."

Me: "I didn't know that Eddie. What three teams would they be then?"

Eddie: Well, there's Scunthorpe FC (sCUNThorpe). Then there's Arsenal (ARSEnal)…"

At which point Mr Edwards paused in the interests of proper comic timing.

Me: "And the third team Eddie?"

Eddie: "Tottenham 'fucking' Hotspur!"

After this European jaunt I didn't play with the band again that same year until flying out to San Francisco to hook up with Charlie, Nicky Garratt and yet another new drummer, Jamie Oliver (a young, talented musician who had debuted with the Subs in 2005) for the North American-wide Fiend Fest – a multi-band travelling festival headlined by The Misfits. As well as these kings of the horror Punk genre – what other outfit would have the perverse imaginative state of mind to compose lyrics like those for their twisted romantic song, Helena: 'If I cut off your arms and cut off your legs, would you still love me anyway? If you're bound and you're gagged, draped and displayed would you still love me anyway?' – five other acts completed the Fiend Fest bill: Osaka Popstar, a weird assemblage purporting to be a Legends of Punk supergroup; our good friends The Adicts; the Subs; Juicehead, a Chicago based group who'd recently signed to Misfit Records; and a London-based band I'd not heard of before called Orange. It was this troupe of players then which took to the stage for the opening Fiend Fest's two night stint at the Galaxy Theatre in Santa Ana, California.

The Misfits had parted ways with their original singer Glenn Danzig and guitarist Doyle Wolfgang von Frankenstein, having now mutated into a three-piece with Jerry Only on lead vocals and bass, ex-Black Flag guitarist Dez Cadena and a former affiliate of the legendary Ramones, Marky Ramone, on the drum stool. During the course of this tour I would become great friends with Jerry and Dez and conversely discover what a miserable, self-centred creature Marky was.

This morose drummer was also a member of Osaka Popstar which additionally featured Jerry and Dez, along with vocalist John Cafiero, who'd hitherto directed various Misfits' videos, plus Ivan Julian who had been a founding member of seminal New York City Punk ensemble, Richard Hell and the Voidoids.

They would play just before the Misfits took to the stage and I found it bizarre that three members of Osaka P would then reappear in their horror-show headline guises a short while after having already performed. Both John and Ivan though were very fine people and we easily bonded as the Fiend Fest progressed. In fact, everyone on that tour, apart from Marky, was as personable a travelling companion as you could wish for.

Four more Californian dates followed – the cities of Modesto, Lompoc, where we had a supplementary gig with The Adicts rather than a day off, Agoura Hills and Morongo. The tour then rolled into Scottsdale, Arizona for a gig, and the next day crossed the border into Tijuana, Mexico.

When I'd lived in Los Angeles, I'd visit Mexico on occasion but this was to be the first time I got to play a show there. The venue was an immense outdoor concrete space with a lot of graffiti – gang related, political or simply artistic – which covered every bit of wall space in the compound. By early evening it was packed with mainly young male Mexican Punks and when it was our turn to shake some action, we fed off their youthful energy and put in a very good performance. Having crossed the border back into California that same night, we played the Key Club in Hollywood the following day with the rest of our touring cohorts, then headed to Denver for a show which consisted of the Subs, The Adicts and Orange to again dodge a payless day off.

Now, when this tour had first been offered to me via a telephone call to France by Nicky Garratt, he'd proposed that instead of the expense of hiring a driver, he and I should share the driving duties. We wouldn't be getting any extra money for our additional labours so I'm still perplexed as to why I actually gave my agreement to this proposition. However, it was only after the Denver show that the true implications of my unthinking acquiescence emerged.

The next Fiend Fest venue was in Hartford, Connecticut, two days hence. When Nicky and I looked at the map at the motel before setting off the next morning, we realised the distance from Denver to Hartford was around 2,000 miles (3,218 kilometres), which roughly translated to more than 30 hours of non-stop driving. This meant forgoing sleeping in motels and only stopping to fuel-up, eat and take the occasional toilet break if we were going to make the next gig. So for two solid days Garratt and I took it in turns to take the wheel for durations of eight hours on, eight hours off as we motored along the I-80 East to our next destination. It was a tough excursion.

Because they'd hired drivers to singlehandedly cover that same distance in whatever vehicles carried their equipment, every other band on the Festival's roster had instead flown by plane to Hartford a day ahead of time to rest-up for the show. Not the U.K. Subs.

The worst part was the nightshift driving. Everyone else in the van would be asleep and silent during the night, but when I changed with Nicky in the morning and then tried to acquire some sleep for myself having laid myself down on a couple of seats at the back of the van, all and sundry would awake and start chatting, begin playing music on the radio and were totally unconcerned about my getting some REMs before my next turn at the wheel.

Harper's backseat driving was also a real source of irritation. He didn't drive himself (thank fuck!), held no licence nor any motoring experience but seemed compelled to continually offer advice and criticism to both Nicky and I throughout this touring period.

On the marathon journey to Connecticut, whilst I was in charge of the vehicle, he started up again with one of his disparaging critiques of my driving, which everybody else in the vehicle thought was exemplary. I'd only got an hour's sleep due to the customary passenger noise after a

Setting up the stage in Tijuana, Mexico, Fiend Fest, 2006.

nightshift and was in no mood for any bullshit from him or anyone else. Having pulled the van over to a standstill on the hard shoulder, I turned round in my seat and yelled at him: "Listen you selfish arsehole, Nicky and I are doing the driving for free so that you can earn extra money. You don't drive, you never have, so shut the fuck up or I will personally throw you out and leave you at the side of this freeway to make your own way to Hartford."

I meant it too.

His wife Yuko also laid into him: "Alvin's right Charlie, you don't drive so shut up, shut up!" He mumbled something about not caring if he was left behind but had the sense to refrain from any more backseat driving for a while, although he couldn't resist starting up again later in the tour.

We made it to the venue in Hartford with a mere two hours to spare before our stage time. We'd endured a similar long distance drive during the North American Social Chaos tour of 1999, but on that occasion, we hired someone to do the bulk of the driving and the Denver to Hartford trip was certainly a much greater distance than had needed to be travelled back then. I took a perverse sense of pride that we had been the only band crazy enough to motor it rather than fly and that Garratt and I possessed the stamina and determination to get us to the venue on time and then directly taken to its stage to play a show after having driven the 2,000 miles between us. I was then 48 years old, Nicky was 51.

As I've already revealed, everybody on the Fiend Fest caper was easy

Alvin, Dez Cadena and Jerry Only.

going and friendly apart from Marky Ramone. His petulant personality first surfaced when we were all individually having photographs taken with the Misfits after a gig. When it was Jamie Oliver's turn to have his pic taken with the headliners, Marky said, "I don't think I want to be in this photo," and walked off in a strop.

The source of his pathetic displeasure was that our drummer was wearing a classic presidential seal design Ramones T-shirt which had the original skin pounder Tommy Ramone's name on it rather than his own, alongside those of Joey, Dee Dee and Johnny. On another occasion I was responsible for his disapproval.

Marky came into our dressing room looking irritated and in a loud and accusatory voice declared: "Hey, somebody went up to our Osaka Popstar's merch table and asked for some signed photos, a badge and a couple of patches. They said they were with one of the bands and so were given them for free when they should have paid like everybody else. Was it one of you guys?"

For some unfathomable reason Charlie turned to me and inquired "Do you know anything about this Alvin?" I laughed and said "No, of course not. Why would I want pictures and patches of Osaka Popstar?"

Marky immediately took offence at my reply: "Yeah right, why would you want those? Why the fuck would you want those, huh? Who the fuck would want that stuff…" as if I'd just impugned the band, their being of so little consequence to me that I wouldn't be interested in any of their merchandise even if it had been offered gratis, which in effect, was the truth.

Adjusting his obvious wig as he left the room in another huff over nothing, Marky Ramone snubbed us for the rest of the tour; apart, that is, from one particular occasion which showcased what a two-faced curmudgeon he truly is.

Garratt and Oliver were playing a game of pool backstage at one of the venues. A camera crew had arrived to video tape the ex-Ramone for a forthcoming documentary. They were filming him as he walked about the large backroom space and seeing the game in progress and recognising an opportunity to aggrandise himself for this future film by appearing affluent and generous, Marky walked up to the pool table, threw down a $100 bill and said "Hey fellas, that's for the winner. Don't spend it all at once."

I nearly dropped my beer in shock. Before that occasion he'd been nothing but dismissive and cold towards us and once the video cameras had departed, he directly resumed his previous icy disposition to the membership of the U.K. Subs. Still, having won the game, Jamie did pocket a nice little earner courtesy of the cheerless ex-Ramone, which was obviously a good thing.

Next up was the Allentown Fairgrounds show in Pennsylvania. As part of the 46 acres on which an agricultural fair takes place each year, there sat a very large building which served as a farmers' market. This was where cattle were bought or sold and farm produce could be purchased. With a newly erected stage at one end of the structure, this would be our venue for show number 12 on the itinerary.

As we arrived, a game of football was in progress between The Adicts and members of Orange. Seeing us enter the building and knowing I'd been a keen soccer player in my youth, Pete Dee called out to me and made an accurate long pass of the ball, which landed at my feet. I immediately put down my gig bag and booted the ball back in his direction. Just as it took flight a uniformed cop walked into the path of its trajectory and took the full force of the football on the side of his skull. His cap and glasses flew off and it certainly didn't help soften the blow that we all started laughing at this comical sight instead of being sympathetic to his situation. He wasn't best pleased.

Now this policeman was an absolute nerd. He was short and skinny with wire-rimmed glasses and looked to be about 12 years-old. I think he must have been bullied at school and joined the police force in order to attain some sense of power and authority to negate his persecuted past and offset his wimpy persona – well, that's my theory anyway – and having some Limey kick a football into the side of his head and losing his cap and glasses in the process was pretty demeaning and must have brought back some bad memories.

I stifled my amusement and did my best to placate him:

"Oops, sorry officer, bit of a miskick. Hope you're alright."

He just glared at me, then picked up his hat and specs and walked off. I then joined the game in earnest. Having scored a goal against the Orange team via a header from a free kick that Pete invitingly floated across, upon resumption, following the reset, one of the opposing team took a fierce shot at our goal which I tried to block with my extended right leg. The ball ricocheted off my shin and looped over my head to continue travelling behind me. I turned around to witness it hitting the nerdy cop full in the face, once more knocking his cap off, although this time destroying his glasses which slid down his face and tumbled to the ground with buckled frames and broken lenses. I know we should have been directly apologetic and sensitive to his plight, but again, it was just too funny not to laugh at.

This time though, the geek reached for his gun.

MISFITS

The cop was such a self-important oddball that, for a brief moment, I thought he might well shoot me for once more belittling his contrived pomposity and disrespecting his ill-fitting uniform in public – they were probably the smallest police garments the precinct could supply, and yet they still looked to be for a far larger man, flapping about on his skinny frame like the loose clothes on a scarecrow. But seeing as I wasn't black or conspicuously Hispanic, I figured my chances were relatively good of getting away with just the threat of being shot rather than taking an actual bullet to the body.

Anyhow, before he could unleash the weapon, another police officer strolled over and intervened by grabbing the angry nerd's arm to prevent the firearm from being unholstered whilst whispering something along the lines of "Don't do it son, they're not worth it" into his ear. This second cop then picked up the dork's cap, placed it on his compatriot's head, gathered up the remnants of his glasses and walked off with our football under his arm to prevent any future reoccurrence of what had already twice happened, to his fellow officer; to which Hoggy, one of the Adicts' road crew, couldn't resist shouting "Hey mister, can we have our ball back," as the two representatives of the law marched off together to the accompaniment of yet more Limey laughter.

The second notable episode at this Pennsylvania gig was the promoter running off with all the takings after the show. When this piece of chicanery was discovered, the Misfits' tour manager, Tank, set off with a venue employee who'd offered to drive him in their car to the supplied address of the thief.

Everybody on that tour liked and admired Tank. As his name implies, he was a large, muscular guy who looked like an American professional wrestler in the mould of Hulk Hogan or Dwayne Johnson, but despite his size and strength, he had a very calm and good natured disposition, always friendly and helpful, an old-school gentleman. Still, you wouldn't want to do something untoward that would initiate his anger, which is what the duplicitous promoter was on the receiving end of when Tank caught him emerging from a vehicle in front of his house just as his own ride arrived there.

The promoter initially proclaimed his innocence so Tank bundled him into the back of the employee's car and had him drive them back to the scene of the crime. On arrival, the burly TM virtually carried his captive onto the Misfits' Nightliner bus – which was parked-up directly outside the farmers market building – and began his interrogation. I wasn't privy to the exact methods employed but after 15 minutes or so of a

Fiend Fest U.K. Subs' line-up backstage, Nokia Theatre, New York City, 2006.

grilling from Tank, the show's organiser started to sing like a soprano and admitted he'd handed all the cash over to his wife to take home and that they'd intended to stiff the bands and keep the entire night's earnings for themselves.

Tank then marched this fraudster back into the car and having escorted him to his house and confronted the wife, returned in triumph with all the absconded cash and paid out what was owing to each of the Fiend Fest groups. Now that's what I call a righteous Tour Manager.

The next day, I drove the band from Allentown to New York City. It became an especially stressful drive once we'd reached the central part of the metropolis – traffic was appalling and yellow cabs would habitually cut up cars and buses and act as if they were exempt from any of the rules and regulations that applied to other road users. Despite succumbing to a large dose of road rage, I got us safely to Times Square where we played a Fiend Fest show at the Nokia Theatre, which has since been renamed the Palladium Times Square.

House of Blues in Atlantic City and the Starland Ballroom in Sayerville followed. The Sayerville gig took place on Halloween, the textbook setting for a Misfits' performance. Sure enough, the majority of the audience came dressed as extras from an Evil Dead film or sported other scary movie related costumes in keeping with the evening's festivities. However, as proceedings commenced, it quickly became apparent they were there solely for the headline act.

After their individual recitals, having already been treated as something to be impassively endured rather than enjoyed, both Orange and Juicehead left the stage to absolute silence. When it was our turn to tread the proverbial boards there was very little applause between songs and the sold-out costumed crowd stood immobile throughout, to which I remarked over my microphone to no effect or humorous understanding: "I think you lot are taking this zombie thing a bit too literally."

We rolled on to play a couple of FF gigs in Canada and subsequently returned to the U.S.A. to perform with our fellow tour participants in Detroit, Cleveland, Mokena and, lastly, Baltimore, where the festival had its finale and we played our concluding American show with the Misfits, et al.

The foremost part of the tour was over but the Subs still had five venues booked for our own headline gigs. However, the annoying thing was Jamie had decided to ditch these remaining dates in order to return to the U.K. to play some pre-booked concerts with a band he occasionally worked with called Toy Town Cash – but which Garratt and I, irritated at Oliver's decision to cut out, referred to as Toy Town Tosspots. Nothing we said could change his mind regarding abandoning us, so we had no other choice but to contact Gizz Lazlo in LA to ask him to take over the drum duties at short notice.

Gizz hadn't played with us since the Social Chaos tour seven years before. Not surprisingly, he was pretty rusty when it came to song arrangements, intros and endings, timings, etc, and the first two shows in Columbus and Downey were pretty haphazard, although by the time we got to The Showcase Theatre in Corona he'd improved considerably and for the last two gigs in Las Vegas and San Jacinto, he was absolutely on it.

We were grateful to Gizz Lazlo for rescuing the situation but conversely resentful of Jamie for taking off to go play with a band of lesser standing which only sporadically gigged. As Nicky Garratt observed at the time, "He's just a kid who hasn't yet worked out where his bread is truly buttered."

I judge the North American Fiend Fest tour of 2006 to be among the best I've partaken in as a U.K. Sub. We'd really bonded with Jerry, Dez and the Misfits' crew, and it was because of the mutual esteem and genuine friendship fostered during that tour that we were invited to be the main support outfit for their 30th anniversary European excursion in 2007.

It was another enjoyable ramble with the New Jersey based group, made even more pleasurable because Marky Ramone had been replaced as drummer by another Black Flag alumnus – Robo. Perhaps the most memorable moments of the sojourn though, featured two of my own band members.

Toy Town Tosspots had already disbanded by the September of 2007, so we were reasonably confident that Jamie wasn't going to jump ship this time around. Following our soundcheck at the spacious Estragon concert hall in Bologna, Italy, and after Garratt and Harper had vacated the stage, I looked out with our drummer from the podium to the front of house and tried to estimate the potential audience capacity of the space. It seemed Oliver was more interested in another sort of 'what do you reckon?'

"See those barriers out there?" he was gesturing towards the tall metal barricade that had been erected some six feet (roughly two metres) from the lip of the stage, "Do you reckon I could clear that if I jumped from here?"

"You might," I replied "but if you didn't make it or landed badly, you would probably break a leg or an arm, or worse, and that would be the end of this tour for the U.K. Subs, so don't even think about trying it," I warned.

"Yeah, you're right" he said, but as we turned in unison to go join Chas and Nicky in the backstage green room, Jamie abruptly spun around and ran for the edge of the stage. I twisted about to see the crazy bastard launch himself off the rostrum. He cleared the top of the barriers alright,

but on landing forcefully on his feet, the room filled with the sound of his screams. I jumped down and saw he was in real pain. Resisting the urge to yell "Didn't I fucking tell you not to," I instead asked, "What's wrong, do you need medical help?"

"I'm OK, I'm OK," he doubly insisted, but I could see that wasn't the case. He then slowly shuffled his way to and through the doors at the side of the stage towards the catering area, still evidently in discomfort and wincing with every step.

When the tour had finished and he'd returned to the U.K., he went to his local hospital for an X-ray. It turned out he'd played out the remaining gigs with two severely fractured feet.

Really, what is it with drummers?

My second abiding remembrance of the 2007 Misfits Euro tour is a more pleasant one which has become a bit of a band legend in the years since it occurred:

Another soundcheck, however this time it was the Misfits testing their equipment and going through a couple of tunes to get the sound balance right for that evening's show in Solothurn, Switzerland.

Nicky Garratt and I had been watching from out front while awaiting our turn to get onstage to do the same with Harper and Oliver. When they'd finished their run through, he turned to me and said "You know that guy John up there who plays Jerry's bass at soundchecks?"

I was puzzled: "What guy John? What are you talking about?"

"You know, Jerry's bass tech John, who always wears a baseball cap and glasses, T-shirt and sweat pants. He was on the Fiend Fest tour too."

"Are you referring to the bloke who was just up on that stage playing bass guitar with Dez and Robo?"

"YES, Jerry's bass tech John!"

After I'd managed to quit laughing, I pointed out the error of Garratt's deluded belief: "There's no bass tech called John, you nutter. That is Jerry."

"What?"

"Yeah, that's how Jerry dresses when he's not in character onstage for the actual show. Fucking hell, you've done two Misfits' tours now thinking all the while that Jerry at soundcheck was a bass tech called John. And where did the name John come from? There is nobody called John on this tour nor was there anybody named John on the Fiend Fest caper. Unbelievable!"

I got a lot of humorous mileage out of Garratt's confusion although to be fair, dressed down like that in his specs, sans his devil lock quiff, without makeup and his horror film superhero stage outfits, the Misfits' singer/bassist did actually look more like a bass tech called John than Jerry Only.

My favourite Misfits memory though is not from a shared tour but the time the band came and stayed at my house in France. The context for this visit was as follows:

The U.K. Subs made our customary appearance at the Rebellion Festival in Blackpool in August 2013. It just so happened that the almighty Misfits were also on the festival's roster that year and having noticed their impressive Nightliner tour bus parked just outside the artists' entrance of the Winter Gardens – the regular location for this festival – I decided to call on Jerry and crew to say "Hi."

Having rapped on the door of the bus with my knuckles, it was Jerry's son, Jerry Junior, who answered. After we hugged, he invited me to come aboard to see his dad and Dez and subsequent to more "How are yas?" and hugs we sat down to catch up with what was new in the Misfits' and Subs' worlds. Having chatted together for over an hour, I got up to leave and casually said "Listen guys, if you're ever travelling down to my part of France, give me a call and come stay at my place. I'll show you around."

"Sure," said Jerry "We would love that," and after another round of hugs I left the bus and thought no more about my invitation, it having been a spontaneous, non-specific 'sometime in the future' type offer. A couple of days later I returned to France and noticed there was a series of messages which had been recorded on the answering service of my home phone.

Message #1: "Hey Alvin, it's Jerry Only, we're driving down to Spain for some shows and passing your place on the way. We've got two free days so thought we would swing by for a visit. We're on our way buddy, can't wait to see yas."

Message #2: "Hey Alvin, Jerry here. Where are you pal? The Misfits are coming to see you and your pops, so get ready for our arrival, we're gonna be hungry so maybe get in some food for us, I'll reimburse yas later."

Message #3: "Its Jerry again, why aren't you picking up buddy? Be careful of what you wish for… ha, ha, ha! We'll get to yours sometime in the afternoon tomorrow, hope that's OK?"

There were a couple more which followed that trio, in which Jerry sounded increasingly sceptical about the validity of my invitation and I could tell by the tenor of his voice that he was concerned I wouldn't be there upon their arrival. When I'd discovered these messages it was already gone 1pm on the estimated day that the Misfits were due to get to Bordeaux. There were also emails from their new tour manager – Tank had unfortunately retired and been replaced – to which I emailed back: 'I've just got home and seen and heard all the messages. Its fine, I'm here now. See you soon.'

Luckily my friend Patrick Kerrane and his wife Sarah, who have a holiday home close to mine in France, stopped by to help me shop for food and to get in more bottles of wine to add to the tally sitting in my sizable wine-rack. Afterwards, in my kitchen, they assisted me in getting a meat sauce and a separate vegetarian one a-simmering to add to the packets of pasta I'd bought for my visitors' meal that evening. Later, having taken a break from cooking to drink a glass of white together in my outside dining area, we witnessed through the gaps in my tall iron gates a huge vehicle towing a large trailer come to a stop in front of my house. The Misfits had arrived.

My invitation had essentially been directed at Jerry and his son, to Dez and their excellent new drummer Eric Arce – who'd previously played with Murphy's Law – but when the band and its entire crew turned up, I realised I would now be hosting 10 people, rather than the four I'd formerly envisaged.

It turned into a wonderful evening. My father got on great with our visitors, regaled them with his army stories, had me uncork numerous bottles of my wine for everyone to guzzle and, post meal, got out his cigars and cognac which we smoked and drank under the stars in the warm August night until the early hours of the next morning.

I was able to put half of our guests up in the house to sleep, whilst the remainder took to their bunks in the bus parked outside. We were all really intoxicated when we'd retired and, as a consequence, it was with a pulsating hangover that I awoke at 9am to the sounds of the Misfits' latest album The Devil's Rain, blasting out of my sound system in the lounge two floors below my bedroom whilst being simultaneously aware of some shouting and activity going on in the courtyard.

Having gently prised myself out of bed and sheepishly descended the stairs to the lounge whilst trying not to puke, I noted the band had turned the room into a temporary gymnasium. Jerry Only, Jerry junior and Eric Arce were taking it in turns to pump iron on a contraption designed for this activity and there were weights and pieces of gym equipment taken from their bus scattered all over the place.

Seeing my pale, hung-over-self framed in the doorway, Jerry shouted over the music to me "Hey Alvin, come join us buddy, you'll feel a lot better if you get some blood pumping around your body." To which, I replied: "Fuck that Jerry, the only thing I want pumping around my body is caffeine. I'm in desperate need of coffee… want some?"

The noises emanating from my courtyard were due to Dez and the crew being in the midst of a game of American football. They were running around, tackling each other, throwing the ball about and yelling "Touchdown!" whenever one of them made it to one or the other end of the outdoor space.

'What is it with these people?' I thought to myself, 'Why can't they just moan and whinge and try to sleep off their hangovers after being on the sauce all night like normal people?'

In the afternoon I took them all on a tour of my town. They were fascinated by the 12th century chateaux which dominates the ville and the churches and other buildings that date back to the time of the crusades. As we walked along one of the narrow streets, a teenage lad and his mother approached us from the other direction. As they got

Me and the Misfits (minus Dez Cadena), out front of my house, France, 2013.

closer, I saw the young man grab his mother's arm and say something to her in an excited way. When they reached us, he looked directly at Jerry and said in perfect English – it turned out his mother was originally from London – "Hey are you in the Misfits?" to which Jerry replied "Yep, sure am, good to meet ya kid."

Still hardly believing his musical heroes were casually strolling about this small rural French town, the 'kid' exclaimed they were his favourite band ever and invited us all to a party which he and his mum were going to attend that evening. We agreed to go and armed with bottles of wine and Misfits' CD albums, T-shirts and posters which Dez and Jerry handed out to any guest who wanted them, we had a good time at the party, drinking Bordeaux red and chatting to the other attendees, with the teenage kid still not quite being able to believe he was hanging out with the Misfits at a social event in the Aquitaine region.

Later that night, when the party had finished, the band and crew left for Spain. They'd all previously done their laundry at mine, purchased food supplies from my local Intermarché supermarket and were taking away a couple of bottles of local wine I'd gifted them for the journey. Before splitting, Jerry gave me and my father a T-shirt, a Devil's Rain CD and a signed poster a-piece. On my poster, along with his signature, he'd inscribed 'Alvin, you rock!' – this being a very Jerry thing to have written.

Even though there has been no return visit as yet, I've stayed in touch with Jerry Only and Dez Cadenza by phone and email. When my father died in 2016, Jerry very kindly called me to commiserate and told me how much he'd enjoyed hanging out with my dad at my place. That same year he joined up with Glenn Danzig, his brother Doyle and, along with Dave Lombardo of Slayer fame on drums, began playing shows under the banner of the Misfits' 'original line-up'.

When he called to tell me about this reunion whilst they were still at the rehearsal stage, I asked him how things were going with Danzig and Doyle, both of whom Jerry had seriously fallen out with in the past and had not spoken to for years. "So far, so good," he told me, and then added "At least no punches have been thrown yet, so I guess you could call that progress."

SINGLE ROOMS

After supporting the Misfits on their 30th anniversary Euro tour, a development occurred which I deemed both underhand and unnecessary. In the late November of 2007 I received a telephone call in France from a friend in the U.K. We chatted about what had recently transpired in our lives and then he said: "By the way, I'm going to see the Subs play in London on December the seventh."

I was surprised by this news: "Really? I didn't realise we were playing in London next month, what's the venue?"

He was astonished at my ignorance: "Oh, don't you know? Charlie has reformed the Garratt, Slack and Davies line-up. I thought he would have told you."

He hadn't. Nobody had; and the person I was most upset with regarding this secretive manoeuvre was Nicky Garratt.

It was characteristic of Harper not to bother telling someone who'd played for so many years in the service of the Subs and had driven the band for no additional money on numerous North American tours; who'd participated in Subs' Canadian and South American ventures and whom he'd travelled with across the length and latitude of continental Europe and the U.K. on multiple occasions, that they were casually being set aside and replaced by a bassist who hadn't had any dealings with the band since 1980. But for some reason, I'd assumed Garratt possessed a greater sense of loyalty than that, and so it was Nicky I called and confronted, to get an explanation as to what was occurring.

Having clarified that I'd just found out from a friend that this reunion was taking place and I was therefore offended that he'd not seen fit to at least inform me about what had been planned, he tried to dismiss the reunification project as something unimportant and not worth notifying me about:

"It's just something Charlie wanted to do which I agreed to be a part of, although I don't see the point of it really; but, you know, it's no big deal," he then added "although I've got to say he's paying each of us (Slack, Davies and himself) far more money for this forthcoming tour than he's ever paid me or you in the past." Which I guess, bizarrely, he thought would somehow make me feel better about having been side-lined. Unsurprisingly, this additional piece of information only engendered the opposite effect.

I didn't know at that point whether it would be just a one-off U.K. tour or a more permanent situation, with European and States-side visits to follow for the museum line-up; but I guess, apart from a well-attended London gig, the tour wasn't the success Harper had been hoping for and following completion of their nine British dates, that same dramatis personae wouldn't play another show together again.

Still, I was sore that I hadn't at least been notified about the reunion ahead of time and was equally mystified as to why Charlie had even thought it was a good idea in the first place. I know nostalgia is a powerful thing and that there would have certainly been a quantity of the band's fans who'd welcomed this simulated recreation of their past – an attempt to relive a time long gone when as energetic young men or women they'd first encountered the Subs in the late-1970s – but the truth is, it would merely be an illusion.

For better or worse, each reasonably stable ensemble of the U.K. Subs throughout the years has been of its own time and possessed its own cyclic value. Trying to recreate the same experience decades later is simply unrealistic, as was proven by the disastrous attempt to reform the early-1980s Harper, Garratt, Gibbs, Steve Roberts line-up in 2002.

The other possible reason for Harper wanting this restoration might have been for the extra money he could charge promoters for a version of the Subs which had not played together for 27 years. As the Misfits had learned, and more recently, The Damned, by suddenly gigging under the banner of 'original line-up' you can significantly hoist up fees and potentially attract a bigger audience from among the nostalgia freaks – even though, when it came to Paul Slack and Pete Davies, this wasn't even the case as the 'original' bassist was in fact Paul's brother Steve, whilst the first Subs' drummer hadn't been Davies but Robbie Harper.

However, if money and attendance were the principal motivations, this too proved illusionary. Charlie himself told me that apart from the London Astoria 2 show which did attract a full crowd and yielded good financial remuneration, all the other gigs were not as well attended and as profitable as anticipated. He even divulged that one of the gig promoters had run off with the ticket money, thereby obliging Harper to pay the other band members and crew out of his own pocket.

As a result of these thwarted expectations, the day after their final reunion show in Leeds, Charlie called to ask if I would go over to the U.K. to play a series of gigs with the Subs, starting in Exeter on the 13th of December, finishing up in Blackburn on the 23rd. Despite my dissatisfaction about the way I'd been shelved without prior notification, I've always considered myself a resolute professional and this was paying work in the service of the U.K. Subs. Moreover, Chas had sweetened the invitation by undertaking to increase my per-gig fee and had assured

Playing a rowdy show at The Barfly, Glasgow, Scotland, 2007.

me hotels had been booked for the band for every city we were going to be playing in.

The band membership for this series of dates was significant. Joining Harper, Jamie Oliver and I onstage for these shows was a guitarist that I'd only played with once before, at the Kanalrock Festival in Norway, roughly four months prior to the tour commencing Exeter gig.

Jet Storm – as he then billed himself – was a Japanese friend of Charlie's spouse Yuko. She'd suggested to her husband using him as a stand-in guitar player in 2006, and he'd filled in on an irregular basis from that time forward whenever Alan Campbell or Nicky Garratt were unavailable until he eventually became the Subs' principal axe-man in 2011.

He wasn't a conventional Punk rock guitarist. His musical influences were more Guns N' Roses and Hanoi Rocks than The Clash or Sex Pistols, and he'd confided to me that he'd seen my 1990s Rock band Cheap And Nasty when we'd played Tokyo in '94, and that he'd humbly asked me to autograph his copy of the Beautiful Disaster album before the show.

Even though at that time Jet's playing was still a bit uneven, I appreciated his more classic rock 'n' roll approach to the guitar work he was providing and the fresh impetus it bequeathed the songs, plus, I got on reasonably well with him as a personality.

This particular assemblage would eventually solidify into a settled

Rosamunde Parsons, the year of our Scottish reunion, 2007.

working unit, a real band that essentially dispensed with the Harper preferred chaotic 'whoever was available' approach, and together we would go on to write and record the critically praised quartet of albums: Work in Progress, XXIV, Yellow Leader, and Ziezo.

The other noteworthy event as a consequence of this December sequence of gigs was my reconnection with Rosamunde Parsons, who turned up for our Barfly show in Glasgow and whom I'd not seen since my Cheap And Nasty tenure back in the early-1990s. Those of you who have already read Volume II of this memoir trilogy might recall Rosamunde and I had enjoyed an intermittent romantic liaison, which would be consummated whenever C 'n' N ventured up to Scotland to perform. We were both happy to be in each other's company again after such a long period of separation and, although she was now in another relationship and I wasn't looking to start one, before she left the venue to return home – as recollected in a future song composed and recorded for my first solo album – we 'joined lips and started our dance.' And that's a volta that has endured right up to the present day.

Despite the extra occupational travel entailed by my relocation to south-west France, I nonetheless truly loved living there; although there were certainly things that I missed as a consequence of no longer being based in London. Shorinji Kempo training for one, as having reached black belt level there were advanced techniques which are only disclosed to Shodan and higher graded students which I could have been learning and adding to my martial arts' cache; and no longer being able to see Crystal Palace F.C. play at Selhurst Park stadium on a regular basis was certainly a downer. Still, the pleasure I got from the warmer climate, culture and lifestyle of the beautiful French region I'd moved to, far outweighed any of the former fixations I'd relinquished.

As for my love life, having been sexually faithful to my wife Trine Karlsen for the duration of our marriage meant that now being divorced, allowed me once more the freedom to enjoy intimacy with other women. It was a liberation I took full advantage of.

There were the usual opportunities for dalliances on tour, which I indulged in from time-to-time, although with a lot more decorum and selectivity than had been the case in my younger days. I also dated a number of women for shorter and lengthier periods, both in France and the U.K.

Having had another marriage end in failure meant I wasn't yet interested in any committed amorous involvements so I would state at the commencement of all my liaisons something along the lines of: "I'm not looking for a long-term romance, so if at any time I want to end our relationship and move on, it's to be accepted. Likewise if you wish to end it at any point, I'll be fine with that too. I'm just being totally honest upfront but, if that's not what you're looking for, then OK, no problem, we won't get together."

Does this declaration strike you as being as taciturn and impersonal as it seems to me now? And yet it eloquently reveals the psychology of

Euro tour, 2008.

my mind during that period – too anxious to commit because of fear of failure; the deluded belief that 'the perfect one' was still out there and would stroll into my life any time soon; my compulsion to undermine a relationship with whoever my femme de jour was, when things were going too well and I'd started to detect some tender feelings ascending on the emotional horizon.

Despite all the women I dated during this aftermath divorce decade of the 2000s, having agreed to my terms of involvement at the start, when I inevitably informed them I no longer wanted to continue the relationship after a few weeks, months, or, in a couple of rare cases, a year or more's duration, they would, with one or two notable exceptions, get upset and accuse me of being an emotional eunuch and a happiness avoider – which is exactly what I thought I'd communicated to them from the off.

My theory for this phenomenon is that there were those who heard what I was saying whilst simultaneously thinking 'I can change this person; I can make them content and whole again via the magic of my personality and the magnitude of my attentiveness', but trying to alter someone to how you want them to be rather than what they are is rarely, if ever, a successful strategy. And in my case, it took many years and a singular woman before I was ready to embark on changing myself for myself, and to be willing and capable of entering into a committed relationship.

After accomplishing another epic Euro tour with the Subs during the first two months of 2008 – 33 gigs in total, taking in territories as diverse as Germany, Croatia, Poland, Czech Republic, Hungary, Switzerland, Slovakia, Spain, France, Italy, Netherlands, Belgium, and Austria – I returned home having, the week before, in Stuttgart Germany, reached the milestone age of the big five-oh.

It had been another energy depleting, sleep deprived campaign but, thankfully, with all the familiar compensations to help lessen the sheer grind of travelling thousands of miles to get to the numerous venues in multiple cities across the European continent. There had also been some additional plusses to commend the tour.

Whilst on the Euro road the year before, I had told Charlie I didn't think he was paying the band a fair wage. In 2000, on my first major European venture with the Subs after having left the band with Garratt and Wylie back in 1983, Harper had paid us a mere €30 apiece per day. Two Euro tours later and it had only increased to a still paltry €60 – that's a combined total of just €180 for Nicky, Jason and I each day with Chas getting much more than that for himself from just the merchandise sales at each show alone – and we were still receiving that same measly amount after Jamie replaced Jason in 2005.

For 2006 and 2007, there was still no increase in our remunerations, so I decided to tackle the subject head-on with Harper and, to his credit, he accepted that what we were receiving was poor compensation for the effort, time and energy we were putting into these tours. Following a discussion with Kurt – still then our Tour Manager – he raised it to €100, although he added that days off would no longer be covered.

At a later date on that 2007 excursion, whilst travelling in the van together, I also pushed for something else I thought was a perfectly reasonable request, a modification which would help make the long and arduous Euro tours more pleasant:

"Charlie, why don't we contact I.B.D. (the Subs' Euro agency of the time) and ask them to get promoters to provide single rooms for every member of the touring party for next year rather than just the double for you and the twins for us? Having to share a hotel room for five weeks with someone is really difficult, you know, waiting for whoever you're sharing with to use the bathroom in the morning before being able to piss, shower or shave; having to put up with their snoring and not be able to bring a woman back after the show or invite people over for a drink out of consideration for the other person. What do you think?"

Harper always had a hotel room for himself with his wife while the rest of us had to negotiate who we would share with in a twin, which wasn't much of a choice really. Say if Garratt happened to be my roommate, even though it was winter with a below zero temperature outside, he would insist on having all the windows open – causing the room to become meat-locker cold – or start up with his incessant coughing whilst claiming he couldn't breathe. On one notable occasion I shared with him, Nicky opened up the skylight windows whilst I was having a shower. When I'd towelled down and walked from the bathroom to my bed, it was covered in a thick blanket of snow. He'd completely ignored the fact that there was a blizzard in progress and had allowed the sleet and snowflakes to descend from the unlocked apertures above.

If it was Jamie I shared with, there were other difficulties. Virtually every night he'd go out after a gig to some club or bar until the early hours of the morning and if he'd not managed to hook up with a girl and mercifully gone to stay at her place, he would always return in a wasted state. On numerous occasions after he had realised he'd forgotten or lost his key, the inebriated drummer would then wake me up by pounding on our hotel room door to gain entry. If Jamie actually managed to get into the room without my assistance, the situation wouldn't be much better. He'd proceed to bang about and knock over furniture in his intoxicated state and then always prolonged the agony by ceaselessly snoring once he'd finally slumped onto his bed, usually while still fully clothed.

This was why I wanted single rooms for the entire band, so that I could have a decent night's sleep without getting pneumonia if sharing with Garratt, and Oliver could go about his post-show socialising without disturbing me afterwards. Charlie, although having been sympathetic to my push for better wages, thought this an insane request:

"Are you fucking kidding, nobody will book us if we ask for single rooms for everybody, and anyway, it's only you that wants this, isn't it?" to which Nicky, Jamie and Kurt immediately disputed Harper's assertion by telling him they too wanted their own room.

"Let's ask," I countered "if you don't ask, you don't get and I'm positive promoters will agree to this in order to book the U.K. Subs."

"Well you contact Andrea then" he snarled, "I'm not asking for something that's going to lead to no one wanting to have the band play their venues."

So that's what I did. Sure enough, for the 2008 European tour which, as I've already reported was one of the most extensive and successful the Subs had undertaken, every single promoter I.B.D. contacted about this

alteration to our usual contract arrangements agreed to the new single rooms policy; and it has remained so ever since.

This reveals another facet of Harper's character from that time. He didn't want to ask or argue for anything that would improve either the earning capacity or the touring conditions of the band – especially if they didn't affect him personally – because Charlie had an odd fear of becoming unpopular with those he should have been assertive with, while conversely, being abrupt and sometimes verbally aggressive to those closest to him who he should have stood up for.

For a long time Chas never truly valued what he and the U.K. Subs provided and represented. It was just a means of scraping a living together for him, happy to accept whatever was offered whilst, mostly, being content to play the same core set of songs with numerous alternating combos devoid of any long term strategy or ambition. He had also mythologised the Subs' years post 1983 up until the stable Gibbs, Oliver, Jet partnership – a fabrication which, no doubt, he will spin in his forthcoming book – recollecting to people how great things were when he was solely in charge of his alternating pack of sidekicks, then recounting the anarchic escapades they had together, some of which can seem funny now, but must have been nightmarish at the time. The stark truth is, during those intervening years things were far from great. In fact they were pretty dire.

Charlie himself told me that an audience of just 50 was considered a good turnout for the group during the late-1980s and early-to-mid

'90s and a mate of mine who used to go see them perform back then, told me he went to a Subs' gig where only five people, himself included, turned up to see them play. When in more recent times the ex-singer of the Adverts, TV Smith, took over from The Vibrators as our regular Euro tour support, he confided to me that the band during that era was considered "a joke" by many within the Punk scene, and the money they earned playing in clubs and bars, was laughable too.

Another friend, who was working away from home in London during this time duration, visited Harper at his bedsit situated above a tube station. Charlie said he would take this mutual pal of ours for a beer at his local pub. He then reached for a large glass bottle that contained loose change, poured the contents on the floor, and started counting out the pennies which had emerged. After a short period of time he ceased his counting and announced "Oh, I'm sorry, I don't have enough here for one beer, let alone two." The friend told him not to worry and instead paid for all the drinks they shared that evening.

Once I.B.D. began to book the annual European tours, the Subs' yearly income improved somewhat; but even when I started playing with the group in the mid-1990s, Harper's then U.K. agent, Toxin, was only able to negotiate fees of around £200 to £250 a show, from which Charlie had to pay him 10%, as well as forking out for van hire, fuel, a driver and the wages of whoever he had managed to prise out to represent the band for whatever gig had been offered. The Subs were hardly dripping in the syrup of success. These were far from being the halcyon days that Chas now recollects.

However, as the first 10 years of the millennium yielded to a second decade, a coalition formed within the U.K. Subs which significantly raised the prestige of the band along with its work rate and earning power. Central to this beneficial alliance would be Charlie's wife, Yuko Morinaga.

FUCK ALVIN AND FUCK HIS DOG!

Yuko Morinaga left her native country of Japan and relocated to the U.K. in 2001, ostensibly to study English language at a London college. A month or so after her arrival a friend introduced her to Charlie Harper. Within a matter of days following their introduction they began dating, and shortly thereafter, living together at Chas' flat in Finsbury Park. One year later, on the 19th of October 2002, to be precise, the couple got hitched at the Islington Town Hall Registry Office on Upper Street, North London.

I first met Yuko during their pre-marriage period and assumed she was going to be yet another one of Harper's short-term girlfriends. Her English was limited at that time so my conversations with her were always restricted to simple phrases – "How are you?", "Would you like a drink?", "Are you enjoying college?" – to which she would give minimal replies without elaboration due to her still limited vocabulary. It came as somewhat of a surprise then when I heard they'd become husband and wife.

As her language skills improved, she was told, and initially believed, the narrative Charlie had constructed and promoted regarding his version of the past and present of the U.K. Subs. How Garratt, Wylie and I had left the band because we wanted to be Rock stars; how it made no difference who was in his backing band, no matter how under-rehearsed, incompetent or unsuitable they were, as long as he, the star, was present; how his chaotic manner of doing business, his insistence in persisting to pay an agent who was only capable of negotiating a gig fee which would mean he'd barely make any money after expenses was, nevertheless, a satisfactory way to continue. And his bizarre contention, which I've heard on numerous occasions, that "allowing people to exploit and take advantage of the Subs has been the making of the band."

But as time moved on and Yuko came to understand the true and stark reality of the Subs' situation rather than the idealistic picture her husband was propagating, she realised things had to change or the band would become so devalued as a professional outfit that its very existence would be in jeopardy and her future life with Charlie would be one of insecurity and penury.

To this end, she slowly started to take over the day-to-day running of the Subs and began instituting a more rational and methodical approach to gigging and business affairs – making sure the transport and participating musicians had been hired in good time and that an offered show actually made financial and logistical sense to play, as well as ordering and then selling the merchandise at venues. It has to be recorded though that these important alterations were not universally appreciated by everybody involved in the band despite the obvious benefits they bestowed, mainly because it was Charlie's wife who was establishing them. Some – no names given – resented her input, saw it as unnecessary interference and started referring to the group as the 'Yuko Subs' as a put down.

There's a popular narrative in Rock music of wives and female partners of musicians gradually gaining control of their spouse's careers and using their intimate proximity to unduly influence decision making and professional direction; and, in some exceptional cases, to even become a band member themselves. Yoko Ono and Linda McCartney for example, and the memorable fictional character Jeanine, who plays the girlfriend of lead singer and guitarist David St. Hubbins in the brilliant 1984 spoof Rockumentary (the director's concocted word, not mine) – This is Spinal Tap.

The movie is about a fabricated British Hard rock band on the slide who tour the U.S.A. in the hope of reviving their former popularity there. At some point during the film, much to the annoyance of lead guitarist Nigel Tufnel, played by actor Christopher Guest, St. Hubbins' needy and pushy lover arrives and after firstly undermining the manager and eventually forcing him to quit, takes over management duties herself and starts dictating where they should play and how they should dress – as signs of the zodiac, it would seem.

Having then destabilised and done away with Tufnel, she ends up playing tambourine on stage with the newly augmented version of Tap who perform an excruciating 40 minute-long freeform musical extravaganza entitled Jazz Odyssey on their debut at a fairground appearance where she'd managed to negotiate them a bigger dressing room than the puppets in the Puppet Show act that'd preceded them.

I'm sure there have been a few Jeanines over the years that have used their relationship with a band member in order to further the ambitions of their partner and themselves and have encouraged challenges to anyone within the group hierarchy who stood in the way of their pursuit of ascendency. But in reality, this Lady Macbeth syndrome is a rarity; and anyway, if the result is increased income, better shows, decent hotels, more comfortable and reliable transportation and greater surety and stability for every member of a band, who cares if the provider is the wife, husband or partner of someone within the group?

Now I have to admit, at first, when Yuko started to get more and more involved in the Subs' affairs, I too raised an eyebrow and was worried that her interest was only in getting the best for her husband and consequently herself, without due consideration for the wider membership of the U.K. Subs. However, as time moved on, I saw the

Yuko and I, at the Jim Sinn store, Tokyo, Japan.

evident advantages of extracting Charlie from the business decision making process, which allowed him to concentrate on what he excels at – writing memorable songs, singing and performing – plus I appreciated her implementation of a more structured and sensible approach to touring and commercial considerations.

To this end, the first controversial move on Yuko's part was to insist her husband ditch Toxin as the Subs' U.K. agent. Toxin is a personable and decent man, but an ambitious and methodical agent he was not. He'd kept the band on a small clubs, bars and pubs level with scant fiscal rewards for far too long, and we all knew it. All, that is, apart from Charlie. Yuko has disclosed to me she had terrible arguments with him about this issue. Chas maintaining Toxin was his friend and he didn't want to change agents on that basis whilst she asserted, friend of not, he was doing the minimum and had no interested in raising the status or fees of the band, and that he only wanted to maintain the same circuit of low paying small venues in order to make some cash to finance his social life and to brag he was the Subs' live show facilitator.

She ultimately won that argument and via recommendations from other bands encountered at festivals and on the road, in November 2006, Yuko asked Darren Griffiths and his Crucial Talent Agency to be sole representatives of the Subs for the British Isles. Darren was immediately able to almost double the group's previous standard fee for a series of shows that same month in Manchester, Glasgow, York, and Mansfield and began working on getting the band out of its tired, repetitive small venues routine. In due course he secured for us some of the most interesting work of the band's career, including a very memorable tour with Motörhead and support slots with, among other notable premiership-level Punk headliners, The Damned, Stiff Little Fingers and Rancid.

Griffiths continues to be the Subs' U.K. agent and he's undoubtedly been another instrumental figure in helping to raise the band's status within the Punk scene and for returning it to the viable, fully professional outfit it had formerly been in the late 1970s and early 1980s.

Although I recognised the value in Yuko taking over the essential running of the Subs, we nevertheless still had our ups and downs and disagreements regarding some aspects of the band's plans and activities. The reformation of the Garratt, Slack and Davies line-up for a tour in 2007 for instance – of which I've already shared I received no notification in advance from Yuko, Charlie or Garratt – and then, a year or so later, Paul Slack suddenly being awarded the bass guitar role for all U.K. shows, this once more having occurred without discussion or notice beforehand. Despite still being able to play the Euro and North American tours I couldn't understand why I was abruptly denied these British dates.

I believe Slack, having enjoyed playing with the Subs during the 2007 reunion tour, had set about campaigning for his return to the group via numerous telephone calls to Charlie and Yuko, and that they eventually acquiesced to his involvement. For their part, this may have been motivated by the opportunity to save some money as Paul lived in England at that time whilst I was based in France, which meant having to pay out for my fares to and from these Channel divided countries.

Considering all the touring, song writing, recording and sheer exertion I'd put into the Subs since the Quintessentials and Riot albums of 1996 and the subsequent Harper, Garratt, Gibbs reunion tour of the U.S.A. in '97, I was again troubled that my hard work and long-term input was being disregarded to save a few quid and that someone who'd had nothing to do with the band, apart from one minor tour over a period of 27 years, was able to tango right back in and take my place. I also found out there was a plan afoot to make a new album with this alternative group of actors, which was a much more serious proposition.

And yet, I had the tangible feeling that things would swing back my way, a powerful intuition which, less than 12 months later, proved to be accurate.

During the Covid lockdown period of 2020, I did the last of a series of phone interviews which had been intermittently taking place over a number of years with Marc Brekau, the author of a forthcoming book on the Subs entitled Born a Rocker, Die a Rocker. As this particular interview proceeded, he asked how I'd managed to again return to playing every tour with the group after Paul Slack had already been admitted back to participate in all the British based shows. Before I gave my answer, he revealed what Slack had stated to him about his ousting – that Yuko had telephoned him and said I'd called her and asked to replace Paul in order to again provide my bass playing for every gig, adding that my pet dog of the time, Jack, was ill and I needed to raise extra money by doing as many shows as possible to pay for his expensive veterinary bills.

This was untrue. The reality is Yuko called my house in France and asked me to resume playing with the Subs. When I enquired why they no longer wanted Paul involved, she disclosed they'd had "problems" with him – I'll not go into details about these 'problems' as some of them were of a personal and private nature and for that reason it would be unfair to reveal them – and they (Chas and Yuko) now wanted me to return to playing all U.K. shows as well everything overseas.

I agreed to perform every live gig with the band and added that the timing was fortuitous as my dog did indeed need an operation and the additional cash would be welcome. Yuko then called Slack and told him what I believe is exactly what he'd claimed to Marc Brekau – that I wanted him ejected and not the other, factual, way around to which, according to Yuko, he angrily exclaimed "Well fuck Alvin and fuck his dog," before terminating the call. This is something he would never have said to my face, with good reason.

It was also during these fading months of the initial decade of the new millennium, that the Subs parted company with Nicky Garratt. The split had been brewing for a while.

Garratt had no interest in playing guitar for any U.K. dates at this point. He was only intent on participating in the Euro, North American and the very rare overseas' visits to territories such as Brazil, Argentina, Australia or New Zealand. He would always chide me when we toured together in Europe by asking "Why do you still want to play those shitholes in Britain? I wouldn't want to be wasting my time doing that."

I explained it was paying work, and anyway, things had improved for the band there since Yuko had effectively become our manager and the Crucial Talent Agency had become involved. But when the gigs with Motörhead came about, Nicky suddenly became very enthusiastic about touring his former homeland and phoned me to ask for my assistance in getting Jet dropped so that he could instead play the prestigious venues where we were due to support Lemmy and co.

My response to this request was unequivocal. I told him it would be totally unfair for the band to drop Jet as he'd been the man who had been prepared to play all the "shitholes" Garratt had scorned and also very disrespectful to deny him the chance to perform on the forthcoming larger stages and replace him with someone who wasn't prepared to do the more insignificant dates. To his credit Nicky told me he absolutely understood and respected my position. But I could tell he wasn't exactly happy with my rebuttal.

OK, we've now touched on the Motörhead cavort, so let's take a brief chronological detour so I can relay to you the highlights of this memorable experience.

When Darren Griffiths informed us of our addition to the 2011 Motörhead touring bill along with the Anti-Nowhere League, I was properly excited at the prospect of playing a series of shows in Britain with Lemmy Kilmister, Phil Campbell and Mikkey Dee.

There were 11 gigs booked – Wolverhampton, Civic Hall; Newcastle, City Hall; Glasgow, O2 Academy; Liverpool, Mountford University; Bristol, Colston Hall; Norwich, UEA; London, Hammersmith HMV Apollo; Plymouth, Pavilions; Southampton, Guildhall; Nottingham, Royal Concert Hall and Manchester, O2 Apollo.

Along with a reasonable portion of already committed Subs' fans attending these shows, each venue would also expose us to a new audience and potentially attract a fresh wave of additional punters to our own gigs from amongst the Motörhead faithful. This turned out to be the case. For years after and up to the present day, we've had young men with long hair and Ace of Spades T-shirts join our mainly Punk-centric crowd to enjoy the music they'd discovered on that tour and which they'd appreciated wasn't so dissimilar to their normally preferred Metal rock noise.

However, before a mile could be travelled or a lick played, there was the subject of the billing of the two support bands to be resolved. Being the more senior and well-known outfit I assumed, as did many others in the Punk scene, that the U.K. Subs would be playing just prior to MH, with the Anti-Nowhere League opening proceedings. But Darren Griffiths, who was agent for both groups, told us that lead singer Nick Culmer (aka Animal) was insisting that they be the main support act and the Subs should be the first group to take to the stage. I countered with a compromise. Each night we would swop places on the bill, ANL opening the first night, the Subs opening the second, then vice versa, and so on.

motörhead

ANTi-NOWHERE LEAGUE

PLUS SPECIAL GUESTS **U.K. SUBS**

NOVEMBER

WED	2	WOLVERHAMPTON CIVIC HALL	0870 320 7000
THU	3	NEWCASTLE CITY HALL	0191 261 2606
SAT	5	GLAGOW O2 ACADEMY	0844 477 2000
SUN	6	LIVERPOOL MOUNTFORD UNIVERSITY	0151 256 5555
TUE	8	BRISTOL COLSTON HALL	0117 922 3686
FRI	11	NORWICH UEA	01603 508 050
SAT	12	LONDON HAMMERSMITH HMV APOLLO	0844 844 4748
MON	14	PLYMOUTH PAVILIONS	0845 146 1460
TUE	15	SOUTHAMPTON GUILDHALL	023 8063 2601
THU	17	NOTTINGHAM ROYAL CONCERT HALL	0115 989 5555
FRI	18	MANCHESTER O2 APOLLO	0844 477 2000

BUY ONLINE AT LIVENATION.CO.UK
www.imotorhead.com   THE ALBUM 'THE WORLD IS YOURS' OUT NOW
A LIVE NATION PRESENTATION IN ASSOCIATION WITH THE AGENCY GROUP

This seemed a perfectly reasonable resolution to me and it may have panned out that way until Charlie decided it wasn't an issue and told Griffiths that he didn't care if we were first on at every show. Such outright capitulation rather than taking a stand and reaching a suitable settlement because he didn't want to be personally unpopular is typical of Chas' character. And the fact is such things do matter.

The music biz is as much about perception as realities. Even if in truth you're not as popular as the group below you on a bill and draw fewer ticket buyers to your gigs, your higher status in a running order gives the impression that you are a more in-demand band. The tangible consequence of that perception is you can command better money and acquire greater prestige than those lower down on the roster.

Nick Culmer, who is a long-time friend of mine – we first met in 1982 when the ANL were the Subs' support act for a North American tour – certainly understood this, and I didn't blame him in the least for pushing for what was in the best interests of his group. It's a pity though that our supposed leader hadn't backed me and held firm in order to achieve the same for the U.K. Subs. Such politics aside, it turned out to be a really enjoyable and insightful fortnight on the road in the company of both bands.

When we arrived backstage for the inaugural show in Wolverhampton, the first person we met was Motörhead's fabled caterer Richie Dunkin. I'd met Richie once before, when Charlie, Yuko, Captain Sensible, and I had attended a MH show together the year before in Brighton. On that occasion, having utilised our passes to make our way to the hospitality room, I noticed there were only bottles of Jack Daniel's available, so I said to Dunkin "Hey pal, it seems there's only JD to drink here," to which he replied, "What did you think you'd find backstage at a Motörhead gig, you daft cunt!" I became good mates with the expletive-lobbing Scotsman there and then. It was a bonus to be reunited with him for the tour, to hang out with the big man, drinking large tumblers of whiskey with just a droplet of Cola and polishing off the fine wines he'd got in especially for me.

As we progressed from city to city, stage to stage, I came to understand the mechanics of the MH touring machine. It was no surprise that Lemmy had written (We Are) The Roadcrew as a thank you to those who assembled the equipment, P.A. and lights each day, and whom he considered "the best roadcrew in the world." They were all, to a chap, decent, industrious people, and I'm happy to report they really appreciated the Subs' down-to-earth, no-nonsense approach to our work. On that basis we quickly bonded with this formidable band of road warriors – at one point during the tour my speaker cabinet lost one of its rubber feet, which caused it to wobble and become unbalanced. Before we took to the stage the next evening, one of the MH crew had spotted this defect and replaced the part without my even having asked for assistance. They were indeed a special group of people.

What I was surprised about though, was the personal dynamic between the members of the band. The only time you saw Lemmy, Phil and Mikkey together was either for the soundcheck – I seem to recall

Supporting Motörhead, Hammersmith Apollo, London, 2011.

the Bob Seger song Rosalie, notably covered by Thin Lizzy, being a regular check tune – or jointly onstage for the actual show. The rest of the time they didn't socialise, had their own separate dressing rooms and groups of friends, and kept apart.

Phil Campbell was the most welcoming and warmest of the trio and it was his personal dressing room which Jamie Oliver and I would routinely visit at the end of the night to do some drinking, trade road stories and hang out in. Phil is an amazing guitarist and a very congenial person. I liked him a lot.

Mikkey was also friendly but there was always a little aloofness there, a touch of distance, which was somewhat understandable. As for Lemmy, I think I ran into him maybe four times during that entire tour. Twice when he was smoking a cigarette in a corridor of one of the venues we were due to play. Once when we fleetingly met as he arrived for a show; and lastly, when the Subs were all individually summoned to his dressing room for a chat and to have photos taken with the great man – I fondly remember on that occasion he had a one-armed bandit fruit machine in there ready to spin, which was conveyed by crew members to every one of his dressing rooms throughout the tour. It was just like the one I would see him feeding money into at the St. Moritz Club in Soho when I'd first met him back in 1979.

On each occasion he would ask me if we were being treated well by his people and how the Subs were faring with the MH audiences. I always replied the same way. That we were being treated exceptionally well by his catering staff and crew and once the crowd realised we played not so dissimilar music to his own, we would get a pretty good reception.

It may seem strange that my communications with Lemmy were limited to just a handful of occasions on such a substantial tour. But what we had no way of knowing at that time is that the primary reason for his low profile was due to him becoming increasingly unwell with the illness that would eventually see him run out of road.

FASCIST RESTAURANTS

As a result of Motörhead's founder and frontman's progressing ill health – eventually diagnosed as prostate cancer and cardiac arrhythmia – the tour's concerts at Bristol's Colston Hall and the UEA in Norwich were cancelled. However, an alternative explanation was given to both the Subs and the Anti-Nowhere League, a bogus account that was then shared with the press and social media.

According to the online Rock music platform Stereoboard.com, who were supplied by Motörhead HQ the same cancellation explanation for the pulled shows they'd conveyed to similar media outlets and to both support bands, the reason for these annulments was 'an injury iconic frontman Lemmy Kilmister sustained to his left hand which has left him unable to play.' Some other news outlets didn't specify Lemmy as the wounded party but simply presented the cause as down to an injury 'to one of the band's members.' Disappointed as we were to lose these two shows, the misfortune was offset a little when MH's management told us that both ANL and the Subs would be paid our playing fees in full. Knowing the reality of Lemmy's health, I guess they'd made sure the tour's insurance policy covered all eventualities.

Despite the minor handicap of having to kick off proceedings every evening, the nine shows we did get to play were pretty good for us. At a couple of gigs there were one or two Heavy Metal Luddites who couldn't resist shouting "Fuck off!" when we took to the stage, but after we'd torn into our ramming speed version of Disease – our nightly opening number – a majority of the audience would warm to us and we always managed to reap a good overall response.

Lemmy used to deal with this negligible Neanderthal clique in a sermon he would nightly preach at the midway point of MH's set:

"Some of you might be wondering why we've invited two Punk bands to join us for this tour rather than a routine Heavy Rock act. That's because there are only two types of music that matter – the music you like and music you don't like – and we like the music of the Anti-Nowhere League and the U.K. Subs."
Amen to that.

Predictably perhaps, the best audience response was at the Hammersmith Apollo in London. There was a hefty contingent of Subs' fans at that show and we really turned it on for them. The entire crowd rewarded us with the "U.K. Subs! U.K. Subs!" chant as we left the stage for the wings. It felt like it was one of our own shows rather than a support slot.

Alvin and Lemmy, 2011.

I celebrated this performance with some glasses of wine back in our dressing room with friends like Gaye Black (aka Gaye Advert), my long-time Croydonian mate Mel Wesson and our West Country contingent, Chris Long, Stubbsy and Darren Griffiths, the latter being the agent who'd skilfully finagled us onto the tour. Later on, having reached a loose and cheerful condition – code for semi-pissed – I went down to watch Motörhead play from a side of stage position where I happened to notice that Flea, the celebrated bassist from the Californian band Red Hot Chili Peppers, was also viewing the show a mere couple of metres or so to my right.

Those who have read my previous two volumes of memoirs will already be aware that when I've had a few drinks I can get a bit mouthy and mischievous. And so, after the Speed rock trio had finished, I walked up to Flea and said: "Listen mate, I've been told you're not a bad bassist; but if you really want to know how to properly play your four string machine, I'm prepared to offer you lessons at reasonable rates."

He looked at me blankly for a second or two until he couldn't suppress his laughter any longer: "Ha, ha, ha! OK man, sounds good, how much do you charge?" A response which conveyed to me that Flea is no stuffed capon – on the contrary, he's an equable fella imbued with a wholesome sense of humour.

The Motörhead tour of 2011 was another significant indicator that the Subs had irrevocably moved on and up from the dark days of small fees and disarray which had damaged the reputation of the band in Britain in the late-1980s and 1990s. It was one of the most memorable and gratifying ventures I've experienced as a Sub, with the only down aspects of the experience being Lemmy's ailing health and those subsequent, though completely understandable, gig cancellations.

He was also suffering from diabetes at the time, so after the wellbeing issues started to really affect his ability to work, the singer/bassist decided to make some changes to his diet and lifestyle. This included eating healthier foods and cutting out the Jack Daniel's in favour of drinking red wine. A year later, at a gig I'd attended where he was providing the catering, Richie told me Lemmy had indeed switched from whiskey to wine, but he was getting through three bottles of the stuff a day having supposed that, as it was his doctor who'd recommended the adjustment, this excessive daily dose was a perfectly acceptable amount. Despite the switcheroo wine therapy, his health and vigour continued to decline and many more Motörhead concerts had to be cancelled in the ensuing years.

Lemmy Kilmister finally succumbed to a combination of ailments on the 28th of December 2015, having only a few days before attained the age of 70. It was a real privilege to have known the man.

He was one of the last of a dying breed of road-hardened Rock musicians who began their careers in the 1960s and played on into the new millennium. I'll never forget his nightly declaration at each venue, delivered in that sonorous, gloriously gravelly voice; an uncompromising affirmation revealing the roots of the music his band proffered to the many thousands around the world who'd treasured their metallic Sturm und Drang for more than four decades: "We are Motörhead, and we play rock 'n' roll."

As I mentioned before we got into aspects of the Motörhead escapade, Nicky Garratt's association with the U.K. Subs had been gradually, but inexorably reaching its cessation with the termination process markedly accelerating during the course of the Subs' winter Euro tour of 2010.

As the tour progressed, Garratt started pushing for the band to make a future album of faster, more Hardcore material and had precipitously chosen a title for the record – Speed. Charlie, on the other hand, wanted to make an album that reflected the more traditional Subs' approach to song writing. He'd also come up with a title for his proposed record, Work in Progress, which also kept to the group's established convention of having the first letter of an album title correspond to its place in the English alphabet.

At this stage, it looked as if Paul Slack might be providing bass for Harper's planned LP, so I really should have been rooting for Nicky's record, but because I didn't like the Speed concept, I just couldn't in good conscience support it.

I write songs in a similar vein to those that Charlie composes – with intros, verses, choruses and middle-eights – exclusive of any predetermined format and which may well end up being stylistically Punk, Reggae, Ska, Hard rock or Blues tinged, but which will always be delivered with a generous and unmistakeable portion of Punk rock attitude. Garratt, on the other hand, wanted us to write in a specific way, utilising lightning-fast riffs and swiftly delivered vocals in order to fit his proposed idea for a Speed driven album, and that is categorically not how I, or Charlie, compositionally roll.

Having gained no endorsements for his suggested conceptual LP from amongst the Subs' membership, Nicky started bickering with Chas and Yuko about Charlie's presumed right to choose the designation of whatever album would eventually emerge, arguing that he and others in the band should also be entitled to put forward title ideas. Moreover, he told them Work in Progress was a terrible name for a record. I kept out of the arguments. It was all heat and no light, so I didn't see much point in joining in with these futile debates. Inadvertently, my refusal to get drawn into taking sides, worked in my favour.

Towards the conclusion of our Euro excursion, after yet another wrangle between the singer and guitarist about the same issue, Yuko pulled me aside and asked, "Would you be willing to play on the next album without Nicky being involved?" To which I answered "Yes."

Having then gone on to play bass, to provide a lead and various backing vocals and to contribute songs to Work in Progress in the Spring of 2010 along with Chas, Jet and Jamie, I knew Nicky Garratt deemed that I'd somehow been disloyal to him in not insisting that he, not Jet, be the guitarist on the new long-playing record. But loyalty, if it's to be equitable, must be a two-way transaction. When Charlie had offered Garratt the reunion tour with Slack and Davies, he hadn't instead insisted Jamie and I play those U.K. dates. Quite the opposite, plus he'd bragged to me about how much more money Harper would be paying them in comparison to the customary line-up.

Additionally, at the start of the 2010 European jaunt, as we were travelling from one particular destination to the next in our Mercedes Sprinter van – just prior to the disagreements which would later emerge over the next album's title and direction – Harper turned around in his seat to inform Nicky he'd been offered very good money for the Another Kind of Blues cast to play at the annual Rebellion Punk Festival in the north of England. He then inquired if Garratt would be prepared to once more work with Slack and Davies. Again, Nicky was quite content to accept Charlie's offer, replying "Absolutely Charlie, whatever you want. I'm very happy to be involved in that."

Having processed Garratt's response, which was made without any reference to me and Jamie and would have resulted in both of us being replaced by a rhythm section that had contributed next to nothing to the band for many years – thereby losing our opportunity to play the most prestigious U.K. Punk festival of the year – I had to conclude that from now on it was every man for himself, which is why I instantly agreed to record an album minus Garratt's involvement when Yuko had first pitched the idea.

Later on, with Yuko's collusion, I also managed to derail the proposed reunion Rebellion appearance, arguing we now had a new album to promote and the festival would be the perfect occasion to play material from the record to publicise it. Charlie saw the sense in my pitch and agreed to drop the Garratt, Slack, Davies reunification idea. It was the Work in Progress recording unit that played on the stage of a packed Empress Ballroom at the Winter Gardens in Blackpool in 2010.

The 2011 January/February tour exacerbated the rift between Harper and Garratt to such an extent it became a certainty this would be the guitarist's last Subs' European campaign. Among other niggles, Nicky had a beef about what he saw as being treated unfairly when it came to rider considerations for himself – a rider is the contracted provision of food, drink and other asks agreed to by a promoter for a hired band.

Nicky is a teetotaller and has, much to his credit, been a vegetarian since his teens. Being a vegetarian in the U.K. or the U.S.A, where Garratt lived and continues to reside, wasn't much of a problem in the early part of the second millennium. But in countries like Spain, Poland, Czech Republic, Hungary, and Serbia, it was much more difficult for him to find the meat-free and fish-free foods he could eat at whatever restaurant the promoter had pre-booked for us and what's more, he had very specific tastes.

If there was brown rice or tofu involved in a dish brought for him, he would sneer at it and disparagingly call it "Hippie food," before sending it back. One time in Spain, post soundcheck, Garratt once again held up the entire ordering process for everyone else whilst he tried to communicate in English to a waitress who only spoke Spanish, what victuals he could and couldn't consume at our hotel restaurant – Garratt wouldn't eat eggs either, so omelettes were also out of the question.

She eventually got the drift of what he was trying to explain to her, went off to the kitchen and later served him a plate of sliced smoked tofu fried in olive oil, roasted peppers and courgettes, sautéed potatoes

Nicky and I, Euro touring, Spain.

and tomatoes, along with a side salad. It looked and smelled wonderful, but by his reaction you would have thought the woman had just presented him with a dog turd to eat.

The "Hippie food" complaint was fiercely invoked along with other criticisms, thus upsetting the poor waitress who had done her best to provide Nicky with an off-menu specially cooked meal which was well within the 'can eat' parameters of what he'd managed to convey to her in a language she had no real understanding of. The rest of us were appalled at his rudeness and said as much, to which he went into his now familiar "You lot always get what you want, why shouldn't I," rant.

Also increasingly frequent at this time was his labelling of any establishment that couldn't provide exactly what he sought to eat as a "Fascist restaurant." What the correlation was between an eatery that didn't cater to vegetarians in the way he expected and the far-right, authoritarian political ideology that rose to prominence in Europe in the first half of the 20th Century, is something I still don't comprehend.

This lack of reasonable latitude for food was also replicated when it came to what he drank. When asked by serving staff what he would like to drink with his meals he always answered, "I think I'll have a glass of dragon fruit juice," only to be predictably told such an uncommon choice of beverage was unavailable. Garratt would then pursue his pointless exercise in asking for exotic nectars nobody else had heard of by replying: "OK, then I'll have a glass of star fruit juice instead." When informed only apple, tomato, orange, and pineapple juices were available, he would again go into a 'woe is me, why aren't I being catered for' spiel, which became increasingly irritating, especially when time was tight and the rest of us just wanted to chow down early enough so that we could digest our meals before we had to take to the stage to play a show.

The apex of this indulgent neuroticism was his new insistence that promoters must provide for him in the dressing room small bottles of sparkling water to drink. If, when we arrived at a venue, he saw there were only large bottles of fizzy water rather than the small bottles he'd prescribed, we would yet again have to breathe-in the scent of burning martyr and listen to his words of resentment towards us, whom he wrongly accused of always getting everything we desired whilst his requests were frequently unfulfilled.

Nicky was also telling people when asked who his favourite bands were, that he only liked Rock music that had emerged before and up to 1972. Playing in a Punk rock band whilst broadcasting that you no longer like Punk rock is tantamount to an admission that you're only doing it for the money and, quite honestly, it became increasingly obvious this was now the case.

Whilst it's true that each member of the band had their own foibles and was trying to make sure their needs were also being catered to within reason, Garratt's growing multiplicity of requirements and resentments were really starting to grind the gears of Charlie, Yuko and me although, with his hedonistic preoccupations to distract him, Jamie didn't seem to be as vexed about these behaviours as the rest of us. In Munich however, something occurred which unified the four of us in our disapproval.

For the obvious reason, Nicky disliked doing any of the new songs we'd added to the set from the Work in Progress album, although he still begrudgingly provided guitar for them, sans any enthusiasm. But at the Feierwerk club in Munich, having once again launched into a track Chas and I had composed entitled Hell is Other People, he bizarrely played the verses where the choruses should be (and vice versa), left out the middle-eight section and generally acted as if it was a song he'd never encountered before, even though we'd performed it more than a dozen times already during the course of the tour.

He screwed it up so badly, Jamie felt compelled to cease drumming and shout through his microphone, "Fuck this, let's do another song," whilst the puzzled München crowd tried to figure out what was going on.

Later that night, when the band, excluding Garratt, gathered to have some drinks in the hotel bar, the prevailing belief amongst us was that it had been an act of deliberate sabotage – the fatuous protest of a man who was still peeved about being omitted from the new record and who no longer had any real interest in being a U.K. Sub. Apart from, that is, the money he could earn and having his round trip air fare to Europe paid by the band so he could spend time at a property he'd purchased in the Harz Mountains of northern Germany and there consort with his most recent German girlfriend. This, I believe, was the defining moment which made up Charlie's, Yuko's and my own mind to replace Nicky with Jet for all future gigging commitments.

If Nicky Garratt hadn't been the consummate guitarist and musician that we all knew him to be, it might have been possible to excuse the unprofessionalism and the disarray of that night; but it had obviously been a deliberate and disrespectful gesture, and that's a bell which simply can't be unrung, no matter who you are or what you once represented.

After the Motörhead tour, prior to the 2012 winter Euro expedition, Garratt again phoned me after Charlie had informed him that he wasn't going to be on board for either that year's European trek or any other future tours. He'd called to ask me to act as an intermediary for him, an advocate for getting this decision overturned and his return to the band resolved. Although I already knew this ruling was non-negotiable, I told him I would talk to Chas.

If he had been more loyal to me in previous years I would have reciprocated and acted in kind. He hadn't, he'd always put his interests first, so I simply passed on to Charlie what Garratt had said without pressing for his restoration.

Sometimes, we reap what we sow.

Despite all I've written about what led up to his dismissal and Nicky's fickleness towards me and Jamie, I nonetheless felt genuinely remorseful for agreeing to cut Nicky loose. We'd certainly had our issues, but we'd also been friends and band mates for a very long time, had travelled thousands of miles around the world together, shared a stage for hundreds of shows and collaborated on some great records. It was a tough decision, but I knew it was the right one. I also believed it was an outcome which would be in his best interest.

Having broken ties with the Subs, Garratt was now free to embrace the categories of music that had first inspired him to pick up a guitar and

play, namely Progressive, Space and Krautrock.

With the Hedersleben band he formed featuring ex-Subs' drummer Jason Willer – which took its name from the municipality where his German property is located – Nicky went on to record and release four albums of Prog-influenced compositions. He also teamed up with one of his early Space rock heroes, Hawkwind's founder Nik Turner, for multiple tours as part of his backing band, additionally playing his axe on, and taking the role of musical director for, Turner's 2013 album, Space Gypsy.

When, in 2022, I heard Nicky had some health issues I called him to see how he was faring. He was fine, had married and moved from San Francisco to a grand house he'd purchased in North Carolina. He was still listening to and playing the music he loved.

Well, Amen to that too.

W, X

Once Nicky Garratt had moved on to Prog-rock pastures new and Jet had been endorsed as our permanent guitarist, the U.K. Subs became a stable working unit that rapidly increased the popularity of the band over the four year period following Garratt's departure. As well as consistency of line-up and uniformly creditable live performances, another major reason for this upsurge in esteem was down to the quality of the four albums the Harper, Gibbs, Jet and Oliver alliance succeeded in delivering during that time span. The next two chapters will reveal the stories behind the inception and creation of each of these pivotal records, beginning with the first album of the quartet:

Work in Progress

As previously revealed, the debut LP from the W, X, Y, Z series of

releases had been the victor in a dispute between Charlie Harper's creative vision for a new album and Nicky Garratt's desire to alternatively make a Hardcore category, fast-paced record. Having rejected Garratt's concept due to his personal antipathy and the general lack of enthusiasm from the remaining membership, Harper decided we should utilise, with my blessing, the affiliate who'd slowly taken over playing all British based shows – Jet Storm – for the forthcoming long player, rather than employ Nicky Garratt's services.

Having already come up with the title Work in Progress for this impending album, Charlie contacted the company which had made available to the record buying public the Subs' Universal LP of 2002 – Captain Oi! – offering them another opportunity to add an additional Subs' product to their catalogue. This primarily Punk rock label agreed to fund and release the results of our studio productivity and so, with Captain Oi! eagerly on board, we began the search for a suitable place to craft the record.

Knox Carnochan, lead singer and guitarist of The Vibrators, suggested we should give serious consideration to his ex-bassist Pat Collier's Perry Vale Studios in South London. He'd just recorded there with the Vibes and loved the results. Following a conversation with Collier by phone, Charlie booked five days, with each of these dates having originally been assigned as days off during our 2010 British Spring tour. This meant, when not playing live music in cities and towns up and down the U.K., we'd be occupied at Perry Vale piecing together the album, devoid of any opportunity for rest and recuperation.

As a result of this limited window of opportunity, there was no way to rehearse any of the new material before we turned up for the first day of the five Chas had reserved. In fact, none of us even got to hear any new compositions offered up for inclusion on the record from other members of the band until we played them to each other in the studio. This set the pattern of how we would briskly roll for all future albums.

Charlie, Jamie and I were accustomed to this way of working. Jet, on the other hand, was used to a much more prepared and systematic methodology when it came to making records, with pre-recorded demos and multiple rehearsals to ensure everybody knew their parts before reaching the studio. We simply didn't have time for any of that, and anyway, I've always thought it stimulating learning unfamiliar material real fast and contributing compatible bass lines and arrangement ideas without any preconceived notions, so that each song magically develops from its austere chord structure to a fully formed creation.

Having to work quickly also awards a natural edginess to the finished product, ensuring that the over-produced feel of some recordings,

Laying down some bass with Pat Collier at the desk.

where too much available time had led to excessive tinkering and unnecessary embellishment, simply wasn't possible.

The studio space was perfect – a large live room where drums, guitar and bass amps were situated and the vocal performances captured, plus a sizeable control room where Collier sat behind his impressive recording console configuring the music we were constructing whilst simultaneously offering astute suggestions. In effect, Pat became the de facto producer of the record and subsequently would be awarded production recognition for WIP and co-production credits for the three albums that followed.

The songs Collier recorded onto his digitalised studio system were a mixture of co-writes, solo compositions and one cover version, entitled Strychnine, which had originally been recorded by the 1960s American Garage rock band The Sonics. My only solo contribution was Guru.

Lyrically about New Age or quasi-religious charlatans who prey on the naïve and emotionally vulnerable, Charlie decided I had the better voice for the song and on that basis, maintained I should provide the lead vocal. It came out pretty good so my supplying at least one principal vocal per LP would become a future tradition for me.

Both of my co-writes were in collaboration with Harper – Children of the Flood and Hell is Other People – with Charlie contributing all the words for the music I'd pre-written for Children of the Flood. However, when I asked Jet to add an intro guitar motif to this track, he simply couldn't come up with anything credible and so, when he went to lunch, I utilised his Gibson Les Paul Junior to put some licks down and added other guitar additions of my own design.

Perhaps understandably, having returned from the café across the road, he felt a little put out by my input, but as I explained to him: "We have to work quickly, there just isn't the time for indulgences or preciousness about respective roles. If you, or Charlie, or I, can't within a short time span produce something that works for a track and somebody else can, then so be it." Jamie would also provide the guitar parts for All Blurs Into One and his other songs for the same reason. Eventually though, Jet came to terms with our necessary frenetic and loose mode of working and turned in some very accomplished and exciting guitar performances.

I'd pre-prepared the music for Hell is Other People, this title having been purloined from the theatrical play No Exit, written by existentialist philosopher Jean-Paul Sartre, and written lyrics for a portion of a verse: 'Maybe it's just me/Maybe it's the age I've reached/I look around/I just see straights or freaks', and all the choruses: 'It seems the world's turned lazy/And that they've all gone crazy/I summon a smile/But all the while, I start to think... Hell is other people.'

Even though it wouldn't have been an effort to complete all the words myself, I wanted to lyrically involve Charlie as I thought HIOP would make a killer live track and if Chas had a direct interest in the song, he'd be more liable to agree to add it to our set when we next toured. After Harper had taken care of the missing lines my hunch proved sound, we started playing it on the 2010 British winter tour and continued to do so for many years afterwards.

Jamie had three co-writes with Charlie: Creation, which was chosen as the opening track of the album, All Blurs Into One and Radio Unfriendly – a varied and skilfully written trio. Jet's writing partnership with our singer resulted in the catchy, stylistically late-1980s American rock threesome Tokyo Rose, Rock 'n' Roll Whore, and Blood.

These songs, along with my contributions and Harper's solo offerings – Eighteen Wheels and The Axe – provided a consistently balls-out, upbeat aspect to the overall sound of the record, as did This Chaos, Charlie's co-composition with Rancid guitarist and ex-U.K. Sub Lars Frederiksen.

I'd relished being back in the studio, devoting myself, alongside my band amigos to the task of making the best possible album in the limited amount of days we could spare from our British tour. The raw results sounded really good to me, but there wasn't enough time to do a definitive mix of the record within the five retained days. This was accomplished over a 48 hour period, post tour, subsequent to my returning to France, although I still had significant input regarding the final musical blend as Pat Collier would send me each track as an attached file to my email address to listen to and then later comment on via video link until we'd all – band and producer – reached a point of mutual satisfaction. This too, became a feature of how we mixed future LPs.

Considering the stringent schedule, Work in Progress turned out to be a fine release with some great songs and quality performances. There were two minor bellyaches for me though. Firstly, Charlie's independent decision to use an artwork piece by Vince Ray whose tattoo-style illustrations are, in my opinion, more suitable for the sleeves of Psychobilly outfits such as Demented Are Go, Mad Sin or The Meteors than for the frontispiece of a U.K. Subs' record. Despite being unimpressed by the image of the cartoon skeleton – complete with Psychobilly quiff, strumming a guitar and singing into a retro 1950s microphone – I wasn't about to get into a row over something which was, after all, just a minor complaint. Especially as I'd only just managed to get myself included as a player on the record and was again working on securing my future position as exclusive bassist for the group.

Further to this, when I saw that alongside Pat Collier's production credit, Charlie Harper had been cited on the cover as executive producer, I experienced another moment of irritation. Jamie and I had been just as involved in the song arrangements, creative ideas and overall sound of the record as Charlie, but only his contribution regarding those aspects was being memorialised. Again, I let it go. Although I made a mental note to make certain that for all future albums, proper accreditation would be given.

XXIV

A contentious debate regarding the concept and title for the next album began raging from the record's inception. Having solidified as a unit and significantly improved the band's standing in the Punk scene in the three years since the release of Work in Progress, Charlie, characteristically, wanted to raze all our hard work and advancement by proposing an idea for the follow-up LP which would have sown confusion and discord on a grand scale.

Aware that the title of this anticipated album would begin with an X, he started spinning the notion that as many ex-members of the Subs as possible should be invited to contribute material and to play on the nascent record, which he'd decided would be titled Exes. It was an insane idea.

Alphabetically, it didn't even make sense. Exes, obviously, begins with an E not an X, and the possibility of drumming up enough of these Exes who'd be interested in taking time out from whatever jobs they now had, to travel from wherever in the British Isles (and beyond) they now lived, in order to contribute to an LP that offered no monetary reward, just the mere possibility of getting a studio performance or a song on the final cut of the record, was negligible.

Add to that, the logistical nightmare of trying to get those who might accept an invitation to arrive at the studio at a specific day and time, whilst trying to get the other musicians who wanted to participate to simultaneously attend on that same day and hour in order to work on whatever song was being touted by whoever was doing the touting. Then combine that hells-broth with the extra difficulty of enmity between certain past and present affiliates of the U.K. Subs, which would hardly make for a good working atmosphere and could well lead to fisticuffs at some heated point of the proceedings.

In order to kill off this crazy proposal I recruited Yuko and Jamie. The three of us argued that Subs' fans, the vast majority of whom had loved Work in Progress and solely wanted to hear another LP with the same performers as per that album, meant Charlie's Exes idea would be a disorderly, disastrous mistake. Harper initially resisted our pleas but was eventually worn down by these persistent urgings, finally agreeing that the current line-up would provide the material and musicianship for our, now nameless, new record.

As with WIP, we recorded at Perry Vale Studios on days off during the course of a U.K. tour. Pat Collier again took care of engineering duties and the band once more had no clue as to how each other's compositions sounded until we got round to playing them to each other at the South London facility. The way song development worked was as follows:

If I, for instance, had a home-written potential album track to submit, I'd play it to the rest of the guys on an acoustic guitar – if a Punk rock tune sounds good when played acoustically, it will sound even better when amplified instruments are employed and the entire band is involved.

Having hopefully garnered a positive response from the rest for my offering, I'd then go into the live room with Jamie to lay down a basic guitar part for the song using one of Pat's electric axes (he had a rack of basses and guitars available for use in the studio), while Oliver simultaneously worked on providing appropriate drums from the soundproof booth his kit had been assembled in. During this process, whilst occupied in getting ourselves a decent take, Jamie and I would communicate with each other about the arrangement and the drum parts via the microphones Collier had provided for that purpose.

Once a satisfactory, mistake-free backing track had been securely captured on the digitalised recorder, I'd go back into the control room and start working on bass lines for the song whilst sat on a stool next to the console using my own personal bass – usually a Fender Jazz – plugged into a DI box that fed the sound into an amp with a mic'd-up speaker in the live room.

I would only have the chord structures and arrangements for my songs pre-prepared, never the bass parts; but it usually didn't take me long to come up with something compatible utilising the four throbbing wires for whatever rudimentary backing track I was focussing on. Once the bass had been added, I'd turn it over to the guitarist (in this case Jet) and give him the option of either keeping or replacing my guide guitar with a six-string rhythm part of his own – sometimes, if my original guitar performance had been viable enough and we were really under the cosh for time, my guide playing would remain on the track and only a bolstering rhythm part would be additionally recorded.

With the rhythm and lead guitar performances in place, vocals were then added. For Charlie's, or my own benefit if I happened to be the designated lead vocalist, I'd have already formulated the lyrics for any self-composed songs. For my co-writes, which were usually with Harper, I'd provide the music and he'd supply the words, these typically being conceived and transcribed onto paper as Jamie and I worked on the backing track. Any supporting vocals and additional instruments were subsequently recorded and adjoined to whatever song was up for consideration.

Meanwhile, Pat, as is his most excellent way, would've been working on preliminary mixes of these components as we'd moved things along. This practise saved us a lot of time and effort when it came to finalising an overall mix at a later date.

The album that would in due course be entitled XXIV was completed using the exact methodology I've just described; as had been the case for Work in Progress and would continue to be the way for the Yellow Leader and Ziezo LPs.

This second album of the quartet eventually tallied 14 tracks, along with a supplementary 12 compositions for a bonus CD featuring acoustic instrumentation rather than the usual big brash electric noise we'd become renowned for.

For the raucous full power record, I submitted three self-composed songs and co-wrote a number with Charlie called Speed; the title of which he may have unconsciously appropriated from Nicky Garratt, as this had been our former guitarist's designated suggestion for the previous album.

My solo-penned threesome, Coalition Government Blues, Black Power Salute and Stare at the Sun were lyrically about three distinctive subjects. CGB mocked the British Liberal Democrat political party for entering into a coalition with the Conservatives which then enabled the Tories to form a government following a hung parliament result in the aftermath of the British 2010 general election – a very rare occurrence in the U.K. as typically one or the other of the two main political parties receive big enough majorities in the House of Commons to form a government outright.

Despite having railed against Conservative policies whilst in opposition, the Lib Dems and their leader Nick Clegg, who was appointed deputy Prime Minister by PM David Cameron as a conspicuous reward for his collusion, hypocritically helped enact some of these same policies as coalition allies in a Tory-led government. It was all about avarice, acquisition of status and power: 'They got a public school cabinet/MPs who've never worked/Liberals who talk like Tories/Clegg who likes his perks.' It should be noted that Charlie's harmonica playing and Dylan-esque vocal delivery on this track were outstanding contributions which really helped solidify the Bluesy ambiance of the piece.

Served over a fast-paced cyclic riff, Black Power Salute – which I sang in my best Iggy Pop meets Glenn Danzig voice – similarly had a political dimension, only this time it centred on the fist-raised protest of two African-American athletes, Tommie Smith and John Carlos, during a medal award ceremony at the 1968 Olympics – an affirmation that became both a potent and controversial symbol of the civil rights movement in the U.S.A. in the late 1960s and early-1970s.

I also provided the lead vocals for the grunge-influenced Stare at the Sun. This was a more personal composition that expressed my disenchantment with my own species: 'I can't seem to catch my breath/I dwell on things that anger and confound me/I have no time for your gods or your governments/My disillusion is a cloak that surrounds me.' Jet's subtle but effective guitar solo perfectly complimented the atmosphere of the song, as did Jamie's muscular, Dave Grohl inspired drumming style.

In fact the entire album was loaded with great songs, inspired musicianship, superlative lyrics and memorable vocal performances, starting with the incendiary assault of the Harper/Oliver opening track, Implosion 77, to the Bo Diddley stomp of Charlie's Wreckin' Ball, and the tuneful Rock-outs of Jet's co-writes with Chas – Monkeys, Las Vegas Wedding and Workers Revolution – all of which had us concluding that the soon to be designated XXIV was definitely going to be a better listening experience than WIP.

From these same studio sessions, the bonus acoustic tracks, which amounted to another album's worth of material and would be released as such on 12 inch vinyl by Captain Oi! in 2021, came about as a suggested idea by Mark Brennan, head honcho of the record company. He'd, no doubt, already calculated it was a way of getting an additional LP out of us at no extra cost. Considering the limited amount of studio time we'd booked for when we were not out on tour, it seemed like a madcap scheme to me. But Charlie was enthusiastic about doing some acoustic material, and so we speedily wrote some acoustic guitar based songs, either together or on our own, and threw in a couple of cover versions for good measure: Angel of Eighth Avenue – one of my favourite Mott The Hoople tunes, for which I played guitar and sang – and Charlie's choice, Ian and Sylvia Tyson's Four Strong Winds.

Moreover, I wrote, played and took the lead vocal on a song about the tragic but inevitably sordid death of guitarist Johnny Thunders called Thunders in the Rain and teamed up with Jamie to co-write Confessions of a Dangerous Mind, this being a song where I again delivered the primary vocal.

There was some good material on the bonus CD, the best of the pick being Charlie and Jamie's beautiful Metamorphosis, the most deficient being Harper and Jet's Stop Global War – a corny protest song with clichéd lyrics and naïve sentiments that's unlikely to put an end to worldwide conflicts any time soon.

Rushed as we were to write and record these extra compositions, they could have turned out a lot shabbier, although I wished we'd had more time to devote to their development and execution.

Once we'd mixed the main album and the supplementary acoustic songs, we were left with the problem of what to call the record. Various ideas were passed around, but when considering something that had to have an X as the first letter of its designation, the possibilities become pretty limited. Enter Mark Brennan, who having realised it was going to be the Subs' 24th official LP, proposed we use the Roman numerals for 24 – XXIV – as the title.

Suggestion accepted, we then worked on finding some fitting artwork for the cover. I'd recently visited Naples and the remarkable remains of the ancient Roman city of Pompeii where I remembered seeing a mosaic called the Wheel of Life and Death – a classic piece of Roman Momento Mori, Latin for Remember Your Mortality, featuring a suspended skull and other kinds of visual symbolism relating to life and death.

Everyone enthused about it, but when Brennan looked into acquiring the image, he discovered it was under copyright control and there was no way the Neapolitan authorities would permit its use for a Punk rock record. Then, following a moment of imaginative genius, Charlie phoned me and proposed the powerful image that would end up adorning the front of the album – an icon depiction of the Madonna where, instead of Mary cradling baby Christ, she would be lovingly supporting an AK-47 assault rifle. This, as I've already observed but strongly feel the need to reiterate, was a truly inspired idea.

Freelance designer Daryl Smith, who also happens to be a member

of the popular Oi band, Cock Sparrer, did a superb job of translating Charlie's outstanding concept into artwork. And I still contend that the imagery, graphics and visual compositions on the XXIV record jacket are by far the most impressive and evocative of the W, X, Y, Z foursome, if not the entire Subs' catalogue – and by the way, I insisted the production credits affixed to this striking sleeve should read: Produced by Pat Collier and the U.K. Subs, my resolve paying dividends as this correct accreditation was duly displayed on our new album and was to be replicated on every Subs' record thereafter.

Y, Z

Yellow Leader

One year after the release of XXIV, we were back at Perry Vale Studios to record the U.K. Subs' 25th and penultimate official album.

Same drill: working during supposed days off whilst in the midst of a Brit-wide tour; still oblivious to the tunes each of us would provide for the song carnival until we'd played them to each other in the studio; having to work quickly because of time limitations; and, as with the previous LP, having no clue as to what the title of the impending record was going to be.

There was one ancillary adjustment. Instead of Charlie and I having to travel back and forth by train to Forest Hill in SE London from his house on the South Coast every recording day, we instead, along with Jamie, stayed overnight at a Travel Lodge hotel in Crystal Palace, a mere 10 minute drive from the Perry Vale facility. The expense of returning to France for down time and having to travel back again to resume gigging just a few days later, was far too financially prohibitive, so I'd taken to sleeping over at Chas and Yuko's when occasional breaks during U.K. tours ensued. Later on, I would stop at Jet's flat in Chiswick, but that's a strange story for another time.

The new album, which would constitute the third of a four-part LP series featuring the 2010 to 2015 line-up, again contained a primarily spirited Rock noise with a couple of striking exceptions. Charlie's hauntingly beautiful acoustic guitar-led composition Rebellion Song was, as far as I'm concerned, one of the best tunes he'd ever written, and it's important to note that it's Jamie Oliver playing all the guitar parts on the recording – rhythm and lead – not Jet.

Harper's Archaeology, was another refreshing change into lower gear via its trippy Jazz feel and lyrical multiple-meanings: 'Every night with her little light/She's digging those bones, digging those bones.'

Once this track was recorded, its originator wanted to insert a breakdown ending, with cymbal taps and strummed open chords, which I thought was a bit hackneyed for such a cool song. When Patrick Collier played the piece back so Charlie could identify where this ending was to be incorporated, he abruptly stopped the playback to hear what Harper was saying. This sudden cut in the music sounded to me like a more sophisticated ending than the extended decaying of instrumentation that Chas had envisioned. When I proposed using this termination of the track in place of Harper's suggestion, Pat was in agreement; and although Charlie was hesitant about our way of thinking, it was this alternative ending that made it onto the record.

There was also a bit of a debate going on regarding Charlie's lines for a song Jet had written the music for. Chas had labelled it Supersonic Girl with a chorus that crowed: 'She's my supersonic girl, my supersonic girl,' ad infinitum. Jet vehemently disliked both Harper's words and title. They got into a verbal knife fight about it with neither man being prepared to yield from their immoveable positions.

The music Jet had provided was pop-catchy – in a light Rock music kind of way – and Harper had followed his lead by adding lyrics which were correspondingly pop-catchy in tone. Now, with the way I write, it's always a case of the sunnier the music the darker the lyric, so I offered up a suggestion to break the deadlock:

"Look, Chas, rather than have this be about a supersonically exceptional woman who's your perfect ideal, how about calling it Suicidal Girl and changing the story to that of a young female who took her life due to social media and peer factors? I'll even give you a first line – 'Die young, die pretty.' What d'ya think?"

It worked. Charlie and a relieved Jet both thought it an acceptable replacement idea to the original and some new words were accordingly written and sung, with Harper slightly altering my suggested first line to 'Die pretty, open a vein.'

I provided three self-composed tracks for the album, plus a co-write with Harper and, uniquely, a collaborative song with both him and Jamie. This three-way composition came about as follows: we'd already recorded all of the music for Oliver's piece, but Charlie was struggling with the lyrical subject matter. I'd been reading a newspaper article about Russia's 2014 invasion and annexation of Ukrainian Crimea, which the Russian government justified with claims that ethnic Russians in Crimea were 'under threat' from 'extremists', even though there was absolutely no evidence to support these allegations – similar false justifications would again be proffered by Vladimir Putin and the Russian Federation to justify the invasion of sovereign Ukraine in 2022.

This article also reported what the then Vice President of the U.S.A. Joe Biden had said to Putin when they'd first met in Moscow in 2011: "I'm looking into your eyes, I don't think you've got a soul," to which Putin chillingly replied, "We understand each other." This seemed like an interesting topic for a word story set to music so I suggested it to Jamie, who was enthusiastic about the idea and asked me to work on the lyrics with Charlie. The end result was Prime Evil with its reference to a 'Czar of pain,' the would-be dictator Putin who 'Strips away your freedoms' and, seeing as it was such a memorable observation, I also utilised the Biden quote to highlight the brutal and dark disposition of the Russian leader.

The first of my solo trio to be recorded, Sick Velveteen, begins with a distorted bass riff that leads into a meaty chord progression, over which Chas delivers my aberrant lyrics: 'Social pariah with a fucked-up head/ You'll find nirvana in her bed/Used, abused and freshly bled/Like all the fools she's misled.' This became the opening track of the album and would be the inaugural live song of our set when we toured the record later that year.

My narrative for Bordeaux Red, the second of my solo offerings to be recorded, was not about my passion for the wines of the region I live in, but an account of a lowly English archer who slays the enemy and risks his life during The Hundred Years' War in service to King Richard I. The dangers and hardships the bowman faced and his devotion to a cause only his Sovereign would profit from, result in the derisory reward of returning to England to live a life of poverty and sickness with the rats and lice in a Cheapside hovel.

Because of the more personal nature of this subject, with its reference to locations close to where I live such as Angouleme, Gascony and Bordeaux, Charlie insisted I should sing it in his stead. I duly obliged.

For my third self-composed track, Feed the Whore, I played the guitars as well as all the bass components. Chas sang it, but many who've heard the song seemed to think it was my vocal performance they were listening to. Charlie agrees with them and has put it down to him somehow having "channelled" my singing voice.

I've tended to concentrate more on the backgrounds behind the words and the musical constructions of my personal donations to the LPs we've been considering so far. This, I think, is reasonable as being the lone composer or co-writer they're the songs I have the most personal knowledge about.

However, despite my deficient awareness regarding what actually inspired the tracks written by my fellow Subs and all the particulars leading to their fruition, it is evident that both the singly and co-written songs Charlie Harper, Jamie Oliver and Jet provided for this yet unnamed album were of an even greater level of quality and creativity than those they'd supplied for the Work in Progress and XXIV records. The production was superior too and as such, alongside the future Ziezo LP, it constitutes for me the cream of the album quartet crop.

The "what's the title going to be?" debate kicked off whilst we were still recording at Perry Vale Studios. Charlie was proposing we call it Yellow

Leader but couldn't explain to us why, apart from the obvious fact it began with a Y, and alphabetically this was to be the letter the album was set to begin with. Whenever I asked, "What exactly does Yellow Leader mean?" he would just look at me blankly and reply "Why does it have to mean anything, it's just a name."

Jamie and Jet were equally perplexed, so I came up with what I believed was an improved appellation – Yes and Now – this being a more positive twist on the ambivalent 'yes and no' phrase, and an affirmative declaration that seemed more in keeping with the spirit of the record than the obscure title Harper was putting forward.

With drummer, guitarist and Pat Collier approving of this replacement handle I pressed Charlie to accept the adjustment. In due course he did consent and we thought the issue was settled. The U.K. Subs' dedicated website uksubstimeandmatter.net even reported this was going to be the name attached to our imminent release. But Harper decided to go back on the agreement and told Captain Oi! to go ahead and call it what he'd wanted in the first place without even disclosing this reversal to the rest of us.

It was a self-centred, underhand move, but what he then instructed the record company to choose in terms of sleeve artwork could have had really serious repercussions for the album.

Charlie and I are admirers of the 1960s Pop Art exponent, Roy Lichtenstein. He instructed Mark Brennan to use a famous piece by this artist entitled Whaam! for the front cover – a comic book styled image of an American jet fighter destroying an enemy plane during aerial combat. Brennan did as he was asked without bothering to consult the rest of the band and accordingly printed up all the packaging for the vinyl and CD versions of Yellow Leader with Lichtenstein's creation at centre stage.

When I eventually discovered this was to be the artwork, it occurred to me that seeing as how my suggested image for XXIV – the Wheel of Life and Death Pompeian mosaic – had been discarded due to legal issues, that I should now look into the permissible situation for the Lichtenstein. And sure enough, I discovered this was also a patent protected picture under the jurisdiction of the Lichtenstein Foundation. Harper, obviously, had not even considered the possibility of a copyright problem for the piece, but I'd assumed Mark Brennan must have checked it out and received permission for its reproduction before going ahead with the costly manufacture of all the sleeves for his new Subs' release. Just to be certain though, I contacted him to make sure he'd attained authorisation and that there would be no legal impediment to duplicating Whaam! on the album jackets.

The contentious artwork for the Yellow Leader album.

"I thought Charlie would have known all this before suggesting the Lichtenstein artwork," he told me in a somewhat shocked tone of voice.

"Are you kidding? You actually expected Charlie Harper to be aware of the copyright implications of anything he'd suggest for an album cover? That's crazy! You obviously don't know Charlie like we know Charlie. I guess then, what you're telling me is you didn't get consent to use this piece before having all the record covers printed, is that right?"

Correct. Brennan then went into an angry rant about how it would cost him thousands of pounds to destroy these sleeves and to order new ones with alternate artwork. It was entirely his own fault for not applying due diligence when Harper had pitched the suggestion but, with a large serving of luck, I figured he just might avoid a financial calamity.

"Contact the Lichtenstein Foundation," I advised, and after supplying

Brennan the relevant contact information continued "see if they're agreeable to you using that particular picture for a Rock record. You never know, they might be OK with it."

A large serving of luck it turned out to be. The foundation got back to him after the board had discussed the matter and informed Mark they were fine with him using it, plus the arty darlings didn't even ask Brennan for as much as a single penny to lease the image. Thus, my estimation of those who administer Lichtenstein's legacy is of a philanthropic group of people who apply the bohemian spirit of the 1960s and put creative collaboration before commercial gain – a rare thing in these grasping, corporate times.

Released in 2014 with a slightly amended version of Lichtenstein's iconic Whaam! graphic on the sleeve's frontispiece, Yellow Leader was celebrated by the media and our fan-base alike as one of the best the Subs had issued since Endangered Species, although just about everyone who procured the record was left wondering: 'what the fuck does the title mean?'

Ziezo

We'd issued three LPs in a row with Captain Oi! and the label was desperately keen to release the 26th and final album of the U.K. Subs' alphabet series, the title of which would, naturally, begin with the letter Z. With this in mind, Mark Brennan approached Charlie with a proposal that we record and Captain Oi! release each month for the 12 months leading up to the recording of our valediction LP, a distinct 45 rpm, 7-inch vinyl single. Harper relayed this proposition to us whilst we were sitting in a dressing room waiting to take to the stage at a U.K. venue. He was very excited about the idea. I was not.

"Have you considered the logistics of us having to get into a studio to record a track every month for a year, or of our getting into the studio to do all twelve tracks simultaneously prior to getting back into Perry Vale for the recording of our final album?"

It was purely a rhetorical question. I already knew Charlie hadn't given a single thought to practical or logistical considerations. I persisted:

"Twelve new songs constitute an album and that's what Brennan is after. He'll pay us pennies for these singles and then later, after the Z record has been released, issue those twelve tracks as an additional LP without having to give us any extra money seeing as he would already own all the publishing rights for the songs. Not only is his single a month scheme impractical, it's also a con."

Jamie agreed with me and basically reiterated in his own words what I'd just relayed to Harper, who still maintained it was a good idea. When Yuko waded in on our side, the single a month swindle was scuppered and we individually started preparing songs for just the one multi-track album.

I was annoyed at Brennan's flagrant attempt at manipulating Harper's predilection to say "Yes" to anything offered without having first thought it through or discussed the pros and cons with the rest of the band. And so when an alternative option to Captain Oi! was bought to our attention by the occasional Subs' tour driver and friend Paul Swinnerton (aka Paul North), I was interested.

Paul had recently organised an album release for first wave 1976 Punk outfit Buzzcocks with the online, direct-to-fan music platform launched in 2009 called PledgeMusic. Pledge worked like this: even before one of their contracted bands had entered the studio to make a record, its fan base and the general public were invited to pay for the product ahead of time, which would then provide the financial resources for studio costs and manufacturing. A pledger could also procure add-ons to their album purchase – T-shirts, hoodies, meet-and-greets, badges, patches, and whatever else a group wanted to offer – with the revenues from all these elements being included in the overall amount collected online by the company. At the end of a campaign, after records and any additions had been posted to their buyers, PledgeMusic would take 20% of the cut and the remainder, after expenses, would go to the band.

Captain Oi! had been an important component in the resurgence of the latter-day U.K. Subs, but the money we'd individually made from the Work in Progress, XXIV and Yellow Leader albums had been pitiful. My personal payment per LP was less than £500 which, considering the time, energy and creative industry I'd put into making those records, was a derisory sum. Pledge, on the other hand, would give us the opportunity to be properly financially rewarded and, even more importantly, to be completely in control of all the mechanics of the album, which encapsulated its recording, its promotion, the photographic material to be used, artwork, vinyl colour choices and packaging options – the whole enchilada.

Jamie, Jet and Yuko didn't take much persuading, although, inevitably, Charlie was humming and harring about us ditching Mark Brennan's label out of fear of the new. To settle this decisive break with Captain Oi!, Swinnerton arranged for the entire band to discuss the matter at PledgeMusic's headquarters in the West End of London. After the

Pat Collier, mixing Ziezo.

meeting, Harper's resistance crumbled and we signed to them as a precursor to the company taking on our campaign for the Subs' farewell record.

In November 2015, we returned to the tried and tested Perry Vale Studios and the excellent engineering and co-production services of

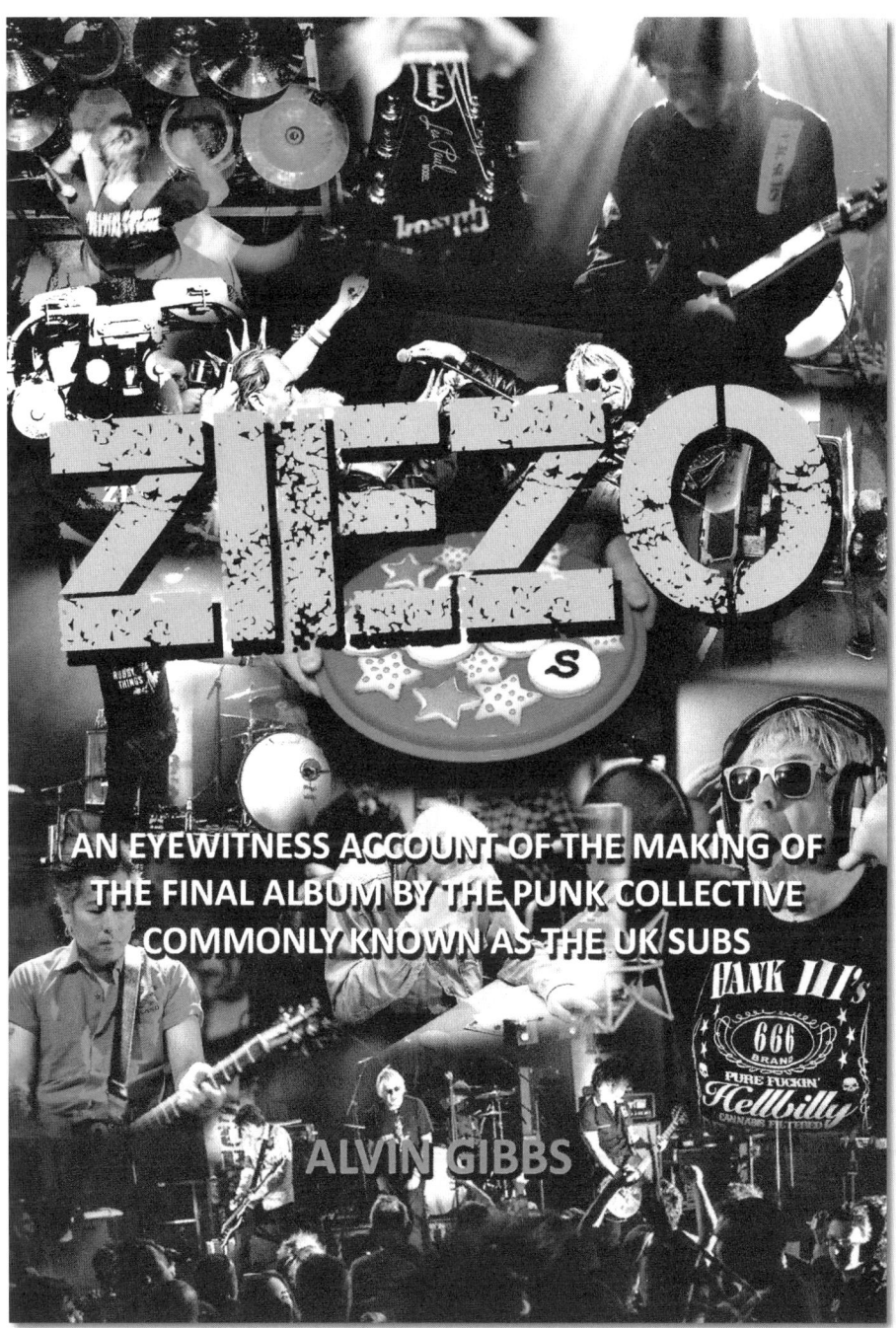

ZIEZO

S

AN EYEWITNESS ACCOUNT OF THE MAKING OF
THE FINAL ALBUM BY THE PUNK COLLECTIVE
COMMONLY KNOWN AS THE UK SUBS

ALVIN GIBBS

Patrick Collier. As before, all the recording dates were meant to be days off during a tour in progress – the annual November/December U.K. winter outing. As part of the pledge extras that the band had decided to offer, there were daily visits to the studio by Subs' aficionados who could observe and listen as we diligently pieced together the album. Most of these visitors even got to participate by providing backing vocals for the songs that required a gang-like auxiliary oral input, as on my self-composed trio: Rise, I Don't Care and I've Got a Gun. We provided wine, beer and snacks for them and made ourselves some new friends as a consequence of these visitations.

It would be only the second time we'd begun recording with an agreed name already in place for an LP. Whilst we were touring in the Netherlands, Charlie had discovered that Ziezo was the Flemish word for 'job done'. We all concurred this admittedly obscure – unless you're Dutch that is – title was a perfect fit for what was due to be our final long-player studio record.

As well as all the other available options, each of us was expected to personally offer something for the public to pledge for. Harper provided an autographed guitar and some hand-written lyrics on parchment paper. Having contributed a number of signed drum skins for this purpose, Jamie Oliver, being the technical computer genius of the band, also took charge of putting up posts, filming and editing video updates and building our dedicated PledgeMusic website. For my part, I wrote a mini-book-type diary for pledgers that detailed the crafting of the album, for which I applied the longwinded title Ziezo: An Eyewitness Account of the Making of the Final Album by the Punk Collective Commonly Known as the U.K. Subs.

As for Jet, despite numerous suggestions designed to get him involved in the wider aspects of the campaign by ourselves and Paul Swinnerton, he refused to offer anything more than his songs and guitar playing for the LP.

This was indicative of a general 'Jet problem' which had been fermenting for a while. Just as with Nicky Garratt prior to his departure, it seemed as though our guitarist was no longer attentive to the band and its music and was merely in it for the money. The truth was Jet had become a semi-detached member of the U.K. Subs, uninterested in socialising with the rest of us and doing the bare minimum to maintain his position in the group.

For the Ziezo sessions Charlie, Jamie and I would make sure we were at the studio by 11am at the latest, each of us eager to work and brimming with creative ideas. Jet would turn up at 2pm, faff about with one of his songs or casually record a guitar contribution for one of ours, then sit around looking bored and removed from the process until departing at 5pm, whilst the rest of us grafted on until gone 8pm. Arguments ensued regarding his lukewarm involvement but there was no positive response to any of the criticisms we pitched his way. He'd become a lost cause that we no longer wanted to save.

Despite his disappointingly unenthusiastic recording conduct, Jet did contribute four very good songs to the LP – World War III, Banksy, Dope Fiend and Oligarchy – plus some fine guitar solos, but studio disagreements were not just confined to Jet versus the rest of the band.

When we'd finished the musical element for my composition I've Got a Gun, I gave Chas the words I'd pre-written for him to sing. The song was about a psychotic American gun-addicted male who fantasises about killing a president, considers firearms 'Gifts from god' and confides that gunfire makes him 'warm inside/Patriotic, misty eyed/Murdering animals just for fun/Maybe a human before I'm done.'

After looking over the lyrics Harper declared "It shouldn't be I've got a gun, it should be she's got a gun." What? I couldn't figure out why he wanted to completely change the narrative so that it was a female killer rather than a man, and so I asked the obvious concise question: "Why?"

"Because we don't have enough songs featuring girls in them," was the reply.

"Really? How about Tomorrows Girls, Fear of Girls, Perfect Girl, Suicidal Girl…"

He cut me off by firmly announcing "I'm not going to sing it like this," and we got into a heated squabble, much to the amusement of our pledging guests. I eventually gave up trying to convince Harper that the version I'd given him was fine as is and yelled: "Do it your fucking way then!" Charlie returned to the live room, took up a position in front of the microphone and then contravened himself by singing the lyrics exactly as I'd written them. When he returned to the control room, he conceded it did work better as originally scripted and with that admission, studio equanimity was restored.

I got to contribute the customary album lead vocal performance for my autobiographical song Disclosure: 'From the slums of Rio to the freeways of LA/I've endured the road for 5,000 days/In the squats of Berlin and the Hilton Paris/Wish you'd tasted all I've seen.'

As with all previous LPs, Charlie and Jamie again supplied some superb compositions, of which City of the Dead, Master Race, Polarisation and what I consider is the best track on the record, Maid of Orleans, are the standouts.

Now I could give a much more detailed account about the construction of Ziezo, but I've already chronicled the minutiae of the making of this album in the published diary that was pledged for at the time and which shifted all 300 of its printed copies. Despite it now being a rare item, occasionally, a second-hand copy does make its way onto a

vending website, so if you see it up for grabs on Amazon or eBay, snap it up and give it a gander. I promise you it will be well worth the cost and whatever time you invest in reading it.

Ziezo was released in 2015. It was an artistically, critically and financially successful album – for this PledgeMusic supervised record we each received tenfold what we would have made with Captain Oi! Unfortunately though, the PM online platform couldn't last out the decade and it folded due to bankruptcy in 2019.

This was to be the last record Jet would contribute to and, supposedly, the last album containing original U.K. Subs' material to be issued. However, what is supposed to be, as opposed to what actually will be, is sometimes as dissimilar as a black knight to a white bishop.

HISTORY

It was around 2007, at a time when I was still unsure about my long-term future as a member of the U.K. Subs in the aftermath of the Harper, Garratt, Slack and Davies reunion tour, that I decided to raise my abiding passion for history to a higher level of understanding. There were a couple of motivational reasons for this.

As some would have gathered from both my previous memoir volumes as well as this concluding one, I've always loved visiting places of historic interest and reading books about the subject. Furthermore, it has continually been my contention that the past is all we have – the present is fleeting, the future has yet to occur – and that personal and broader histories are decisive in shaping ourselves and human societies, and will continue to influence all events, advancements, and regressions to come.

The first president of the United Arab Emirates, Zayed bin Sultan Al Nahyan, put it succinctly when he said, "He who does not know his past cannot make the best of his present and future, for it's from the past we learn." This is the reason I believe history to be the most important branch of study from the group of educational disciplines referred to as the humanities.

So, seeing that I was possibly in a situation where I would have a lot more additional time to exploit, I decided to progress from enthusiastic amateur to academic intensity in order to substantially broaden and extend my knowledge of the subject.

Another impetus was that if everything went tits-up and playing music professionally was no longer an option for me, a good, educationally recognised qualification in this field would give me the means to get a job either teaching history at an English language school in France or as a private tutor to the children of expats. Well, that was the expectation. The reality was once I'd signed up to do a Bachelor of Arts Honours degree with the Open University, the reunion tour I'd mentioned at the top of the page came to nothing and I was back to consistent gigging and travelling with the Subs.

This meant I was going to be undertaking a university degree course whilst living the nomadic life of an itinerant Punk rock musician, which would obviously serve up some serious challenges. But before we get into those difficulties and other aspects of the scholastic six-year journey I undertook, here's some background on the academic institution I'd picked to help me achieve my original goals of deeper historical understanding and a potential new career.

Envisioning it as an important aspect of his party's commitment to modernising British society in the mid-1960s and in breaking the monopoly of moneyed, elitist institutions such as the Oxford and Cambridge universities, the then Labour Party Prime Minister, Harold Wilson, became a proponent for a new all-inclusive government-funded academy which he believed would lead to a more competitive economy, promote additional equality of opportunity and deliver greater social mobility. Launched as The Open University in 1969, it accepted students from all economic backgrounds and dispensed with the need for any prior educational qualifications.

Anyone from the age of 16 onwards could apply to take a degree course or choose a lesser qualification curriculum while remaining in regular employment. This is why the undergraduate degree programs with the OU takes six years to complete rather than the average three years of full-time study at conventional universities. Another disparity is that there's no campus as such for students to attend classes. There are physical structures owned by the OU in Milton Keynes, most notably Walton Hall, where the vice-chancellor's office is housed and some of the permanent salaried academic employees are based; but instead of fixed study centres for scholars, the OU utilised a variety of methods to instruct its BA and MA students – the course books each learner receives every term containing all primary reading for the assignments they'll submit, and for their yearly hand-written examination in allotted towns and cities; DVDs, audio materials, computer software and even, at one time, television programmes: British readers of a certain age may remember the very dry, yawn-inducing late night OU broadcasts on BBC 2 back in the 1970s and '80s which always seemed to feature a bearded uber-nerd presenter operating cheap props whilst wearing an even cheaper suit. These televisual geek-fests ended in 2006.

Face-to-face learning is also included and encouraged at a variety of regional locations where part-time OU academics offer regular tutorials during term time for those students willing to travel. Unfortunately, living in France and being on the road with the Subs for close on six-months of the year, meant I was unable to attend a single tutorial during my entire six years of study.

Apart from being able to work on the degree whilst travelling and gigging with the band, the other attraction for choosing the Open University was financial outlay. The average cost of a BA degree in a campus-based Uni back in the first decade of the new millennium was around £20,000, and that's just for the tuition. Taking into account the auxiliary books I had to buy from a supplied reading list separate to the materials provided by the OU, the fees for my stays at a hotel in Colchester on the nights before my annual three-hour exams at the town hall there, and, most importantly, the cost of the degree course

On the Euro road, the year I began my OU degree, 2007.

itself, I figured I paid around £9,000 in total – less than half the cost of going to a conventional university, which would have been impossible for me anyway due to my touring schedules and where I lived.

Because I hadn't studied in any official educational capacity since leaving school at 16, my first term with the OU was occupied in taking a foundation course. This entailed a range of humanities subjects: art history, sociology, ethnographic studies (learning about the remarkable Benin Bronzes from West Africa was fascinating), philosophy, science topics and, as you would expect, a large dose of general history. The main reason for this foundation program was to get me used to writing assignments in an academic way rather than the creative style I'd been used to.

Scholastic writing entails exploring ideas in clear prose, the use of factual evidence from reliable sources to support claims and providing correct attributions for quotes and other extracts from reference material – the OU uses the Harvard Referencing Method, a particular way of attributing authors, publications and their dates, page numbers or internet URLs for all cited data in every written assignment.

Because of the specific nature of this foundation course, I was spared having to take the dreaded examination at the end of my first term in 2008. However, for the conclusions of my five terms thereafter, I had to travel to stay in a hotel in Colchester and then get down to its town hall early the next day to sit through a three-hour long written exam with a room full of other History BA Hons students. Luckily, these important annual exam assessments – worth 60% of my overall term's mark – always occurred on a day off during a U.K. tour, otherwise I'd be unable to attend and would've scored a pathetic yearly grade.

Having got the foundation part out of the way, my history degree started in earnest in my second term with Classical Studies. This was an in depth analysis of the cultures, conflicts, architecture, philosophers, writers, poets, and other notable movers and shakers from the ancient Greek and Roman worlds. I'd previously read a lot of related books on Greek and Roman history and already had a reasonable knowledge of the subject; but because it was the second term of my educational journey, which always applies a much stricter criteria than that of year one, my Classical Studies tutor gave me a paltry 38% in total for the six assignments I'd submitted to him for assessment. Additionally, whoever had evaluated my examination for that year awarded me a similarly low score.

I'd garnered a very healthy 78% for my foundation course so was gutted to receive these disappointing figures, which was essentially because I'd not properly applied the strict Harvard Referencing Method and was still trying to write like the originator of Neighbourhood Threat: On Tour With Iggy Pop, rather than the author of A Brief History of Ancient Greece – one of my many set text books. These were mistakes I would not repeat.

I was having to read and absorb the information from my books, then write and send in wordy assignments via an online link as I travelled in a van with the rest of the band; or whilst trying to block out the noise in a dressing room before a gig; or, after show, back at our hotel in the early hours of the morning. None of these locations were conducive to focusing on my work with their inherent distractions or, in the case of a 3am hotel room writing situation, the impairment of tiredness. It made the process of obtaining a good degree grade infinitely more difficult.

In fact, after I'd sent an email to one of my tutors containing that term's travel and gigging itinerary as the reason I'd be unable to attend any of her tutorials, she wrote back saying that with such an intensive schedule she hadn't a clue how I could possibly study at university level at all; and that volume of travel/gigging intensity was replicated for every term I undertook.

But difficult is not impossible, and for the rest of my study duration I trained myself to identify the most relevant data as opposed to immaterial passages and commentaries in my text books and to write essays in an academically competent way. Plus, I made sure all my work was sent in via my online Student Homepage well before the given deadlines. This disciplined approach resulted in my overall third term score increasing to a much improved 76%; and every term thereafter I received anywhere between a creditable 75 to 79% as a total yearly tally.

The most gratifying aspect of the whole OU degree experience though was just how much pleasure I was getting from studying and learning about the different time periods, their values, impacts, and influences, as each term brought with it a new field of enquiry. Term three came under the heading 'Empire: 1492-1975' – the Spanish conquests in South America, the foundations of the British and other European empires and their impacts on indigenous peoples; the much-pondered question 'why do empires fall?' For my fourth term 'Medieval to Modern: 1400-1900' I studied, among other related topics, the European Reformation and challenges to the established church, the War of Three Kingdoms (formerly known as The English Civil War) and slavery and its abolition. Term five focused on 'Enlightenment to Romanticism: c.1780-1830' – the French Revolution and The Age of Reason; rejection of religious belief in favour of rational and scientific explanations, the rise of Napoleon and the counter-Enlightenment sentiments of the Romantic movement.

And, for my final year, 'The Renaissance', I delved into the cultural shift which originated in Europe in the late-13th century and ended with The Sack of Rome in 1527, after the army of the Holy Roman Emperor, Charles V, pillaged the city – this violation engendered economic collapse and, in turn, led to the withdrawal of patronage money on which leading Renaissance artists, philosophers, writers, and architects were dependent on to work and live.

Renaissance means rebirth in French. It was coined as a term for this progressive era of European history by the French writer Jules Michelet in his book of 1855, which advanced the opinion that the art of Italy in the 15th century had 'rebirthed' the sculpture and painting styles of the Classical World by reclaiming their authentic compositional perspectives and accurate depictions of the human form. This was in contrast to the archetypal paintings of the medieval period, where a knight on a horse might be portrayed as being the same height as the castle he was sieging and which, typically, produced images lacking perspective depth whilst simultaneously accentuating disproportionate scale.

As well as its distinctive classical approach to art, the Renaissance also generated Humanist philosophy, the Protestant reformation, advancements in astronomy and anatomical knowledge – autopsies to determine causes of death were a Renaissance innovation – plus, a more common use of written vernacular language in preference to Latin and a number of significant mechanical innovations; the most momentous being the invention of the first printing press by Johannes Gutenberg circa 1436, which allowed for the transmission of new ideas in pamphlet and book form to rapidly reach all parts of literate Europe.

All these yearly modules had fascinated and increased my depth of knowledge about their themes, but this concluding subject was the one I found the most captivating. Consequently, for my final year's dissertation (this being a much larger research project which formed the concluding part of my undergraduate degree course), I chose to investigate and write about a famous Renaissance painting housed in the National Gallery in London – the Arnolfini Portrait, rendered by Jan van Eyck in 1434. There's a degree of controversy about what the picture signifies with some art historians claiming it's a wedding portrait, whilst others assert it represents an engagement scene. Counter to both opinions, one particular professor claims it commemorates the bestowing of legal authority from the merchant Giovanni di Nicolao Arnolfini to his wife so she could lawfully conduct business in his absence overseas.

Whatever the actual reason for its execution, it's nonetheless an intriguing work of art, loaded with symbolism and hidden meanings. For instance, the small dog situated between the couple in the portrait is a sign of their mutual fidelity (dogs are known for loyalty to their owners, hence its symbolic inclusion), while the fruit on the side-table and their windowsill is one of a number of Renaissance cyphers used in memento mori – fruit eventually loses it freshness, becomes overripe and rots, just as the human body does.

Having completed my dissertation on the portrait and sent it into the OU for evaluation, I had to wait some months before I found out what level of degree I'd been awarded.

Undergraduate degrees are graded at four levels of distinction, a

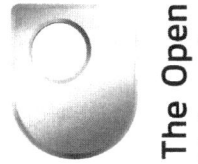

The Degree of

BACHELOR OF ARTS (HONOURS) IN HISTORY

having been conferred

Alvino Gibbs

has been granted
Upper Second-class Honours

31st July 2014

Vice-Chancellor

Secretary

561906

1st being the top rating; then a 2.1 (or upper second), which despite not having the prestige of a 1st, is still considered a good degree pass category; a 2.2, which is often referred to in academic circles as a Desmond – Desmond Tutu, ho, ho, ho! – is the pass classification that the majority of undergraduates will attain, and, lastly, what is known as a Bare Pass Grade, which is given to students who'd only just managed to reach the minimum percentage level allowing them to claim a Bachelor of Arts degree.

In view of all the challenges I'd had to overcome and the difficult conditions in which I'd worked on my assignments, you'd have thought when I received the news that I'd achieved a 2.1 level BA Honours degree I'd have been more than content with this achievement. But I wasn't. Three percentage points more would have given me a first-class degree, and it really ached my balls to think that if I'd not let things slide in my second term, I would have passed with distinction and bagged myself the ultimate graduation grade.

Still, it was with a measure of self-pride in the company of a woman, whom I was dating at the time, that we made our way together to the Barbican Centre on the 31st of July 2014 so I could take part in the OU graduation ceremony and collect my degree certificate from the vice chancellor on the stage of the great hall, in front of the 1,000 or so other students who'd attended for that same purpose.

I'd rented the traditional graduation cloak for the occasion, which displayed the Open University colours of light-blue and gold, although I'm pretty certain I was the only attendee there who teamed it with a black open-neck shirt, jeans and suede brothel creeper shoes.

After a celebratory lunch, my then girlfriend drove me to a club in Southend, Essex, where later that evening I played a punter-packed show with the U.K. Subs in a hot and sweaty venue. We were yet again in the midst of another long tour of the British Isles.

It was a day of contrasts.

So, six years and £9,000 later, what had I got out of my studies with the Open University? Answer: more than I could ever have anticipated. It had demonstrated that I could apply myself to a long-term task with discipline and determination, overcoming the various challenges and difficulties I encountered along the way – though this shouldn't have been a total surprise as it had been that same level of fortitude which initially gained and then maintained my career as a professional Rock musician over a considerably longer period of time.

As well as infinitely broadening my knowledge of the eras covered, my degree course in history also taught me to think critically and analytically – not to simply accept a popular historical, political, religious, or scientific narrative unless, after proper examination, the evidence supported its credence. Another lesson learned from the OU modules was how to access the reliability of evidence to avoid the trap of accepting and subsequently spreading propaganda, a skill which has been very useful in recent times due to the increase in disinformation and conspiracy theories on social media along with those so called 'news networks' with little regard for facts or actualities, such as

America's Fox News and the Russian Federation's mouthpiece, Russia Today.

Perhaps the most surprising part of this education though, was discovering what a historian truly is. A sizeable number of people still think of historians as a nerdy breed who wear specs and tweed jackets with elbow patches (or, in the case of the female variety, tweed skirts and blue stockings) and whose purpose is to recall, recite and comment on the dates of battles and events of the past via dreary books and articles whilst concurrently giving tutorials in schools, colleges and universities. It's a perception that is way off the mark, and here's why…

Were you aware that Jack Ryan, the lead character in the Tom Clancy series of political thriller books and adapted films – among them, Clear and Present Danger, The Hunt for Red October and Patriot Games – is no special forces' assassin or undercover espionage operative but a history professor who teaches at the U.S. Naval Academy in Annapolis, Maryland? How then did this fictional character become a valued member of the CIA and an advisor to the President of the United States?

The answer is that, being a historian, Ryan has been trained to rapidly analyse given information and to subsequently identify its substance and significance. Having taken into account all the evidence, he is thereafter able to offer an informed opinion to his military and political superiors – this occurs in The Hunt for Red October, where he rightly deduces from the data he's been given that an absconded Soviet Union nuclear submarine heading towards the U.S.A. is not about to unilaterally start World War III, but that its captain and crew have gone rogue in order to defect to the West.

That's essentially what historians do. They look at documents and data, assimilate and analyse them, then form judgements based on what the information points to and the evidence endorses. When I was in the midst of my degree studies, it seemed to me that being a historian is a bit like being both a detective and a lawyer. Suppose the question you'd been given to write an assignment on was: 'To what extent did Cleopatra influence the fall of the Roman Republic and assist in helping the rise of imperial political power in its stead?'

Well, first off, you would go into detective mode and try to find as much primary and secondary evidence in books, articles and all available info online as possible – primary evidence is that which comes from the time period under investigation (in Cleopatra's case 69 BC to 30 BC) whilst secondary evidence is anything relating to the subject after those dates, up to the present. Now this can be really tricky as everything we know about this legendary Queen of the Nile from that time period in written form, comes to us via a number of ancient Roman authors who offered their opinions about Cleopatra after her death. In some cases, well over a hundred years later.

Each of these writers would also have had a vested interest in portraying her as Augustus Caesar had proscribed and made widespread throughout the Roman world – namely that she was a foreign seductress who'd firstly used her beauty and charm to bewitch Julius Caesar, before going on to seduce, emasculate and corrupt Marc Antony who, having been turned native by Cleopatra, then turned against Rome and committed suicide after losing the battle of Actium in an attempt to defeat his once fellow ally and co-Triumvir, Octavian Caesar – later self-rebranded as the first Roman Emperor, Augustus Caesar.

Despite, even before encountering Caesar and Antony, Cleopatra being an immensely wealthy and powerful ruler in her own right with an empire that included Egypt, Cyprus, Syria and other middle eastern territories, nevertheless Plutarch, Suetonius, Dio, Horace, et al, essentially portrayed this last Pharaonic Queen as a social climbing, ball-breaking, wanton sexual predator and blamed her for Marc Antony's downfall, with no contradictory written testimony available from the Egyptian side to challenge this.

In fact, the only thing we know about Cleopatra from the primary evidence available to us is her physical representations on wall friezes and two statues, plus her profile image on some Egyptian coins, each of which refute the claim that she was the gorgeous woman that most Roman writers contend Julius Caesar and Marc Antony found irresistible.

Much of what is written by these Roman authors could therefore be dismissed as Augustinian fake news, but not entirely. Despite Plutarch largely supporting the misogynistic foreign she-devil narrative, he also eliminates the myth of Cleopatra's stunning physical attractiveness by writing her beauty was not the type 'that would astound those who saw her' but rather 'interaction with her was captivating.' This author also doesn't entirely pin the responsibility for Marc Antony's ruination on her either, noting that earlier in the Triumvir's existence he'd been corrupted by an associate called Curio who 'plunged him into a life of drinking and dissipation.' As I've already stated, tricky, isn't it?

Still, a judgement must be made and an answer to the question given, which is when the historian switches into lawyer mode and becomes an advocate for their conclusions, using the most reputable and convincing evidence and data to bolster their claims. And that, in a proverbial nutshell, is what a historian does.

Now I know some of you may have continued reading this chapter as it sluggishly progressed whilst all the while thinking 'when the fuck is

With my OU degree scroll at the Barbican, London, 2014.

he going to return to recounting his adventures with the U.K. Subs, the gigging and recording stories and all the other good Punk rock stuff', which, I promise you will resume shortly. Nonetheless, I thought it important to devote an entire chapter to the subject of history as, apart from anything else, taking on the challenge of obtaining a degree with the Open University has been one of the most fulfilling and gratifying ventures of my life.

The OU is one of those U.K. institutions, like the NHS, which all Brits should be proud of. It has offered the chance of studying at university level to a huge number of people who wouldn't be able to afford attending a conventional campus – if you're in receipt of benefits the degree courses are free and if on a low income, you pay very little – as well as for those who'd believed that further education and universities were only the preserves of the affluent and the young.

The late Labour politician Tony Benn had been one of the early enthusiasts for the establishment of the OU. When I attended my graduation ceremony, the guest speaker was his son, Hilary Benn MP, who said that his father had written an article for a newspaper in 1969 in which he proclaimed it would provide the opportunity for people from all social backgrounds between the ages 16 to 80 to study for an undergraduate degree. A week later he received a letter from an incensed man who'd read the article and fumed "I'm 82, why the hell am I being excluded from studying with this splendid new university!?"

The Open University is the People's University, and if you've got a subject you're passionate about and would like to really get seriously under the skin of, along with a constitution to stick at it through all its necessary years of study, I can't recommend it enough.

COW'S TONGUE

History lesson over, now back to the more recent past and the post-Nicky Garratt edition of the U.K. Subs, with all its fluctuations, vicissitudes, warm breezes, and storms.

With Jet now firmly established as Subs' guitarist numero uno in 2012 we persisted with our regular tour of continental Europe in January/February. However, instead of subsequently moving onto our customary extensive spring gigging excursion of the British Isles in April through to May, we all flew separately to Tokyo to play seven shows in diverse venues and locations around Japan.

This wouldn't be my first time in the country that had given the world Manga comics, Akira Kurosawa's movies, karaoke and the remarkable, if sometimes twisted, books of Yukio Mishima, among many other excellent meticulously wrapped gifts. I'd been there for the first time as a traveller; then some years later whilst playing bass for Iggy Pop, and, moreover, as a member of Cheap And Nasty for three visits; but this was to be my first time in Nihon with the U.K. Subs.

Having endured a very long flight from Paris to Haneda Airport I discovered in the arrivals building waiting patiently for me to appear, Jamie, Jet and our Japanese promoter, Katsu. Yuko had told me we would be staying overnight in a hotel in Tokyo and then travelling to the location of our first show of the tour the next day. Katsu had other plans. He shared the bombshell that we would immediately be driving to the northern city of Sendai.

"How far is Sendai from Tokyo?" I asked.

"Oh, maybe a five-hour drive," was the reply.

I'd already been journeying without sleep for over 24 hours and here was our promoter telling us we were going to be directly travelling another five – owing to piss stops and a snack and coffee break, it would extend to seven – Jamie, Jet and I sitting elbow-to-elbow in the backseat of his small car as the front passenger side had become occupied by Katsu's girlfriend, who he'd invited along for the ride. The journey seemed endless. When we'd reached Sendai, we checked into our hotel and went straight back out to eat and drink at the restaurant across the road from the hostelry.

Having requested beers and flasks of hot sake, Jet got excited because the city is known for a particular speciality food called Gyutan, which he was extremely keen to sample and ordered for everyone. When large plates of this brown, pungent matter arrived at our table garnished with pickled vegetables, I figured it was some kind of indeterminate meat dish, but it was only after Jamie had interrogated our Japanese guitarist further that we discovered the gourmet treat Jet was salivating over was grilled cow's tongue.

"Try some," he recommended "it's delicious." So we did.

Now, I love Sushi, Sashimi, Miso soup, Tempura, Ramen noodles and all that other good stuff I'd tasted and enjoyed in Japan during each of my previous visits, but this so-called delicacy was akin to trying to chew and swallow a sliced, diced and barbequed time-worn truck tyre, which over its lengthy existence had absorbed copious amounts of leaked engine oil and road tarmac. It really was that bad.

Jamie and I loathed it. Jet adored it, which meant he happily ended up with our portions whilst my rhythm-section comrade and I picked out something actually edible to eat from the menu providentially printed in the English language as well as the vernacular.

I was reaching the point of becoming over-tired as our evening in the restaurant stretched out, so I hatched a cunning plan with Jamie, one which we believed would ensure we'd have a good night's sleep and simultaneously counter the onset of any jet lag the following day. It was a simple strategy; one that only a couple of travel-weary knuckleheads who'd been in transit for over 30 hours might believe had a chance of success.

It went like this – drink vast amounts of beer and sake until reaching a point of near physical collapse, then stagger back to our respective hotel rooms to finally crash out. Problem was, despite ordering round after round of Kirin beers with hot sake chasers, we just couldn't drink enough of them to reach that desired state of sleepy inebriation.

We kept requesting, the waitress kept delivering, we kept imbibing. After the fifth round, and each subsequent time this sequence of events occurred, an audience consisting of Katsu, his girlfriend and a quartet of their Sendai acquaintances who'd joined us at the table, would let their jaws plunge downwards in disbelief and exclaim "Shinjirarena!" ("Unbelievable!") Or, as transpired, when we'd reached and decanted down our throats round nine in our quest for oblivion, "Fukanō!" which doesn't translate to what you might think, but instead means "Impossible!"

The reason for their astonishment was due to the low tolerance to alcohol that many Japanese have a genetic disposition for – Yuko being the exception. This is owing to a common absence of an enzyme that breaks down alcohol called aldehyde dehydrogenase. Not being

Japanese, Jamie and I obviously didn't have this deficiency, and so we added yet another couple of rounds to the tally before heading back to the hotel still feeling disappointingly sober.

Our cunning plan was not a success. It took me quite a while to fall asleep and when I did, it only lasted a couple of hours before I was fully awake again, lying in my bed waiting for the dawn to arrive so I could leave the hotel in search of some strong coffee. Jamie had endured the same experience and we both suffered from acute sleep disorder for the rest of our stay in Japan.

Charlie and Yuko on the other hand, had already been in the country for a week and breezed into the venue for our inaugural show having caught the bullet train from Tokyo to Sendai, which had taken them a mere one hour and 30-minutes to accomplish.

The performance was good and we were pretty happy with how well we'd gone down, especially considering Japanese audiences have a reputation for being notoriously passive; but I couldn't quite believe it when Katsu informed us afterwards that we were returning by road to Tokyo the following day for the next gig. We'd all arrived in the Japanese capital from Europe, so why hadn't the first show been there – which would have allowed time for Jamie, Jet and I to properly rest – rather than having to straightaway travel so far north to play an opening show, then drive all the way back again. It didn't make sense.

The reality was Katsu's not a professional tour agent. He's a friend of Yuko's, who'd put together these dates as a favour to her rather than as a means of making some money for himself. This meant we couldn't be openly critical, and anyway, despite the persistent jet lag and other glitches, it turned out to be a really interesting trip, with perhaps the most thought-provoking experience being our visit to the city of Hiroshima, where we performed our trademark variety of Punk rock music at a venue there called Club Border.

There was a beautiful, luminous day in progress upon our arrival in Hiroshima and having some hours to spare before soundcheck, we collected our room key-cards from the hotel and headed off together to take a look at the city.

As many of you will know, Hiroshima was where the first atomic bomb was detonated on the 6th of August 1945, this being one of the conclusive acts of World War II – Nagasaki also suffered similar significant devastation and huge loss of life when a second A-bomb was dropped on its unsuspecting civilian population three days later – and this tragic piece of 20th Century history necessitated our visiting the most iconic remnant of those appalling events, the Genbaku Dome.

Situated in Peace Park, adjacent the Motoyasu River, this domed building is the only edifice to survive partially intact within the

U.K. Subs visit the Atomic Bomb Dome, Hiroshima, Japan, 2012.

destruction zone due to the bomb detonating directly overhead (the hypocentre), which allowed the former exhibition hall to structurally resist most of the blast's intensity. Seeing it in person was chilling enough but as we surveyed the relic, a local man approached us and asked Jet in Japanese if we were Americans or British?

Having told him that apart from himself, Katsu and Yuko, we were all Brits, this aging Nihonjin then disclosed in good English that his mother had been pregnant with him in Hiroshima on the day the B-29, named Enola Gay, dropped its nuclear device on the city. He then went on to explain to us in graphic detail the horrific consequences of both the initial explosion and its long-term aftermath, which our indigenous witness and educator believed the American government and its military has tried to minimise in the post-war period. Both himself in utero, and his mother, were lucky to survive the blast, although they mutually suffered lifelong disorders connected to radiation poisoning, including various forms of cancer and being unable to procreate thereafter.

It was a harrowing tale; but when you take into consideration just how infinitely more powerful the latest breed of nuclear weapons are, along with Russia's President Putin's recent casual threats to use them, both tactically on the battlefields of the Ukraine and intercontinentally, I can only fervently hope that sense will prevail, and the bombs of Hiroshima and Nagasaki will prove to be the only hyper-destructive devices of their kind to be used in a conflict. Conventional war is hell enough.

As well as the uncomfortable experience of seeing Hiroshima's structural testament to its near destruction, and then learning about the death and desolation which had taken place there 67 years before our visit from a man who'd been directly affected by it, there were also, naturally, some lighter occasions to enjoy during the course of our Japanese excursion. One which freely comes to mind was the time I was booked into a Love Hotel in the city where the penultimate show of the tour transpired.

Nagoya is located in a central part of Honshu Island and its Love Hotels, along with those situated elsewhere in the country, are a quintessentially Japanese phenomenon. They're essentially hostelries that cater to those who want to spend some time with a lover for the purposes of clandestine sexual congress – perhaps a married man with his secretary, a wedded older woman with her toy-boy, plus every other combination of carnal togetherness you can imagine. Rooms there can be rented by the hour as well as for overnight stays and, as I was to discover, are fully equipped for all their target customers' needs.

How Charlie, Yuko and I got to stay at such an establishment is a bit of a mystery, but I think it's likely that Katsu attempted to book our accommodation last minute, and due to a business convention or a big sporting event going on, there were no longer rooms available at any of Nagoya's conventional hotels. As a result, he, Jamie and Jet stayed at a friend's house – Katsu seemingly had friends and acquaintances in every Japanese city – whilst the Harpers and I were dispatched to a site where undercover lascivious activity was the name of the game.

When we entered the hotel lobby to check-in, Yuko told Chas and I that the convention was not to look directly at any other guests we might encounter. This was because if we'd actually lived in the city, we

U.K. Subs, Japan tour, 2012.

might embarrassingly recognise somebody we knew staying there, or even shockingly, spot a spouse or boyfriend/girlfriend in the company of their confidential paramour. We didn't reside in Nagoya, so that wasn't going to be an issue for us, although I kept thinking when we reached the front desk the receptionist might presume we were renting a room for a kinky threesome, which was a distressing enough notion. Thankfully, Katsu had got us separate rooms, so Charlie and wife headed off to theirs to get ready for that evening's show, and I retired to mine.

My first impression of my hotel room was just how enormous the bed was and how pink the walls were. Big scarlet love hearts had been liberally applied to the blush-painted plaster and there were mirrors strategically affixed to the ceiling directly above the bed. There were dispensing machines on either side of the room – one that offered, if fed with the correct amount of Yen banknotes, champagne, beer, boxes of chocolates or bunches of fake flowers, whilst the other contraption dished out, for similarly overpriced fees, condoms, aphrodisiac potions, handcuffs, a selection of sex toys, and what purported to be some erotic underwear.

In a corner was a small stage on which a karaoke machine with a microphone attached had been set up for me to sing to my non-existent lover, complete with a spinning disco ball overhead and some multi-coloured ceiling lights. In the bathroom I discovered a Jacuzzi big enough for a dozen swingers to splash about and swing in, a penis and balls shaped bathmat and a stack of towels, on which couples engaged in various sexual acts had been skilfully embroidered.

Thinking I'd catch up with the news by watching BBC World or CNN on the widescreen TV, I was mortified to ascertain that all I could find when utilising the remote control was channel after channel of pornography – fuck and suck films, some dull stripteases, even S&M, fetish and weird water-sports stuff – and there I was, without a date to enjoy this fine cornucopia of tack-tastic offerings, all on my lonesome, in a Love Hotel, in downtown Nagoya.

I really should have nicked that bathmat and a couple of those towels though – they were class.

This may seem strange – unless you happen to be a bassist that is – but for me personally, one of the best things about the Subs' 2012 Japanese tour was my acquisition of what was to become my signature bass for many years. It came about in Tokyo, after our soundcheck at a venue called The Loft, which just so happened to be where we played our final show of the tour.

Jamie had only one pair of battered drumsticks remaining and so had asked Katsu for directions to a nearby musical equipment retailer to purchase a couple of new pairs. It was no more than a 15-minute walk away, so I said I would keep him company. Having set off, we arrived at the three-floored, very well stocked shop after following the given route and within the given time.

Whilst the drummer was sorting out his sticks, I wandered up to the first floor to check out the bass guitars, where I discovered row upon row of four-string instruments. The one that really caught my eye though was displayed on a wall: a brand new, black-lacquered Fender Aerodyne Jazz. Unlike a standard Jazz bass which, due to its weight, can be a real strain on the strap shoulder and the lumber region, the Aerodyne version has a thinner body and is consequentially much lighter to handle and less of a burden to the upper body than the stock version.

If it sounded as good as it looked I was having it, impulse-buy warnings in my head be damned. After the shop assistant had taken it down from the wall for me to try, I plugged into a nearby amp and heard what I was desperately hoping to hear – a really meaty tone with a soupçon of growl for good measure. I was smitten, the credit card was

Pre-show pic, Japan tour, 2012.

duly deployed, and I returned to the venue clutching my brand-new instrument, which I used that evening in preference to the Fender Jazz Charlie owned and loaned me, this having previously been stored at Yuko's parents' house in Tokyo for the band's use whilst in Japan. The difference in richness of tone between the two basses was remarkable and categorically dismissed any buyer's regret from my mind.

I retired the Aerodyne from U.K. Subs' touring and recording duties a couple of years back out of consideration for its long service and its accumulation of road scars. It now rests on its stand at my home in France although, last summer and again this year, I did give it an outing at a series of French gigs with my solo band The Disobedient Servants. It still sounds amazing, so maybe I'll bring it back as my number one for some futures dates with the Subs to give my left shoulder and spine a reprieve whilst at the same time awarding some ear therapy to those who appreciate a fine sounding bass.

It would be seven years before I revisited Japan. By then, we had a new guitarist playing with us in the shape of the lean, Punk rock machine, Steve Straughan. On the way there, we stopped off in Hong Kong to play the first ever U.K. Subs' show in that former British colony whilst protests raged all around us at the planned introduction of a bill that allowed extraditions to mainland China and a general clampdown on free speech by the authoritarian Chinese government.

After this four-day HK stay, we flew to the largest of Japan's four islands, Honshu, and lodged for a week at the Tokyo Inn hotel in the Shinjuku district of the city, whilst we played four shows in the capital during the month of October 2019 – a venue called Nutty's on the 10th, then Anti Knock on the 11th, and two performances (12th and 13th) at The Loft, for which one of Birmingham's finest Punk bands and our good friends, Drongos for Europe, travelled over to be part of the supporting line-up for this final duo of shows.

This time around, having been spared the sleep deprivation and jet lag problems that had plague me on my last visit, I had a much more enjoyable experience, although there was the matter of the little local difficulty which caused the cancellation of a fifth planned gig Katsu had arranged for us on the 14th.

Typhoon Hagibis reached landfall in Japan on the 12th of October 2019 and was the deadliest and largest to strike Japan since Typhoon Fran decimated parts of the country in 1976. It destructively made its way across the islands and reached Tokyo in the late hours of the 13th, where it persisted up until the 15th, after which it began to dissipate and move on to other regions. At its full-strength Hagibis' winds reached speeds of anywhere between 120 mph (195 km/h) to 185 mph (295 km/h) and I can personally attest to the potency of its rage having been in my hotel room situated on the seventh floor of the Tokyo Inn when the typhoon descended on the city.

The first thing I became aware of was the incredibly loud animal-like howl of the gale's intensity, before later noticing that my room windows were occasionally curving inwards, which had me concerned they might shatter from the sheer power of the cyclone's air pressure. Figuring I'd be safer at street level than my present high position in a swaying building, I grabbed the bottle of wine I'd purchased earlier and headed down to the dining room on the ground floor, which is where I discovered Yuko and the rest of the Subs eating snacks and drinking beers they'd bought from one of the vending machines in the lobby.

The rugby world cup was taking place in Japan during this time and there was an international selection of rugby aficionados staying at the hotel who'd also decided the ground floor dining room was the best place to wait out the tempest. Most of them were likewise imbibing alcoholic beverages and I struck up a conversation with some French team supporters which then widened to include a couple of Irish and Australian fellas. Soon bottles of whisky, glasses of wine and cans of beer were being shared about and it turned into a typhoon party, which took our minds off the extreme weather outside and was a lot of fun – although next morning I did have a pretty sizeable hangover, one which required several cups of green tea to help counteract the bastard of a headache and the nausea, along with what little food I could bring myself to consume at breakfast.

As well as being the most destructive for decades, typhoon Hagibis was to be the most financially costly on record, with an estimated $17.9 billion worth of damages. The human cost was high too. Japan's Fire and Disaster Management Agency reported that 98 people had died, seven were missing and 346 had been injured by the storm. We'd lucked out. The worse of its destructive energy had lessened by the time it reached Tokyo, so I can only imagine how frightening the typhoon's impact must have been in high-risk areas such as the cities of Nagano and Ichihara, where the tropical cyclone wreaked severe havoc.

I'd survived a tour van crash in Germany in 1981 which if it hadn't been for the stout oak tree we'd luckily collided with, would have seen us plummeted 20 feet onto the road below resulting in certain death; been in a near-plane crash during an electrical storm in Newark, New York in 1983; a 5.9 magnitude earthquake in Los Angeles in 1987; outlived a serious neurological illness in London in the late 1990s; and, upon conclusion of our 2019 Tokyo visit, could now add one of the largest typhoons to make landfall in Japan since records of such phenomena began, to my list of feasibly life-threatening experiences.

And that should have been enough high drama for anyone in a lifetime, don't you think?

Think again.

MICHELIN-STAR CHEF

From 2012 until Jet's departure from the Subs in 2016, we primarily kept to the yearly routine of dedicating January/February to touring Europe; April/May for the towns and cities of the U.K.; festivals in Britain and fly-in, fly-out festival appearances in differing locations around the EU during the summer months, before ending the year with our traditional November/December British Isles tour. There were the album recordings of course and other exceptions to this systematic touring cycle of which the Japanese caper of 2012 has already been covered, although that still leaves a few ventures well worthy of consideration…

We were invited by one of Germany's foremost Pop-Punk bands, Die Ärzte (The Doctors), to play two shows with them in their homeland in the high summer of 2013. Formed in Berlin in 1982 and heavily influenced by the British Punk outfits that would perform at SO36 and other Berlin clubs, by the time the request came for the Subs to open for them they'd got so big over there that playing in large outdoor locations where they could satisfy the overwhelming demand for tickets became their only sensible option. We'd also had a trio of our own gigs booked for the trip – Tilbury in the Netherlands, Regensburg and Münster in Germany. As satisfying as those shows were, they turned out to be insignificant in both size and prestige to the Die Ärzte duo.

I'd not even heard of Die Ärzte before the offer to support them arrived and so, just prior to heading off to the second-most populous country in Europe after Russia, I contacted a couple of my German acquaintances via social media to find out what this band was about. The replies were essentially the same: that DÄ were in a similar position to their Deutsch Punk rivals Die Toten Hosen, in the sense that they were both massive in Germany but apart from a limited number of places in the rest of the world where there was a significant German ex-pat population, both remained largely unknown and incapable of attracting audience numbers anywhere near as substantial as those they could command in their native land.

Just how popular they were there was made vividly apparent when we arrived to play the first of our two shows with them at the Schlossplatz in the Bavarian town of Coburg. As it name implies, the Schlossplatz was a vast square dominated by a medieval castle – the Veste Coburg – and on the August day we arrived to play with DÄ, it was heaving with more than 25,000 punters, many drinking Bavarian brew in the sun, all seemingly in good spirits and excited at the prospect of seeing and hearing their favourite band, but also refreshingly curious as to what the opening act from England would sound like.

Onstage, Die Arzte shows, Germany, 2013.

It turned out to be a very accepting crowd, appreciative of our music, generous in their applause between songs and more than willing to enjoy what we were offering them from onstage in the evening twilight. Charlie even got them all clapping along in unison during the breakdown part of Warhead, which looked impressive from my lofty stage-right position.

Before we'd taken to the large rostrum erected in the Schlossplatz, Die Ärzte drummer, Bela B, and bassist Rodrigo González visited our dressing room to thank us for agreeing to join them for these shows. It was a nice gesture and, being a fellow bass player, I especially got on with Rodrigo, discussing our favourite instrument and equipment choices – plus those that we'd tried in the past but hadn't liked – and forming a fellowship based on our parallel roles in our respective bands and similar Rock music preferences.

Bela surprised us by apologising for the catering provided for the gig. We'd already been in the circus-sized tent where lines of tables supported dozens of trays containing varying kinds of food and where fridges housed numerous bottles of beer, wine and other cold beverages – all of which we thought was a more than plentiful provision – thus prompting me to ask the drummer the obvious question: "What exactly is wrong with the catering?"

"Usually we have a Michelin-star chef cook all the meals," Bela explained, "but he wasn't available for today's concert. He'll be doing our catering for the Bremen show though and then you will see and taste the difference."

Fuck me, a Michelin-star chef! And I'd thought our regular U.K. rider – Tesco sandwiches, crisps, other snacks, chocolates, fruit, a case of beer, bottles of wine and water, and a cash buyout for hot food – was pretty impressive. Just how superior this part of their performing contract was in comparison to our own rider requests became amply demonstrated when we got to the location of the final DÄ show.

This second gig, in the city of Bremen, was at the vast outdoor Bügerweide fairground site and had attracted an audience of over 35,000. Upon arrival, we were immediately escorted to a building which constituted the backstage area for both bands. Having located our dressing room and placed our instruments and bags there, we followed the signs for the dining area and walked into a large space which had been set up to look like a regular restaurant, with various tables and chairs scattered about but without any food or drink to be seen.

Having chosen a table to sit at with Jamie, we'd only been seated a couple of minutes before a waiter came over and asked us what we wanted to eat?

"Well, have you got a menu we could look at?" I asked.

"No," he said, and then reiterated, "What do you want to eat?"

"I don't understand," I replied.

"You can ask for anything you want and if for some reason we don't have what you've requested in the kitchen, we will send someone out to buy the ingredients and the chef will cook it for you. Likewise, with whatever you wish to drink with your meal."

Resisting the urge to ask for Dragon or Star fruit juice, I instead asked for a bottle of Cote de Provence wine and a plate of spaghetti de mare, with some extra garlic and chilli in the sauce. Sure enough, a chilled bottle of my preferred rosé was shortly delivered to our table, along with my plate of seafood pasta. Both were delicious and you could really discern the disparity between the dish I'd ordered having been prepared by a master chef and the usual offerings from the bloke who knocks out the pizza and pasta at your local Bella Italia chain restaurant.

The show was also sublime. Again, Charlie got the crowd clapping

Facing towards a puny crowd in Bremen, Germany, 2013.

during Warhead and there's a cool photo from that moment where I'm swigging from a beer bottle in front of 35,000 raised hands with my bass slung behind my back, waiting for the solo kick-drum passage to end and the entire band to re-enter with the chorus sequence.

I also got to spend the night with a young blonde German woman after we'd returned to our hotel. She had earlier been invited by Chris Long to the backstage area – Chris was on the trip with Stubbsy, both taking care of gofer and roadie duties – and afterwards, in the company of a female friend, she'd come back to drink wine in the hotel bar, later resulting in the friend ending up with Jamie, whilst the blonde stayed overnight with me. It was another one of those perfect days, made even sweeter when I obtained my fee for the two shows which, to date, has been the most money I've ever received for a pair of gigs at any point during my entire playing career.

Jet was excited again, although this time not at the prospect of eating the grilled tongue of some unfortunate Japanese cow, but because he was about to embark on his first U.S. tour. I was pretty happy too as even though I'd been on many, many North American playing excursions before, this wasn't going to be one of those exhausting coast-to-coast-and-back-again fifty-date grinds of the past, but an agreeable ten-show visit, exclusive to the West Coast of the U.S.A. The other pleasing aspect of this particular escapade was that we would not be taking any of our own equipment with us, not even instruments, which meant no loading in or loading out at venues.

Paul Swinnerton, who would be driving for us throughout, had arranged for a Marshal head and an Ampeg bass SVT amp along with a bass guitar and a six-string for Jet's use, to be transported by an LA friend to Long Beach for the first show. The rest of the backline, including the drum kit, would thereafter be waiting for us at each venue as part of the agreement between our American booking agent and promoters. This meant we could dispense with hiring the usual tour van and instead travelled in comfort in a Chevy Suburban SUV which was a sturdy, evil looking beast with an ultra-glossy black finish and tinted windows.

The opening salvo of our West Coast tour took place at the Ink 'N' Iron festival in Long Beach, California, on the 12th of June 2015, at a location which was scenically spectacular – the festival's main stage had been erected directly in front of where the decommissioned 1936 ocean liner The Queen Mary was moored, which consequently provided an impressive backdrop for each band as they performed. Californian Punk rock outfit Pennywise were the headliners with the Subs in fifth spot of a hefty fifteen-band festival bill.

After The Dickies had finished their set, it was our turn to play music to the thousands who had gathered in the audience space afore and below the stage. We turned in a good show and afterwards spent the rest of our time there drinking beer and exploring the iconic art deco interiors of the passenger ship which had sailed its last voyage to Long Beach Harbor in 1967 and had subsequently been converted from a seafaring vessel into a floating hotel.

After next day's drive to Las Vegas, we checked into the casino/hotel which the promoter of our venue there – The Dive Bar – had pre-booked for us. The Silver Sevens was situated in old Vegas, a mile east of its famous Strip. It certainly didn't have the prestige or opulence of the more upmarket establishments such as Caesars Palace or the MGM Grand, but it was a perfectly fine stay over with everything you'd want in a Vegas hotel – swimming pool, gym, a bar, restaurants and all the same gambling options of the more swanky places on the main Strip, but on a much smaller scale. Jamie and I were given a cavernous twin room to share with two huge double beds and all mod cons, after which we ditched our suitcases and headed down to grab a beer and try our luck at one of the roulette tables.

Being out of pocket by $200, or thereabouts, after a mere 20 minutes of playing, I stopped bestowing on the house more of my hard-earned

Jamie, film director Susan Dynner and Alvin, pre-festival performance, Long Beach, CA, U.S.A. 2015.

cash and returned to our seventh floor room. Jamie continued to gamble, winning then losing to the wheel of chance in equal measure, so that he ultimately ended up in a break-even position.

The Dive Bar was a comparatively small but atmospheric venue and considering we've never really been any kind of a draw in Vegas, the 120 or so punters that turned up and clearly enjoyed the gig seemed a reasonable outcome and one, thankfully, that our promoter also seemed entirely satisfied with.

After our performance, Oliver and I got chatting to two women who'd attended the show. They wanted us to go with them to sample the delights of Las Vegas, to take us to their favourite clubs and bars. They were both very attractive but it had already gone 1am and, in all honesty, I was just too tired to contemplate roaming around Vegas, drinking and flirting into the early hours in the company of these admittedly alluring females – I guess it was the definitive sign that I was getting older and that sleep had now become more important to me than drinking more alcohol and gadding about on the premise that there was a real possibility of casual sex with one or other of these shapely Nevadans. So, I declined the offer. "Such wastefulness," was how Paul Swinnerton described my decision...

"But you're Alvin Gibbs!" he exclaimed, in a manner that indicated I was not only letting myself down, but somehow simultaneously letting him and the rest of the world down too, then adding "Clearly, one of those beauties fancied you, and all you had to do was go out with her and then you'd have definitely got laid. Do you know what a guy like me would have given for an opportunity like that?" It was a question I couldn't be bothered answering.

Jamie, on the other hand, being almost half my age, disappeared into the night with the duo to do what I would have done if I was still as correspondingly energetic and promiscuous as I'd been in my twenties and thirties. Thing was though, come the morning and our planned 9am departure for our subsequent show in Los Angeles, Mr Oliver had still not returned to our allocated hotel room nor was he answering his phone or replying to text messages.

Now, I may well have regularly gone out partying after playing a show until the onset of first light when I was his age, but I always made it back to the hotel for the hour set for departure, no matter what dire condition I happened to be in. It was a sacrosanct act, the mark of commitment and professionalism to which I remain devoted.

This 'Jamie's missing', situation was hardly an uncommon event. There had been many previous occasions where Jamie had gone out drinking after a gig and then wouldn't be in the lobby of whatever hotel we were staying at when the agreed setting off time came around the following day. Getting no response to calls or messages to his mobile, Yuko would then have to phone round his friends to try to discover where our errant drummer might have crashed out for the night, which could take up to a couple of hours to accomplish and would put us way behind schedule.

In this particular case, he eventually wandered into the Silver Sevens an hour-and-a-half late – still evidently drunk, face covered in the multiple lipstick kisses of one of the previous night's women which, having not looked into a mirror that morning, he was still totally unaware of. After encountering the wrath of the rest of the band and our driver, he then attempted to placate us in the way he always petitioned our forgiveness when this annoying, amateurish behaviour transpired by earnestly pleading "Sorry, so sorry guys, oh shit, I know I fucked up, but it won't happen again, I promise."

But it would occur again, and again, and again, and sure enough each time we forgave him, which in due course awarded him a sense of invulnerability, of being able to do as he wanted whilst believing there would be no consequences because he'd got away with it so many times before. This was a reasonable assumption on his part, but ultimately a succession of more serious misdemeanours would shatter Jamie's perceived immunity, and the outcome of that would be a sad,

Day off, California, U.S.A. West Coast tour, 2015.

difficult, but necessary day for both the U.K. Subs and its longest serving drummer.

The tour kicked on – San Diego, Seattle, Portland and Eugene Oregon, Berkley California – with the West Coast's balmy June temperatures and daily sunshine warming the flesh and spirits of us travellers and which provided some fantastic topography to enjoy as we travelled from one venue location to another in the spacious air conditioned four-wheel drive vehicle. There were some very minor metaphorical bumps in the road, one of them being the bad attitude and belligerence shown to us by the morons who worked at the venue we'd played at in Seattle called the El Corazon – if you're ever offered a gig there do try to swerve it if possible – but on the whole it was a really gratifying tour that concluded in Lancaster California on the 21st of June.

Even Jet looked like he'd been enjoying himself, smiling and chatting to us rather than constantly looking at his smartphone and withdrawing into his own mute, interior world, as had been the case for near an entire year by that point. It was the first time in a long time he'd actually seemed happy to be a part of the band. Unfortunately, this improved attitude deteriorated as soon as we resumed our familiar touring cycle in the U.K. and Europe. I guess the band's return to the common grind was too much to take after all that U.S. West Coast sun and glamour. If only he could have sustained his renewed positive attitude, post America, then perhaps what would occur the following year might never have needed to transpire.

Further into 2015, we were again solicited by an overseas based band to provide support for one of their prestigious concerts, this time in my adopted home country of France. Les Wampas were a Punk-Alternative outfit who had formed in Paris in 1983, and their invitation was for the U.K. Subs to play just prior to them in the French capital at the renowned Casino de Paris which is not, as its name might suggest, a venue for gambling but instead a beautiful 19th Century music hall theatre.

We were again treated very well by both our hosts and the substantial audience who attended. Having submitted our set to an approving full house, Les Wampas notched it up a level with their brand of humorous Punk songs, their lead singer, Didier Wampas, taking full advantage of the stairway on stage with its internal illumination system which under-lights every step as you descend it, these being the very same stairs Sid Vicious had used in his legendary My Way video.

This concert took place in Paris on the 3rd of October 2015. The following month, at an Eagles of Death Metal gig at the Parisian Bataclan Theatre, ISIS terrorists stormed the show and began randomly shooting the audience with automatic weapon fire. They killed 89 and seriously injured more than a hundred concert goers. It was the worst of a series of co-ordinated attacks in the city that evening, and it's chilling to consider that if these murderous Islamic fundamentalists had planned their atrocities for the month before, it could well have been the Casino de Paris show which was targeted and us, the victims.

CHANGING OF THE GUARD

I've already mentioned it didn't make financial sense for me to either fly home to France on days off during our annual duo of five-week-long U.K. tours or to pay out for hotels, the costs of which would have severely diminished my earnings. For a number of years, I'd stayed over at Charlie and Yuko's place on the English south coast during the three, sometimes four days, of downtime each week; but when they had some building work done to their house it became the perfect excuse to be rid of me, which was fair enough. Although I always kept out of their way, spending most of my time in the spare room reading or working on my Open University assignments to give them maximum privacy, I know that having a long-term guest can nevertheless be a difficult and distracting thing. So I took to sofa-surfing at various friends' flats and houses for a while, which quickly became stressful and tiring.

Everybody else in the band could return home to rest and recuperate whilst I had to travel up and down the country from place-to-place trying to find somewhere to stopover for a day or two before going back on the road again. I wasn't a young man anymore – in my fifties – and the situation really started to demoralise me. Hence, in an act of desperation, I asked Jet if I could occasionally stay at the flat he rented with his girlfriend Cindy, to which request he kindly, if unenthusiastically, said "yes."

They had a small additional room in their spacious apartment where Jet had constructed a recording studio with a mixing desk and all the other equipment necessary to demo his songs. There was a strip of floor by the desk where he said I could sleep. No bed, not even a mattress, just hard floor to kip on. He didn't supply any bedding, cushions or even a towel for me to use, so the first night I spent in there I rolled up my leather jacket and used it as a pillow and slept fully clothed as it was a cold night.

When I asked him if I could buy a small, thin, roll-up mattress and duvet in order to be more comfortable and warmer, Jet told me there was no room to store these items in the flat, so I continued to sleep either fully clothed or with an overcoat as a blanket on the floor, although he did eventually let me borrow a pillow and a towel. Now, I don't want to appear ungrateful here, I was certainly appreciative that he allowed me to stay over at his home at all, but in contrast, when Jet had lodged at my place in France on a couple of occasions with the rest of the band, I'd given him a room of his own which contained a bed, pillows, duvet and towels, and made sure he was comfortable throughout his stay. I toughed it out for a while, but then a more serious piece of weirdness transpired.

Cleopatra Records in Los Angeles offered the Subs some money to provide a track for a compilation album entitled Punk Rock Christmas, and we thought the song we always encored with in the December portion of our annual U.K. winter tour – Kevin Bloody Wilson's Hey Santa Claus – would be the perfect fit for this record. I subsequently asked Jet if I could leave one of my basses at his place for when I returned to London to record this track. Once again the "There's no room for it" excuse was deployed to which I replied "Just put it on top of your wardrobe or lean it against a wall in the spare room until I get back," but he was having none of it: "I don't want to take responsibility for your bass," he insisted.

"OK," I said, "seeing as leaving my bass in your flat is such a problem, what if I manage to find someone to lend me a bass, can they deliver it to yours on the day of the recording?"

"No," was the unequivocal answer.

I discussed this with Jamie, and his response was equally unequivocal: "Fuck him! Let's get someone else to play guitar for the track." And that's what we did. Instead of Jet, we got my friend Steve Crittall to lay down the axe parts at his Racknophobia home studio in the Soho district of London. I also recorded my contribution there using his Fender

Euro festival, circa 2014.

Mustang bass, whilst Jamie programmed the drums and, via the marvel of the WAV file, sent them on to Steve to be attached to the sparse backing track. Charlie then added his vocals at a later date.

Some months subsequent, as we sat in the tour van waiting for Chas and Yuko to arrive from the south coast to join us, Jet suddenly asked: "Oh, what's happening with the Christmas song for Cleopatra?"

"You didn't seem interested," I told him "you wouldn't let me leave a bass at your flat or allow a borrowed one to be delivered, so we got someone who loaned me a bass to play guitar on it instead."

His response was indicative of the indifferent attitude he now showed towards the band: "That's fine; it doesn't matter to me anyway."

You've already read about Jet's tardy, lethargic approach to recording the Ziezo album, and this new signal of his disinterest in being a member of the Subs only compounded the situation. But before things reached their inevitable conclusion, something occurred that made these interpersonal band issues seem insignificant.

Before I travelled to the U.K. to embark on the Subs' 2016 spring tour, I'd said goodbye to my father at my house in France, not knowing it would be a final farewell. He seemed in fine health and promised to take good care of my dog Jack whilst I was away – a formerly abandoned feral Jack Russell terrier I'd adopted some years before.

We were three gigs into the tour when the first of a trio of show-free days occurred. Not wanting to stay at Jet's anymore, for all the reasons I've previously disclosed, I headed down to East Sussex to spend my downtime with long-time friend Mel Wesson and his wife Nicola at their home set in a country village, not so far from where Brian Jones was discovered dead in his swimming pool in the summer of 1969.

On the second free day, Mel and I visited Bodiam Castle. As we explored this medieval structure with its castellated towers, portcullis and moat, my mobile phone began spewing out its familiar ringtone notification. I saw the caller was another mate of mine, Patrick Kerrane, so I answered in expectation of an invitation to visit him and his wife Sarah at their place in Dawlish in Devon during my next measure of downtime.

Patrick seemed upset, his voice was distressed and quivering and it was obvious something bad had occurred. After he'd explained he had received a call from a woman I'd hired in France to check in on my dad and who regularly house cleaned for us, he passed on the news that my father had died that morning of a massive heart attack. There had been no indication of ill health before leaving Bordeaux, no sign that he was anything but a robust 82 year-old. I was in total shock.

My stepfather – my mother had divorced my father and then remarried in the early 1980s – had tragically died of cancer in 2002. It was a very upsetting time for us but not an unexpected event. Leroy had been receiving treatment for thyroid cancer for over a year before it metastasised and spread to his lungs and other organs. He was eventually admitted to a hospice and my mum, my sisters and I would regularly visit him to harrowingly witness his slow but foreseeable decline. My father's death on the other hand was not anticipated, so my grief was significantly intensified as a result.

Although there were aspects to my dad living in my house with me that were challenging at times – the classic father and son story – I was nevertheless very close to him. He had instigated my love of history and literature whilst I was a young boy, and it should be noted, he later introduced me to the pleasure of imbibing intoxicating beverages, for

The Alvin, Jamie, Charlie and Jet line-up.

which I'm also indebted to him. Having not been with my dad when he passed on was a difficult thing to come to terms with. I felt guilty, even though there was no rational reason to be upset with myself.

Having explained the situation to Charlie and Yuko by phone, they were nothing but empathetic and completely understood that I needed to abandon the tour and return immediately to France to organise my dad's funeral and take care of all the other inescapable unsavoury necessities which needed to be sorted in a situation I had neither anticipated nor wanted to deal with. I flew back to Bordeaux the next day. The U.K. Subs played on with replacement bassist Jon Ayre, who was a friend of Jamie Oliver's and did a fine job considering the short notice he'd received to deputise.

It was an emotionally turbulent time for me, and for my sisters, brother-in-law and nieces, all of whom travelled over to attend my father's farewell ceremony and cremation in France. We nonetheless got through it in a supportive and affectionate familial way and made the best of a difficult period by sharing stories exemplifying my dad's sometimes quirky nature or recalling his common decency and loving attitudes towards us all. We also drank a lot of wine in his honour, which is something he would definitely have approved of.

Despite the residual sorrow which would take a long time to dissipate, I wanted to return to the tour as soon as possible. I badly needed the distraction and camaraderie and so, once the funeral was completed and my family had returned to England, I made sure I got myself to the Queen's Hall in Nuneaton for the launch party of the Ziezo album.

I was truly touched by the huge cheer that went up when I went onstage just prior to our performance to check on my equipment, and by the high levels of sympathy and compassion directed my way not just by the Queen's Hall audience, but at each of the venues we played for the remainder of the 2016 spring excursion.

It was to be the last tour Jet participated in. I know Charlie and Yuko – she had effectively got him the job with the Subs and had been his friend for a number of years – were done with what Yuko described as "having a disinterested passenger in the band," and certainly Jamie and I had reached the same conclusion. Our drummer then took it upon himself to call Jet to tell him his services were no longer required on the grounds he'd obviously become entirely unenthusiastic about playing for the Subs, adding that he'd be much better off finding another outfit to join which more suited his personality.

Jamie additionally told Jet that we would be willing to state on our social media platforms that he'd left the band of his own volition, rather than having been pushed out. Oliver later reported our former axe man actually sounded happy about moving on, said he felt no ill towards us and appreciated that we were going to frame it as a resignation rather than a sacking.

Jet had gone; the search for a replacement guitarist began.

Various names were ventured. I put forward a candidate who I'd seen performing with the Angelic Upstarts – Steve Straughan. I knew our sometimes driver Paul Swinnerton had worked regularly with Steve's group, Hi-Fi Spitfires, so I phoned him to find out what he thought about Straughan's possible membership of the U.K. Subs. He told me there was no more suitable contender than Steve, that he was a good musician and, as importantly, would make a very reliable and enthusiastic addition to the group. It was a glowing reference and it convinced me to push for his admission into the band.

Eventually Chas, Yuko and Jamie agreed to my giving Steve a call to offer him the job. He was delighted, said the Subs were one of his all-time favourite Punk outfits, but there was a downside – he'd already pledged to do some shows with the Upstarts and wouldn't be available for our forthcoming Hellfest appearance in Clisson, France in June, nor for our September Canadian tour. The fact that he wanted to honour these commitments spoke of his innate sense of integrity and loyalty so we told him we would get stand-ins for those two separate outings, but thereafter he had to put the Subs' interests first and be available for every other future event or tour. He readily agreed; and that's how it's been ever since.

Hellfest is a huge event, a veritable fabricated city made up of various sized stages and performing areas, food and drink outlets, numerous vendors selling leather-heavy clothing, skull rings, studded belts and massive amounts of band T-shirts and hoodies, along with the obligatory CD and vinyl record stalls. Over 400,000 mainly tattooed and pierced folk attend it every year, and it's by far the biggest festival annually held in France.

We decided to ask Tony Morrison (aka Tony Feedback) if he'd be up for stepping into our new guitarist brothel creepers for this important appearance – Tony had, like Steve, formerly played with the Angelic Upstarts and occasionally still employed his Stratocaster in the service of Mod outfit Long Tall Shorty. He was all for the challenge, and so he drove to my house in SW France from his holiday home in the French North and we ran a few times through the set we'd be playing the following day. The next morning, we got into our respective cars – Tone in his classic Jaguar, me in my humble Citroën Picasso – and separately made the four-hour journey to Nantes.

Yuko and the rest of the Subs were already at the hotel booked for us just outside the festival enclave and after being picked up by the shuttle service for performing musicians, we got ready in our dressing room close to the Warzone stage, which had been reserved for all the Punk rock outfits playing that year.

I would estimate about 25,000 people witnessed our recital and seeing as he had just one day to learn the entire set, Tony did a sterling job of employing his axe for us in front of such a large crowd, which has got to have been an especially unnerving experience for the fella. We later celebrated together in style in the artists' catering building, where food and fine wines were in plentiful supply, and where I solidified my friendship with Tony and began a new one with Rainy – the most excellent bassist of Discharge, who also happened to be on the bill at Hellfest.

For the later Canadian tour we utilised the guitar prowess of Finny McConnell, leader of the Celtic-Punk band The Mahones. Around that beautiful country, 10 cities were visited including Toronto, Ottawa, Montreal, and Ontario. The entire trip was an essentially happy one with good shows and the impressive abundance of wildlife and spectacular forest terrain daily framed in the passenger windows as we drove from place-to-place, coast-to-coast during the still warm and sunny commencement of the Canadian autumnal season.

2016 was moreover the year that the Urban Dogs reformed to record a new album. It had been 18 years since the release of the previous Dogs' LP – Wipeout Beach, in 1998 – so a follow-up was long overdue. Rob Cook and Mark Chadderton of Time & Matter Records were enthusiastic about this irregular band getting together in a studio to make a record; so with their financial support Charlie Harper, Knox Carnochan, Matthew Best and I assembled in the early part of May to lay down tracks at Pat Collier's Perry Vale Studios.

12 songs were recorded. I contributed three of them – Sidewalk Baby and Goddamn Liar, both on which I sang lead vocals and played the guitars as well as providing the bass parts; plus my elegy to Vivienne Westwood: World's End Apocalypso. On this track I again took responsibility for the guitars – as was the case for our cover version of You Can't Put Your Arms Around a Memory – although at my behest, it was Knox who delivered the main vocal on our interpretation of this Johnny Thunders' classic.

Harper also offered up three songs – Pawn Shop Special, The Whisky Song and, what is for me one of the best tunes on the album, the Rolling Stones influenced Dancing on the Heads of Snakes – as well as a fine co-write with Knox entitled Trick or Treat. The ex-Vibrator likewise bestowed three excellent solo tracks, and in addition we added one more cover version to the overall tally in the shape and sound of (I'm Not Your) Steppin' Stone: the memorable Monkees' song which was also recorded in idiosyncratic fashion by the Sex Pistols for a 45-rpm vinyl single issued in 1980.

Released under the title Attack by T&M later that year, this Urban Dogs' album is perhaps the best we've offered up for consideration to the record buying public. I was really gratified with how it turned out and was equally pleased when it was decided we should book some shows to promote it.

The Attack album launch party gig was set for London's fabled 100 Club on the 17th of November. However, just prior to this important debut show, Knox phoned Charlie to say he'd decided to pull out of all future Dogs' commitments due to his poor physical and mental health. It was a huge setback. Knox had been an essential part of the band and his withdrawal left us flummoxed as to who could successfully fulfil the vacant role. Once again, Tony Morrison came to the rescue.

Having contacted him, Tone threw himself into becoming the latest member of the Urban Dogs, applying all his typical positivity and due diligence to the task. He quickly learned the entire repertoire for our future gigs and put in a solid performance at the 100 Club – although bizarrely, completely unexpectedly, Knox turned up as we were finishing our set and decided to join us for the encore section after which, via his

Alvin, Charlie and Jamie back row, with Yuko and Tony Morrison, Hellfest, France.

microphone, he told the rest of us not to give up our day jobs (I resisted retorting that playing music was my day job) before disappearing into the West End night.

Tony went on to play further shows with the Urban Dogs – including a support slot with the Damned in Cambridge and, the following year, for an appearance at the Opera House situated in Blackpool's Winter Gardens multi-venue edifice, as part of the annual Rebellion Festival line-up. He was really excited about being on the Opera House stage as it was the very same rostrum that Jimi Hendrix had performed on with his Experience backing band in 1967. In tribute to that occasion he played his white Fender Stratocaster – the same make and colour of instrument Hendrix had used there – which Tone threw across the stage at the end of the gig in a classic piece of 1960s-style Rock theatre.

During this collaborative period, I'd become very good friends with Tony Morrison and his wife Zara; but yet another fatal and unforeseen event in the not so distant future was going to catastrophically deprive us of Mr Feedback, along with an estimated 6,927,378 other human beings worldwide.

CRAWL FOR DADDY!

Steve Straughan had debuted with the Subs at a BrewDog AGM appearance in Aberdeen in 2016 – the company had plans to manufacture a beer called Warhead, but nothing came of it – and he subsequently played a few Euro festivals prior to Finny McConnell taking on the guitar duties for a Canadian trip. Steve really didn't have enough time to practise the songs beforehand and was essentially thrown in the proverbial deep end of the pool as an unschooled swimmer, minus water wings – apologies for the prolonged aquatic metaphor.

We could have cancelled these festival gigs and rehearsed with him instead; but despite Steve's lack of reasonable learning time, we took the view it was better to commit rather than forsake, and trusted he'd be able to cope.

Although he was generally on the case there were a couple of shaky guitar solos and the occasional mistake during these initial performances, but nothing horribly grating or embarrassingly obvious.

After a couple of these shows were video-downloaded to social media platforms, the usual suspects thought they had every right to slate our new guitarist for not being note perfect, even though it wasn't his fault he'd been unrehearsed for these preliminary public performances. On the U.K. Subs' Facebook Fan Page some of these critics – few, if any, actually play an instrument themselves nor would have any knowledge of Straughan's lack of preparation due to our decision to go ahead and play these events regardless – took it upon themselves to whine about how much of a better guitarist whatchamacallit was or how Steve was a pale musical shadow of so and so and to query why we hadn't instead rehired such and such, ad infinitum.

Now, I've got to admit I've never been an admirer of this particular online fan forum. Too many of its members – or rather the ones that are its most frequent contributors – are myopically preoccupied with putting up posts, pictures and articles from the so called, 'good old days' of the band, which in their estimation were the years 1977 to 1982. Their unfair condemnation of Steve angered me so much I felt compelled to write a post in his defence, which I then dispatched to the website.

Having disclosed the lack of rehearsal time for our new member, I hit back at the critics by comparing them to a bunch of morose pensioners who extol the virtues of the past whilst bellyaching about the iniquities of the present. Although this wasn't directly related to the Steve situation, I moreover reminded them that the U.K. Subs was not a museum piece but a changing, evolving band which had released 26 albums and consistently toured for over 40 years, not just the five LPs recorded and the tours undertaken during its initial five-year history – an era the old fart contingent ceaselessly obsessed about and would consequently recycle the same old videos, pictures, songs, posters, articles and items from, over and over and over again, like some online seventh circle of hell.

You may have detected I've strong views on the subject of futile nostalgia, and you'd be right.

My post actually received a good response. The critics – at least on this occasion – remained mute and we pressed on with the more important business of touring for a living and getting Steve properly established as the new guitarist of the U.K. Subs.

To this end we saw out the year with our traditional British Isles winter tour, and then embarked on a European-wide excursion which consisted of multiple shows in France, Italy, Switzerland, Germany, Austria, Poland, Czech Republic, Slovenia, Belgium, and the Netherlands, beginning on the 18th of January 2017, concluding with a performance in Oberhausen, Germany, 17th of February.

In April we returned to the U.S.A., this time disregarding the West Coast to exclusively tour the eastern seaboard. Mo, who was the singer of the band Riots – which would be the Subs' support act throughout – had booked us eight gigs, starting on the 2nd with a festival appearance in St. Louis, Missouri. We thereafter performed in Chicago, Pittsburgh, Baltimore, and Philadelphia before reaching New York City on the 8th, where a trio of engagements awaited.

That same arrival evening we played a seamless show at a super-cool venue called Berlin in the Alphabet City district of NY, and the next day performed twice (an early evening recital for the under 21s, plus a much later one for the legal age imbibers) at another excellent club, Bowery Electric, which was situated in the East Village.

After soundcheck, prior to the first of our pair of Bowery Electric appearances, Steve, Jamie and I walked a couple of blocks along from the venue to visit the location where CBGBs had once proudly stood. It had morphed into a men's clothing store which sold a luxury label brand I'd never heard of before called John Varvatos. There was still a preserved portion of the graffiti-covered wall from the infamous CBGBs' toilet to be seen, but that was the only aspect of the joint that you could connect to the previous incarnation of the building.

The clothes were crazy expensive – the cheapest thing I found for sale was a silk scarf priced $240, with leather jackets around $1,500 to $2,500 a pop and T-shirts going for $300 to $500. Forget about the suits and overcoats, you'd need to take out a mortgage to purchase those items. As

a gag I went up to the twenty-something sales assistant and asked "Do you give discounts for CBGBs' veterans? I've played here at least a dozen times." He looked at me vacantly awhile and then replied: "No, why would we?"

"Yep," I answered "why would you?"

Those Electric Bowery shows were exceptional. A bunch of long-time friends like Jimmy Gestapo from NY-based band Murphy's Law, Bronx pal Frank Visone, my cousin Carlos Marolo and others, turned up and joined the sell-out crowds for these shows. They were the perfect conclusion to what had been a fine tour.

The following year we embarked on what will almost certainly be the very last American excursion by the U.K. Subs – unless, that is, a major outfit over there offers us vast sums of money to be their future support band in the U.S.A., in which case we'd happily reverse this decision.

Having played a succession of shows on the eastern side of the country in 2017, we had a Californian-based agency book us a series of co-headline shows with Surf-Punk band Agent Orange for West Coast venues only. They came back with an itinerary which had the tour starting in San Jose on the 11th of October 2018, and ending the 28th of that same month in San Diego, with 12 further gigs confirmed for in-between these bookend dates.

A driver had been recommended to us by the agency; but having agreed terms with him on the phone he called me a couple of days before we were due to arrive in Los Angeles to profusely apologise because he couldn't now be involved due to a family emergency. I understood, asked him to propose a replacement and he told me to call a friend of his, Steve King, who'd been behind the wheel on numerous band tours over a number of years.

Steve was hired. I got myself to Paris, stayed overnight at a Charles de Gaulle Airport hotel and flew out of there the next morning. Having landed at LAX Airport and made it through homeland security and customs checks, our driver was waiting outside to whisk me off to the Long Beach motel where Charlie, Yuko, Jamie and Steve Straughan were already ensconced.

King had got a friend to let me borrow his Fender Precision bass on the condition I had a photo taken of myself playing it onstage with the band, which I then had to send to him via an email along with written confirmation I'd used it for the tour – I guess he thought the pictorial and written evidence would somehow make the instrument more valuable if he sold it on at some point in the future. Our driver also sourced a guitar for Straughan to use.

Agent Orange would be loaning us their drum kit shells and backline which meant, as with the last two American tours, we were able to travel in a people carrier-type vehicle rather than having to hire a large van for ourselves and for the transportation of amps, drums, speaker cabinets, etc.

After two days of acclimatising in Long Beach, we set off to the house of the man who we'd originally engaged to drive us, as Yuko had organised having our tour T-shirts delivered there a week before he'd suddenly withdrawn his services. He lived on the fringes of Beverly Hills in Los Angeles, which entailed us cruising along the I-710 freeway heading north before turning east into West Hollywood.

As we drove through this part of the city, I recognised a building with a memorable story attached to it…

Back in 1987, when I was living in LA – cue swirling mist and the theme tune to Doctor Who as we travel back to a time when I was playing the clubs and bars of the city with a band called Revolver – I became friends with one of the guitarists from an outfit that once had actor Johnny Depp as a member – Rock City Angels. The guitarist in question, Mike Barnett, used to hang out with me and a group of other mutual friends and acquaintances, drinking beer and bourbon and talking mainly about Rock music-related stuff at the Rainbow Bar and Grill, the Frolic Room and various other prime Los Angeles spots habitually frequented by resident musicians.

One afternoon he turned up at my apartment to invite myself and my former wife Mary Jordan to a get together that evening to celebrate his girlfriend Abby's birthday at the very building I recognised 31 years later whilst being driven with the rest of the Subs' contingent to Beverley Hills. This location was now being used by a retailer to sell upmarket, pricey furnishings; but back in '87, this edifice had been the site of an establishment called Aladdin's Cave which, at that time was a striptease joint competing for clientele with its more famous competitor, the Seventh Veil, on Sunset Strip.

We accepted the invitation and around 9pm the lead singer of Revolver, Ike Baruch, picked Mary and I up from our flat in his beat-up 1950s Plymouth Fury to drive us to the venue for Abby's birthday bash. During the ride Ike told us Mike's girlfriend actually worked at Aladdin's Cave, which had me assuming she'd be one of the waitresses there. This looked to be the correct assumption as after entering the place and taken our seats at a table reserved for the occasion, she immediately carried over a tray of drinks and thanked us all for attending – there had been some other friends of the couple already seated there when we arrived. Everybody clinked glasses and wished Abby a happy birthday, and she utilised the situation to take time off from her work awhile, to sit and chat with her guests, whilst sipping on a celebratory cocktail.

Meanwhile, as we drank and talked, up on a stage no more than 12 metres away from where we were sitting, a topless young black woman was gyrating and rubbing her crotch up and down a metal pole positioned mid-rostrum, which she then proceeded to wrap her legs

around before expertly inverting herself and inviting any customers – most of whom were middle-aged Mexican males – onto the stage to put dollar bills in her panties. Having accrued a hefty amount of money in her knickers, she eventually disposed of the underwear, this being the climax to her act, and then proceeded to shimmy and wiggle about the platform accompanied by the music of the Rolling Stones' tune, Brown Sugar, until her time was up and she could again take a break from her exertions.

Abby finished her drink and sighed "Birthday or not, it's time for me to get back to work guys," then ascended from her seat and headed towards the bar. A few minutes later another waitress arrived to garner our drinks order. In a moment of misplaced generosity, I offered to purchase a round of beverages for everyone and then discovered upon their arrival, that I was required to pay over four-times the amount of money for these drinks than the exact same order would have cost me in one of the bars and clubs we usually frequented. Still in shock from the hefty tab, a second traumatic event then promptly transpired.

Over the house PA, a baritone voice boomed:

"Ladies and gentlemen, please welcome to the stage, the beautiful and talented Abby Rose."

It can't be, not that Abby, surely? But it was indeed 'that Abby' who emerged from behind the velvet curtains at the rear of the stage, clad in a flimsy silver lamé bra and a G-string which looked to be made of the thinnest needlepoint thread. She then proceeded to cavort and hip-thrust in time-honoured striptease fashion on the performance platform, whilst sitting directly beside me to my right – my mortified wife was on my left – Mike Barnett started shouting words of encouragement to his partner, exhortations such as: "Oh yeah honey, shake that money maker, woo, woo!" And most notably, "Work it baby, work that sexy butt."

Once she'd dispensed with her bra and begun inching around the stage on her hands and knees whilst having dollar bills stuffed into her microscopic underwear by those eager members of the clientele who'd originated from south of the border, Barnett then surpassed himself by yelling "That's it baby! Crawl for daddy, crawl for daddy!"

The whole situation was as embarrassing and awkward as it was compelling. I mean, do you look at the naked body of your mate's girlfriend in an admiring way – inevitably the G-string was ultimately whipped off to reveal that Abby wasn't a natural blonde – or do you try to ignore the show and start up a polite conversation with one of the other birthday guests about how awful the freeway smog has become?

During her performance I was doing my best not to appear overly interested in the proceedings but it was near impossible to avoid Abby's erotic capering due to being seated directly facing the action; and anyway, her boyfriend seemed perfectly relaxed about having us all ogle the revealed body of his lover; so I viewed a portion of the show whilst surreptitiously exchanging glances with my wife which conveyed our shared disbelief at what was occurring.

After Abby had finished her fleshy display and Mike had stopped narrating her movements, he asked me: "Well, what did you think?"

How the fuck do you respond to a question like that? – "Yeah Mike, great tits, bet you've had some fun with those?" or perhaps, "Fabulous

U.K. Subs, West Coast tour U.S.A. 2018.

arse mate, she sure knows how to highlight that gorgeous tail of hers."
But of course, I didn't articulate any of those observations, instead
reverting to good old British understatement for my review of Abby's
birthday performance – "It was very visual," I reassured him.

Fast forward to Los Angeles 2018 and having picked up those boxes
of T-shirts from Beverly Hills, we drove on in a northerly direction
towards the host city for that evening's show, San Jose. There, at a venue
called The Ritz, we met up with our co-headliners, the power trio Agent

Orange, whose line-up of the period consisted of lead singer/guitarist Mike Palm, bassist Perry Giordano and drummer Dave Klein, each man being as pleasant and helpful as we could have hoped for. Over the days ahead I also came to the conclusion that Perry was not just a very fine bass player, but without doubt the nicest, generous and most decent individual I've ever encountered in all my years of touring, with his dedication to the causes of animal welfare, the environment and social justice being verifications of the validity of this appraisal.

San Francisco followed on from the inaugural Jose gig where, at a venue called Slims – owned by renowned singer/songwriter/guitarist Boz Scaggs – both bands performed with fire and proficiency to a sell-out crowd. The following day we drove to Reno, Nevada. Upon arriving at the weirdly named Jub Jub's Thirsty Parlour, our club for that evening's frivolities, Jamie realised he'd left his kick pedal, snare and cymbals back at Slims in Frisco, these being the only pieces of equipment he was required to provide for the tour.

He tried to blame Steve King for this mishap, saying he'd asked him if everything had been loaded into the Toyota mini-van, to which our driver had replied "Yeah I think so." But as I pointed out to our drummer: "It's not Steve's responsibility to make sure your stuff makes it into the van, it's yours. You should have checked the dressing room yourself and not just relied on what other people think is the case."

I knew the real reason he hadn't ensured his gear had been safely squared away was because, post show, he was more interested in chatting to an attractive girl he'd noticed at the bar. This oversight meant we would have to drive four-hours back to SF to retrieve his percussion paraphernalia before pushing on for a further eleven-hours to reach Portland Oregon, this being the next destination cited in the itinerary book.

Luckily, the following day was gig-free. Nevertheless, it was still going to be a long and arduous fifteen-hours of freeway travel and with this in mind, before Jamie left the venue after our Reno performance in the company of yet another young woman he'd met there, I reminded him he had to be back at the motel for no later than 9am, to which he assured me "No problem mate, I'll be there."

I should have known better.

At 9am Charlie, Yuko, the two Steves and I were ready to roll, but Jamie was missing. I got the motel receptionist to let me into his room. His bed had not been slept in and a suitcase lay unopened on the floor. I grabbed the case and took it down to the lobby, where I shared with the rest of my travelling companions the news that our drummer had not returned to the hotel last night and was now officially AWOL. Yuko immediately started calling his mobile phone, but despite several attempts to reach him, she only succeeded in communicating with his network server's answer service.

There was a Denny's restaurant down the road, so we decided to have breakfast there and, having eaten, checked back at the motel to see if our errant stick man had turned up. There was still no sign of Jamie and still no responses to Yuko's calls and text messages. Having hung around for an hour or so at the hostelry in the forlorn hope of his arrival, Charlie insisted on driving off without him, saying "He can fucking make his own way to Portland and if he doesn't get there, we'll get another drummer in for the rest of the tour," which was an entirely reasonable point of view.

During the return journey to San Francisco, calls where regularly made to his mobile, but with the same negative outcomes. Five hours later we reached Slims and had to wait yet another hour for someone to arrive to open the club so we could collect Oliver's forgotten items. Having retrieved his drum equipment, we got back on the freeway and motored on towards Oregon where another piece of needless folly unfolded – an irrational series of actions which might have led to deadly consequences.

Whilst travelling in the fast lane of the I-80 freeway out of San Francisco, Steve King inexplicably wouldn't pull over into the adjacent slower lane to allow the car behind us – now almost bumper-to-bumper with our vehicle in the hope of getting him to budge – to overtake. Instead, he maintained the cruising speed he'd adopted, which was anyway too slow for the express lane, and continued to disregard freeway protocol in order to deliberately frustrate and annoy the driver at our rear.

I decided to tackle King about it:

"Steve, pull into the slower lane and let that guy pass us."

He didn't respond, just kept looking into his mirror with a grin on his face, seemingly enjoying aggravating the total stranger who simply wanted to forge ahead.

"Didn't you hear what I said Steve, pull the fuck over…"

At which point, the understandably exasperated tail-gaiter decided to overtake us in the adjoining slower lane. As he drew alongside us to our right, I realised King had made a bad mistake. Sitting at the

American West Coast tour, 2018.

steering wheel was a young black man bearing all the characteristics of a Californian gang member – red bandanna, braided hair, cut-off hoodie emblazoned with DEATH ROW RECORDS and with enough gold chains around his tattooed neck to make Mr T from the 1980s' A-Team TV series incandescent with envy. Having lived in LA for five years, I knew that look well and the trouble it could spell.

Steve on the other hand, despite having lived in Long Beach all his life, seemed impervious to the danger his actions had engendered and decided to further provoke the situation by suddenly accelerating so that the gang banger couldn't complete his overtaking manoeuvre. This, in turn, had the edgy individual heavy footing his pedal so that he was again level with us, whereupon King made the calamitous decision to flip him the middle finger as a gesture of defiance before immediately speeding up again to block the neighbouring vehicle from passing.

I saw the guy reach into his glove compartment and pull out a handgun. Yuko saw it too. We both screamed at Steve to immediately cut the macho shit and let the man through, but it was too late to withdraw – the gangsta had lowered his side window and was pointing the gun directly at us. I was anticipating multiple bullets tearing through the windows and side panels at any second. However, as he took aim, I saw him glance across at a sign that indicated the name of the next fast approaching exit road. Mercifully it was his turn off. Instead of unleashing lead, he threw down his weapon onto the front passenger seat and veered his ride onto the off ramp and out of our lives.

I ordered Steve King to pull over at the next gas station and there, gave him a furious dressing down.

"You could have got us all killed, you fucking idiot. What were you thinking of?"

He apologised and told me he'd been scared as it was the first time anyone had levelled a gun at him.

"Yeah, you should have been frightened alright, although if that guy had started firing lead it would have been Charlie or me or Yuko that would have taken the bullets seeing as we were sitting on the right-hand side whilst you were relatively safe sitting over there on the left at the wheel. If you ever act like that whilst on the road with us again, you're off the tour, do you understand?"

He said he understood, apologised some more and assured me he'd learned his lesson. Having survived a near freeway shooting, and still with no knowledge of our drummer's whereabouts, we returned to the mini-van and carried on driving towards Oregon.

What did I remark about having had enough dangerous high drama for one lifetime three chapters ago?

DISOBEDIENT SERVANT

Once we'd reached Portland after what turned out to be the arduous road trip we'd anticipated, Jamie finally deigned to respond to Yuko's assorted phone messages and attempts to reach him. Typically, he was super-apologetic about screwing up, after which he told her he'd stay over another night with his new female friend in Reno at the casino hotel they'd been residing at, and then, the next day, take a flight to Portland.

I wasn't happy about any of this. We'd had to travel eight-hours out of our way to retrieve his equipment which he'd left behind in SF whilst all the while Jamie continued to enjoy himself with his short-term girlfriend in a swish hotel in Reno. He'd then added audacity to amateurism by remaining there for yet another night of pleasure, thereafter, to make the comfortable and brief journey by air to the city which it had taken us fifteen-hours to get to by road. Following a taxi ride from the airport, he breezed into the Wonder Ballroom just before show time, having left the rest of his band to attempt an unsatisfactory drummer-less soundcheck and to set up everything for the gig without his assistance. "Unbelievable fucking cheek," was my summation of the situation.

Of course, many 'sorries' were deployed, plus the usual promises to delete his unprofessional conduct from all future tours. I didn't speak to him for a while. Sometimes giving someone the silent treatment is more thunderous than employing verbal uproar – but I was relieved he'd at least made it for the gig and we'd not had to cancel that evening's performance, nor had to start hunting around to source a replacement drummer for the remainder of the trip.

With the Portland show accomplished, we moved northwards to Seattle to endure the natural hostility of the staff who work at the Corazon Club, their innate levels of sour-faced enmity having attained even greater heights since the last occasion we'd been unfortunately obliged to play there – I actually heard the manger refer to us as "Those fucking Limeys," to one of his bartenders, and it was impossible to raise a smile or even some semblance of reasonable attitude out of anyone who worked in that building.

From there we drove on to play shows in Salt Lake City and Fort Collins before performing in two separate venues (the Black Sheep and the Oriental Theater) on two alternating evenings in the city of Denver.

Albuquerque and Mesa Arizona were our next host municipalities, after which we returned to California for our final trio of gigs of the tour, in Long Beach, Santa Ana and San Diego.

After our early-evening Alex's Bar show in Long Beach, Steve King

U.S.A. 2018.

suggested we go see former Minutemen and Iggy Pop and the Stooges bassist, Mike Watt, perform at a pizza joint which also functioned as a music venue at weekends and which just so happened to be a short ride down the road from Alex's. Having got there and entered the establishment along with a couple of our own audience members in tow, we virtually doubled the number of people in the room. With our entry there were now a total of 20 attendees, perhaps even less. After getting drinks at the bar, we sat at a table in this almost empty room to listen and view what was occurring on stage.

Rather than look towards the mere handful of people who'd paid to get in, Watt and his guitarist instead faced each other from opposite sides of the stage, whilst a drummer sat behind a kit and bounced his sticks around its skins directly between them. There were no songs as such, just some random bass noodling from Mike Watt who peered over his wire rimmed glasses at the manifestly drunk or drug-fucked guitar player – this six-stringer would regularly stagger forward and look to be about to fall over, before regaining his balance and resuming his original upright position, although somehow throughout always managing to churn out the discordant noise which emanated from his Marshall speaker cabinet.

As this pair went about their incoherent business, the centre stage drummer provided a series of unconnected rhythmic beats which suggested he was either totally unaware of what the other two were playing or that it didn't much matter to him.

The entire performance was bizarre. Maybe it was supposed to be some kind of jazz inspired freeform experiment or an indulgent extended jam session. Whatever the threesome's objectives, Jamie's view of the proceedings after we'd listened to their purposeless drivel for 10 minutes was a straightforward evaluation that I was in complete agreement with: "This fucking sucks!"

Eventually the whole sorry performance came to an end when the guitarist finally succumbed to gravity and whatever alcohol or chemicals he'd earlier indulged in to plunge downwards, face-first, onto the stage floor. He was thankfully unharmed, given a pizza for his troubles and sent on his way by the restaurant owner. This was not what I'd been expecting.

Still, Watt had played with Iggy Pop, and as a fellow Iggy veteran I felt compelled to say a few words to him. My opportunity to do so came as he started loading his bass gear into a car outside the venue.

"Hey Mike, my name is Alvin Gibbs and we both have two noteworthy things in common," I told him.

"Oh yeah?" he replied.

"Yep, we are both professional bassists and we've both played with Iggy Pop, or rather Jim, as we know him."

He gazed at me for a couple of seconds, shrugged his shoulders and answered "Oh, OK," before getting in his vehicle and driving away. Like the unmusical offerings we'd endured, this too was not what I'd been expecting.

You'd have thought Watt would have at least been curious about when I'd played with Iggy and what the band configuration I'd been a part of had been; but just "Oh, OK," and then he departs – really! Perhaps he was embarrassed about the sorry spectacle I'd just witnessed and wanted out of there fast, or he truly wasn't interested in who I was or what mutual connection to Iggy we shared.

In retrospect, as I had done with Flea from the Red Hot Chili Peppers, I should've just offered him bass lessons.

The year before the worldwide Covid plague began taking millions of lives and 'lockdowns', 'mandatory mask wearing' and 'keeping social distance' became familiar words and phrases, the U.K. Subversives fulfilled their annual British Isles and Euro touring commitments with the bonus additions of visits to Hong Kong and Japan; plus, the recording of a second album featuring other artists' songs, all of which were given the Subs' makeover treatment.

This idea for a record of other people's material had been pitched to us the year before (2018) by Cleopatra Records and following five-days of effort at Perry Vale Studios with Pat Collier at the technical helm, we dispatched to them 12 recreated tunes by such diverse acts as the MC5, Humble Pie, David Bowie, Queens of the Stone Age and Jonathan Richman, as well as several additional modified classics from the Rock genre canon.

Thereafter, Cleopatra released this collection using the title I'd suggested to them – Subversions – and this departure from the normal recorded output of the band garnered good sales and reviews which, in turn, led to an offer for a second album of alternative versions to be digitally captured for transfer onto CDs and vinyl.

Again crafted at Perry Vale Studios, Subversions II provided another dozen tracks from an eclectic selection of sources and managed to equal the sales figures and achieve the same positive media responses as the first.

I was pleased for Steve Straughan. Even if this duo of LPs only contained unoriginal songs, he'd at least made it onto two U.K. Subs' albums, the only other record he'd played on prior to the Subversions series being the five-track Screaming Senile EP of 2018.

For me personally though, the most significant diversion from the familiarity of the conventional Subs' cycle was the release of my solo album and the tour to promote it.

The idea of my doing a solo record had been kicking around for some years. Charlie often told me he thought I was more than capable of making a fine DIY LP and whenever we gigged in Poland our promoter, Krzysztof Lach, would also encourage me by saying "A lot of people think your songs are very good. You really should make a record featuring your own material. I'm sure it would turn out great and do very well." But despite their support, I continued to resist the notion for a long time due to three specific reasons fuelling my reticence: One – I always thought solo albums smacked of vanity and were a form of ego-massaging for their creators; Two – I truly believed there wouldn't be many takers for any record I was principally responsible for; Three – although I'd provided lead vocals for U.K. Subs, Urban Dogs and Cheap And Nasty LPs in the past, I'd never esteemed my own singing voice, and still don't.

However, having canvassed others about the possibility and received similar encouraging responses I started thinking: 'Well, if I'm going to do this it's now or never' – I'd already fully circled the sun on 60 occasions and came to the realisation that there wasn't a hell of a lot of time left to waste if I was going to take a chance and attempt something new. So, having put aside my former reservations, I set about writing a collection of songs for my prospective solo project.

The first two tunes I conjured up were Ghost Train and Camden Town Gigolo, which I would play to whoever would listen to them in the dressing rooms at Subs' gigs on Charlie's acoustic guitar. Receiving keen approval for this pair of tunes inspired me to rapidly write 10 more – I'd also just come back from a trip to Venice to discover that my visit to the Serene City had helped get the artistic juices flowing and inspired the creative impetus for composing additional songs.

Next up were the issues of where and when to record the LP. Some free days were available during the Subs' U.K. spring tour and would provide the optimal blocks of time for laying down the tracks. As for where, my first thought was to use the familiar, quality proven Perry Vale facility; but after contacting my friend Steve Crittall to discuss the possibility of using his Racknophobia home studio in Soho, I decided on this more chancy option instead.

There was no live room at Racknophobia, so I contacted Jamie and asked if he'd be up for programming the drums for the album, to which he replied in the affirmative. With Oliver on board, I thought it would also be good to have some other guest players contributing, especially on lead guitar. The first player I contacted was ex-Damned axe supremo Brian James, who I'd recorded and toured with in the 1970s. Having sent him, via the magic of the internet, the backing track of a song entitled Clumsy Fingers to a studio he regularly used in Brighton, Brian dispatched his contribution back to us a week later. It was a bit sketchy in places but after Steve applied some editing wizardry, Brian James' guitar donation sounded suitably manic for this particular track, which lyrically was a summation of my on-going friendship with Rosamunde Parsons.

Other friends, such as Mick Rossi of Slaughter and the Dogs fame; Ruts DC's Leigh Heggarty; guitarist with The Saints, Barry 'Barrington' Francis; ex-Generation X and Chelsea axe man James Stevenson; and my former band comrade from Cheap And Nasty, Timo Kaltio, were either emailed or telephoned to ask if they'd be interested in participating. Each enthusiastically agreed to play, with Rossi summoning up some Mick Ronson-style licks for Deep as our Skin, Heggarty supplying his superb six string abilities on Ghost Train and Polemic, Stevenson infinitely improving the song duo of Camden Town Gigolo and Dumb, and Barrington adding some extra swing to I'm Not Crying Now via his vintage Gibson SG.

ALVIN GIBBS & THE DISOBEDIENT SERVANTS

YOUR DISOBEDIENT SERVANT

I'd asked Timo Kaltio to add a guitar solo to a song I'd written about a mutual friend of ours, Dave Burns, who'd died of a heroin overdose some years before. Dave had lived down the road from me when I'd resided in West Hampstead in the 1990s/early 2000s and we would regularly meet up with Timo, Dave Tregunna and others to socialise in the local pubs or to go off to see a gig together in central London. I'd actually first met Burns at a much earlier time due to his association with Hanoi Rocks. He would occasionally be the opening act for them, fearlessly playing his songs on acoustic guitar to an indifferent Glam rock audience whilst utilising his Desperate Dave stage name. It was after one such performance in 1983, at the Marquee Club, that we'd originally become acquainted.

His death was a shock to us all. Dave's girlfriend had left him and in short order he'd lost his job as a video editor at the BBC and consequently had to vacate his flat. Down on his luck, he gravitated towards the wrong sort of company and as an ingredient of their seedy culture, joined in using opiates to soften the dark emotions engendered by the recent setbacks in his life. One night Burns injected a lethal dose of brown into his body. Desperate Dave was dead.

Kaltio did an excellent job of supplying the appropriate lead parts for the track, but during the course of the recording session I became worried for his own health. He was sweating profusely throughout and seemed a little shaky. I'd got him a really good bottle of wine to take home but he insisted we open it up and share it with him whilst we worked on the track. After finishing, I took Timo and Steve to a pub in Soho and got in a round of beers. The ex-Cheap And Nasty guitarist was subdued, hardly touching his pint. I asked him if he was OK, he answered that it would be better for him to go rather than stay any longer, but having raised himself up, he fell directly back into his chair again.

Crittall and I helped Kaltio out onto the street. I waved down a taxi to drive him home and after he'd literally fallen into the cab and ended up sprawled out on the floor beneath its passenger seats, I had to convince the driver that he was ill, not drunk. After handing Timo £40 for the fare I told him he needed to see a doctor urgently to discover what was wrong with him. He promised he would go to his GP the following morning.

When I got back to France, I phoned him to make sure he'd done as promised. He told me everything was fine and the following year even came onstage to play Desperate Dave is Dead with me at the 100 Club in Oxford Street. But everything was not fine. I later learned Timo had severe liver damage and that the cirrhosis he'd acquired from his constant large daily intake of alcohol was incurable and degenerative.

He moved to his native Finland with his girlfriend Beki in 2021 and we made plans to make a Cheap And Nasty reunion record, which the other original members of the band similarly committed to. Tragically that reunification album never came to fruition – Timo's death in Helsinki the following year saw to that. How poignant then that the last recorded testament of Timo Kaltio's guitar playing was in the service of a song that commemorated the life and demise of a friend.

Another contributor was Mel Wesson, my Croydonian mate of many years who'd attained a degree of fame and fortune composing film music on behalf of Hans Zimmer for such films as the twenty-fifth in the James Bond series, No Time to Die, Ridley Scott's Black Hawk Down and for the various movies that emerged from the Batman and Pirates of the Caribbean franchises. Mel provided piano and sound augmentation for what is perhaps the most filmic and atmospheric track on the record, Heaven and the Angels.

As well as engineering duties, Steve Crittall also co-mixed and co-produced the album with me. He moreover played some fine guitar on

The last time I would share a stage with Timo Kaltio, 100 Club, London, 2019.

my elegy to Joey Ramone, Arterial Pressure, and likewise on Heaven and the Angels. Ditto for our co-written fast and metallic Back to Mayhem track too, as well as submitting what I consider one of the best guitar solos on the entire record for my protest song No!

Naturally, I played all the bass parts, along with electric rhythm guitar throughout and was responsible for every lead and backing vocal performance. I also bestowed the title and artwork for the original release of the LP on the Time & Matter record label – Cleopatra Records would later reissue it in the U.S.A. with alternative packaging of a more vivid and commercial nature which, while being very different from the initial artwork, I really liked. As for the title, I'd already decided to call the project Alvin Gibbs and the Disobedient Servants and so, recalling that in the 18th and early 19th centuries gentlemen would sign off their correspondence to a friend with a customary 'Your obedient servant,' I decided to subvert that archaic tradition and call my solo record, Your Disobedient Servant.

The front cover of the T&M sleeve featured my suggested, officially leased black and white photograph from the 1960s film The Servant, with lead actor Dirk Bogarde serving his employers at the dining table,

Disobedient Servants headline the 100 Club, 2019

an image which I made more obviously deviant by having blood stains applied to Bogarde's shirt collar and white gloves, and the addition of deliberately over poured wine which flows from the glasses onto the table top. Any of you who've seen this classic British movie will already know it's about a retainer who slowly undermines the master and servant relationship so that eventually the servant becomes the master, and his employers the servants.

Before Your Disobedient Servant was made available for purchase in 2019, a single was issued. Ghost Train was selected as the A-side, with Clumsy Fingers as the B-track. For this 7-inch vinyl release I got my friend Gaye Black (aka Gaye Advert) to provide the artwork. She did a sterling job and would go on to deliver equally excellent cover art for two more Disobedient Servants' records – The History EP and the State of Grace three-track 7-inch, each being released in 2020 and 2021 respectively.

Upon its release the album elicited fine reviews and good sales figures. The first pressing sold out within a couple of months and a second batch featuring alternative coloured 12-inch vinyl was duly ordered and made available to buy online. All the CDs sold too, which amazed me. I really thought there would be very little interest for my debut solo record but was delighted to discover that my original negative estimation of my still admittedly limited commercial viability had been proven incorrect.

Bolstered by the encouraging reception for the album, I organised a tour of England starting at the Waterloo bar in Blackpool on the 4th of June 2019, thereafter travelling on to perform in York on the 5th, Manchester 6th, Birmingham 7th, Nottingham 8th, Bristol 9th and concluded this first Disobedient Servants' series of live performances with our grand finale at the 100 Club on the 10th. Bristol Punk outfit Criminal Mind were our support band for the entire tour, with the Servants' line-up consisting of Jamie Oliver playing drums, Leigh Heggarty on expertly deployed guitar, and me, myself and I taking care of the bass and lead vocals tasks – it has to be noted that Steve Crittall joined us for the Birmingham and 100 Club gigs and that Timo Kaltio and Barry 'Barrington' Francis both had guest spots at the 100 Club, as did Charlie Harper, who got up to sing the breakdown part to Warhead, which we'd incorporated into the mid-section of our cover version of the Ruts' anthem, In a Rut.

The tour didn't get off to the most auspicious of starts. Having lived in southern France for many years I'd forgotten that June in the U.K. was not always as consistently summery as it normally is in the Bordeaux region. For the Blackpool show there was a veritable monsoon in progress and we were lucky to get the one hundred or so people who braved the strong winds and torrential rain to attend. However, from then on, despite the continuing poor climate, we got a decent crowd at each subsequent venue and I was very pleased with our 100 Club turnout, especially considering this important show took place on a very wet Monday evening, which was hardly the most favourable day of the week, nor the category of weather liable to draw people out of their homes to a Rock concert.

Four days later we played our debut show in Europe. We were on just before the headliners (Das Moon) at the DNI Miasta Festival in Poland; but the day before we flew to Warsaw demonstrated that Jamie was going to be a sporadically unreliable member of The Disobedient Servants, as he had been for the U.K. Subs.

REVERSE ENGINEERING

Seeing as we were due to fly out to Poland from there the following day I'd booked Leigh, Jamie and I single rooms at a hotel, just a 20 minute taxi ride from Stansted Airport. The strategy was for all three of us to meet up at 5pm at Liverpool Street Station and then take the express train to the airport after which a taxi would be procured to drive us to the hotel. On the way to Liverpool Street our designated drummer contacted me to say he wasn't going to convene with us at the station and would instead make his own way to the hotel for around 7pm.

"OK," I said "no problem. Get there for seven and we'll go find a place to have dinner together near the hotel."

"Fine," he said, "see you at seven."

7pm came and went, no Jamie. 8pm, 9pm, ditto, no Jamie. Leigh and I had a meal during which I repeatedly called Oliver to discover his whereabouts and any news regarding his altered time of arrival. True to Jamie's past methodology, he didn't answer any of my calls and Heggarty and I were starting to consider the possibility that he wouldn't turn up at all.

The women's World Cup Final was in progress and the pubs were open til late to accommodate the matches. We found a suitable place to drink beer and watch the England game whilst I continued my efforts to reach Jamie by phone.

Around 12.30am, after 20 (or more) attempts to speak to him directly, he finally answered. I figured from the background noises that he was in a bar or pub and still gadding about in London; hence the second part of my question was rhetorical:

"Where are you Jamie? You're still in London, aren't you?"

He was the worse for drink, didn't deny he hadn't yet left the Smoke and claimed he'd texted me earlier to let me know he was going to be even later than he'd previously stated. I checked my phone, there was no text. When I told him this he sneered: "Then get yourself a phone that works!" before hanging up on me. I tried calling back several times but his mobile had been switched off.

The next morning I checked his room. There were no signs of anyone having spent the night there, nor had he bothered to contact us to explain what he now intended to do about travelling to Poland. Leigh and I took a cab to Stansted not knowing if he was going to make the flight or not. Apart from the obvious stress of the situation, I was angry that I'd paid out for a single room for him in a good hotel which hadn't been utilised, instead choosing to get intoxicated with whoever he'd been trawling the pubs and bars in London, rather than joining us as agreed.

When Leigh and I got to the airport, we were at least thankful that Jamie had made it to the gate for our flight prior to boarding. He acted as if nothing untoward had occurred and then told me he'd invited a woman he'd recently met to fly over to attend the festival. When I asked him where she was going to stay, seeing as only two rooms had been secured by the promoter at a hotel close to the festival site, he said he would get them their own room which he would pay for himself. "Chances are that the hotel will be fully booked seeing as it's adjacent to where the action is," I cautioned. "You need to contact them now to check availability and if all their rooms have been taken, find yourselves another place to stay."

Naturally, he didn't, and when his 'guest' arrived in Poland – a young Brazilian women who he'd later discover believed herself to be a spell-casting, curse-dispensing black magic sorceress, although really nothing more than a deluded nut job – they discovered that no rooms were available to rent, which meant I was compelled to let them have the single room the promoter had held for me.

Annoying as this was, I wouldn't have considered it such a problem if it hadn't been for the fact he'd already triggered so much stress and uncertainty by his non-appearance the night before which had left Leigh and I speculating whether he'd turn up at all. This latest act of inconsideration therefore doubly pissed me off.

Now you've already learned Mr Oliver had been guilty of instances of unprofessional conduct whilst drumming for the U.K. Subs. There'd been occasions when he hadn't turned up for the agreed following day's set-off time after he'd departed into the night to party and find some female company following a gig. Yuko would then have to contact all his friends in whatever country we happened to be via Facebook Messenger or WhatsApp in the hope someone might know of his whereabouts whilst the rest of us, who'd all made sure we were ready to leave at the prearranged hour, sat around in a foul mood in the lobby waiting for him to eventually sanctify us with his presence.

However, the most noteworthy incident occurred during a U.K. tour in the spring of 2018.

Having established a pickup point at a London tube station for the drive to our next gigging destination, we all managed to arrive there on time apart from Jamie. Having waited in the van for an hour, the inevitable round of telephone calls and internet messages were

Alvin playing with the Disobedient Servants, 2019.

implemented, all to no avail. Jamie's then live-in girlfriend Beka, his mother, and every friend and acquaintance known to Yuko were contacted. No one had knowledge of Jamie's whereabouts and Beka told Yuko she hadn't heard from him since he'd phoned her the day before. Another hour passed. Charlie's patience waned and he insisted we take off for the venue without our drummer.

On the drive north we phoned around in the hope of finding a replacement for that evening's appearance. Being so last minute, inevitably all the professional stickmen we asked to deputise were already engaged in other activities and so, in a desperate attempt to salvage the show, we called a couple of amateur drummers who were Subs' fans and might just be capable of playing along with the classic songs. The only person available that evening turned out to be long-time pal, Richard Copcutt, who'd been head of U.K. Converse shoes and an enthusiastic follower of the band since first seeing the Subs perform at the Lyceum in London in 1981.

Now Richard hadn't even been near his home drum kit in some time but was nonetheless willing to help us out and give it a go. We consequently phoned in advance to get the permission of our assigned support band to utilise their kit and went ahead and performed a much altered set which consisted of the simplest and most well-known titles for Copcutt's benefit. Considering he hadn't had any rehearsal time and had to be content with just a necessarily brief soundcheck, Richard did as good a job as any unprofessional musician might be expected to in such haphazard circumstances.

Richard Copcutt had heroically come to our aid, but it was Jamie's disappearance which had put us in a position where we had to turn to an unprepared and merely recreational player in order to fulfil our obligation to those who'd purchased tickets.

After arriving at the hotel where we'd be spending the night, we learned via a call from Beka, why our errant drummer had been a no-show. Jamie was caught scoring something he shouldn't have by a police officer in London on the evening before the gig. Consequently banged-up overnight in a cell, he was to be released in the morning.

Now most bands I know would consider a member missing a show due to such folly as an immediate sacking offence. But after he was driven by Beka to our hotel the next day and having hyper-apologised and claimed this most recent piece of unreliability had been "a wakeup call," never to be repeated, we again forgave; whilst I continued to rationalise to myself: 'Maybe, just maybe, the experience of his being held overnight in a police cell and facing a charge that could jeopardise his future entry into the U.S.A, might prove to be the sobering experience that finally brought home the realisation that it was time to put the work first and the partying second.'

I've previously touched upon an episode of band misconduct on Jamie's part, which was in fact connected to the release of the Screaming Senile 12-inch EP in 2018. Now, on reflection, and because in recent times I and the remainder of the Subs have fully reconciled with our former drummer as a friend, this here author no longer wants to reveal the details pertaining to this regrettable incident. We've moved on, and life is too short to dwell on something that has now become an unfortunate component of the past.

However, what I will disclose is this occurrence deeply stunned and upset Yuko, Charlie and myself, and was deemed serious enough by Steve Straughan to have him threaten to quit the Subs unless Jamie was sacked. I managed to talk Steve down, told him not to do something rash that he might later regret, promised I'd speak to Yuko and assured him we'd immediately get on with trying to find a replacement drummer for the forthcoming Japanese and winter U.K. tours.

Yuko and I did contact a couple of possible candidates for the drum role in the Subs, but both players were already engaged for the months we'd needed them. We subsequently decided to press on with Jamie after having given the absolute guarantee to Steve that if Oliver screwed up one more time, he would be our drummer no more.

Over the years I worked with him I'd grown close to Jamie. We were the rhythm engine; the essential heartbeat of the U.K. Subs plus we'd also had a lot of fun and good times together whilst travelling through the numerous nations we played Punk rock in over multiple continents. He can be a very generous person, charming, funny, smart, and endearing, and I developed an almost parental protective mind-set towards him – one evening, in a pub near where we were staying over with Vibrators' drummer Eddie Edwards, an aggressive, obnoxious drunk picked on Jamie who retaliated by punching the bullying irritant in the face, to no noticeable effect. The now enraged stranger grabbed Oliver by the throat and pushed him in the direction of a nearby wall at which point, I dived in and used a karate technique that unbalanced Jamie's attacker, before delivering a palm strike under his chin which sent him crashing to the floor. It gave the landlord of the pub, in conjunction with Jamie and me, the opportunity to surround the instigator and, after dragging him up from the ground, to throw him out of the door of the establishment, whereupon the proprietor locked him out and called for last orders.

It had been an unthinking instantaneous reaction on my part, engendered by both my protective sentiments towards my band mate and my fear that the man he was tussling with might eventually get the upper hand and do him some serious harm – Jamie could usually handle himself in a fight, but in my experience it's better to act than stand back and assume a favourable outcome.

This protectiveness had been one of the reasons I'd been the main protagonist for arguing he be given multiple chances to change his ways. Consequently, it was the reason I'd felt let down by what had occurred;

U.K. Subs Zoom video meeting during the Covid pandemic.

plus I just couldn't figure out what he thought the outcome would be?

However, we'd promised Steve Straughan that this categorically was going to be Jamie's final chance to start acting with professionalism and to become a dependable member of the Subs. Anything less and he'd be out.

His reasonable behaviour on the tours that followed helped sustain the feeling that he'd at last altered his ways and that he'd now become aware that he was no longer immune to being dismissed from the band. The onset of the Covid pandemic in early 2020 likewise prolonged this belief as gigs and tours were cancelled and the band's lack of activity led to weekly group video chats instead. Jamie was also essential to the making of the Reverse Engineering album during this plague-riven period, the whys and the hows of which I'll share with you now:

We'd released what had ostensibly been touted as the final U.K. Subs' album – Ziezo – in 2016. Nevertheless, everybody in the band independently continued to write more material, much more than could be accommodated on a mere EP or a single release. Hence, during one of the Covid lockdown periods, whilst engaged in a collective video call, I suggested we should think about recording and putting these songs out there in a format large enough to encompass them all. Charlie was excited about the idea of making an additional album to Ziezo and put forward the obvious title Encore for the prospective record; but during this period of worldwide pestilence and movement constraints, there were significant problematic issues regarding manufacturing and distribution; and, for sure, we didn't want a repeat of the Screaming Senile fiasco.

Hence, I decided to call Cleopatra Records to see if they'd be interested in a new, original long playing U.K. Subs record for their roster which, if they assented, would take care of both the manufacturing and distribution difficulties.

Turned out they were very interested; but only if we agreed it would unequivocally be the last ever original material studio album from the band – any future live albums or cover song LPs in the mould of Subversions being exempt from this stipulation. Having consented to their terms, we then considered how we were going to record this backlog of songs at a time when travel was severely restricted and most studios weren't even open for business due to the pandemic.

The only solution was for Jamie, Steve and I to record all the backing tracks, guitar solos and any vocals we might be required to provide at our individual homes in London, Sunderland and Bordeaux via technology we'd downloaded to our laptops, thereafter to be sent on as WAV files to a studio near Charlie's house in Sussex, which the owner had agreed to specially open up for him so that Chas could add his vocals to our backing tracks.

I went with a digital recording platform called Reason, although in order to have bass, guitar and vocal input for this workstation, it was also necessary for me to purchase online a good vocal microphone and the all-important interface module into which you plug any instrument that you want to connect to the downloaded software on the computer. Via simultaneous video communications Jamie and I then affixed my bass lines and guide guitars to his pre-programmed drum parts and once that process had been completed, we'd send these files to Steve so he could adjoin his contributions from his home in Sunderland.

It was a very different but surprisingly easy way to make a record, with the added bonus of not having to pay out for studio costs (apart from the couple of days Harper required), nor for hotel rooms or travel expenses.

I ended up, as was now traditional on a Subs' album, providing two lead vocals for my self-written tracks – Vision and Sound plus Slavery – whilst Charlie took care of all the other primary vocals for the remaining 10 songs at his local studio. Jamie engineered each backing track recording session; but after adjudging we needed a fresh set of ears for the final mix, we sent the 12 tracks on to Patrick Collier for a concluding polish. It was the right move; as per usual Pat did an outstanding job of achieving the punchiness and power to compliment the material.

Arguing that Harper's idea of entitling the record Encore was a bit obvious, I instead offered up Reverse Engineering as an alternative – I based this on the proposition that we'd reversed our former decision not to make another original album after the release of Ziezo. This alternative title for the album was unanimously given the thumbs up by my fellow Subs and the entire project was then dispatched to Cleopatra Records to be converted into 12-inch vinyl and CD formats.

Released in 2022, Reverse Engineering received significant critical acclaim and achieved excellent sales, although only an authentic soothsayer could have foreseen it was to be the last ever U.K. Subs' record Jamie Oliver would have the opportunity to contribute to.

CONTROVERSY

The U.K. Subs were no strangers to controversy even before our drummer inexplicably decided to submit a Facebook post offering his views about the murder of a British Member of Parliament by an extremist Islamic terrorist. Some years before the uproar created by these ill-judged lines in the public domain, we'd already been attacked by hostile critics on social media, although on that occasion it was a very different dispute which initiated the uproar…

In 2012 we'd played a show at the Witchwood Live music venue in Ashton-under-Lyne. This appearance subsequently led to a social media storm with multiple accusations from manifold keyboard warriors that the Subs had given a band, with alleged far-right political leanings, a platform to preach their ideology by allowing them to be our support act.

The truth was we didn't even know there was going to be an opening band for this show. All the posters and promotional material for the gig had indicated that it was to be a Subs only event and I was actually pleased that we were due to be the sole outfit playing that evening – during this particular tour we'd already had a couple of opening groups overrun their time slots, which put our stage time back to an even later hour; plus, a couple of these ensembles had deemed it perfectly OK to take over our dressing room with their friends, to help themselves to our wine and beer whilst we were onstage and, once offstage, generally made such a fucking nuisance of themselves that Jamie and I were forced to physically eject them. It therefore came as an unwelcome surprise when the promoter informed us that a band called Pressure 28 were going to be opening proceedings.

I'd never heard of Pressure 28, nor had any other member of the Subs. After our equipment had been set up, Jamie received a message from someone who'd somehow discovered they were on the bill and alleged one of their members had once been connected to a politically far-right organisation.

When they arrived, we kept a cautious eye on them but they seemed friendly and respectful enough, and during their set I listened out for any lyrics or pre-song speeches that might have indicated they were advancing some kind of extremist right-wing agenda. There was nothing sung or said which could remotely be construed as rightist or racist – if there had been, I would have immediately got the promoter to sling them off stage and refused to play until they'd been evicted from the building.

Post show, I was further reassured when chatting to their young bassist to learn he used to date an Afro-Caribbean woman and that he'd recently met an American Skinhead Oi! band called The Templars who had two black members which he thought was cool, seeing as it's unusual for Skinhead groups to have black musicians. If one or more of Pressure 28 had been active in far-right politics in the past, there were no indications that the band was now their vehicle to spread this ideology in the present – at least not at the show they'd played with us.

The next day a post appeared on Facebook which claimed the U.K. Subs had provided a dais for extreme right-wing Oi! band Pressure 28 to propagate their Nazi dogma after having already been forewarned that their membership included a known British Movement supporter and racist. This accusation was obviously inaccurate for multiple reasons.

We rarely got to choose our own support bands for gigs – they were pretty much always selected by local promoters based on what these organisers considered suitable as complimentary acts to the Subs whilst simultaneously being the most likely to sell extra tickets; and, as I've already clarified, on that particular night we were under the impression only ourselves would be providing the music for the Witchwood punters. It follows then we could not have invited Pressure 28 to be part of the gig; the promoter, who'd perhaps deliberately kept their name off all the promotional information knowing the pandemonium that their inclusion might unleash, was entirely responsible for that.

Nor had the one message Jamie received about their political disposition provided any hard facts or evidence regarding what it alleged. We'd received countless messages over the years claiming certain groups attached to our bill contained members with dubious pasts, among them such friends as the Anti-Nowhere League, The Cockney Rejects, The Business, Discharge and others; all of which we'd dismissed as nonsense based on our first-hand knowledge of these excellent bands.

The U.K. Subs also had a long tradition of anti-fascism, which would have been absolutely clear to anyone who'd taken the time to listen to the song Nazi Cunts (how blunt a declaration is that?) from the 1996 album, Occupied. But, unfortunately, facts don't much count on social media, a forum which has become increasingly open in recent years to hard line opinions aimed at creating division, disputes and sustained outrage to the detriment of reason, complexity and nuance.

It has also become the go-to medium for the most outlandish propositions, with perpetrators knowing full well there will always be an audience out there for any spurious bullshit, no matter how uninformed or irrational. The tragic reality is that sensationalism, prejudice and ignorance has greater currency on social media platforms these days than evidence-based facts or educated views.

Founded on one contentious post, we suddenly found ourselves in the eye of a social media storm which quickly enlarged and could have had severe consequences for the future of the band – Yuko started to receive calls from U.K. promoters asking if it was true the Subs had deliberately chosen a Nazi band to be their support act in Ashton-Under-Lyne; and when our Berlin based Euro tour agent Mutti, phoned to say he'd been contacted by various European promoters who'd read the accusations and were considering cancelling our shows, I realised it was time to start hammering the laptop keys in our defence and push back against the ridiculous accusation that the band had become sympathetic to the ideology of the political far-right.

Based on one post taken at face value, it's amazing just how many people felt compelled to comment on a situation of which they had no factual understanding and had shown no curiosity concerning the accused party's side of the story. I waded through the multiple criticisms from those who wanted, for diverse reasons, to berate us and make the Nazi tolerant claim stick as well as from those outraged by the allegation and who provided many declarations of support for the band. I then got on with writing my rebuttal, an abridged duplicate of which I've provided below:

OK, usually I don't get involved in disjointed, sporadic, ill-informed debates on Facebook but when your band is being accused of being Nazi sympathisers and thereby by implication, I find myself being tarred with the same brush it's time to hit a few keys and defend the honour and integrity of the U.K. Subs and point out a few facts to the perpetrators of this ridiculous theory.

First off, in all the years I've been associated with the Subs we have never deviated from a collective point of view that has been anything but clearly anti-Nazi. I, as a member of the band, have played at least 20 anti-Nazi events around Europe in recent years including performing on the back of flatbed truck in Italy while fascists hurled a paving stone at us when we intentionally disrupted their rally.

Listen to our lyrics and you will find copious amounts of evidence to support our conscious intentions to act on Nazi theology and the spread of other totalitarian systems (of the left or right) in the same manner as kryptonite upon Superman – surely my self-penned song on the new album 'Coalition Government Blues' demonstrates that we are not even conventionally centre-right wing.

On a personal level it's well known that I'm half Portuguese, with my mum's mother being Brazilian and her grandfather having been a black emancipated Brazilian slave. When my mother remarried after divorcing my father, she took a husband who was black Jamaican. He was one of the finest, kindest men I've met in my life and my sisters and I loved him dearly… Leroy unfortunately died of cancer in 2002. Together we would go to see Crystal Palace FC play with his Caribbean mates, drink together in the South Norwood pubs and attended parties where white & black mixed happily.

During WW II my great uncle helped liberate Belsen concentration camp. There he met & eventually married my great aunt Gunter who was the only member of her Jewish family to emerge from that terrible place alive. She became a very close member of our family. There is not a racist bone in my body & anyone who knows me knows that. Why then, with my mixed-race genealogy and hatred of Fascism, would I choose to play in a band with Nazi sympathisers? The answer is of course the accusation is both foolish and beneath contempt.

Let me now deal with how this 'theory' evolved: yesterday we played a show in Ashton-under-Lyne. The promoter had booked a support band that we had no knowledge of. They were evidently Skinheads, but so what? Punks & Skins should be comrades. Jamie then got a report from someone that they might have Nazi associations. I listened closely to their lyrics for signs of a far right agenda but there was nothing at all to indicate they were in any way promoting views that we would have found risible. They even played a version of Secret Affair's 'Time For Action', a pop Mod anthem and hardly a white power call-to-arms.

Someone then Facebooked Jamie to say their name was somehow contrived from a 'known' Nazi lexicon, when in fact it's nothing more than the tyre pressure of a well-known Italian scooter! If you go to their webpage you can see there is no suggestion of an association with Right Wing causes & they claim to be simply a Skinhead Oi, Cockney Rejects, type outfit. But of course none of this satisfied the minority hysterical contingent that inhabit planet Facebook. So, let me make this plain and simple: We would never play with a band with a Nazi agenda and/or affiliations; but based on what I saw and heard this was no Nazi preaching outfit. Of course, I cannot ascertain the personal political theology of each individual member, but it's from observed behaviour and what I hear and see for myself that I make up my mind, not from the rumour mill of social media.

I can't fucking believe I'm having to defend the U.K. Subs and myself against charges of being Nazi tolerant. What band recorded and released a song entitled 'Nazi Cunts'? It's time for this irrational and unnecessary 'debate' to end so we can all move on to more pressing issues that need our attention in the real world. A.

It was by no means a perfect refutation to the charge which had sucked in so many uninformed critics – as well as those who habitually peruse social media just looking to wade into any controversy with artificially incensed diatribes fabricated by inflated egos – but once my post had been replicated on various online platforms and shared by hundreds of Facebook friends (which in turn was then shared by their friends), it definitely helped take some of the heat out of the situation; which, in turn, allowed the storm to abate and eventually evaporate as other unrelated online disputes involving other bands and artists came to the fore.

The Jamie Oliver controversy, on the other hand, proved to be a much more difficult problem to settle.

On the 15th of October 2021, Sir David Amess, a British Conservative Party politician and Member of Parliament for the constituency of Southend West, was killed after being stabbed multiple times by Ali Harbi Ali, a 26 year-old man who had been radicalised by online propaganda videos loaded up onto YouTube by the fanatical Islamist death cult known as ISIS. The perpetrator had contrived a meeting with Amess claiming to be a NHS worker who needed his advice, and this murder of an MP, who had offered to help the man who then took his life in such a brutal manner, shocked and angered people of all political persuasions. Jamie, however, had another take on it.

On the day after this tragedy, in his initial Facebook post, Oliver inferred that Amess should bear some responsibility for his own murder by the mere fact he was a Conservative politician. After reading it I

U.K. Subs with Robert Plant of Led Zep fame and his band.

knew it was going to ignite yet another U.K. Subs' social media shit-storm and, sure enough, comments of outrage and disbelief quickly started to mount up to which Jamie compounded the issue by initially trying to defend what, to my mind, was an indefensible position.

The controversy then took over the Subs' Fan Club and Official Facebook pages with many commenting that Oliver should be dismissed from the band – there were even messages threatening the drummer's physical safety if he remained as a member – whilst others maintained he had every right to express himself.

In order to try to calm things down I subsequently spoke to Jamie by phone and advised him to write a secondary post apologising for inferring Amess had in some way 'had it coming to him' by the mere fact of his political orientation. He half-heartedly made an apology for any offence which might have been caused by his original written offering in this subsequent post, but then exacerbated the issue by trying to make out his initial piece was nothing more than a spoof in the style of the satirical comedy TV show, Brass Eye, which I, nor many others who reread his original words, believed.

Still, I felt compelled to write a post in defence of Jamie pointing out he'd now apologised and thereafter pleaded for everyone to move on and to let the band get back to playing Punk rock to the masses rather than having to waste more misplaced energy on yet another social media scandal. These words had no effect on the situation whatsoever.

The general response to my post from those who were outraged was 'Not good enough', whilst the alternative online voices continued to insist in evermore vociferous tones that 'Jamie should write whatever he wants' with no consequences for putting forward a view the rest of the band didn't share and which was now turning our personal and group web pages into verbal warzones.

I knew then we were essentially fucked whatever we decided to do in trying to end this increasingly vehement online squabble.

As the arguments raged and grew ever more hostile, Mark Chadderton, who together with Rob Cook, oversaw the uksubstimeandmatter. net website, as well as administrating the Subs' Fan Club and Official Facebook pages, called me to say that the verbal aggression between those incensed at Jamie's post and those who continued to defend it was now so bad that Facebook had contacted them threatening to remove our pages unless some action was taken. These important online platforms were where the band kept fans informed about forthcoming records and tours, plus all other essential Subs' related news. The Official page had accumulated over 150,000 followers whilst the Fan Club page had more than 10,000 adherents. Losing these online platforms would be a serious blow to the group.

Mark did his best to erase the most vociferous comments as they were hourly added but it became a losing battle as it simply took too much time and effort to police every new judgement and critique appended to the general furore. Shortly thereafter Yuko phoned to tell me someone we knew connected to a band that we were good friends with, had informed her that he'd discovered certain people connected to the political far right were going to target Jamie when he next played with the Subs. If his claim was credible, and there was no reason to disbelieve this person, she, understandably, was concerned about Oliver's future safety as well as that of her husband and the remainder of the band.

I discussed the options with Yuko and Charlie – Chas' take on the fiasco was that Jamie, as the youngest and most internet savvy member of the group, should have known better than to put up such a provocative post on Facebook and ought to have anticipated the ferocious repercussions it had caused. We decided to have a conference call with our drummer to discuss the situation.

Yuko told him that our online platforms were in danger of being taken down due to the uproar caused by his post and disclosed what she learned from our contact about his personal safety. I suggested he do the forthcoming French mini-tour but then sit out the more extensive

U.K. one, as this was where any reprisals against him were most likely to occur.

He said that if people were truly after him, they could communicate with their likeminded thuggish compatriots in France and get them to affect some physical retribution, so it was for the best that he actually quit the band and we find ourselves another drummer. We agreed that if that was what he truly wanted we'd start looking for a replacement stickman straight away. He seemed fine about it and wished us well.

I then got in touch with Steve to tell him what the outcome of our telephone conversation with Jamie had been. He, you may recall, believed Oliver should have been sacked following the Screaming Senile debacle and I'd only just managed to stop him leaving after his 'him or me' ultimatum by promising our guitarist that one more difficulty with Jamie and the drummer would be automatically replaced. I think Steve Straughan saw this as a karmic resolution. He was very relaxed about Oliver effectively quitting the band and was looking forward to working with someone that he'd consider more reliable and trustworthy.

Yuko asked me to write a post explaining that due to the backlash following Jamie's missives on Facebook we'd received information that his safety was in jeopardy if he continued playing with the Subs; and that consequently, after talking with Jamie, the band and the percussionist had reached a mutual decision to part ways. I also added in my post that we were saddened this had occurred and paid tribute to our now ex-drummer and the immense contribution he'd made to the recordings, live work and improved status of the group since he'd first played with the Subs in 2005.

One of the most important things I've learned during my 65 years of living is not to assume because you behave and think in a certain way that it necessarily follows that everybody else does. Some of the reactions to my post proved to be a textbook example of that miscalculation.

If I, as an outsider, had read my explanation as to why Jamie Oliver was no longer an affiliate of the U.K. Subs, I'd have thought 'Oh well, this was an internal band matter, mutually agreed upon with the group and the now ex-member and completely understandable', thereafter, to continue scrolling down through my Facebook feed, with no compulsion to leave a comment or click on an offered emoji.

However, I'd foolishly forgot there are individuals who habitually scan Facebook looking to get involved in disputes that have nothing to do with them as well as those who aspire to breed their own agendas and want to big themselves up by wading into any evolving internet saga – despite having no real understanding of the issues involved whilst still unreasonably feeling entitled to pass judgement. And that is exactly what happened.

People that had never been to a Subs show in their lives were suddenly present in the commentary section under my post deriding me personally for sacking Jamie for such a minor offence while deliberately forgetting, as I had clearly written, that it was a mutually agreed resolution between the band and drummer. Some old anarchist who claimed he used to blow up police stations as part of 'the cause' in the 1970s, attacked us for caving in to the right wing, as did many others who termed us 'Tory boys in St. Pauli clothing' (St. Pauli is a German football team which is identified with left-wing politics) and other accusations of a similar nature that inferred we were secretly sympathetic to the political right.

I've never voted Tory in my life and had been an active member of the Labour Party for 14 years, right up to relocating to France. We weren't capitulating to the right wing, just taking the threats to Jamie by elements from an extreme faction of that political ideology seriously; but none of that, of course, was of interest to those who wanted to join in the shrill chorus of the disdainers.

Things then went from uninformed to ridiculous – one idiot put a photo of me dating from 1982 on the Subs' fan page. In this pic I'm wearing a Canadian policeman's cap which I'd augmented with a skull and crossbones badge. The fool claimed it was a Nazi SS emblem and proof positive that I was a fascist sympathiser – I'd purchased that pin from a mainstream Punk store called Fans after seeing Lemmy of Motörhead wearing the exact same badge on his leather jacket at the St. Moritz Club.

One of the last pics of the Oliver, Straughan, Harper, Gibbs version of the Subs.

A singer of a well-known Punk outfit felt the need to declare, like some high priest of the scene: "I disagree with this decision." So what? I wouldn't have dreamed of telling him how to run his band, nor who to hire or fire, so why the fuck was he offering us his unwanted pronouncement regarding something he knew so little about? Another singer, who had only weeks before sacked his entire band on Facebook, called me a hypocrite for having a guitarist in the Disobedient Servants who regularly put up anti-Tory posts – he obviously couldn't tell the difference between someone who writes missives against a political entity and its policies, and somebody who suggests a democratically elected MP should bear some responsibility for being stabbed to death by a terrorist.

However, the main repetitive criticism which the Subs received during this debacle was 'How can you possibly dismiss Jamie Oliver over this one transgression?'

Without even taking into account the fact that we didn't actually fire him – you may recall it was his choice to quit outright rather than do the French tour – by Jamie's own admission he should have been righteously ousted from the Subs on at least two previous occasions.

I've already listed all the infractions (greater and lesser) he'd been responsible for over the years and how we always forgave and offered him another chance. So it was certainly no case of having just let the band down on this one occasion; but the dilemma for me was should I reveal online the more serious offences Jamie was responsible for as our defence against the 'one mistake' charge – which would have tarnished his reputation and could have had serious repercussions for his career as a professional musician – or do I just stay mute and ride it out. I chose the latter.

A lot of vitriol was heaped on me personally, mainly because I had been the spokesperson for the Subs regarding this issue and was therefore the easiest target to lash out at – it really was a textbook case of 'shoot the messenger'. Hundreds of individuals contacted me privately (understandably, they didn't want to be sucked into the crazy squabbles by joining the fray on social media) to check that I was OK and to advise me to take down my post and resulting commentaries as a means of ending the abuse. However, I didn't do as they kindly counselled for a couple of reasons.

Firstly, I'm more mentally tougher than most people realise. No one wants to be thought badly of, but I consider verbal attacks, especially those online, to be nothing more than cowardly, feeble attempts to diminish me and therefore I never give my detractors the pleasure of prising from me a rejoinder – put your hands on me though and you'll find my response will not be as indulgent or passive, and that's guaranteed.

The people who sniped away at me from the safety of an online platform are undeserving of the energy I'd have to expend on a rebuttal, and so I have a blanket policy of not engaging with morons on the internet having realised full well that's exactly what they're angling for. It's better to disregard their claims and attacks in the knowledge that on the fast-moving, ever fluctuating internet, their words will soon be superfluous history as new controversies move to the fore.

Secondly, I actually found the whole furore very instructive. I learned who my true friends were as opposed to those who claimed friendship but were nothing more than acquaintances that went with what was seemingly popular at the time. Fuck 'em! They're nothing more than spineless arse-wipes and having now revealed their identities to me I know their names and their games.

I did, after some months, delete the post and its resulting comments from my Facebook page having let it run its course without interference. Just before the U.K. tour began, which would see new member Dave Humphries taking on the drum responsibilities, I visited Jamie at his flat in London. We quickly transferred ourselves to a nearby pub and over pints of beer talked about what had occurred.

He told me he'd anyway considered leaving the Subs to focus on a new band – UltraBomb – which he'd formed with ex-Hüsker Du bassist Greg

Norton and Mahones' singer/guitarist Finny McConnell. He considered what had happened as being in the best interests of both the U.K. Subs and himself. We parted as friends and remain so.

If our detractors had thought Jamie's exit would create a backlash in terms of live attendance and enthusiasm for the Subs, they were very much mistaken. That subsequent British Isles tour saw us have more sold out shows than ever as the whole overblown controversy dissipated. We played on as if nothing of any consequence had occurred knowing full well what really counts is what happens in the genuine physical world rather than the here-today-gone-tomorrow background noise of the Metaverse.

As I noted earlier, it had all been very instructive.

COVID, BREXIT AND ME

The Covid virus took the lives of millions of people worldwide from the years 2020 to 2022, among them, from the Punk rock community, my friend, the Urban Dogs and Long Tall Shorty guitarist Tony Morrison (aka Tony Feedback), frontman of the Angelic Upstarts, Thomas 'Mensi' Mensforth, Soft Boys bassist Matthew Seligman and the keyboard ace of The Stranglers, Dave Greenfield.

As well the appalling loss of life, this plague also ended the possibility of touring again for an excruciating length of time, made all but essential travel unfeasible and saw us having to spend long periods confined to our homes. My income stream dried up as tour after tour was cancelled and I even succumbed to the virus myself after a lockdown was briefly lifted and the Subs were invited to play a special one-day Rebellion event at the Winter Gardens in Blackpool.

I'd ignored all the noise regarding vaccination risks and disregarded the other Covid-related conspiracy theories which were rife on the internet. Having already been inoculated, I made a speedy recovery without any long-term issues – I have since been re-jabbed three times and although these immunisations didn't prevent my acquiring the virus again on two subsequent occasions, each additional infection was a milder experience than the previous which I'm convinced, was due to the extra protection the vaccines awarded me.

People made their own choices. I understand that; but my advice is always to choose science over speculation.

Despite the many negative elements associated with this unfortunate phase of recent history there were, for me at least, some positives too. This enforced break from the touring routine I'd relentlessly submitted myself to for more than two decades, bestowed the time to finish Volume I of my memoir series entitled Diminished Responsibility: My Life as a U.K. Sub, and other strange stories, as well as the opportunity to complete Volume II – Volume I was published by Tome & Metre (the book division of Time & Matter Records) in 2020 whilst Volume II was made available for acquisition the following year.

Henry Rollins graciously provided the very flattering Foreword for the first of these books whilst Ginger Wildheart gifted the subsequent tome with an equally well-written and complimentary introductory piece. Both editions achieved unanimous critical acclaim, with Volume I even earning the distinction of being Vive Le Rock! Magazine's Book of the Year for 2020.

With Jamie Oliver's assistance, I also managed to record a new Disobedient Servants' single, which featured a reworking of my 1990s

My houses in SW France:
the main house on the left, smaller house on the right.

Urban Dogs Wipeout Beach album contribution, State of Grace, along with two freshly written B-side tunes entitled Too Bad She's in Love, and, Brother, Sister. By utilising the computer software we'd employed for the Reverse Engineering LP, Jamie and I put together the backing tracks from our respective locations in Bordeaux and London, after which I added the vocals. We then sent on the results to guitarist Leigh Heggarty for his home input. This 7-inch vinyl offering was then released by Time & Matter Records in 2021, and again showcased some superb sleeve cover artwork by Gaye Black.

The other advantage to being powerless to tour was that for the first time in many years I could properly relax and enjoy the beautiful house I owned in South-West France. Previously I'd only got to intermittently spend time at the Bordeaux homestead between lengthy excursions dispensing Punk rock music around the world, but the various lengthy lockdowns which were imposed over a two year period, ensured I could finally, fully, appreciate and enjoy its many rooms with high ceilings and marble fireplaces, its large 19th century windows, to take full advantage of the exterior terracotta roof-tiled dining area and to witness the amazing sunsets and the ensuing constellations of stars which would emerge after twilight from the vantage point of my courtyard with its grape vines, pomegranate and fig trees.

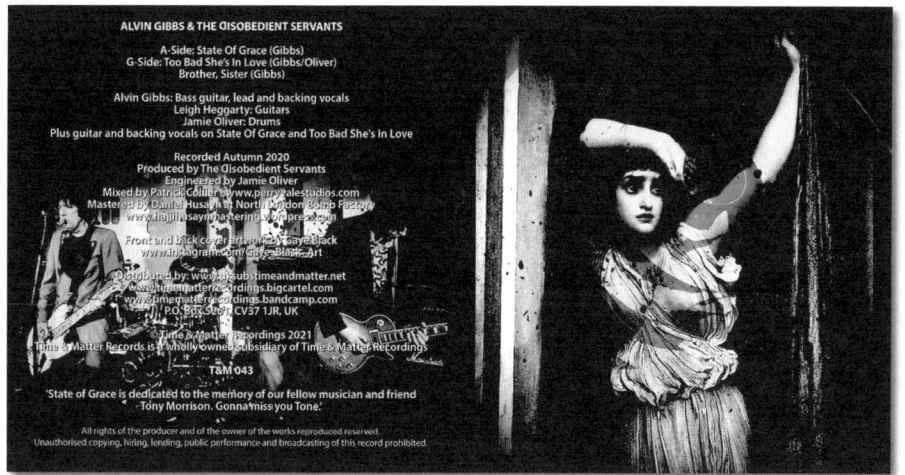

It was certainly true there wasn't any income forthcoming as these months elapsed and I consequently had to live on my savings; but there again, with the non-essential shops shut and all music venues, cinemas, bars, and restaurants closed, plus the imposition of severe travel restrictions, there wasn't that much to spend my money on either – just a weekly shop for food supplies and, naturally, some consoling bottles of good wine.

Socialising with other households was restricted too, so in order to avoid feeling isolated or lapsing into depression from lack of social interaction, I took part in weekly video group chats with Yuko and my fellow Subs; with family members and friends, and the woman I'd first met in Edinburgh when playing for Cheap And Nasty in the early 1990s, Rosamunde Parsons.

Rosamunde told me she still was residing with her partner but they were no longer romantically involved. It had developed into a purely platonic friendship. They'd not been amorously or physically intimate for a couple of years and she had also become disenchanted with living in western Scotland and was looking for a significant alteration to her life. The more we talked, the more I realised I was willing to take the chance of living with her and for us to become a permanent couple.

When I touted the idea, Roz disclosed it was what she wanted too. This would obviously entail her leaving the house she still shared with her former partner and relocating to my place in SW France. However, the strict travel restraints which had been imposed as a result of the pandemic meant this wouldn't be possible until the virus had peaked and waned. Plus there was another major hindrance – Brexit.

Britain's thorny relationship with the European project goes back to its membership of the EEC (European Economic Community) in 1973.

Following its inclusion after two previous attempts to join had been blocked by the then President of France Charles de Gaulle, both Euro-sceptic Labour and Conservative politicians immediately started to argue for withdrawal, which eventually led to Labour Prime Minister Harold Wilson's decision to hold a national referendum on whether to remain in the EEC in 1975. The result was a resounding 67.23% of votes cast for the Remain campaign.

When in 1983 the Labour Party led by Michael Foot offered withdrawal without a referendum, it was heavily defeated in that year's General Election, with the party thereafter reversing its policy to a pro-EEC stance when Foot's replacement, Neil Kinnock, became leader. Foot had lost the election to Margaret Thatcher who, although prone to Euro-sceptic bluster, actually became one of the architects of greater European integration during the 1980s.

Despite being unenthusiastic about political union, Thatcher was passionate about the introduction of a Single Market – as a free-marketer she saw the economic advantages of the U.K. being in a European free-trade zone devoid of import tariffs and barriers. She made numerous concessions to achieve implementation of the Single Market which jarred with her reputation for being an uncompromising political negotiator (her Tory press nickname was, after all, 'the Iron Lady'), with her biggest compromise being acceptance of the Single Market's enshrinement in a compulsory legal treaty rather than her preferred option of a non-binding agreement. The resulting document which Thatcher signed up to – The Single European Act – came into effect in 1987 and not only engendered implementation of the Single Market, but also bought about the closer monetary and political union that Thatcher had originally hoped to swerve.

Having resigned in 1990, Margaret Thatcher's Conservative successor, John Major, implemented a policy of further integration by signing the Maastricht Treaty in 1992, despite criticism from a small but increasingly vocal and media-savvy group of backbench MPs and a trio of cabinet ministers who he famously referred to as "The Bastards." This treaty introduced, among other closer union steps, the idea of European Citizenship, legal guarantees for civil, political and economic rights within the EU, the creation of a central bank and evolution from a purely economic institution to that of a more profoundly political one.

However, as a concession to the increasingly strident minority of euro-sceptic MPs within his parliamentary party and to counter a newly formed anti-EU political organisation UKIP (U.K. Independence Party) – founded by the wealthy, tax-avoiding, non-dom tycoon James Goldsmith – Major negotiated Britain's opt-out from the treaty's European Social Charter. As previously touched upon, this part of the

Maastricht Treaty pledged fundamental EU-wide legal rights relating to employment, housing, education, social protection and welfare. Nonetheless, Major's shameful attempt to placate "The bastards" and others on the right of his party, failed. It merely emboldened the Euro-critics and led to deeper divisions within his government and the wider Tory party.

It's a proven dictum that divided political parties do not win elections; and the exposed schisms and discord within the Conservative Party over the question of the U.K.'s continuing relationship with the EU became one of the notable factors why John Major lost the General Election to Tony Bair in the Labour leader's landslide victory of 1997 – incidentally, UKIP failed to win a single seat in this election, despite having fielded candidates in 547 nationwide constituencies.

As PM, Blair adopted a solidly pro-European integration policy to the extent that he even considered replacing the British pound with the Euro as the country's common currency. Gordon Brown, having become PM after Blair had stepped down in 2007, continued the enthusiastic EU stance of his predecessor. Three years later, Brown narrowly lost his premiership to Conservative leader David Cameron who, following a hung parliament result at the 2010 General Election, formed a governing coalition with the Liberal Democratic Party.

Cameron inherited the rising tide of Euro-cynicism in own his party which had dogged John Major during his term in office and as a strategic act of appeasement to the malcontents and despite still firmly believing in the advantages of continued membership of the European Union himself, he agreed to an in-out U.K. referendum vote to be included as a Conservative manifesto pledge for the 2015 General Election. The Tories won a slender outright victory at that election with a majority of just 12 seats after which, Cameron set about trying to reform EU policy in certain areas – particularly regarding the topic of rising immigration. He then claimed he'd made headway in his negotiations and believed this progress would be enough to counter Euro-scepticism and deliver a decisive vote for Britain continuing its membership of the European Union.

On the 23rd of June 2016, the U.K. held the promised referendum on whether to leave or remain in the EU. The result was 52% voted for withdrawal whilst 48% voted to remain. The immediate aftermath of Britain's decision to leave the world's largest trading bloc was turmoil in both the stock and money markets (the pound lost 15% of its value against the dollar in the weeks following thc Brexit decision) and having led the Remain campaign and failed, David Cameron resigned as Prime Minister. After a Conservative leadership election, he was replaced as PM by the former Home Secretary, Theresa May.

Although May had campaigned for Remain, she was obliged to initiate the process for Britain's secession from the bloc, a fraught and very complex procedure which eventually led to her own downfall and resignation in 2019.

Now I know some of you are thinking: 'Here he goes again, what the hell has all this historical background information about Britain's long-term relationship with the European Union got to do with either the U.K. Subs or his career in Rock music or the man's life in general?' Well, being a historian, I know the importance of providing context before offering analysis or opinion, and having now provided you with the context here's my take on the whole Brexit saga and, in the chapter that follows, how it affected me personally…

The Brexit referendum should have never taken place. Even as late as December 2015, there was, according to the polling organisation ComRez, 'a clear majority in favour of remaining in the EU'. David Cameron only agreed to it as a means of neutralising those who wanted to leave the union in his own party and to counter external spivs and chancers, such as the former leader of UKIP Nigel Farage who, for a couple of years prior to the referendum, seemed to be on just about every political British TV and radio talk show spouting his 'the EU is the root of all evil' views despite standing for election to the House of Commons several times and being rejected by the voters on each occasion. Another chancer getting excessive media attention was the de-facto leader of the Leave campaign, Boris Johnson.

Having already acquired a reputation for being a proven fabricator and ambitious political actor – a man capable of taking any side deemed useful in his pursuit of becoming PM, even if he personally disagreed with it – Johnson set about trying to induce xenophobia and pandered to the worst prejudices of the British public by repeatedly making false claims in newspapers and during TV/radio appearances. The more ridiculous the falsehood the more news coverage he got – it's an unfortunate truth that every branch of the media would much sooner report fictional sensationalism than laborious but verifiable factual information on the grounds it believes the former arouses greater public interest.

They lapped up the bullshit he propagated, such as his absurd claim that the EU Commission wanted to outlaw bent bananas and (wait for it) were preparing a directive regulating condom size to a one-fits-all based on the average length of an Italian man's penis; and let's not forget his shameful comparison of EU goals as being the same as those of Napoleon Bonaparte and Adolf Hitler.

However, the reality was, up until he saw the opportunity to undermine Remainer Theresa May's premiership by becoming the poster boy for the Leave campaign, Boris Johnson had previously been a supporter of the European Union.

In his book published in 2001 entitled Friends, Voters, Countrymen, he argued that Britain should stay in the EU because, among other given reasons: 'We would lose influence in the designing of the continent.' In 2005 he described himself as "A bit of a fan of the European Union," and added "If we didn't have one, we'd invent something like it." In 2013, bumbling Boris wrote: 'our problems are not caused by Bwussels (his deliberate misspelling of the city where the EU parliament is situated), but by British short-termism.'

Even at the beginning of the referendum year 2016 he stated that "The membership fee [of the EU] seems rather small for all that access. Why are we so determined to turn our backs on it?" And yet, just a few months later, having calculated he'd become the heir apparent leader of the Conservative Party by switching allegiance even if, as was likely, the vote would go Remain's way, he was suddenly spouting, among other nonsense, that the EU was draining Britain financially dry – he blatantly lied that the U.K. was paying £350m a week for membership, a figure that even arch Leaver Nigel Farage now gleefully admits was a total fabrication – and that the money saved should instead be used to properly fund the NHS and other social services.

All horseshit of course as after the vote was won and the U.K. Statistics Authority pointed out the gross inaccuracy of this claim, Johnson, in typically insincere style, maintained he was "Shocked" that his words had been taken at face value and to believe he was seriously suggesting £350m might be available for extra public spending, was "a wilful distortion" of his true meaning: this being an outright admission that what was written on the side of his Brexit campaign bus – 'We send the EU £350m a week: let's fund our NHS instead' – was nothing more than a counterfeit slogan designed to mislead the British public.

Another great Leave lie was the 'take back control of our borders' solution to what was seen by many in the U.K. as unacceptable levels of immigration. The Leave campaign insisted the high degree of migrants was due to the EU's flimsy border controls and its applicable laws, which made stopping the influx of foreign workers and illegal immigrants, impossible for the British government to implement. Repeating this spurious allegation as he toured the country to promote the supposed benefits of Brexit, Johnson told voters that "leaving the European project would allow the U.K. to take back control of its money, its laws and its borders," thus, he insisted, giving the British government the means to drastically reduce and control immigration. We will examine the validity of that claim shortly.

As well as playing the 'fear of the foreigner' card to great effect, the Leave campaign also successfully convinced a large percentage of referendum voters that the bad economic situation prevailing in Great Britain was due to its membership of the European Union. Like the immigration issue, this was also a case of deliberate misdirection. The real architects of the U.K.'s dismal fiscal condition and its resulting social depravations and inequities were in fact a lot closer to home.

Conservative Prime Minister David Cameron and his Chancellor, George Osborne, instigated a decade-long policy of austerity which they sold to the country as a necessary response to the 2008 financial crash. This punitive policy of high taxes coupled with big reductions in government spending, led to greater inequality, poverty and injustice. The Marmot Report for the Institute of Health Equality revealed that during this period: 'for the first time in a century, life expectancy had stopped growing and for women in poor areas actually fallen.'

Those most affected by these austerity measures were living in the poorer parts of the country. They were therefore understandably angry and looking to take out their electoral rage on whomever they perceived as being part of the political establishment. Cameron, as the instigator of austerity and head of the Remain campaign, was an obvious target, whilst other wealthy Old Etonians such as Boris Johnson and Jacob Rees-Mogg – looking like some 1930s PG Wodehouse fictional character made flesh – were absurdly seen as anti-establishment, populist Brexiteers.

These perceived mavericks, along with Nigel Farage, the owner of the Wetherspoon chain of pubs Tim Martin, and others, were alleging that austerity had been the direct result of membership of the EU; and no matter how untrue this contention may have been, those in a mood for change (any kind of change, for good or bad) were disposed to listen to them and vote accordingly. And so the hellish cocktail of misinformation, selfish personal political ambition, crude nationalism mixed with the innate British distrust of foreigners, utter ignorance of how EU institutions work and how its laws actually benefited Great Britain, social depravation and societal desperation, led to the U.K.'s certified withdrawal from the European Union in 2020.

For my part, although I believed the EU parliament needed some reforming to bring it closer and make it more transparent to the people in (the then) 28 democratic countries it served, it seemed to me that the U.K. leaving the world's largest trading bloc was economic madness. Departure would also mean the British people relinquishing their entitlement to live and work anywhere within the union, plus having to give up guaranteed rights relating to employment, housing, education, and welfare, all of which were legally enshrined in EU law but would expire once Britain had exited, with no similar sureties forthcoming from the British government.

Even on a basic level, if terrorist organisations such as ISIS along with personages like Donald Trump and Vladimir Putin – who instigated a Russian 'malign influence' campaign on social media to try to manipulate the vote Leave's way – as well European far-right politicians in the foul variety of Marine Le Pen of France and the recent Islamophobic victor of the general election in the Netherlands, Geert Wilders, were all openly supporting Brexit, then surely it should have been obvious that voting Leave was going to be the wrong choice – actually, after she'd witnessed the chaotic political and economic fallout from Britain's withdrawal from the EU, Le Pen dropped her original promise of a Frexit vote if elected president and concentrated on her as-per-usual anti-immigration, France First policies instead.

I was therefore utterly dismayed when the result was declared and rapidly became angry when the morning following the referendum, people who had voted Leave, were asked on television as to why they had done so. Their answers veered from the moronic – "I voted to leave because I thought most people would vote remain" – to the pathetic – "We voted leave just because it was something different" – to the ugly – "I've had enough of foreigners coming over here and stealing our jobs and taking our housing. They'll all have to go back now we've left the EU."

One particular smartly dressed, middle-class, middle-aged woman gave her reason for voting for Brexit as: "I was sick and tired of the European Union telling us what to do. They seemed to be deliberately picking on Britain with their ridiculous directives and were forcing the British people to do things they didn't agree with." This answer is very illuminating. It demonstrates just how ignorant even supposedly educated people were regarding how the EU works.

That woman seemed to think EU commissioners sat around in offices in Brussels week-in-week-out discussing 'How can we annoy the British people now? I know, let's send out a directive compelling the U.K. to ban the eating of fish and chips on the grounds of promoting a healthier diet. That should really fuck with their heads!' If she had actually taken the time to find out how a directive becomes EU law, she would have realised just how hollow her reasoning for voting Leave was.

Directives are introduced by EU commissioners to initiate, among other important reforms, infrastructure improvements, health and safety issues, the promotion of equality and civil rights, construction projects, consumer protection, working conditions and the raising of multiple standards throughout the union. Commissioners are proposed by member states in consultation with the commission president, who thereafter chooses a panel of nominated commissioners who are given individual hearings at the European Parliament to estimate their suitability before a vote is taken on who joins the commission.

Any proposed ordinance emitting from this body is firstly subjected to an impact assessment to evaluate how it will economically and socially affect each member state. Having made these assessments and, if necessary, amended the original directive, the Commission will then liaise with the national parliaments of each EU country and take on board their input. Once an agreed version of the directive is achieved it is then accorded the process known as the Consent Procedure, where the European Parliament – which consists of democratically elected MEPs from all member states – can exercise its power of veto or approval via a vote.

If approved, it is then sent on to all national parliaments for scrutiny before ratification or rejection. Even then, in certain areas, the EU can only adopt new laws with the unanimous support of every member state, which naturally included the U.K. before its exit.

As now revealed, the truth is very different from that latter Leave voter's conviction of an undemocratic, cavalier EU law making process which was purely designed to madden her and the British people. But of course the vast majority of the U.K. population has no real knowledge of how their own parliamentary legislative system works, let alone that of the EU. And certainly the preponderance was unaware that less than 30% of British law emanated from the European Parliament, most of which former Prime Ministers John Major, Tony Blair and Gordon Brown all agreed they'd happily adopted, as these laws were all beneficial to the British nation and its citizens.

As I always say, you can come to an opinion from a position of knowledge or a position of ignorance. Unfortunately, when it came to the Brexit referendum, too many people voted without any knowledge of the realities of our relationship with the European Union, and that's an unfortunate legacy which has already negatively impacted peoples' lives and will continue to do so way into the future.

So, at the time of writing, seven years on from the referendum and three years after the U.K. officially left its nearest and biggest trading partner, how has 'go it alone Britain' fared? Let's start with the economic situation:

Britain currently imposes the highest tax burden on earners since the 1940s – it was 32.8% in 2012 when the then Chancellor, George Osborne, was inflicting austerity on the country, it's now at 36.8%

and is expected to reach 37.7% by 2026, according to Office of Budget Responsibility. Wage rises have stagnated and inflation, although having decreased recently, is still running at around 4.6% whilst the Eurozone average is 2.9%. When I first purchased my house in France in 2002, a pound sterling got you €1.50, today it averages €1.14.

It has to be conceded that some of the U.K.'s economic woes are down to other factors – primarily Covid related – but the prevailing experience in the country as I write this is that for the vast majority of the British people, living standards have not improved post-Brexit. In fact they've got worse. This would explain the latest poll findings of 55% who now think it was the wrong decision to leave the EU compared to 33% who still believe it was the right choice.

Immigration was a major factor in the Brexit vote, perhaps the biggest motive for choosing Leave. Remember the Leave campaign's claim that high immigration was due to the EU's soft laws and attitudes to migration and that once the country had exited the union and taken back control of its borders, the influx of economic migrants and asylum seekers would be swiftly halted? Well, the figures as they stand show that ending June 2023, net migration has reached a record high of 676,000, and it's still climbing. The figure for small boats crossing the English Channel up until September 2023 stands at 436 vessels, on which 20,973 'illegal migrants' travelled to Britain. This is in line with the sharp rise in migrant Channel crossings since 2018, with the return rate for those who make it unlawfully to British shores being a mere 2%. How is this possible?

When the U.K. was still a member of the EU it could utilise a Euro-wide mechanism known as the Dublin III Regulation which allowed it to return migrants to other EU countries if it could prove they passed through safe European nations before reaching Britain – this proof was achieved via the Eurodac fingerprint database which, in the majority of cases, was able to verify those countries asylum seekers had travelled through in order to reach Britain. Once the U.K. had seceded from the union it lost both the Dublin system and its access to the Eurodac database.

Whatever the actual reasons, it's an indisputable fact that immigration has significantly risen, not decreased, since Britain supposedly took back control of its borders.

And the political fallout? Since the referendum, Great Britain has seen four Prime Ministers come and go: David Cameron resigned in 2016, Theresa May 2019, Boris Johnson 2022 and Liz Truss, who lasted just 49 days and who even managed to crash the economy via her kamikaze mini-budget during her brief premiership, also stepped down in 2022. The U.K. is presently on its fifth Conservative Party elected PM since

2016 – little Rishi Sunak – who inherited the office from Truss in 2022. Two of those previous PMs quitted as a result of Brexit (Cameron and May) and since the 2016 vote, the country has seen seven Chancellor of the Exchequer's enter and leave 11 Downing Street.

Meanwhile, Britain's political influence in Europe has greatly diminished – which is what Boris Johnson warned of before he switched to the Leave camp; the Northern Ireland-Republic of Ireland border conundrum, which no Leaver seemed to have even considered prior to it slapping them in the face once the withdrawal agreement had been signed, is still on-going and fragile; and the last seven years has been marked by multiple ministerial resignations and dismissals, Conservative Party political plotting, ineptitude, lies and arrogance, rule breaking and disorder; and the absence of any workable ideas at the highest levels of government that might actually improve people's lives in the U.K.

Is that what was meant by Taking Back Control?

THE LAST TOUR

The personal repercussions of the Brexit debacle were equally messy and prejudicial. I'd chosen to live in France believing that my right to do so would remain un-changed throughout my lifetime (as did many thousands of other ex-pats who'd chosen to live and work in European countries), but now, as a British citizen – actually, we're not even true citizens, merely Subjects of whatever constitutional monarch inherits the throne – I'd suddenly lost my right to reside anywhere within the EU. As a reaction to the U.K.'s withdrawal from the union, the French government decided that only British nationals, who'd been continually residing in France for five years or more, could legally carry on living and working full-time in the country.

I'd been a resident of France for far longer than that but was nonetheless obliged to prove it. This entailed digging up at least five years-worth of bank statements, proof of French local and national tax payments, household bills, home and car insurance documents, verification of ownership of my house, getting an officially written and stamped affirmation from the Marie (my local town hall) to confirm the date when I'd first registered with them; photocopies of my medical card, my passport and driving licence, all in time-honoured triplicate, as per the ever bureaucratic à la Française.

An appointment at the applicable office of the prefecture for an interview then had to be secured and subsequently, having offered up my bloated dossier of required paperwork, I got to see someone handling applications to examine and register my documents and to whom I had to verbally make my case for remaining in the country which had been my home for close on 18 years. The pleasant woman who interviewed me was very sympathetic to those of us who'd been caught up in the Brexit madness and having looked at my stack of evidence, told me there was nothing to be anxious about, that my Titre de Séjour would be approved quickly and that, at least as France was concerned, my status would remain just as it had been prior to the U.K.'s secession from the European Union.

Sure enough, a month or so after that interview, I discovered my Carte de Séjour in the post, this being a permanent residence card which awarded me all the rights of a French citizen. It was one Brexit worry taken care of, but there were other concerns. As I disclosed in the previous chapter, Rosamunde and I had decided to establish a stable, enduring relationship which would require her to live permanently with me in France. Prior to 1st February 2020, this would have been a simple procedure – she would have bought a plane ticket from Scotland to Bordeaux. I would have picked her up at the airport in my trusty

Citroën and driven her to mine, and there our life together would have begun in earnest. But Brexit had destroyed such simplicity and instead, placed a series of expensive and difficult hurdles for us to surmount.

U.K. nationals could no longer, as a legal right, perpetually live and work in EU countries. This meant Roz could only remain with me for 90 successive days in a 180 day period before having to leave the Euro zone – and that's if she remained exclusively in France and didn't use any of those days travelling to other Schengen nations as per the Withdrawal Agreement negotiated by the British government. As a result, she had to fly back to Scotland and arrange for an interview in order to apply for a year-long renewable visa at the French consulate in Edinburgh – an expensive document, which will annually continue to be so right up until she can finally apply for a permanent residency card like my own in five years' time.

Even more costly than the renewable yearly visa was her health insurance. Previously, Roz could have purchased Euro-wide cover for around £150 a year. Post Brexit, the cheapest health protection which we could get her for France only was £2,500, annually…

Yeah, I know, I've taxed your patience enough about this subject already and so, whilst I'm still behind, I'll abandon my prolonged Brexit lament while leaving my British readers with this final question about the issue – to what extent has your nation having quit the EU in 2020 personally improved your life in the U.K. as of now? I predict that the majority of you have seen no social or economic improvements to your lives and, in actuality, for many, things have got worse, rather than as promised by the Snake Oil sellers, considerably better.

With Jamie Oliver no longer part of the band and with the Covid curse rescinding, a measure of travel and live work became feasible. It was imperative then that the Subs recruit a new drummer as quickly as possible to meet our impending gigging commitments for the latter part of 2021. Four French shows, in Caen, Vauréal, Dijon, and Sélestat, were fast approaching, so we needed someone who could step in on a short-term basis whilst we considered who would be best suited to be our full-time stickman.

A few names were suggested, among them Kevin Nixon who I'd known since 1980 when his band, Anti-Pasti, were one of the support bands on my first British tour with the U.K. Subs. I called him and discovered he was happy to step in for this quartet of shows, despite having a regular job which he assured me he could get the necessary time off from. As per the Subs' norm, Kevin wasn't afforded the luxury of a rehearsal beforehand but did a worthy job of hitting the skins

and bashing those flat metallic discs that trigger hearing loss in his temporary role as drummer during this brief French excursion.

After that fleeting French live performance taster, Yuko contacted various acquaintances in the Punk scene to relay the news we were now looking for a permanent skin beater and requested recommendations for someone they thought might be compatible. When our U.K. agent, Darren Griffiths, suggested contacting the man who occupied the drum stool for the Cheltenham Punk band 4ft Fingers, she took his advice. Following a lengthy phone conversation with 'Magic' Dave Humphries, Yuko called me and asked that I check out his drum work on some live videos on YouTube in order to assess his viability for being a prospective long-term member.

Most of the footage was from Dave's side-line Metal rock band Reign of Fury, so it was a little difficult to decipher if his drumming style would be suitable for the Subs' more R&B influenced Punk sound. Still, it was obvious he was a competent player, plus I thought his image was OK. I reported back that I'd concluded Dave was worth a shot and we invited him to join us for our appearance at the Sinner's Day Festival in Belgium, on the 1st of November 2021.

As you've all now learned is customary procedure with the Subs, Humphries was not offered any rehearsals with the band prior to his debut show. Nonetheless, he put in a sturdy enough performance to seal his entrée into the group, after which he went on to tour with us in the U.K. During the period he was in the band I discovered Dave was a very reliable person, always ready to roll on time and, if travelling on his own to an overseas festival or an individual gig, would without fail arrive exactly when and where he'd been instructed to be. Although still a young man, he was happily married and showed no interest in pursuing extramarital short-lived relationships whilst on the road with other women. Additionally, he hardly touched alcohol nor smoked or took drugs.

These were all positive personality attributes, especially considering the wayward reliability and undesirable habits of some of our previous band members. But there were also a couple of issues that, although I considered minor irritations rather than major problems, quickly started to grind Charlie and Yuko's gears and instigated some friction within the band.

For his first British tour, Dave brought for the initial gigs a drum kit covered in fake fur. This may have been an appropriate affectation for his Metal outfit, but it certainly wasn't a fitting look for the U.K. Subs. Charlie made it ice cube clear that the hairy kit had to go and Humphries quickly exchanged it for another set of shells, sans fur. Despite this swift amendment, it still gave the impression that Dave wasn't aware of what the culture of the Subs was about, and there were other situations where this proved to be the case.

Another source of touchiness was his in-ears monitor equipment and soundboard. It took a long time to finalise what he wanted to hear via this apparatus, which was fine if we had plenty of time to soundcheck, but quickly became annoying if we arrived late at a venue due to an unusually long day of travel, traffic issues or, as happened from time-to-time, mechanical or delay problems relating to our transport. On those occasions we wouldn't have enough time to get a good overall sound for the entire band once he'd finished with the lengthy setup and adjustment period needed to achieve a good personal sound for himself.

His playing was mostly OK, but his timing could sometimes be erratic and erred towards him speeding up which would intermittently throw Steve and I into a state of musical confusion and leave Charlie wondering where to sing his next line. Still, overall, I liked Dave and having personally pointed out these concerns to him, believed the discrepancies in all of these departments would improve after a reasonable portion of time. Charlie, on the other hand, was not prepared to wait for the necessary corrections to occur and relayed both directly and through his wife, his dissatisfaction with our latest member.

Yuko called me just prior to a series of gigs set for the U.K. in December 2022 to say that Harper wanted to find an alternative drummer for all future live and studio work – regarding the latter, Dave Humphries had contributed his drumming to a recording we'd made of the AC/DC song, Hell's Bells, which was then released on a Cleopatra

The short-lived 'Magic' Dave line-up and Krzysztof Lach.

Records' compilation album entitled High Voltage Punk: A Tribute to AC/DC. This record also consisted of other idiosyncratic versions of well-known tracks by the platinum-selling Hard rock band, contributed by, among others, such Punk luminaries as Fear, Anti-Nowhere League, 999, and The Vibrators. It would be the only CD and vinyl testament to Magic Dave's time with the Subs.

I understood Charlie's unease in persevering with a member of the band he no longer had confidence in, but argued for Dave to be offered the forthcoming shows even though Harper wanted to ditch him straight away. There were two motives behind my case for keeping Humphries on a while longer: firstly, with these gigs almost upon us, I didn't want to rush into getting someone in who wouldn't have enough time to correctly learn the set – at least Dave knew all our live material, having played with us for over a year at that point – and secondly, I hoped a good series of performances by him might yet save his job.

Whilst Chas did agree to let Dave play this sequence of shows after relaying to Humphries that they would be his valediction appearances; it became evident Harper's mind was irrevocably made up. Despite Dave showing improvement during those December gigs, especially in the area of drumming speed, we again started the search for yet another replacement percussionist after we'd played our final show.

As I've already stated, I liked Dave Humphries and appreciated his professionalism and dedication to the work. Steve Straughan had also become very attached to the drummer and was saddened by his departure. However, if a collective finds itself in a position where a senior member is resolutely unwilling to work with a junior colleague, there's nothing more that can be done to alter this fact and ultimately, it's for the best to accept the situation and move on.

Although I had no way of knowing it at the time, Dave's departure actually proved to be an instance of good fortune. I write this because after all the usual name swapping and brainstorming regarding who should succeed him, Yuko suggested approaching someone we'd seen playing drums for TV Smith's occasional backing band, The Bored Teenagers, when they'd supported us for a duo of Euro shows a couple of years beforehand. We'd all been impressed by Stefan Häublein's abilities and I readily admit I couldn't top her suggestion. I was all for finding out if he would be interested in becoming a U.K. Sub, and we were all subsequently delighted when Stefan said he'd be honoured to join the band.

Stefan was invited to join the Subs at a pivotal juncture in the group's history. Even before Humphries' exit, we'd started discussing the best way to wind down band business before it became enforced retirement due to illness or physical problems on Charlie's part. We were well aware that Chas would be hitting his 80th birthday in May 2024, and although he was still amazingly sprightly and energetic for a man approaching an eighth decade of living, he did have health issues – diabetes, prostate concerns, occasional debilitating sciatica and arthritis. It therefore made sense to control the process by firstly lightening the workload, starting with a drastic alteration to the culture of relentless touring we'd pursued for decades.

To this end we decided to truncate the customary European Winter Tour at the beginning of the New Year and to designate and publicise it as our final European mainland tour. This concluding multi-gig Euro caper would be Häublein's first on the road experience as a Sub and it became quickly apparent, right from the opening show in Utrecht in the Netherlands on the 13th of January 2023, that he was a perfect fit for the band in the all-important areas of reliability, superb playing and personality – a revelation which had the rest of us wishing we'd recruited him much sooner.

It was an excellent tour, with Nasty Rumours – a wonderful Powerpop/Punk quartet based in Bern, Switzerland – being our support band throughout. There were 21 gigs in total, as compared to the usual 35 to 40 which we'd usually be obliged to play; and instead of

Farewell Euro tour 2023.

travelling all over continental Europe in order to unleash our music on the attending punters of around 12 to 14 individual Euro countries, we only performed at venues in Germany, Switzerland, Netherlands, and Belgium. This made the whole affair less stressful and tiring; and, as a welcome bonus, virtually all of these shows were sold out, which easily made up for what could have been a big financial deficit in choosing to play fewer venues. In fact, we made far more money from this concluding European campaign than we'd ever made there before.

Our routine U.K. spring tour was then intentionally ditched and we instead concentrated on a series of festivals both in the U.K. and Europe, including our regular spot at the Rebellion Festival at Blackpool's Winter Gardens in August 2023. The following month we embarked on what was billed as the U.K. Subs' last ever tour.

I had mixed emotions about the prospect of ending all those years of relentless international travel, of relinquishing the near daily performances and the intense highs and lows that are innate components of being on the road. I'd embarked on my first tour with the Subs in 1980 and now, 43 years later, that part of my life was coming to an end.

Despite the misplaced nostalgia regarding the way I'd worked and subsisted for so long, the truth was that being on perpetual tour for prolonged stretches of time over countless years had been a near-impossible way to live. The decades of unremitting motion, with only limited opportunities to down tools and sample the comforts of a home existence before again having to take the rollercoaster ride of hotels, venues and show times; to once more drift into excessive drinking of alcohol and the eating of unhealthy foods out of tedium, necessity or convenience; of having to endure the lengthy, monotonous motorway drives where the only reference to your location in time and space was the fleeting images to be discerned from the dirty windows of a fast moving motor vehicle, or, if on a commercial flight conveying you to your next destination, the ever changing landscapes that shift and transform below the hull of your aircraft.

Then there are the mostly reasonable although sometimes strained, interactions between you and your constant travel companions, plus the barrage of strangers or familiar faces from outside the band's intimate bubble that drift in and out of your subjective reality on a daily basis. And let's not forget the hells-broth of excitement, boredom, stress, fatigue, elation, adrenaline rushes, disappointments, and triumphs that influence your daily touring mood on an hour-to-hour cycle as you transfer from one continent to another, from one nation to another, from city to city, venue to venue as part of a seemingly endless existential journey.

Even the raw numbers are perilously excessive: hundreds of thousands of miles travelled via road, sea and air, with the likelihood of an eventual serious or fatal accident due to mechanical failure or human error ever increasing as the tours mount up and the years dissolve. Then there's the personal cost.

I've paid the penalty of two failed marriages and many unsuccessful attempts at romantic partnership as a consequence of my addiction to touring and the inevitable infidelities and relationship atrophy inherent in spending months away from a wife or potential partner. As I've already affirmed, it's a near-impossible way of life, and yet no band that I know of has been more devoted to this arduous and problematic regime than the U.K. Subs.

It had become time to alter the pattern of our characteristic working reality in order to try to reach a more balanced way of enjoying what mattered most to us – namely playing our music in a live setting – but simultaneously retaining the ability to make a reasonable living for ourselves from our efforts. Trading in touring for an occasional few gigs here, a couple of gigs there, and by focusing on the money spinning festivals and events that maximised band income, would mean we could ditch the negative aspects integral to unrelenting road work and accordingly enjoy making music together again without any of the shortcomings, whilst at the same time maintaining our professional status.

Consequently, the last touring will and testament of the U.K. Subs was set for September/October 2003, commencing with a show in Tunbridge Wells and concluding with five consecutive nights at the legendary 100 Club on Oxford Street, London.

It was an extraordinary tour, perhaps the best I'd been involved in as a U.K. Sub. Every ticket for every show had either been sold beforehand or would be sold on the night; and the appreciation and sheer love for the band was generously and enthusiastically demonstrated by each capacity audience as we made our way around the British Isles. As a band we responded to all this revealed passion and affection by putting in some very solid performances, with Charlie in great voice, dancing, leaping, and interacting with the punters like a man less than half his age.

However, our final touring hurrah didn't completely roll along without a hitch. We did have a reminder of the wisdom of our decision to quit touring after Chas was suddenly stricken with a bout of painful sciatica on the morning of our Blackpool appearance. Although he manfully got through the show without anyone apart from Yuko and the band being aware of his extreme discomfort, it was a large slice of luck that we had three days off following Blackpool, which provided the necessary time for Harper to fully recover in time for our next appearance onstage at the largest room of the Waterfront venue in Norwich.

The final five dates at the 100 Club were each, in their own distinctive way, classic Subs shows. Having originally envisioned playing a single decisive concert at a big, prestige venue in London such as the Roundhouse, or at what had been called back in my day Hammersmith Odeon – now rebranded The Eventim Apollo – we quickly came to the conclusion that a far more appropriate location to end our farewell tour in would be the venue which had staged the first ever British Punk rock festival back in 1976 – featuring Sex Pistols, The Clash, Siouxsie and the Banshees, and Buzzcocks.

Audience capacity for the 100 Club is around 350 punters so we knew even two shows there, would be nowhere near sufficient to accommodate all those who would want to attend our tour-terminating swansong.

Having initially booked three sequential evenings, we learned all the tickets had been snapped up for this trio within a few days of going on sale, which necessitated adding a fourth, and thereafter a fifth show, as yet again demand outweighed expectations. Five successive sold out nights was a club record, with the band closest to matching this historic statistic being a three gig capacity residency by Siouxsie and the Banshees nearly 20 years beforehand, in 2004.

The audience ambience for these shows was exceptional – joyous, friendly, emotionally charged, loud, and demonstrative. Along with

CRUCIAL TALENT PRESENTS...

PHOTO CREDIT TO RAVEN

PUNK ROCK LEGENDS

UK SUBS

THE FINAL TOUR!

SEPTEMBER

07 – TUNBRIDGE WELLS, THE FORUM SOLD OUT!
08 – BRISTOL, THE FLEECE SOLD OUT!
09 – EXETER, THE PHOENIX SOLD OUT!
10 – SOUTHAMPTON, 1865
11 – READING, SUB 89
12 – CARDIFF, GLOBE SOLD OUT!
14 – MILTON KEYNES, CRAUFURD SOLD OUT!
15 – LEEDS, BRUDENELL CLUB SOLD OUT!
16 – DERBY, HAIRY DOG SOLD OUT!

17 – BLACKPOOL, WATERLOO SOLD OUT!
21 – NORWICH, WATERFRONT
22 – BIRMINGHAM, O2 ACADEMY 2
23 – NORTHEAST CALLING FESTIVAL
24 – EDINBURGH, LA BELLE SOLD OUT!
27 – LONDON, 100 CLUB SOLD OUT!
28 – LONDON, 100 CLUB SOLD OUT!
29 – LONDON, 100 CLUB SOLD OUT!
30 – LONDON, 100 CLUB SOLD OUT!

DUE TO DEMAND FINAL LAST EXTRA DATE ADDED!
OCTOBER 01 – LONDON, 100 CLUB SOLD OUT!

WWW.UKSUBS.CO.UK

sundry long-term fans that'd been following the Subs since the late 1970s/early 1980s, every evening also enticed plenty of more recent devotees to the band to join the capacity crowds, with a smattering of fellow professional musicians from the Punk scene in attendance too – all present to help us take it home in style. It proved to be the perfect way to accomplish a lingering bow and to celebrate our decision to turn away from the relentless road – a once desirable, ostensibly infinite highway, which had been a home, a playground, a passion, and an infatuation, for the preponderance of this author's lifetime.

So, where do we go from here? Well, the Subs may have completed their last tour, but we certainly haven't played our last show. For 2024 we've lined up several festival appearances and in May, will be celebrating Charlie Harper's 80th birthday with a special show at the Shepherd's Bush Empire Theatre in London. This will be followed by further gigs to commemorate this notable anniversary at some of our favourite European haunts – two nights at the SO36 in Berlin, an evening apiece at the Fabrik, Hamburg and the Melkweg (the Milky Way), Amsterdam.

And what do you know? We've even accepted an invitation to headline a festival in Los Angeles in 2025. This may turn out to be an act of supreme optimism, but we're nevertheless determined to fulfil this commitment and play one final show in the U.S.A. – band members' good health and desire withstanding.

Abandoning touring has also provided the opportunity for each of us to pursue other projects in a more significant way. Charlie has his acoustic solo career; Stephen Straughan will be devoting more time to his Hi-Fi Spitfires trio and I'm going to put additional time and effort into my solo outfit, Alvin Gibbs and the Disobedient Servants – we've already played a show at the 100 Club in January this year and have further English dates with the early-doors Punk group Chelsea set for the spring of 2024. The Servants will also record a follow-up album to our Your Disobedient Servant debut in the near future.

Inevitably though, the U.K. Subs' shows will dry up and that measure of income will evaporate along with the work. It's a legitimate concern although, according to the internet, I shouldn't be too worried about matters of a financial nature. Roz recently discovered a website via Google called Net Worth, which reveals the supposed fortunes of musicians, actors, TV personalities, and suchlike. She typed my name into its search box:

"Honey," she said, "according to this website your net worth is eighteen million dollars!"

"Really" I replied, "eighteen million?"

"Yep," she confirmed.

"Wow, eighteen million dollars, that's a lot of money… if only I was me."

Alvin Gibbs net worth is
$18 Million

THINGS TO COME

There is a small town close to where I live in France where you'll find a warehouse situated just off the route de la ville, marked by a banner bearing the words Bric à brac et Brocante (Flea market and Antiques). This building is crammed to capacity with all manner of objects – huge armoires, ancient chests, chandeliers, prints and paintings, precariously tall columns of books, masses of glass and dinner ware, old clocks and candlesticks, along with all the additional paraphernalia its proprietors have amassed from the various house clearances they've conducted over many years.

Because of the immense and haphazard proliferation of items to be seen in this space – so many that even a slim person can hardly find enough room to navigate its narrow passages to view the miscellaneous pieces for sale without having to walk sideways – the effect on your senses when you first enter the building is of overwhelming disorder and mystification. However, if you resist the urge to flee and instead buckle down to seriously searching amongst the debris, there's treasure to be uncovered.

Since I first happened upon this place over a decade ago, I've purchased many wonderful things as a consequence of my combing through the discarded possessions of those who've passed on: a 19th century wood carved and glass display cabinet; a Louis XV gold-leafed framed mirror; a decorated medieval 14th century floor tile; some original prints from the time of Napoleon I and his nephew, Napoleon III; two beautiful armoires; a velum-bound book of prayers, dated 1692; an oak dining table and six chairs; a gilded bronze replica Napoleonic regimental eagle on a marble base, which I paid €150 for but later discovered was being sold at the Louve Museum shop in Paris for over €1,000; plus a number of other modestly-priced gems.

However, perhaps the most illuminating discovery I've unearthed during my various visits to this bonkers warehouse of hidden wonders wasn't something that I wanted to buy and keep, although it has perhaps been the most affecting and insightful artefact I've uncovered there.

I noticed a cardboard box resting on a cabinet. After I looked inside, I saw it contained a stack of photographs. Out of curiosity, I began examining the contents of this unexpected find. They were the photographic relics of a person's life – monochromatic baby and infant plates from the 1920s; wedding pictures from the 1940s, some faded portraits which, in consideration of the clothes being worn, were evidently taken in the '50s; dozens of later colour family snapshots of birthday parties and holidays, of siblings and children, grandchildren, celebrations and dinner parties, all discernibly from the 1960s to the 1990s.

There was one particular woman who featured in a number of these images. She had been the pre-World War II child in the pretty dress, the young vivacious bride, the mother, the middle-aged grandmother, the smiling elderly grey-haired matriarch surrounded by the newer generations of her blood, some of whom cradled babies or had their arms draped around their own children... and I thought to myself: 'sometime in the future, the photographic chronicles of my life may well end up in some cardboard box in a place like this too – discarded, worthless, resting on a dead man's cabinet.'

It was an austere reminder of my mortality. The poet WH Auden wrote: 'Behind it all is death, like the sound of distant thunder at a picnic.' Now that I've reached the age of 66, Auden's thunder has grown louder in recent years and its initiating storm seemingly approaches at an ever increasing rate.

Still, let me be clear, I do not fear death any more than I feared being born. And as for what happens after our demise, why would anyone be concerned about that? What occurs after death will not be altered by people's anxiety or convictions. I'm pretty sure we all return to the nothingness we originated from but would be delighted to discover I'm wrong and that there's in fact an alternative higher existence awaiting me when I eventually flee my cage of flesh, blood and bones.

In part, my relaxed acceptance of the reality of death is because I've already had an incredible life. I took a supremely naïve idea: to become a professional Rock musician, make records and play music to thousands of people worldwide, and then somehow managed to turn that cracked aspiration into an enduring reality. As a result of fulfilling those ambitions, I was also able to travel the globe to look, taste, touch, and fully partake in the human experience in a way that few people get to emulate. If I was a person with religious convictions – which I decidedly am not – I would deploy the word 'blessed' to describe the remarkable measure of time I've already spent here on planet earth.

However, despite my general satisfaction with how my past has informed my present – and notwithstanding being aware that I do not have a huge amount of time left – there is still much that I'm determined to achieve in whatever subsequent years may be available to me.

Having a stable, romantic partnership with Rosamunde Parsons has made a huge difference to my outlook. I'm excited about our current plan to sell the Bordeaux house and move to the Cote de Azure in the Mediterranean south of France. It will enliven us; deliver new scenery, new opportunities, new challenges and no doubt, new friends and acquaintances. I believe fresh experiences are even more important for people in their later years. Changing routines and environments

provoke visual and metabolic renewal; helps maintain mental agility and provides an escape mechanism from the stagnation which inevitably thwarts creative and intellectual growth.

Despite this contented association with Roz progressing along nicely at present, I'm also experienced enough in such matters to know that there are no guarantees when it comes to long-term relationship success – as a great line from a bad movie once put it: "Happy endings are just stories that haven't finished yet." But despite my characteristic soupçon of scepticism, I'm pretty confident that based on our mutual maturity and the fact I will no longer be obliged to again spend six months of the year on the road, that we can last the course and construct a fulfilling and enduring life together – if not, I vow to you now, I will never succumb to joining an online dating site. I'd much rather meet someone in the old fashioned way: via alcohol and bad judgement.

As already disclosed, the future also offers numerous shows with the band that has been such an essential part of my identity for so long, I've often joked that Charlie Harper is my canary in the gigging mineshaft – all the while he's capable of getting up on stage and performing, then so am I. Once the Subs' concerts incrementally decrease to an eventual point of termination, the Disobedient Servants will become my main musical outlet and concern. It's my intention to enlarge the status of the band in Europe – particularly in my adopted homeland of France – rather than just rely on a modicum of acceptance and work in the U.K.

I'm also resolved to continue writing books and articles. In fact I have two finished historical novels which, now this final memoir tome has been completed, I will endeavour to get published. I've also got a number of other ideas for novels and magazine pieces, all to be brought to fruition in the coming months and years.

Just this week I've received the news that I'm now entitled to both British and French pensions, the combined amounts from which, due to my being absent from both countries for many years, will just about cover my wine bill for a fortnight…

… On the subject of wine let me readily admit to my addiction to this magnificent elixir, it being a substance that raises the spirits, thins the blood, fuels heroic thoughts and conjures up creative ideas. There are gods of wine (the Roman deity Bacchus and his Greek counterpart, Dionysus) which is more than can be said for other forms of alcohol. Are there gods of beer, gin, tequila, rum, vodka, or whisky? Not to my knowledge, and this detail accordingly gives us an insight into the special esteem the gorgeous stuff has been held in history, with my personal admiration for the liquid versions of red, white and rosé being why I'm averse to eating grapes – I dislike taking my wine in pill form…

And so, having now officially become a pensioner, albeit one that neither behaves, dresses, nor cares for the typical interests of a senior person (my intense dislike of golf comes to mind), I want to declare that I also have no interest in what is often referred to in conjunction with pensionable age as 'retirement'. Retire from what? The things I do are a product of what I am, hence the idea of withdrawing from them is tantamount to saying: "I'm going to retire from myself," which makes no sense at all.

If you've followed my story from Volume I, through Volume II, and on to this final edition of my memoir trilogy, you'll already be aware that my fascination with Rock music began in the 1960s, metamorphosed in the early-1970s to an obsession that overtook that of wanting to become a professional footballer and, in turn, saw me forming a school-based Glam rock band in 1973. Come the advent of Punk and my witnessing many of the renowned first-wave outfits of that genre, I became an active participator in the scene by means of joining my first Punk rock group in 1978, The Users.

Following a stint with The Users, I experienced touring at a higher level supporting The Police in Europe and Thin Lizzy in the U.K. with ex-Damned guitarist Brian James and The Physicals respectively. My becoming a U.K. Sub in 1980 raised the bar even higher: I initially recorded two albums and four singles with the Subs, appeared on Top of the Pops, and travelled all over the British Isles, Europe and North America to play and perform prior to swapping London for San Francisco and thereafter, relocating to Los Angeles. Whilst living in the city of fallen angels I became Iggy Pop's bassist and embarked on an eight month-long global tour with one of the seminal figures of napalm hearted Rock 'n' Roll. During that same period, I played a show with the actor Johnny Depp, became a friend of and hung out in New York City with Joey Ramone, spent time in the company of David Bowie, Alice Cooper and Michael Hutchence, as well as experiencing many other 'pinch me' moments.

Upon my return to London, I gigged in the U.K., Japan and Scandinavia and also supplied instrumentation and compositions for two LP records plus three single releases with the Hanoi Rocks' spin-off band Cheap And Nasty. After four years of C 'n' N I returned to active duty with the Subversives, and subsequently played an inestimable number of world-wide tours, gigs, and festivals, plus contributed, both as a musician and songwriter, to a further nine studio albums and 11 single/EP records.

Perhaps the biggest Rock band of the late-1980s/1990s, Guns N' Roses, covered one of my songs for a platinum-level selling LP, the royalties from which paid in part for my house in France.

During the large slab of time these accumulated events took place, there were certainly other instances of Diminished Responsibility and enough additional Strange Stories to fill another three volumes. And, no doubt, there will yet be a couple of lapses of appropriate conduct and a twisted tale or two to be accrued in future days; but I'm satisfied with what is already available in the public domain and have no desire to keep ploughing the same literary ground beyond this final instalment.

What a ride. What an incredible journey. Although the question should nevertheless be asked: if I had my time all over, would I still pursue the same course of action and again set about obliterating the hurdles, the insecurities, the objections and uncertainties, and all the other difficult demolitions necessary, in order to escape the straight and narrow world and attain such an uncommon life?

Oh yes, annihilate them all, I most certainly would… with a wrecking ball!

APPENDIX I: ALVIN GIBBS DISCOGRAPHY

This is by no means a complete account of all the recordings I have contributed to over the many years I've been a professionally active rock musician. There is a sizable number unnamed here for reasons of concision or because I'm simply unaware they've been released.
This is especially the case with compilation albums. There seems to be at least another half-a-dozen or so of these issued by a variety of record companies every year containing either a song or songs I've composed, sung or played bass guitar on, and I frankly do not have the time nor inclination to catalogue them all. Still, this discography does provide a chronicle of the bulk of my career's recorded output, and I hope and anticipate there will be yet more titles for inclusion in this list over the coming years.

THE USERS

Album (Compilation): *Secondary Modern*
Released 2008 - Bin Liner Records (RUBBISHCD009)
Contributions – bass guitar, backing vocals.

PHYSICALS

Album (Compilation): *Skulduggery*
Released 1999 - Overground Records (OVER 80CD)
Contribution – bass guitar.

U.K. SUBS

Album: *Diminished Responsibility*
Released 1981 - GEM/RCA Records (GEMLP 112/PL 43507)
Contributions – bass guitar, backing vocals, songwriter.

Album: *Endangered Species*
Released 1982 - NEMS Records (NEL 6021)
Contributions – bass guitar, backing vocals, lead vocal, songwriter.

Album: *Killing Time*
Released 1988 - New Red Archives (NRA06)
Contributions – bass guitar, backing vocals, lead vocal, songwriter.

Album: *Quintessentials*
Released 1997 - Fallout/Jungle Records (FALL LP 054)
Contributions – bass guitar, backing vocals, songwriter.

Album: *Riot*
Released 1997 - Cleopatra Records (CLP9929-2)
Contributions – bass guitar, rhythm guitar, backing vocals, lead vocals, songwriter.

Album: *Time Warp*
Released 2001 - Anagram Records (CDPUNK 120)
Contributions – bass guitar, backing vocals.

Album: *Work In Progress*
Released 2010 - Captain Oi! Records (AHOY CD310)
Contributions – bass guitar, guitar, backing vocals, lead vocal, songwriter.

Album: *XXIV*
Released 2013 - Captain Oi! Records (AHOY HBCD315)
Contributions – bass guitar, acoustic and rhythm guitar, backing vocals, lead vocals, songwriter, co-producer.

Album: *Yellow Leader*
Released 2015 - Captain Oi! Records (AHOY LP 317)
Contributions – bass guitar, guitar, backing vocals, lead vocal, songwriter, co-producer.

Album: *Ziezo*
Released 2016 - U.K. Subs Records (001ZCD)
Contributions – bass guitar, backing vocals, lead vocal, piano, songwriter, co-producer.

Album (Live): *Staffordshire Bull*
Released 2003 - Invisible Hands Music (IHCD 28)
Contributions – bass guitar, backing vocals, songwriter, sleeve notes.

Album (Live): *Violent State*
Released 2004 - Combat Rock Records (DPR023)
Contributions – bass guitar, backing vocals, songwriter.

Album (Live): *Bremen 82*
Released 2016 - French Connection Records (FC 01)
Contributions – bass guitar, backing vocals, songwriter, sleeve notes.

Album (live): *The Last Will & Testament Of*
Released 2024 - Cleopatra Records (CLO 5461)
Contributions – bass guitar, backing vocals, songwriter.

Album (Compilation): *Recorded: 1979-1981*
Released 1982 - Abstract Records (AABT 300)
Contributions – bass guitar, backing vocals, songwriter.

Album (Compilation): ***Demonstration Tapes***
Released 1984 - Konexion (KOMA 7880005)
Contributions – bass guitar, backing vocals, lead vocal, songwriter.

Album (Compilation): ***A.W.O.L.***
Released 1987 - New Red Archives (NRA05)
Contributions – bass guitar, backing vocals, lead vocal, songwriter.

Album (Compilation): ***The Singles 1978 - 1982***
Released 1991 - Abstract Sounds (AABT 800)
Contributions – bass guitar, backing vocals, songwriter.

Album (Compilation): ***Down on the Farm - A Collection of the Less Obvious*** Released 1991 - Streetlink Records (STR CD 017)
Contributions – bass guitar, backing vocals, lead vocal, songwriter.

Album (Compilation): ***Scum of the Earth***
Released 1993 - Music Club (MCCD 120)
Contributions – bass guitar, backing vocals, songwriter.

Album (Compilation): ***The Punk Singles Collection***
Released 1995 - Anagram Records (CD PUNK 66)
Contributions – bass guitar, backing vocals, songwriter.

Album (Compilation): ***Punk Can Take it – Rare and Unreleased***
Released 1996 - Cleopatra Records (CLP 9703-2)
Contributions – bass guitar, backing vocals, lead vocal, songwriter.

Album (Compilation): ***Self Destruct - Punk Can Take it II***
Released 1997 - Cleopatra Records (CLP 9826-2)
Contributions – bass guitar, backing vocals, lead vocal, songwriter.

Album (Compilation): ***Punk Rock Rarities***
Released 1998 - Captain Oi! Records (AHOY CD 93)
Contributions – bass guitar, backing vocals, lead vocal, songwriter.

Album (Compilation): ***Sub Mission***
Released 1999 - Fallout/Jungle Records (FALLLP055)
Contributions – bass guitar, backing vocals, lead vocal, songwriter.

Album (Compilation): ***Before You Were Punk – The Very Best of***
Released 2004 - Anarchy Music (ARY 8001-2)
Contributions – bass guitar, backing vocals, lead vocals, songwriter.

Album (Compilation): ***Stranglehold***
Released 2007 - Pegasus Records (PEG CD 627)
Contributions – bass guitar, backing vocals, songwriter.

Album (Compilation): ***Complete Punk Singles Collection***
Released 2011 - Captain Oi! Records (AHOY DCD 312)
Contributions – bass guitar, backing vocals, songwriter.

Album (Compilation): ***AD 1979 – 1981***
Released 2014 - Edsel Records (GEMBOX01)
Contributions – bass guitar, backing vocals, songwriter.

Album (Compilation): ***Friends And Relations***
Released 2016 - Cleopatra Records (CLO 0186)
Contributions – U.K. Subs tracks: bass guitar, backing vocals, songwriter. Target Generation tracks: bass guitar, backing vocals, songwriter, co-producer.

Album (Compilation): ***4 Ways to the Center***
Released 2016 - Cleopatra Records (CLO0437CD)
Contributions – bass guitar, backing vocals, lead vocal, songwriter.

Album (Compilation): ***Fear to Go***
Released 2024 - Cleopatra Records (CLO 4958)
Contributions – bass guitar, lead and backing vocals, songwriter

Albums (Collection): ***The Albums Volume 1 (A to M)***
Released 2018 - Edsel Records (UKSUBSAM001)
Contributions – bass guitar, backing vocals, lead vocals, songwriter.

Albums (Collection): ***The Albums Volume 2 (N to Z)***
Released 2018 - Edsel Records (UKSUBSSNZ001)
Contributions – bass guitar, guitar, backing vocals, lead vocals, songwriter, co-producer.

Album: ***Subversions***
Released 2018 - Cleopatra Records (CLO 0834)
Contributions – bass guitar, backing vocals, co-producer.

Album: ***Subversions II***
Released 2019 - Cleopatra Records (CLO 1297)
Contributions – bass guitar, backing vocals, co-producer.

Album: ***Reverse Engineering***
Released 2022 - Cleopatra Records (CLO 2843)
Contributions - bass guitar, backing vocals, lead vocals, songwriter.

Single: ***Party in Paris***
Released 1980 - GEM Records (GEMS42)
Contributions – bass guitar, backing vocals.

Single: ***Keep on Running (Til you Burn)***
Released 1981 - GEM Records (GEMS45)
Contributions – bass guitar, backing vocals, songwriter.

Single: ***Countdown***
Released 1981 - NEMS (NES 304)
Contributions – bass guitar, backing vocals, songwriter.

Single: ***Sabre Dance***
Released 1988 - New Red Archives (NRA07)
Contributions – bass guitar, backing vocals, lead vocal, songwriter.

Single: ***War on the Pentagon***
Released 1997 - New Red Archives (NRA46)
Contributions – bass guitar, backing vocals.

Single: ***Day of the Dead***
Released 1997 - New Red Archives (NRA47)
Contributions – bass guitar, backing vocals, songwriter.

Single: ***Cyberjunk***
Released 1997 - New Red Archives (NRA48)
Contributions – bass guitar, backing vocals, songwriter.

Single: ***The Revolution's Here***
Released 2000 - Combat Rock Records (CRO50)
Contribution – bass guitar.

Single: ***Product Supply***
Released 2011 - Time & Matter Recordings (T&M 005)
Contributions – bass guitar, backing vocals, songwriter.

Single: ***Yellow Leader EP Limited Edition***
Released 2015 - Captain Oi! Records (AHOYEP317)
Contribution – bass guitar.

Single: ***For Pledgers Only***
Released 2016 - (no label or catalogue number)
Contributions – bass guitar, backing vocals, lead vocal, songwriter.

Single: ***Predator***
Released 2017 - U.K. Subs Records (no catalogue number)
Contribution– bass guitar.

Single: ***The Beast***
Released 2017 - U.K. Subs Records (no catalogue number)
Contributions – bass guitar, backing vocals, lead vocal, songwriter.

Single: ***Screaming Senile***
Released 2018 - U.K. Subs Records (no catalogue number)
Contributions – bass guitar, backing vocals, lead vocal, songwriter, co-producer.

Single: ***Sensei***
Released 2021- Cleopatra Records (CLO 2576)
Contributions – bass guitar, backing vocals, co-producer.

U.K. SUBS & DEAD BOYS

EP: ***Carnaby St. EP***
Released 2024 – Cleopatra Records (CLO 5452)
Contributions – bass guitar, backing vocals, co-producer.

KNOX

Single: ***Troops of Tomorrow***
Released 1982 - Quiet Records (Troops 1)
Contribution – bass guitar.

URBAN DOGS

Album: ***Urban Dogs***
Released 1983 - Fallout Records (FALL LP012)
Contributions – bass guitar, guitar, backing vocals, lead vocal, songwriter.

Album: ***Wipeout Beach***
Released 1998 - Raw Power Records (RP003)
Contributions – bass guitar, guitar, backing vocals, lead vocals, songwriter.

Album: ***Attack***
Released 2016 - Time & Matter Records (T&M 026)
Contributions – bass guitar, guitar, backing vocal, lead vocals, songwriter, co-producer.

Single: ***New Barbarians***
Released 1982 - Fallout Records (FALL 008)
Contributions – bass guitar, backing vocals.

Single: ***Limo Life***
Released 1983 - Fallout Records (FALL 011)
Contributions – bass guitar, backing vocals.

Single: **_Millenium Dome_**
Released 1998 - Raw Power Records (RP006)
Contributions – bass guitar, guitar, backing vocals, lead vocal, songwriter.

Single: **_Trick or Treat_**
Released 2016 - Time & Matter Records (T&M 025)
Contributions – bass guitar, backing vocals.

IGGY POP

Contributions to all Iggy Pop albums/single – bass guitar, backing vocals.

Album (Live): **_Live at the Channel Boston M.A. 1988_**
Released 1990 - Revenge Records (CAX 7)

Album (Live): **_Cold Metal_**
Released 1991- Living Legend Records (LLRCD 119)

Album (Compilation): **_Best of... Live_**
Released 1996 - MCA Records (MCD 84021)

Album (Live): **_Live on the King Biscuit Flower Hour_**
Released 1997 - King Biscuit Flower Hour Records (KBD 88033)

Album (Compilation): **_Greatest Hits Live_**
Released 2003 - King Biscuit Flower Hour Records (KBFR 40022 2)

Album (Compilation): **_Where the Faces Shine – Volume 2_**
Released 2008 - Easy Action Records (EARS S018)

Album (Live): **_Search and Destroy: Live in Chicago 1988_**
Released 2016 - Live on Vinyl Records (LOVLP2002)

Single: **_Live at the Channel Boston M.A. 1988_**
Released 1990 - Revenge Records (WM 106/SS19)

CHEAP AND NASTY

Album: **_Beautiful Disaster_**
Released 1991 - China Records (WOL 1002)
Contributions – bass guitar, backing vocals, songwriter, co-producer.

Album: **Cool Talk Injection**
Released 1994 - Canyon International (PCCY 00546)
Contributions – bass guitar, backing vocals, lead vocal, songwriter, co-producer.

Single: **Mind Across the Ocean**
Released 1990 - China Records (CHINA 318792907)
Contributions – bass guitar, backing vocals, co-producer.

Single: **Beautiful Disaster**
Released 1991 - China Records (CHINA 348795107)
Contributions – bass guitar, songwriter, co-producer.

7" Flexi Disc: **Internal Action**
Released 1991 - Kerrang! Magazine (BENDER 3)
Contributions – bass guitar, songwriter, co-producer.

GUNS N' ROSES

Album: **The Spaghetti Incident**
Released 1993 - Geffen/Uzi Suicide Records (GEF-24617)
Contribution – songwriter.

Single: **Ain't it Fun**
Released 1993 - Geffen Records (GFSTD 62)
Contribution – songwriter.

CHARLIE HARPER AND THE SUBSTITUTES

Single: **E For England**
Released 2002 - Nutopia Music (no catalogue number)
Contributions – bass guitar, backing vocals.

SEX DRUGS AND HIV

Album: (charity compilation, various artists)
Released 2015 - Mat Sargent (LMGM017)
Contribution – bass guitar.

ALVIN GIBBS AND THE DISOBEDIENT SERVANTS

Album: *Your Disobedient Servant*
Released 2018 - Time & Matter Records (T&M 032) and
2020 - USA edition, Cleopatra Records (CLO1565VL)
Contributions – bass guitar, guitar, lead vocals, backing vocals,
songwriter, co-producer.

Single: *Ghost Train*
Released 2018 - Time & Matter Records (T&M 031)
Contributions – bass guitar, guitar, lead vocals, backing vocals,
songwriter, co-producer.

Double Single: *History EP*
Released 2020 - Time & Matter Records (T&M 036)
Contributions – bass guitar, lead vocals, backing vocals, songwriter,
co-producer.

Single: *State Of Grace*
Released 2021 - Time & Matter Records (T&M 043)
Contributions – bass guitar, lead vocals, backing vocals, songwriter,
co-producer.

ANDY MCCOY

Album: *Jukebox Junkie*
Released 2022 – Cleopatra Records (CLO3113)
Contributions - songwriter.

APPENDIX II: ALVIN GIBBS BIBLIOGRAPHY

Neighbourhood Threat: On Tour with Iggy Pop
Published 1995 - Britannia Press
ISBN 978-1899784103

Destroy: The Definitive History of Punk
Published 1996 - Britannia Press
ISBN 978-1899784004

Neighbourhood Threat: On Tour with Iggy Pop (2nd edition)
Published 2001 - Codex Books
ISBN 978-1899598175

Destroy! L'Histoire Définitive du Punk (French edition)
Published 2007 - Camion Blanc
ISBN 978-2910196516

Iggy Pop: La Menace Intérieure: En Tournée Avec L'Iguane (French edition)
Published 2010 - Camion Blanc
ISBN 978-2357790742

ZIEZO – An eyewitness account of the making of the final album by the Punk collective commonly known as the UK Subs
Published 2016 – U.K. Subs in association with Time & Matter Recordings for PledgeMusic
No ISBN number

Some Weird Sin: On Tour with Iggy Pop
Published 2017 - Extradition Publishing/Cadiz Music
ISBN 978-0957171787

Diminished Responsibility - My life as a U.K. Sub, and other strange stories. Volume I
Published 2020 - Tome & Metre Books
ISBN 978-1-8380116-0-4

Diminished Responsibility - My life as a U.K. Sub, and other strange stories. Volume II
Published 2021 - Tome & Metre Books
ISBN 978-1-8380116-2-8

Diminished Responsibility - My life as a U.K. Sub, and other strange stories. Volume III
Published 2024 - Tome & Metre Books
ISBN 978-1-8380116-5-9

ASSOCIATE DISOBEDIENT SERVANTS

Alvin would like to thank the following 'Associate Disobedient Servants' for their invaluable and much appreciated help in bringing about the publication of this book:

John Abercrombie
Peter Ahlers
Steve Ainley
Magnus Andersson
Glyn Aspinall
Nick Ball
Gary Barton
Paul Beck
Dominique Bellenger
Matthew Bentham
David Bignell
Andy Briggs
Ed Briggs
Neil Brookshaw
Dave Brown
Christina Brzezinska
Dave Burdon
Simon Burrough
Richard Carter
Juan Christian
Matt Clarkson
Chris Coleman
Pat Collier - R.I.P
Coppo & Lynda Copson
David Cowie
Liz & Steve Creech
Dominic Daley
Steve Dalley
Mark Dineen-Bolton
Aidan Doherty
Chris Damien Doll
John Dowson
Quintin Drake

William Ellefsen
Alex English
Mark Freeman
Billy James Fry
Roddy Goodman
Chris Gouck
André Gourdon
Mark Greatorex
Anne Green
Tony Ham
Jason Hardcastle
Brian Harkness
Harve the Marve
Sue Hathaway
Grant Heath
Mark Henshaw
Hugo, Minnie & Lenny
Brian Hutchinson
Phill Jackson
Martyn Janes
Jürgen Januschowski
Dave Jones
Kev Jones
Russell Jones
Graham Jordan
Oliver Kamnitzer
Jez Keefe
Patrick Kerrane
Andrew Ketley
Dave Kitson
Mark Kockelbergh
Thomas Kreutz
Rafael Kwasigroch

Michael Kwasigroch
Carl Lawson
Ludovic Leleu
Paul Levick
Nigel Linger
Paul Lobban
Simon Lochead
Karolina Lundberg
Ulf Lyraan
Paul Maile
Danilo Mariucci
Gary Mccrindle
Mark McCulloch
Dave McKenzie
John McVey
Michi Scott Medley
Neale (Bardar) Milam
Andrew Miller
Graham Morris
Gary Mortimer
Mark Moylan
Erik Nilsson
Ian Palmer
Jim Paterson
Steve Payen
Tony Phipps
Rob Pietrucha
Chris Plume
Krzysztof Przednowek
Keith Rainbow
Matthew Rayner
David Rhodes

Gary Rugless
Pete Sadler
Chris Saville
Sten Sawicz
Smell Segregates
Ian Fleming Shap
Mandy Sharpe
Tracie Slade
Armitage Smith
Graham Smith
Melvin Snell
Jon Stewart
Mark & Jayne Stickings
Taki
Mike Talbot
Keith Thomson
Ronay Thomson
Andy Thorn
Tony Uzzell
Paul Van Acker
Jem Wallace
Boudewijn Warbroek
Dominic Warwick
Mick Waters
Neil Watson
Liz West
Tony Whatley
Darren Williams
Philip Wilson
Mark Winch
Mitchell Woodland
Rafal Zimn

PHOTOGRAPHIC CREDITS

Rob Cook, Silvy Maatman, TCB-Chris Hill photography, Claire Taylor, Dave Uglypunk, Rosamunde Parsons, Jez Keefe, Chris Long, Yuko Morinaga, Steve Crittall, Krousky Peutebatre Pictures, Dunja Dopsaj.

THE T&M STORY SO FAR...

Time & Matter (T&M) is an independent record label and book publisher originally set up to work with U.K. Subs members old and new.

The T&M HQ / Distribution is based in Bedfordshire, England.

Initially, Time & Matter Recordings was set up as a 'not for profit company' in February 2010, putting out previously un-released or no longer available U.K. Subs material with all the proceeds going to charity.

These charitable causes are personally chosen by the legendary Subs front man Charlie Harper, and have included individuals in need, those directly affected by the Japanese tsunami and earthquake in March 2011 and also the RNLI, to whom we have been making regular donations since 2013.

We have so far raised over £25,000 for various charities…

In May 2012 we launched a subsidiary label called Time & Matter Records to deal with commercial ventures, and then in 2017, another subsidiary label was launched to release non-U.K. Subs related material which is called Thyme & Mattar Records.

April 2020 saw another venture started, TOME & METRE BOOKS and TOME & METRE PUBLISHING, of which we have so far published critically acclaimed books by Alvin Gibbs, Del Greening and Andrew Brooksbank.

All three labels and our book publishing venture share the same T&M catalogue number prefix...

Time & Matter Recordings and its subsidiaries are run under a partnership by the uksubstimeandmatter.net website editors, who have been U.K. Subs fanatics since they were school friends in Kenilworth, Warwickshire, aged 12, in 1979.

Mark Chadderton (Swanage) | Rob Cook (Stewartby)

T&M RELEASES:

Time & Matter Recordings *
Time & Matter Records +
Thyme & Mattar Records #
Tome & Metre Books <>

T&M 001 - **U.K. SUBS**
Dance & Travel In The Robot Age - CD Album *

T&M 002 - **U.K. SUBS**
Soft Lights & Loud Guitars - DVD *

T&M 003 - **U.K. SUBS**
2011 Official Calendar *

T&M 004 - **U.K. SUBS**
Tour In Progress - Double DVD *

T&M 005 - **U.K. SUBS**
Product Supply - 7" Single *

T&M 006 - **U.K. SUBS**
2012 Official Calendar *

T&M 007 - **URBAN DOGS**
Bonefield - CD Album +

T&M 008 - **U.K. SUBS**
2013 Official Calendar *

T&M 009 - **CHARLIE HARPER & CAPTAIN SENSIBLE**
Too Much Reality EP - 7" Single & CD Single +

T&M 010 - **U.K. SUBS**
2014 Official Calendar *

T&M 011 - **T&M MERCHANDISE**
I Stick In A Car - Time & Matter Car Sticker *

T&M 012 - **A.M.I**
Anti Meathead Inc - CD Album +

T&M 013 - **U.K. SUBS**
The Revolution's Here - 10" Mini LP +

T&M 014 - **U.K. SUBS**
2014 Tour Programme – Celebrating Charlie Harper's 70th Birthday *

T&M 015 - **FEATURING CHARLIE HARPER #1**
The Berlin Lights / The Dugz - 7" Single +

T&M 016 - **URBAN DOGS**
Rebellion Song - 7" Single +

T&M 017 - **U.K. SUBS**
2015 Official Calendar *

T&M 018 - **U.K. SUBS**
Amoeba Sounds EP - 7" Single +

T&M 019 - **T&M MERCHANDISE**
T&M Records T-Shirt #1 +

T&M 020 - **CHARGE 69**
Much More Than Music – LP/CD +

T&M 021 - **T&M MERCHANDISE**
Time & Matter Patch #1 +

T&M 022 - **U.K. SUBS**
2016 Official Calendar *

T&M 023 - **U.K. SUBS**
Summer 1977 Demo - 7" Single +

T&M 024 - **U.K. SUBS**
November 1977 Demo EP - 7" Single +

T&M 025 - **URBAN DOGS**
Trick or Treat - 7" Single & MC +

T&M 026 - **URBAN DOGS**
Attack – LP/CD/MC +

T&M 027 - **CHARLIE HARPER & FRIENDS**
Stop Hobophobia - 7" Single +

T&M 028 - **THE EMBEZZLERS**
Under The Microscope - 7" Single #

T&M 029 - **THE EMBEZZLERS**
Another Girl Another Planet - 7" Single #

T&M 030 - **MARTIN NEWELL**
Wireless Wivenhoe - CD Album #

T&M 031 - **ALVIN GIBBS & THE DISOBEDIENT SERVANTS**
Ghost Train - 7" Single +

T&M 032 - **ALVIN GIBBS & THE DISOBEDIENT SERVANTS**
Your Disobedient Servant – LP/CD +

T&M 033 - **LONG GOOD FRIDAYS**
Amplified/End Of Days - 7" Single #

T&M 034 - **LONG GOOD FRIDAYS**
Off With Their Heads EP - CD Single #

T&M 035 - **JANUS STARK**
Angel In The Flames – LP/CD +

T&M 036 - **ALVIN GIBBS & THE DISOBEDIENT SERVANTS**
History EP - Double 7" Single +

T&M 037 - **T&M MERCHANDISE**
10th anniversary badge *

T&M 038 - **ALVIN GIBBS**
Diminished Responsibility:
My life as a U.K. Sub, and other strange stories - Volume I - Book <>

T&M 039 - **JANUS STARK**
Rewind To A – CD Album +

T&M 040 - **JANUS STARK**
Chez Wrong – CD Album +

T&M 041 - **GIZZ BUTT**
Free Digital EP – Digital Download EP +

T&M 042 – **CHARLIE HARPER & THE SUB MACHINE**
Panic / Post War Punks - 7" Single +

T&M 043 – **ALVIN GIBBS & THE DISOBEDIENT SERVANTS**
State Of Grace - 7" Single +

T&M 044 – **LONG GOOD FRIDAYS**
Gone – CD EP #

T&M 045 – ANDREW J BROOKSBANK
From Arthaus To Bauhaus 1972 – 1979 - Book <>

T&M 046 - ALVIN GIBBS
Diminished Responsibility:
My life as a U.K. Sub, and other strange stories - Volume II - Book <>

T&M 047 – JANUS STARK
Face Your Biggest Fear – LP/CD +

T&M 048 - FEATURING CHARLIE HARPER #2
The Mistakes / The Ramonas - 7" Single +

T&M 049 – DEREK GREENING
Jinxed – How Not To Rock 'N' Roll - Book <>

T&M 049-2 – DEREK GREENING
Jinxed – How Not To Rock 'N' Roll – (Revised) Book <>

T&M 050 – THE MISTAKES
A Good Hill To Die On - LP/CD +

T&M 051 – LONG GOOD FRIDAYS
Kill The Angels So We May Sing - Digital Download Album #

T&M 052 – JANUS STARK
The Flags Of Discontent - Digital Download EP +

T&M 053 – FLESH FOR LULU
Cosmic Mind Fuck - CD Album *

T&M 054 – JANUS STARK
Amplified & Unified – Live At The Unity Fest - Digital Download
Album +

T&M 055 – LONG GOOD FRIDAYS
Closure - CD Album #

T&M 056 – JANUS STARK
Headhunter - Digital Download Mini Album +

T&M 057 – SAFETY PIN MAGAZINE SPLIT SINGLE
U.K. Subs / The Mistakes - 7" Single +

T&M 058 – THE MISTAKES
5-track session for Neil Crud on Louder Than War Radio +

T&M 059 – **JANUS STARK**
Whatever Happened To The Harold Smith Demos?
- Digital Download Mini Album +

T&M 060 – **JANUS STARK**
Exploding On Stage! Live at the Pitz, Milton Keynes - 9th July 1999
- Digital Download Album +

T&M 061 – **JANUS STARK**
OK Chicane, Here I Come - Digital Download Mini Album +

T&M 062 – **JANUS STARK**
Live At Wessex Studios 1998 - Digital Download Mini Album +

T&M 063 - **ALVIN GIBBS**
Diminished Responsibility:
My life as a U.K. Sub, and other strange stories - Volume III - Book <>

T&M 064 – **JANUS STARK**
Panic Attack - The 'lost' 'Great Adventure Cigar' pre-production
recordings (Part One) - Digital Download Album +

T&M 065 – **JANUS STARK**
White Man Speak With Fork Tongue - The 'lost' 'Great Adventure
Cigar' pre-production recordings (Part Two) - Digital Download Album
+

T&M 066 – M**ARK CHADDERTON**
Charlie Harper – Songwriter - 1977 Metamorphosis <>
(Manuscript work in progress – to be published)

T&M 067 – **DESTRUCTORS**
Bullshit The 'lost' pre-production recordings (Part One) -
Digital Download Album +

T&M 068 – TO BE CONFIRMED
To Be Confirmed

T&M 069 – TO BE CONFIRMED
To Be Confirmed

T&M 070 – TO BE CONFIRMED
To Be Confirmed

T&M 071 – TO BE CONFIRMED
To Be Confirmed

T&M 072 – TO BE CONFIRMED
To Be Confirmed

T&M 073 – TO BE CONFIRMED
To Be Confirmed

T&M 074 – TO BE CONFIRMED
To Be Confirmed

T&M 075 – TO BE CONFIRMED
To Be Confirmed

T&M 076 – **U.K. SUBS**
Live 1977 – Full Details To Be Confirmed

T&M 077 – **U.K. SUBS**
Live 1977 – Full Details To Be Confirmed

Additional info:
T&M 002 - Joint release with Radar Proof Recordings
T&M 020 - Joint release with Combat Rock
T&M 028 - Joint release with Seventeen Records
T&M 057 - Joint release with Safety Pin Magazine

Tome[1] & Metre[2] [3]Publishing[4] - 2024

---

[1] A book, especially a large, heavy, scholarly one.
[2] The rhythm of a piece of poetry.
[3] The basic rhythmic pattern of beats in a piece of music.
[4] To make information available to people, especially in a book.